Amsterdam

written and researched by

...d, Phil Lee and Karoline Thomas

with additional contributions from

Suzanne Morton-Taylor

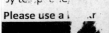

ROUGH
GUIDES

www.roughguides.com

Contents

Amsterdam on the water colour section following p.112

Architecture in Amsterdam colour section following p.176

RUSLAND
SLIJKSTRAAT
University of Amsterdam

Colour maps following p.312

◀◀ Amsterdam gables ◀ Oudeschans canal

Introduction to Amsterdam

Amsterdam has grown up in the past decade or so. It is a slicker, more cosmopolitan place than it once was, more business-minded, less eccentric, and overall more integrated into the European mainstream. Yet it still enjoys a reputation as one of Europe's most relaxed cities – and with some justification. There's a laid-back feel to the streets and canals (and its people) that you just don't get in any other European city. Of course, it remains a place for Sixties throwbacks who just want to get stoned, and for well-oiled gangs of blokes on the prowl in the still notorious Red Light District. But it also has a small-city feel: it doesn't take long to get from place to place, and – thanks to its canals – many parts of the centre are uncongested and peaceful.

Amsterdam's welcoming attitude towards visitors has been shaped by the liberal counterculture of the last four decades, but it's emphatically no longer the hippy haven it once was. In fact, in the last few years the city has been more or less absorbed into the rest of Europe, with not only high-end bars and clubs muscling in on its more traditional haunts, but also with the emergence of crime and drug problems that for decades seemed to have passed Amsterdam by. However, some things haven't changed, and it's hard not to feel drawn by its vibrant, open-air summer events, by the cheery intimacy of its cafés, and by the Dutch facility with languages; just about everyone you meet in Amsterdam will be able to speak good-to-fluent English, and often more than a smattering of French and German too.

Amsterdam is still far from being as diverse a city as, say, London or Paris; despite the huge numbers of immigrants from the former colonies in Surinam and Indonesia, as well as from Morocco and Turkey, to name but a few, almost all live and work outside the centre and can seem almost invisible to the casual visitor. Indeed, there is an ethnic and social homogeneity in the city centre that seems to counter everything you may have heard about Dutch integration. It's a contradiction that is typical of Amsterdam. The city is world-famous as a place where the possession and sale of cannabis are effectively legal – or at least decriminalized – and yet for the most part Amsterdammers themselves don't really partake in the stuff. And while Amsterdam is renowned for its tolerance towards all styles of behaviour, a primmer, more conventional big city, with a more mainstream dress sense, would be hard to find. Indeed, these days the city is trying to reinvent itself, geared towards a more up-market kind of tourist who is a little less fixated on smoking and drinking. In recent years, a string of hardline city mayors have had some success in diminishing Amsterdam's image as a counterculture icon, instead touting it as a centre for business and international high finance. Almost all of the inner-city squats, which once defined local people-power, are gone or legalized; many coffeeshops, especially those in the Red Light District, are closing; and the Red Light District itself – for years the beacon of the city's laissez-faire attitude – is being cleaned up, and many of its sleaziest establishments closed down. The cityscape, too, continues to evolve, with large-scale urban development on the outskirts and regeneration within.

Nevertheless, Amsterdam remains a casual and intimate place, and Amsterdammers themselves make much of their city and its attractions being *gezellig*, a rather overused Dutch word roughly corresponding to a combination of "cosy", "lived-in" and "warmly convivial". Nowhere is this more applicable than in the city's unparalleled

▼ Canal house on Prinsengracht

So much to see, so little time...

Amsterdam is perfect for short breaks: it's small, so you can amble about almost everywhere and see pretty much everything; there are very few must-see sights, so you don't have to spend half your time feeling guilty about the cultural icons you should be visiting; and there are literally hundreds of enticing bars, cafés and restaurants where you can take the weight off your feet between attractions. The itineraries below give an idea of how to plan your time. Mostly designed around key sights, they cover everything from a flying visit to a full week in the city, and can be used as rigidly, or as flexibly, as you like.

Two days
Dam Square • Anne Frank Huis • Red Light District • Oude Kerk • Rijksmuseum • Van Gogh Museum • Leidseplein • Grachtengordel South • Museum Van Loon/Museum Willet-Holthuysen • Rembrandtplein

Three days
As above, plus:
Westerkerk • Koninklijk Paleis • Brouwersgracht • Western docklands

Five days
As above, plus:
Rembrandthuis • Waterlooplein • Verzetsmuseum • Artis Zoo • Tropenmuseum • Heineken Experience • De Pijp • Vondelpark • Museumtramlijn • Amsterdamse Bos • Amsterdam ArenA

Seven days
As above, plus:
Stedelijk Museum • Esnoga • Joods Historisch Museum • Eastern docklands • Amsterdam Noord • Haarlem • Keukenhof Gardens

CANAL BOAT TRIP

selection of **drinking** places, whether you choose a traditional brown café or one of a raft of newer, more stylish bars. The city boasts dozens of excellent **restaurants** too, with great Indonesian options and a host of increasingly adventurous Dutch establishments. As for **cultural attractions**, the city holds its own in contemporary European film, dance, drama and music; it harbours several top-notch jazz venues, as well as the Concertgebouw, home to one of the world's leading orchestras, and the state-of-the-art Muziekgebouw, the city's prestigious venue for opera and orchestral music. The club scene is relatively restrained, although a wealth of **gay bars** and clubs partly justifies Amsterdam's claim to be the "Gay Capital of Europe".

Where to go

The city's layout is determined by a web of canals radiating out from a historical core to loop right round Amsterdam's compact centre, which takes about forty minutes to stroll from one end to the other. Butting up to the River IJ, the **Old Centre** spreads south from **Centraal Station** bisected by the Damrak and its continuation, the Rokin, the city's main drag; en route is the Dam, the main square. The Old Centre remains Amsterdam's commercial heart, as well as the hub of its bustling street life, and also holds myriad shops, bars and restaurants. The area is also home to the **Red Light District**, just to the east of the Damrak, and contains dozens of fine old buildings, most memorably the Oude Kerk, the Amstelkring and the Koninklijk Paleis.

The Old Centre is bordered by the first of the major canals, the Singel, whose curve is mirrored by those of the Herengracht, Keizersgracht and Prinsengracht – collectively known as the **Grachtengordel**, or "Girdle of Canals". These waterways were part of a major seventeenth-century urban extension and, with the interconnecting radial streets, form the city's distinctive web shape. This is Amsterdam's most delightful area, full of the handsome seventeenth- and eighteenth-century canal houses, with their decorative gables, and narrow, dreamy canals, that most people associate with the city; a well-worn image, perhaps, but one that is still entirely authentic. Here you'll also find perhaps the city's most celebrated attraction, the **Anne Frank Huis**, the house in which the young Jewish diarist hid away during the German occupation of World War II, now a poignant reminder of the Holocaust.

▶ Leidsegracht

Immediately to the west of the Grachtengordel lies the **Jordaan**, one-time industrial slum and the traditional heart of working-class Amsterdam, though these days almost entirely gentrified. The same applies to the adjacent **Western docklands**, although the origins of this district are very different; the artificial islands of the Westerdok were dredged out of the river to create extra wharves and shipbuilding space during the seventeenth century, and only in the last few decades has the shipping industry moved out.

On the other side of the centre is the **Old Jewish Quarter**, home to a thriving Jewish community until the German occupation of World War II. Postwar development laid a heavy hand on the quarter, but nonetheless there are a couple of significant survivors, principally the **Esnoga** (Portuguese Synagogue) and the **Joods Historisch Museum** (Jewish Historical Museum). The adjacent Plantagebuurt is greener and more suburban, but it does possess one excellent museum, the **Verzetsmuseum** (Resistance Museum); the neighbouring **Eastern docklands**, in particular Zeeburg, is another formerly industrial area that has undergone rapid renewal – as have some parts of Amsterdam Noord, just across the river from Centraal Station. Amsterdam's **Museum Quarter** contains, as you might expect, the city's premier art museums, principally the **Rijksmuseum** with its wonderful collection of Dutch paintings, including several of Rembrandt's finest works, and the excellent **Van Gogh Museum**, which holds the world's largest collection of the artist's work. Both lie just a stone's throw from the city's finest park, the **Vondelpark**.

▶ Traditional café

Finally, the residential suburbs – or **outer districts** – spreading beyond Singelgracht – are relatively short of attractions – notable exceptions being the wooded parkland of the **Amsterdamse Bos** and the **Amsterdam ArenA**, home to the city's celebrated Ajax football team.

Talk to Amsterdammers about visiting other parts of their country and you may well

be met with looks of amazement. Ignore them. The Netherlands is a small nation, and the Dutch have an outstanding public transport system, an integrated network of trains and buses that makes a large and varied slice of the country easily reachable. Consequently, the choice of possible **day-trips** is extensive; the towns of **Haarlem** and **Alkmaar**, the old Zuider Zee ports of **Marken** and **Volendam**, and the pretty town of **Edam** are all worth a visit – not to mention the much-touted **Keukenhof Gardens**, which are at their best during spring and early summer.

When to go

Amsterdam enjoys a fairly standard, temperate **climate**, with warm summers and moderately cold and wet winters. The weather is certainly not severe enough to make much difference to the city's routines. That said, high summer – roughly late June to August – sees the city packed to the gunnels, with parts of the centre almost overwhelmed by the tourist throng, whereas spring and autumn are not too crowded and can be especially beautiful, with mist hanging over the canals and low sunlight beaming through the cloud cover. At any time of the year, but particularly in summer, try to book your accommodation in advance.

Average daily temperatures (°C) and monthly rainfall (mm)

	Jan	Feb	Mar	Apr	May	Jun	Jul	Aug	Sep	Oct	Nov	Dec
Amsterdam												
Min°C	1.2	0	3.7	4.8	8.2	12	13.5	13	10.9	7.7	4.8	3.5
Max°C	5.1	6.4	8.5	12.6	16.8	19.2	21	21	18.3	14	8.8	6.7
mm	78	43.6	89.3	39.3	51.2	60.1	63.4	60	80.1	104.7	76.4	72.3

20

things not to miss

It isn't possible to see everything Amsterdam has to offer on a short trip, and we don't suggest you try. What follows, in no particular order, is a subjective selection of the city's highlights, from elegant canal-side architecture and vibrant markets to outstanding art collections and traditional bars – all arranged in colour-coded categories to help you find the very best things to see, do and experience. All entries have a page reference to take you straight into the guide, where you can find out more.

01 **The Jordaan** Page **83** • The Jordaan holds many of the city's most diverting secondhand and bric-a-brac shops – and some of its prettiest canals.

02 Bloemenmarkt Page **82** • Masses of colourful blooms for sale, including – of course – tulips.

04 The Begijnhof Page **52** • The fourteenth-century Begijnhof is one of the quietest and prettiest corners of the city centre.

03 Coffeeshops Page **196** • Nowhere else in the world can you smoke high-quality dope in such comfortable – and legal – surroundings.

05 **The Grachtengordel** Page **64** • The elegant bends and handsome canal houses of the city's seventeenth-century extension are what makes the city unique.

06 **Concertgebouw** Page **122** • One of the finest concert halls in Europe, attracting some of the biggest names n classical music and opera.

07 **Brown cafés** Page **176** • Amsterdam is famous for its brown cafés – dark, cosy and very traditional.

08 **Koninklijk Paleis** Page **48** • Co-opted by the Dutch royals but originally Amsterdam's town hall, this building speaks volumes about the city during the Golden Age.

10 **The Vondelpark** Page **123** • The leafy Vondelpark, with its ponds, footpaths and colony of parrots, is the city's most attractive park.

09 **Anne Frank Huis** Page **68** • The museum created in the Secret Annex – home to Anne Frank and her family for two years during World War II – is the city's most moving sight.

11 Van Gogh Museum
Page **119** • The world's most comprehensive collection of the artist's work – simply unmissable.

13 Oude Kerk Page **56** • The city's oldest and most venerable church, slap-bang in the middle of the Red Light District.

12 Queen's Day Page **35** •
Amsterdammers let their hair down on Queen's Day (Koninginnedag), the city's biggest and wildest municipal knees-up.

14 Indonesian food Page **175**
• Fill up on Amsterdam's ethnic food speciality.

15 **Amstelkring** Page **58** • The last of the city's clandestine Catholic churches now holds a fascinating museum.

17 **Cycling** Page **25** • Get around the city like a local by renting a bike for the day.

16 **The Eastern docklands** Page **107** • The city's most resurgent district, with some of its coolest bars and restaurants, and landmark contemporary architecture.

18 **Proeflokalen** Page 87 •
Served ice-cold, jenever, the Dutch version of gin, is the nation's favourite spirit, and these "tasting-houses" are the traditional places to sample it in its various flavours.

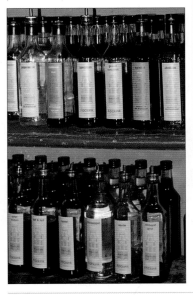

19 **The Heineken Experience** Page 127 •
Although this is no longer a working brewery, the compensation is an excellent museum devoted to the art of brewing – with a few beers thrown in along the way.

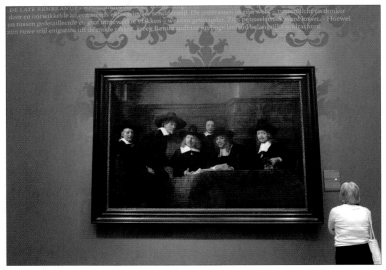

20 **Rijksmuseum** Page 113 • The city's greatest museum – featuring everything from paintings to furniture and applied arts – is undergoing restoration, but you can still see the best of its paintings in the Philips Wing.

Basics

Basics

Getting there

UK travellers are spoilt for choice when it comes to deciding how to get to Amsterdam. There are plenty of flights, from all over the UK, and taking the train through the Channel Tunnel is just as easy – not much cheaper, but almost as quick. Bus travel is probably the most affordable option; and by car, deals for drivers on ferry routes into Dutch and Belgian ports are particularly competitive. From North America and Canada the main decision is whether to fly direct – easy enough as Schiphol is a major international air travel hub, served by dozens of short- and long-haul airlines – or to route via London, picking up a budget flight onwards from there. From Australia and New Zealand, all flights to Amsterdam require one or two stops on the way; from South Africa, direct flights are available.

Flights from the UK and Ireland

Amsterdam is one of the **UK**'s most popular short-haul destinations, and you'll find loads of choice – in carriers, flight times and departure airports. Aside from the major full-service carriers (KLM, British Airways and BMI), there are plenty of no-frills airlines operating flights to Amsterdam, including EasyJet, BMIbaby, Transavia and Jet2.com, as well as a few business-oriented, smaller carriers such as VLM.

Flights to Amsterdam's **Schiphol Airport** (pronounced skip-oll) take roughly an hour from London, or ninety minutes from Scotland and the north of England. There's a good number of daily flights out of London – Heathrow, Gatwick, Stansted, Luton and London City – plus nonstop flights from many of the UK's **regional airports**, including Birmingham, East Midlands, Cardiff, Southampton, Norwich, Liverpool, Manchester, Leeds-Bradford, Humberside, Newcastle, Teesside, Edinburgh, Glasgow and Aberdeen.

Whichever route you choose, it's hard to say precisely what you'll **pay** at any given time: the price depends hugely on when you book and when you fly, what offers are available – and how lucky you are. However, flying to Amsterdam with one of the low-cost airlines between April and September, you'll pay around £120 return travelling at convenient times at the weekend, including taxes, as opposed to £160 with one of the full-service carriers. Weekday travel will cost £50–70 with a budget carrier, £100 or so

with a full-service airline. If you want more flexibility with your ticket you'll pay more, as you will if you book at the last minute – economy return tickets from London to Amsterdam can cost anything up to £400. All carriers offer their lowest prices online.

Flying to Amsterdam from **Northern Ireland**, the most economical option is with EasyJet out of Belfast International (fares are around £100). From the **Republic of Ireland**, Aer Lingus flies five times daily to Amsterdam from Dublin and twice daily from Cork, for a minimum €80–100 return, depending on the season, with fares rising at peak times.

Flights from the US and Canada

Amsterdam's Schiphol Airport is among the most popular and least expensive gateways to Europe from **North America and Canada**, and finding a convenient and good-value flight is rarely a problem. **Direct flights** are operated by KLM/Northwest, Continental and Delta Airlines; many more fly **via London** and other European centres – and are nearly always cheaper because of it.

Virtually every region of the US and Canada is well served by the major airlines. KLM and Northwest, which operate a joint service, offer the widest range of flights, with direct or one-stop flights to Amsterdam from eleven US cities, and connections from dozens more. From elsewhere in the US, the Dutch charter firm Martinair flies year-round from Miami direct to Amsterdam. United also flies direct to Amsterdam from Chicago,

Six steps to a better kind of travel

At Rough Guides we are passionately committed to travel. We feel strongly that only through travelling do we truly come to understand the world we live in and the people we share it with – plus tourism has brought a great deal of **benefit** to developing economies around the world over the last few decades. But the extraordinary growth in tourism has also damaged some places irreparably, and of course **climate change** is exacerbated by most forms of transport, especially flying. This means that now more than ever it's important to **travel thoughtfully** and **responsibly**, with respect for the cultures you're visiting – not only to derive the most benefit from your trip but also to preserve the best bits of the planet for everyone to enjoy. At Rough Guides we feel there are six main areas in which you can make a difference.

- Consider what you're contributing to the **local economy**, and how much the services you use do the same, whether it's through employing local workers and guides or sourcing locally grown produce and local services.

- Consider the **environment** on holiday as well as at home. Water is scarce in many developing destinations, and the biodiversity of local flora and fauna can be adversely affected by tourism. Try to patronize businesses that take account of this.

- Travel with a purpose, not just to tick off experiences. Consider **spending longer** in a place, and getting to know it and its people.

- Give thought to how often you **fly**. Try to avoid short hops by air and more harmful night flights.

- Consider **alternatives to flying**, travelling instead by bus, train, boat and even by bike or on foot where possible.

- Make your trips "**climate neutral**" via a reputable carbon offset scheme. All Rough Guide flights are offset, and every year we donate money to a variety of charities devoted to combating the effects of climate change.

while Delta operates from Atlanta and New York; Continental from Houston.

Booking far enough in advance, you should be able to find a **fare** between April and September for $700–900 return from New York (flight time 8hr 10min) or Chicago (8hr), $900–1000 from Atlanta (10hr), and around $1000 from LA (10hr 30min), though booking less than a couple of weeks in advance can push these prices up considerably.

From **Canada**, KLM flies direct to Amsterdam year-round from Vancouver (9hr 30min) and from Toronto (7hr 10min). There are also plenty of one-stop options via Frankfurt, London and Paris. **Fares** from Toronto go for around Can$1100, from Vancouver around Can$1400.

Flights from Australia, New Zealand and South Africa

There are **no direct flights** to the Netherlands from **Australia and New Zealand**: all involve at least one stop. Singapore Airways

and Malaysian offer the most direct routes out of Sydney (stopping in Singapore and Kuala Lumpur respectively). Thai, Austrian and Qantas all have two stops (Bangkok/ Munich, Bangkok/Vienna and Singapore/ London). Flights from Christchurch go via Sydney and London and from Wellington via Melbourne or Sydney and London. One further option is to pick up a cheap ticket to London, and then continue your journey to Amsterdam with one of the no-frills budget airlines (see p.22).

From **South Africa**, KLM offers **direct flights** to Amsterdam, with services from Cape Town and Johannesburg. South African Airways offers one-stop flights via London and Frankfurt or Munich; Lufthansa via Frankfurt; and Virgin Atlantic via London.

Fares from Sydney or Melbourne are around A$1800–2000, and from Auckland A$2200. A return flight from Christchurch or Wellington will set you back around NZ$3000. Flights with KLM from Cape Town cost around R8600; from Johannesburg,

R7300. Indirect flights via London or Frankfurt cost around R8000.

By train

The simplest and quickest way to travel from the UK to Amsterdam by **train** is to take the **Eurostar** service from London nonstop to Brussels. Trains depart from St Pancras International station (1hr 59min) in central London; and from Ebbsfleet International station (1hr 48min), off Junction 2 of the M25. Trains arrive at Bruxelles-Midi station (Brussel-Zuid in Dutch), from where plenty of fast trains – including the **Thalys** high-speed services (⊛ www.thalys.com) – head on to Amsterdam (around 2hr 30min). The total journey time from London is around six hours, and Eurostar can arrange a through ticket from any point in the UK.

A standard return **fare** to Amsterdam costs around £150, but special deals are commonplace, especially in the low season; and you can also sometimes reduce costs by accepting certain ticket restrictions. Book through Rail Europe or directly through the Eurostar website (for both, see p.22).

The Dutch Railways website (⊛ www.ns.nl) can give full **timetable** details (in English) of trains from stations in the UK to any station in the Netherlands.

A much longer – but cheaper – **rail-and-ferry route**, the **Dutchflyer**, is available through Stena Line in conjunction with National Express East Anglia trains. The journey operates twice daily (early morning and evening) with **trains** departing London's Liverpool Street station bound for Harwich, where they connect the **ferry** over to the Hook of Holland – the Hoek van Holland. The whole journey takes between nine and eleven hours. From the Hook, there are frequent trains onto Rotterdam (every 30min to 1hr; 30min), where you change for Amsterdam (1hr). As for **fares**, a standard return costs £70, £90 on an overnight sailing, cabin included – cabins are compulsory on overnight sailings. Tickets are available from National Express East Anglia trains or you can book online with Stena.

By bus

Travelling by **long-distance bus** is generally the cheapest way of reaching Amsterdam

from the UK, but it is very time-consuming: the journey from London to Amsterdam takes twelve hours or more. **Eurolines** (see p.23) operates four services daily (8am, 10am, 8pm & 10pm) from London to Amsterdam, all using Eurotunnel. A standard fare is £56 return (under-26s and over-60s pay £53) though promotional return fares can be snapped up for much less.

By car

To reach Amsterdam **by car or motorbike**, you can either take a ferry, or – preferable for its hassle-free crossing – use **Eurotunnel**'s shuttle-train through the **Channel Tunnel**. Note that Eurotunnel only carries cars (including occupants) and motorbikes, not cyclists or foot passengers. Amsterdam is roughly 370km from the Eurotunnel exit in Calais.

There are two shuttle trains per hour (only three in total from midnight–6am), taking 35min (45min for some night departure times); you must check in at Folkestone at least 30min before departure. It's possible to turn up and buy your **ticket** at the tollbooths (exit the M20 at junction 11a), though it's a

good idea to book in advance through the website (see p.23) at busy times.

Fares depend on the time of year, time of day and length of stay (the cheapest ticket is for a day-trip, followed by a five-day return); it costs less to travel between 10pm and 6am, while the highest fares are reserved for weekend departures and returns in July and August. Prices are charged per vehicle; short-stay savers between April and October for a car start at around £110. If you wish to stay more than five days, a standard return costs from around £130, while a "Flexiplus" fare, which entitles you to change your plans at the last minute, costs more still. Some special offers are usually also available.

By ferry

Three operators run **ferries** from the UK direct to ports in the Netherlands, and all offer year-round services. The fastest route is with Stena Line, which sails from Harwich in Essex to the Hook of Holland; the journey time is 6 hours 15 minutes; travelling at night always takes longer and you have to book a cabin. P&O North Sea Ferries operates from Hull to Rotterdam (11hr). DFDS Seaways sails once daily from Newcastle (North Shields) to IJmuiden (14hr), half an hour's drive from Amsterdam.

Aside from the options direct to Dutch ports, you might want to consider the ferry routes to Belgium and France. P&O sails once a day from Hull to Zeebrugge in Belgium (14hr 30min), while Norfolkline operates a year-round service from Dover to the French border town of Dunkerque (2hr).

Fares vary hugely, depending on when you leave, how long you stay, if you have a car, and the number of passengers. Discounts for students and under-26s are available.

Airlines and agents

Airlines

Aer Lingus Ⓦ www.aerlingus.com.
Air Canada Ⓦ www.aircanada.com.
Air France Ⓦ www.airfrance.com.
Air New Zealand Ⓦ www.airnz.co.nz.
American Airlines Ⓦ www.aa.com.
bmi Ⓦ www.flybmi.com.
bmibaby Ⓦ www.bmibaby.com.

British Airways Ⓦ www.ba.com.
Cathay Pacific Ⓦ www.cathaypacific.com.
Continental Airlines Ⓦ www.continental.com.
Delta Ⓦ www.delta.com.
easyJet Ⓦ www.easyjet.com.
KLM (Royal Dutch Airlines) Ⓦ www.klm.com.
Lufthansa Ⓦ www.lufthansa.com.
Malaysia Airlines Ⓦ www.malaysiaairlines.com.
Martinair Ⓦ www.martinair.com.
Northwest Ⓦ www.nwa.com.
Qantas Airways Ⓦ www.qantas.com.
Ryanair Ⓦ www.ryanair.com.
Singapore Airlines Ⓦ www.singaporeair.com.
South African Airways Ⓦ www.flysaa.com.
Thai Airways Ⓦ www.thaiair.com.
Thomsonfly Ⓦ www.thomsonfly.co.uk.
United Airlines Ⓦ www.united.com.
Virgin Atlantic Ⓦ www.virgin-atlantic.com.
VLM Airlines Ⓦ www.flyvlm.com.

Agents and operators

ebookers UK ☏ 0800/082 3000, Republic of Ireland ☏ 01/431 1311, Ⓦ www.ebookers.com. Low fares on an extensive selection of scheduled flights and package deals.
North South Travel UK ☏ 01245/608 291, Ⓦ www.northsouthtravel.co.uk. Friendly, competitive travel agency, offering discounted fares worldwide. Profits are used to support projects in the developing world, especially the promotion of sustainable tourism.
STA Travel UK ☏ 0871/2300 040, US ☏ 1-800/781-4040, Australia ☏ 134 STA, New Zealand ☏ 0800/474 400, SA ☏ 0861/781 781; Ⓦ www.statravel.com. Worldwide specialists in independent travel; also student IDs, travel insurance, car rental, rail passes and more. Good discounts for students and under-26s.
Trailfinders UK ☏ 0845/058 5858, Republic of Ireland ☏ 01/677 7888, Australia ☏ 1300/780 212; Ⓦ www.trailfinders.com. One of the best-informed and most efficient agents for independent travellers.

Rail contacts

Dutchflyer UK ☏ 08705 455 455, Ⓦ www.dutchflyer.co.uk.
European Rail UK ☏ 020/7619 1083, Ⓦ www.europeanrail.com.
Europrail International Canada ☏ 1-888/667-9734, Ⓦ www.europrail.net.
Eurostar UK ☏ 0870/518 6186, outside UK ☏ 0044/12336 17575; Ⓦ www.eurostar.com.
National Express East Anglia UK ☏ 0845 600 7245, Ⓦ www.nationalexpresseastanglia.com.

Rail Europe UK ☎0844/848 4064, US ☎1-800/622-8600, Canada ☎1-800/361-RAIL, ⓦwww.raileurope.co.uk, ⓦwww.raileurope.com/us.

Bus contacts

Eurolines UK ☎0871/781 8181, ⓦwww .eurolines.co.uk.

Ferry contacts

DFDS Seaways UK ☎0871/522 9955, ⓦwww .dfdsseaways.co.uk.

Norfolkline UK ☎0844/847 5042, ⓦwww .norfolkline.com.
P&O Ferries UK ☎0871/664 5645, ⓦwww .poferries.com.
Stena Line UK ☎0870/570 7070, Northern Ireland ☎0870/520 4204, Republic of Ireland ☎021/427 2965, ⓦwww.stenaline.co.uk.

Channel tunnel

Eurotunnel UK ☎0870/535 3535, ⓦwww .eurotunnel.com.

Arrival

Arriving in Amsterdam by train and plane could hardly be easier. Schiphol, Amsterdam's international airport, is a quick and convenient train ride away from Centraal Station, the city's international train station, which is itself just a ten-minute metro ride from Amstel Station, the terminus for long-distance and international buses. Centraal Station is also the hub of Amsterdam's excellent public transport network, whose trams, buses and metro combine to reach every corner of the city and its suburbs.

By air

Amsterdam's international airport, **Schiphol** (☎0900/0141, ⓦwww.schiphol.nl), is located about 15km southwest of the city centre. It's one of the busiest airports in Europe, and one of the best organized, with an efficient **transfer** system to the city and indeed the rest of the country. Arriving passengers are channelled through to a large and well-signposted plaza, which has all the **facilities** you would expect – car rental desks, banks, exchange offices, left-luggage facilities, ATMs and a **VVV** (tourist office) with accommodation booking service, as well as a Netherlands Railways ticket office and access to the **train station**.

Trains run from the airport's train station to Amsterdam's **Centraal Station** every ten minutes during the day and every hour at night (midnight–6am); the journey takes 15–20 minutes and costs €3.90 one-way, €6.70 return, with a 50c surcharge if you buy from the ticket office rather than the ticket machines. Be aware that you cannot buy tickets on the train; if you are caught without a valid ticket, you have to pay the regular fare plus a €35 fine. **Hotel shuttles** are another option; the Connexxion service (☎038/339 4741, ⓦwww.schipholhotelshuttle.nl) departs from the designated bus stop outside the Arrivals Hall every thirty minutes (on the half-hour) from 6am to 9pm at a cost of €14.50 one-way, €22.50 return. The route varies with the needs of the passengers it picks up at the airport, but buses take about thirty minutes to get from the airport to the city centre. Tickets are available from the Connexxion desk in the Arrivals Hall. There are also plenty of taxis; the fare from Schiphol to most parts of the city centre is €40–45.

By train and bus

Amsterdam's **Centraal Station** (CS) has regular connections with key cities in **Germany**, **Belgium and France**, as well as all the larger towns and cities of **the**

Netherlands. Amsterdam also has several suburban train stations, but these are principally for the convenience of commuters. Centraal Station is still undergoing a much-needed face-lift but does have lots of **facilities**, including left-luggage lockers and a staffed left-luggage office (see p.34). There's also a VVV (tourist office) on platform 2 and a second directly across from the station entrance, plenty of ATMs and a GVB exchange office, more shops than you can shake a stick at, and

lots of places to eat too, including a good and atmospheric restaurant-café, *Restaurant 1e Klas*, open all day on platform 2 (see p.36). For all rail enquiries contact **NS** (Netherlands Railways; international enquiries ☎0900/9296, domestic enquiries ☎0900/9292, ⓦ www.ns.nl).

Eurolines' (see p.21) long-distance, international **buses** arrive at **Amstel Station**, about 3.5km to the southeast of Centraal Station. The metro journey to Centraal Station takes about ten minutes.

Getting around

Almost all of Amsterdam's leading attractions are clustered in or near the city centre, within easy walking – and even easier cycling – distance of each other. For longer jaunts, the city has a first-rate public transport system run by the GVB, comprising trams, buses, a smallish metro system and four passenger ferries across the River IJ to the northern suburbs (see p.137). Centraal Station is the hub of the system with a multitude of trams and buses departing from outside on Stationsplein, which is also the location of a metro station and a GVB public transport information office.

Tickets

The most common type of **ticket**, valid for all forms of GVB transport, is the **strippenkaart**, a card divided into strips: fold your *strippenkaart* over to expose the number of strips required for your journey and then insert it into the on-board franking machine or get it stamped by the conductor (located in a booth at the rear on most trams). Amsterdam's public transport system is divided into **zones**, and one person making a journey within one zone costs two strips. The "Centre" zone covers the city centre and its immediate surroundings (well beyond Singelgracht), and thus two strips will cover more or less every journey you're likely to make. If you travel into an additional zone, it costs three strips, and so on. More than one person can use the same *strippenkaart*, as long as the requisite number of strips is stamped. After franking, you can use any

GVB tram, bus and the metro for up to one hour. At the time of writing, a two-strip *strippenkaart* cost €1.60 and a three-strip €2.40; you can buy these on the bus or tram. However, you're better off buying tickets in advance, from tobacconists, magazine stores like Bruna or AKO (both located on Centraal Station), the GVB, the VVV and metro stations; a fifteen-strip costs €7.30 and a 45-strip €21.60. If you're over 65 you can buy a reduced *strippenkaart* for €4.80. Alternatively, you can opt for a **dagkaart** (day ticket), which gives unlimited access to the GVB system for up to a maximum of three days. Prices are €7 for 24 hours, €11.50 for 48 hours and €15 for 72 hours.

At the time of writing, the **OV-Chipkaart** was being introduced – a rechargeable payment card which you can buy at the station and use on all forms of public transport – to eventually replace the *strippenkaart* completely. From August 2009 only

Water transport

Cruising along Amsterdam's canals might not be the fastest way of getting from A to B – but it's certainly picturesque. The following options give you the freedom to hop on and off as you please; for guided tours, see p.37.

Canal Bus (☏020/623 9886, ⊛www.canal.nl) operates on three circular routes – coloured green, red and blue – which meet at various points: at the jetty opposite Centraal Station beside Prins Hendrikkade; on the Singelgracht opposite the Rijksmuseum; and by the Stadhuis on Waterlooplein. There are fourteen stops in all and together they give easy access to all the major sights. Boats leave from the jetty opposite Centraal Station every half an hour or so during high season between 9.15am and 7.25pm, and a day ticket for all three routes, allowing you to hop on and off as many times as you like, costs €20 per adult, €10 for children (4–12 years old). It's valid until noon the following day and entitles the bearer to small discounts at several museums. Two-day passes cost €30.

Museumboot (☏020/530 1090, ⊛www.lovers.nl) operates on two routes – the North/South line and the Golden Age line. All jetties of both lines are located at or near many of the city's major attractions. It departs from opposite Centraal Station (every 30min; 10am–6.45pm) and a come-and-go-as-you-please day ticket costs €20, children €10 (4–12 years old).

Canal Bikes (☏020/626 5574, ⊛www.canal.nl) are four-seater pedaloes which take a lifetime to get anywhere but are nevertheless good fun, unless – of course – it's raining. You can rent them at four central locations: on the Singelgracht opposite the Rijksmuseum; on the Prinsengracht outside the Anne Frank Huis; on Keizersgracht at Leidsestraat; and behind Leidseplein. Rental prices per person, per hour are €7 (3–4 people) or €8 (1–2 people), plus a refundable deposit of €50. They can be picked up at one location and left at any of the others; opening hours are daily 9am–6pm, till 9.30pm in July and August.

the OV-Chipkaart will be accepted on the metro. Check ⊛www.ov-chipkaart.nl for more information.

Finally, note that the GVB tries hard to keep **fare-dodging** to a minimum, and wherever you're travelling, and at whatever time of day, there's a reasonable chance you'll have your ticket checked. If you are caught without a valid ticket, you risk an on-the-spot fine of €35.

By tram, bus and metro

The city centre is crisscrossed by **trams**. Two of the more useful are trams #2 and #5, which link Centraal Station with Leidsestraat and the Rijksmuseum every ten minutes or so during the day. You can either get on the trams via the front door or – if the tram has a conductor booth – at the back where you can get your ticket stamped. **Buses** are mainly useful for going to the outskirts, and the same applies to the **metro**, which has just two city-centre stations, Nieuwmarkt and Waterlooplein.

Trams, buses and the metro operate daily between 6am and midnight, supplemented by a limited number of **nightbuses** (*nachtbussen*), which run roughly every half hour from midnight until 7am. All tram and bus stops display a detailed **map** of the network. For further details on all services, head for the main **GVB information office** (Mon–Fri 7am–9pm, Sat & Sun 10am–6pm; ☏0900/8011, ⊛www.gvb.nl) on Stationsplein; the website has a useful journey planner. The GVB's free, English-language *Tourist Guide to Public Transport* is very helpful, and it also provides a **free transport map**. A map of the city's tram, metro and bus routes is included at the back of this book.

By bike

One of the most agreeable ways to explore Amsterdam is by **bicycle**. The city has an excellent network of designated **cycle lanes** (*fietspaden*) and for once cycling isn't a fringe activity – there are cyclists everywhere. Indeed, much to the chagrin of the city's taxi drivers, the needs of the cyclist often take precedence over those of the motorist, and by law, if there's a collision it's always the driver's fault.

Bike **rental** is straightforward, with lots of rental outlets (*fietsenverhuur*) in central Amsterdam. Among the best are: Bike City at Bloemgracht 70 (☏020/626 3721, ⓦwww .bikecity.nl; daily 9am–6pm); Damstraat Rent-a-Bike at Damstraat 20–22 (☏020/625 5029, ⓦwww.bikes.nl; daily 9am–6pm); Orange Bike at Single 233 (☏020/528 9990, ⓦwww .orangebike.nl; daily 9am–6pm); and Macbike, which has branches at Centraal Station (Eastpoint), Stationsplein, Mr Visserplein 2 and Weteringschans 2 (☏020/620 0985, ⓦwww .macbike.nl; daily 9am–5.45pm). Most places charge around €7 for three hours, €9–13 per day or 24 hours, €25 for three days and €35–40 for a week for a standard bicycle; 21-speed cycles cost about half as much again. Everyone asks for some type of security, usually in the form of a cash deposit (some will take credit card imprints) and/or passport.

Finally, if you want to **buy a bike**, a well-worn boneshaker will set you back about €100, maybe less, while €150 and up should get you a fairly decent secondhand machine; see p.216 for a list of recommended **bike shops**. Never buy a bike from someone off the street or in a bar as it will almost certainly have been stolen. **Bike theft** is in fact a real problem, so make sure you have a good lock – they can be bought cheaply at the city's flea market (see p.229) among other places. For useful **cycling terms** in Dutch, see p.291.

By car

The centre of Amsterdam is geared up for trams and bicycles rather than **cars** as a matter of municipal policy. Pedestrianized zones as such are not extensive, but motorists still have to negotiate a convoluted one-way system, avoid getting boxed onto tramlines and steer around herds of cyclists.

Driving into the city is strongly discouraged by the authorities; parking your car in the outer suburbs and entering the city by tram or metro is a better idea. If you do take your car into the centre, you'll find that on-street **parking** is very limited – with far too many cars chasing too few spaces – and can be quite expensive. Every city-centre street where parking is permitted is metered

Amsterdam addresses

For the uninitiated, Amsterdam addresses can be a little confusing. Addresses are written as, for example, "Kerkstr. 79 II", which means the second-floor apartment at Kerkstraat 79. The ground floor is indicated by **hs** (*huis*, house) after the number; the basement is **sous** (*sousterrain*). In some cases, especially in the **Jordaan**, where streets have the same name, to differentiate between them, **1e**, **2e**, **3e** and even occasionally **4e** are placed in front; these are abbreviations for *Eerste* (first), *Tweede* (second), *Derde* (third) and *Vierde* (fourth). Many **side streets** take the name of the main street they run off, with the addition of the word *dwars*, meaning "crossing"; for instance, Palmdwarsstraat is a side street off Palmstraat. Furthermore, and for no apparent reason, some dead-straight cross-streets change their name – so that, for example, in the space of about 300m, 1e Bloemdwarsstraat becomes 2e Leliedwarsstraat and then 3e Egelantiersdwarsstraat.

T/O (*tegenover*, or "opposite") in an address shows that the address is a boat: hence "Prinsengracht T/O 26" would indicate a boat to be found opposite Prinsengracht 26.

The main **Grachtengordel canals** begin their numbering at Brouwersgracht and increase as they progress anticlockwise. By the time they reach the Amstel, Herengracht's house numbers are in the 600s, Keizersgracht's in the 800s and Prinsengracht's in the 900s.

---

between 9am and at least 7pm every day, until midnight in the city centre. The **standard rate** is between €4–5 for one hour within the Grachtengordel and city centre, around €30 for the day (9am–7pm) and €20 or so for the evening (7pm–midnight). An entire day's parking (9am–midnight) costs €45, and you can buy a ticket for the whole week for a whopping €180. Tickets are available from meters if you are paying by the hour, or from **Stadstoezicht** offices around town – call ☎020/553 0333 for details of the nearest one to you. If you overrun your ticket, you can expect to be clamped by eager traffic wardens, who can give you a fine of around €55. The good news is that signs on all the main approach roads to Amsterdam indicate which of the city's car parks have spaces. **Car parks** in the centre charge comparable rates to the metered street spaces. Some of the most central 24-hour car parks are: Amsterdam Centre (Prins Hendrikkade 20; €4 per hour, €55 per day); De Bijenkorf (Beursplein/Damrak; €4 per hour, €50 per day); De Kolk (NZ Voorburgwal/NZ Kolk; €4.20 per hour, €50 per day); Muziektheater (Waterlooplein, under City Hall; €4 per hour, €48 per day). Those on the outskirts are a good deal less expensive and are invariably but a short journey from the centre by public transport. Finally, note that some of the larger

hotels either have their own parking spaces or offer special deals with nearby car parks.

Car rental agencies

Adams Rent-a-Car ⓦ www.adamsrentacar.nl.
Avis ⓦ www.avis.com.
Budget ⓦ www.budget.com.
Diks Autoverhuur ⓦ www.diks.net.
Europcar ⓦ www.europcar.com.
Hertz ⓦ www.hertz.com.

Taxis

Due to the various obstacles that Amsterdam motorists face, **taxis** are not as much use as they are in many other cities. They are, however, plentiful: there's a taxi rank on Stationsplein outside Centraal Station, and other ranks are liberally distributed across the city centre; they can also be hailed on the street. If all else fails, call ☎020/677 7777. **Fares** are metered and are reasonably high, but distances are small; the trip from Centraal Station to the Leidseplein, for example, will cost around €12 (€7.50 for the first 2km, €2.20 per km after that), €2 more to Museumplein. Be warned that there are taxi drivers who will try to set a fixed price for a ride – especially late at night – usually to their own advantage. Don't argue, but ask them to turn on the meter instead.

The media

English-speakers will find themselves quite at home in Amsterdam, as Dutch TV broadcasts a wide range of British programmes, and English-language newspapers from around the world are readily available.

Newspapers and magazines

British newspapers are on sale at most newsagents on the day of publication, for around €4. Current issues of UK and US **magazines** are widely available too, as is the *International Herald Tribune*.

Of the **Dutch newspapers**, *NRC Handelsblad* is a right-of-centre paper that has perhaps the best news coverage and a liberal stance on the arts; *De Volkskrant* is a progressive, leftish daily; the popular right-wing *De Telegraaf* boasts the highest circulation figures in the country and has a well-regarded financial section; *Algemeen Dagblad* is a right-wing broadsheet; while the middle-of-the-road *Het Parool* ("The Password") and the news magazine *Vrij Nederland* ("Free Netherlands") are the successors of underground Resistance newspapers printed during wartime occupation. The Protestant *Trouw* ("Trust"), another former underground paper, is centre-left in orientation with a focus on religion.

Bundled in with the weekend edition of the *International Herald Tribune* is **The Netherlander**, a small but useful business-oriented review of Dutch affairs in English. For events listings in English, see "Tourist information" (p.36).

Television and radio

Dutch **TV** isn't the best, but English-language programmes and films fill up a fair amount of the schedule – and they are always subtitled, never dubbed. Many bars and most hotels have at least two of the big pan-European **cable and satellite** channels

– including MTV, CNN and Eurosport – and most cable companies also give access to a veritable raft of foreign television channels, including Britain's BBC1 and BBC2, National Geographic, Eurosport and Discovery, and a host of Belgian, German, French, Spanish, Italian, Turkish and Arabic stations, some of which also show un-dubbed British and US movies. Other Dutch and Belgian TV channels – cable and non-cable – regularly run English-language movies with Dutch subtitles.

Dutch **radio** has numerous stations catering for every niche. Of the **public service stations**, Radio 1 is a news and sports channel, Radio 2 plays AOR music, Radio 3 plays chart music and Radio 4 classical, jazz and world music. Of the **commercial stations**, some of the main nationwide players are Radio 538, Veronica, Sky Radio and Noordzee FM, and pretty much all play chart music. The Dutch Classic FM, at 101.2FM, plays mainstream classical music, with jazz after 10pm.

There's next to no **English-language programming**, apart from the overseas-targeted Radio Netherlands (@www.rnw.nl), which broadcasts Dutch news in English, with articles on current affairs, lifestyle issues, science, health and so on, and the BBC World Service (@www.bbc.co.uk /worldservice), which broadcasts pretty much all day in English on 648kHz (AM) around Amsterdam; it also occupies 198kHz (long wave) and 101.3 (FM) – as do the Voice of America (@www.voa.gov) and Radio Canada International (@www.rcinet .ca), whose frequencies are listed on their respective websites.

Travel essentials

Crime and personal safety

Though Amsterdam is relatively untroubled by crime in comparison with other European cities, there is nevertheless more street crime than there used to be, and it's advisable to be on your guard against **petty theft**; secure your belongings in a locker when staying in hostel accommodation, and never leave any valuables on view in a car. On the street, beware of the distraction ploys that petty thieves can try, such as someone asking for directions while an accomplice puts their hand in your bag; if you're in a crowd be wary of people moving too close to you. Be cautious when using ATMs, especially late at night, and be wary of suspicious devices fitted around the card slot. If you're on a bike, make sure it is well locked up; bike theft and resale is a major industry here – as is the usual mobile phone theft – keep your network provider's number handy in case you have to bar your phone.

If you are robbed, you'll need to go to a **police station** to report it, not least because your insurance company will require a police report; remember to make a note of the report number – or, better still, ask for a copy of the statement itself. Don't expect a great deal of concern if your loss is relatively small – and don't be surprised if the process of completing forms and formalities takes ages. If your credit card is stolen, report the theft immediately to your card company (see p.34 for contact details).

As for **personal safety**, it's generally possible to walk around most parts of the city without fear of harassment or assault, but wherever you go at night it's always better to err on the side of caution. In particular, Amsterdam's **Red Light District** can have an unpleasant, threatening undertow (although the crowds of people act as a deterrent), as can the area around **Centraal Station** and certain quiet parts of **De Pijp**. In general, try not to wander around looking lost. Using **public transport**, even late at night, isn't usually a problem, but if in doubt take a taxi.

If you're **detained by the police**, you don't automatically have the right to a phone call, although in practice they'll probably phone your consulate for you – not that consular officials have a reputation for excessive helpfulness (particularly in drug cases). If your alleged offence is a minor matter, you can be held for up to six hours without questioning; if it is more serious, you can be detained for up to 24 hours. For details of foreign embassies and consulates, see p.32.

Electricity

The Dutch electricity supply runs at 220v AC. British equipment needs only a plug adaptor; American apparatus requires a transformer and an adaptor.

Entry requirements

Citizens of the EU/EEA, including the UK and Ireland, plus citizens of Australia, New Zealand, Canada and the US do not need a visa to enter the Netherlands if staying for **three months or less**, but they do need a current **passport**. Travellers from South Africa, on the other hand, need a passport

In an **emergency** – police, fire or ambulance – call ☏112. ☏0900/8844 is the number to call if it's not an emergency; they'll give you the details of the nearest city-centre police station. There are police stations at the following locations: NZ Voorburgwal 104; Beursstraat 33; Elandsgracht 117; Marnixstraat 148; Lijnbaansgracht 219; Prinsengracht 1109; Ferdinand Bolstraat 190.

Drugs

Thousands of visitors come to Amsterdam just to get stoned. This is the one Western country where the purchase of **cannabis** is de-criminalized, and the influx of people drawn to the country by this fact creates problems: many Amsterdammers, for instance, get mightily hacked off with "drug tourism". The Dutch government's attitude to soft drugs is more complex than you might think: the use of cannabis is tolerated but not condoned, resulting in a rather complicated set of rules and regulations that can be safely ignored as long as you buy very small amounts for **personal use only** – which means possession of up to 30g and sales of up to 5g per purchase in coffeeshops, though in practice this is pretty relaxed, and many places will happily sell you much more than this (as they will space cakes, although these are also technically illegal).

Current **prices** per gram of hash and marijuana range from €10 for low-grade stuff up to €25 for top-quality hash and as high as €60 for really strong grass. Buy in bulk, or sell to other people, and you become liable under Dutch criminal law. Never, ever buy dope on the street – if you do, you'll likely become a magnet for some pretty unsavoury characters, plus you may find yourself not buying dope at all; in any case there's really no need with the delights on offer in the city's many **coffeeshops**. Since July 2008, smoking tobacco is no longer permitted in bars, restaurants and coffeeshops. You can, however, smoke pure joints or use tobacco substitutes, which are widely available.

Needless to say, the one thing you shouldn't attempt to do is take any form of cannabis out of the country. A surprising number of people think (or claim to think) that if it's bought in Amsterdam it can be taken back home legally; this story won't wash with customs officials and drug enforcement officers, who will happily add your stash to the statistics of national drug seizures, and arrest you into the bargain.

As far as **other drugs** go, Dutch government has recently enforced a new law surrounding magic mushrooms, making them just as illegal as hard drugs after a series of serious incidents. You can still purchase the "grow-your-own" kits or buy truffles, which are claimed to have a similar effect. Despite the existence of a lively and growing trade in cocaine and heroin, possession of either could mean a stay in one of the Netherlands' lively and ever-growing jails. Ecstasy, acid and speed are as illegal in the Netherlands as they are anywhere else.

and a tourist visa before they leave for the Netherlands for a visit of less than three months; these are available from the Dutch embassy (see p.32).

EU/EEA residents (with the exception of Bulgaria and Romania) planning on **staying longer than three months** do not need a residence permit, but they do need to register with **IND**, the Immigration and Naturalization Service (ⓦwww.ind.nl). In Amsterdam, go to the Vreemdelingenpolitie (Foreign Police), Johan Huizingalaan 757 (ⓣ020/889 3045, ⓦwww.immigratiedienst .nl) armed with your birth certificate and proof that you have the funds to finance your stay, a fixed address, and health insurance. Other nationalities wishing to stay in the Netherlands for more than three months need an **entry visa** and a

residence permit. The rules are complicated – so consult your Dutch embassy at home before departure. EU and EEA citizens (with the exception of Bulgaria and Romania) no longer need a permit to be able to **work** in the Netherlands, but pretty much everyone else does – again enquire at the nearest Dutch embassy before you depart for the latest regulations.

Wherever you're from, a good source of information if you're planning a long-term stay is a non-profit organization called **Access** (ⓣ020/423 3217, ⓦwww .access-nl.org). They operate a very useful English-language information line on everything from domestic services to legal matters, as well as running courses on various aspects of Dutch administration and culture.

Dutch embassies abroad

Australia 120 Empire Circuit, Yarralumla, ACT 2600 ☎02/6220 9400, ⓦwww.netherlands.org.au.
Canada 350 Albert St #2020, Ottawa, ON K1R 1A4 ☎1-877/388 2443, ⓦwww.netherlandsembassy.ca.
Ireland 160 Merrion Rd, Dublin 4 ☎01/269 3444, ⓦwww.netherlandsembassy.ie.
New Zealand PO Box 480, Ballance/Featherston St, Wellington ☎04/471 6390, ⓦwww.netherlandsembassy.co.nz.
South Africa 210 Queen Wilhelmina Ave, New Muckleneuk, Pretoria ☎012/425 4500, ⓦwww.dutchembassy.co.za.
UK 38 Hyde Park Gate, London SW7 5DP ☎020/7590 3200, ⓦwww.netherlands-embassy.org.uk.
US 4200 Linnean Ave NW, Washington, DC 20008 ☎1-877/388 2443, ⓦwww.netherlands-embassy.org.

Embassies and consulates in the Netherlands

Australia Carnegielaan 4, 2517 KH The Hague ☎070/310 8200, ⓦwww.netherlands.embassy.gov.au.
Canada Sophialaan 7, 2514 JP The Hague ☎070/311 1600, ⓦwww.canada.nl.
Ireland Dr Kuijperstraat 9, 2514 BA The Hague ☎070/363 0993, ⓦwww.irishembassy.nl.
New Zealand Eisenhowerlaan 77, 2517 KK The Hague ☎070/346 9324, ⓦwww.nzembassy.com.
South Africa Wassenaarseweg 40, 2596 CJ The Hague ☎070/392 4501, ⓦwww.zuidafrika.nl.
UK Lange Voorhout 10, 2514 ED The Hague ☎070/427 0427, ⓦwww.britain.nl; Consulate-General: Koningslaan 44, PO Box 75488, 1070 AL Amsterdam ☎020/676 4343.
US Lange Voorhout 102, 2514 EJ The Hague ☎070/310 2209, ⓦwww.usemb.nl; Consulate General: Museumplein 19, 1071 DJ Amsterdam ☎020/575 5309.

Gay and lesbian travellers

Amsterdam is one of the top **gay destinations** in Europe: attitudes are tolerant, bars are excellent and plentiful, and support groups and facilities are unequalled. The national organization for gay men and women, **COC** (ⓦwww.coc.nl), dates from the 1940s and is actively involved in gaining equal rights for gays and lesbians, as well as informing society's perceptions of homosexuality. The national HQ is in Amsterdam, at Rozenstraat 8 (Mon–Fri 9.30am–5pm; ☎020/623 4596); it can offer help, advice and information on events around the city.

For more help and advice contact Amsterdam's **Gay and Lesbian Switchboard** on ☎020/623 6565. Gay legislation in the Netherlands is streets ahead of the rest of the world; same-sex marriage and adoption by same-sex partners were legalized in 2001, and within six months over two thousand couples had tied the knot. The age of consent is 16.

Consider timing your visit to coincide with **Amsterdam Pride** (ⓦwww.amsterdamgaypride.nl) on the first weekend in August, **Queen's Day** (not solely a gay event) on April 30 or **Leather Pride** (ⓦwww.leatherpride.nl) in late October and November. For more information on gay festivals and events, as well as gay accommodation and nightlife, see Chapter 12.

Health

As a member of the European Union, the Netherlands has free reciprocal health agreements with other member states. **EU citizens** are entitled to free treatment within the Netherlands' public healthcare system on production of a European Health Insurance Card (**EHIC**), which you can obtain by picking up a form at the post office, calling ☎0845 606 2030, or applying online at ⓦwww.dh.gov.uk; allow up to 21 days for delivery. The EHIC is free of charge and valid for at least three years, and it basically entitles you to the same treatment as an insured person in the Netherlands. **Australians** are able to receive treatment through a reciprocal arrangement with Medicare (check with your local office for details).

In an **emergency** phone ☎112. If you're reliant on **free treatment** within the EU health scheme, try to make this clear to the ambulance staff, and, if you're whisked off to hospital, to the medic you subsequently encounter. If possible, it's a good idea to hand over a photocopy of your EHIC on arrival at the hospital to ensure your status is clearly understood. As for describing symptoms, you can be pretty sure that someone will speak English. Without an EHIC you won't be turned away from a hospital, but you will have to pay for any treatment you receive and should therefore get an official receipt, a necessary preamble to the long-winded process of trying to get at least some of the money back.

You can get the address of an **English-speaking doctor** from your local pharmacy, tourist office or hotel. If you're entitled to free treatment under EU health agreements, double-check that the doctor is both working within, and regarding you as a patient of, the public health care system. Bear in mind, though, that even within the EU agreement you may still have to pay a significant portion of the prescription charges (although senior citizens and children are exempt). Most private health insurance policies don't help cover prescription charges either, and although the "excesses" are usually greater than the cost of the medicines, it's worth keeping receipts just in case.

The **main hospitals** (*ziekenhuis*) are: Academic Medical Centre (AMC; Meibergdreef 9, ☎020/566 9111), VU Medical Centre (De Boelelaan 1117, ☎020/444 4444), Onze Lieve Vrouwe Gasthuis (Oosterpark 9, ☎020/599 9111) and Sint Lucas Ziekenhuis (Jan Tooropstraat 164, ☎020/510 8911).

Minor ailments can be remedied at a drugstore (*drogist*). These sell non-prescription drugs as well as toiletries, tampons, condoms and the like. A pharmacy or *apotheek* (usually open Mon–Fri 9.30am–6pm, but often closed Mon mornings) also handles prescriptions; centrally located pharmacies include Dam Apotheek (Damstraat 2, ☎020/624 4331), Lairesse Apotheek (De Lairessestraat 40, ☎020/662 1022) and Apotheek Koek, Schaeffer & Van Tijen (Vijzelgracht 19, ☎020/623 5949).

Dental treatment is not within the scope of the EU health agreement; enquire at the local tourist office or your hotel reception for an English-speaking dentist.

Insurance

Even though EU health care privileges apply in the Netherlands, you'd do well to take out an **insurance policy** before travelling to cover against theft, loss, illness or injury. A typical policy usually provides cover for the loss of baggage, tickets and – up to a certain limit – cash or cheques, as well as

cancellation or curtailment of your journey. Many policies can be chopped and changed to exclude coverage you don't need: sickness and accident benefits can often be excluded or included at will. If you need to make a **claim**, you should keep all receipts, and in the event you have anything stolen, you must obtain an official statement from the police.

Visitors planning **longer stays** (at least three months) are required by Dutch law to take out private health insurance. Taking out private insurance means the cost of items not within the scope of the EU scheme, such as dental treatment and repatriation on medical grounds, will be covered.

Non-EU residents, apart from Australians, will need to insure themselves against all eventualities, including medical costs. In the case of major expense, the more worthwhile policies promise to sort matters out before you pay rather than after, but if you do have to pay upfront, make very sure that you always keep full doctors' reports, signed prescription details and all receipts.

Internet

Amsterdam has a healthy supply of **internet cafés** and most hotels provide internet access for their guests for free or for a small charge; many have also installed wi-fi networks. A central option is Internetcafe at Martelaarsgracht 11 (daily 9am–1am, Fri & Sat until 3am; ☎020/627 1052, ⊛www.internet cafe.nl), just 200m from Centraal Station, serving alcoholic drinks as well as the usual juice and coffee. Rates are reasonable – €1 per half hour, including a drink. There's also **free internet access** at the main library (Bibliotheek; see p.109) near Centraal Station.

Laundry

Larger hotels generally provide a laundry service, though this tends to be expensive. The city's best **self-service laundry** is Clean Brothers, Westerstraat 26 (Jordaan and Western docklands; daily 8am–8pm), charging €7 for a wash and dry. They also do service washes, dry-cleaning, ironing and so on. Other laundries are to be found at Kerkstraat 367 (Grachtengordel South) and Warmoesstraat 30 (Old Centre).

Left luggage

There's a staffed left-luggage desk in the basement of Schiphol Airport, between Arrivals halls 1 and 2 (daily 7am–10.45pm), as well as left-luggage lockers. Small items cost roughly €3 per day, medium €4, large €5 and very bulky items €7.50; the maximum storage time is seven days. At Centraal Station, you'll find coin-operated left-luggage lockers (daily 7am–1pm), as well as a staffed left-luggage office (daily 7am–11pm). Small coin-operated lockers cost €4.50 for 24 hours, the larger ones €7.

At train stations outside Amsterdam, left-luggage lockers cannot currently be used without a Dutch debit card.

Libraries

The main public library, the Bibliotheek, is at Oosterdokskade 143, just west of Centraal Station (daily 10am–10pm).

Lost property

For items lost on the trams, buses or metro, contact GVB Head Office, Prins Hendrikkade 108–114 (Mon–Fri 9am–4pm; ☎0900/8011). For property lost on a train, first go to the service office at Centraal Station (24hr). After five days all unclaimed property goes to the Central Lost Property Office in Utrecht (☎0900/321 2100). If you lose something in the street or park, try the police lost property office at Korte Leidsedwarsstraat 52 (Mon–Fri 9am–4pm; ☎14020). Schiphol Airport's lost and found desk is in the Arrivals Hall (daily 8am–6pm; ☎0900/0141).

Mail

As part of a gradual scheme, all **Dutch post offices** are scheduled to close by 2012, and postal transactions will be carried out at the new **TNT** stores or places with the TNT logo. **Stamps** are sold at a wide range of outlets including many supermarkets, shops and hotels. **Postboxes** are everywhere, but be sure to use the correct slot – the one labelled *overige* is for post going outside the immediate locality.

Maps

The **maps** in this guide should be more than adequate for most purposes, but if you need one on a larger scale, or with a street index, then pick up *The Rough Guide Map to Amsterdam*, which has the added advantage of being waterproof and rip-proof. This marks all the key sights as well as the location of many restaurants, bars and hotels. If you want a map covering the outer suburbs as well, the best bet is the **Falk** map of Amsterdam (1:15,000). Other options include the city maps sold by the VVV, which come complete with a street index, and the handily compact, spiral-bound street atlases produced by Falk (suburbs: 1:12,500; centre 1:7500).

Money

The **currency** of the Netherlands – like much of the rest of the EU – is the **euro** (€), divided into 100 cents. At the time of writing the exchange rate was €0.75 to $1 and €1.10 to £1. There are **notes** of €500, €200, €100, €50, €20, €10 and €5, and **coins** of €2, €1, 50c, 20c, 10c, 5c and 2c. Euro coins feature a common EU design on one face, but different country-specific designs on the other, but no matter what the design, all euro coins and notes are legal tender in all of the following countries as well as the Netherlands: Austria, Belgium, Finland, France, Germany, Greece, the Republic of Ireland, Italy, Luxembourg, Portugal and Spain. Note that bills of €200 and €500 are almost impossible to change anywhere other than in an official bank.

The Netherlands is a **cash** society; as a general rule, people prefer to pay for most things with notes and coins. However, **debit cards** are becoming increasingly popular, and most shops and restaurants accept these and **credit cards**. You can use many Visa, Mastercard and UK debit cards (within the Cirrus, Plus or Maestro systems) to withdraw cash from **ATMs** – often the quickest and easiest way of obtaining money. There are dozens around the city and they give instructions in a variety of languages.

In the event that your **credit card is lost or stolen**, call ☎020/504 8666 for American Express (☎0800/022 0100 for traveller's cheques); ☎0800/022 5821 for MasterCard; and ☎0800/022 3110 for Visa.

Dutch banks usually offer the best deals on changing money. Banking hours are Monday to Friday 9am to 4pm, with a few big-city banks also open Thursday until 9pm or on Saturday morning; all are closed on public holidays (see below). Outside these times, changing money is rarely a problem; there's a nationwide network of **GWK exchange offices**, which are open late every day, and at Amsterdam Centraal Station and Schiphol Airport, 24 hours a day. GWK offers competitive rates and charges reasonable commissions, but some other agencies do not, so be cautious. VVV tourist offices also exchange money, as do most hotels and campsites and some hostels, but their rates are generally poor.

Opening hours and public holidays

The Dutch weekend fades painlessly into the working week with many smaller shops and businesses, even in Amsterdam, staying closed on Monday mornings until noon. **Normal opening hours** are, however, Monday to Friday 8.30/9am to 5.30/6pm and Saturday 8.30/9am to 4/5pm, and many places open late on Thursday or Friday evenings. **Sunday** opening is becoming increasingly common, especially within the city centre, where most shops are now open between noon and 5pm.

Most **restaurants** are open for dinner from about 6 or 7pm, and though many close as early as 9.30pm, a few stay open past 11pm. **Bars**, **cafés and coffeeshops** are either open all day from around 10am or don't open until about 5pm; all close at 1am during the week and 2am at weekends. **Nightclubs** generally open their doors from 11pm to 4am during the week, though a few

open every night, and some stay open until 5am at the weekend. A handful of **night shops** – *avondwinkels* – stay open into the small hours or round the clock.

Museums are usually open from Monday to Friday from 10am to 5pm (some smaller museums are closed on Monday, the main tourist drags have longer opening hours), and from 11am to 5pm on weekends. Though closed for Christmas and New Year, state-run museums adopt Sunday hours on the remaining public holidays, when most shops and banks are closed. **Galleries** tend to be open from Tuesday to Sunday from noon to 5pm. Precise opening hours are quoted throughout the guide.

Public holidays (*nationale feestdagen*) provide the perfect excuse to take to the streets. The most celebrated of them all is **Queen's Day** – *Koninginnedag* – on April 30, which is celebrated throughout the Netherlands but with particular gusto in Amsterdam. The rest are as follows: New Year's Day, Good Friday, Easter Sunday and Monday, Liberation Day (May 5), Ascension Day, Whit Sunday and Monday (seven weeks after Easter), and Christmas (December 25 and 26).

Phones

The **international phone code** for the Netherlands is 31. Numbers prefixed ☎0800 are free; those prefixed ☎0900 are premium-rate – a (Dutch) message before you're connected tells you how much you will be paying for the call, and you can only call them from within the Netherlands. **Phone booths** are rapidly disappearing as a concomitant of the irresistible rise of the mobile phone, but there is a light scattering at major locations, like Centraal Station. **Phone cards** can be bought at outlets like

Calling home from abroad

Note that the initial zero is omitted from the area code when dialling the UK, Ireland, Australia and New Zealand from abroad.

UK international access code + 44 + city code.
Republic of Ireland international access code + 353 + city code.
US and Canada international access code + 1 + area code.
Australia international access code + 61 + city code.
New Zealand international access code + 64 + city code.
South Africa international access code + 27 + city code.

The VVV

Once in Amsterdam, any of the city's tourist offices, the **VVV**s (pronounced "fay-fay-fay"), will be able to help with practical information.

There's a VVV on platform 2 at Centraal Station (Daily 11am–7pm) and a second, main one directly across from the main station entrance on Stationsplein (daily 9am–6pm). These two offices share one premium-rate **information line** on ℡0900/400 4040, and a **website**: ⓦwww.iamsterdam.com. They offer **advice and information** and sell a range of **maps** and guidebooks as well as **tickets** and passes for public transport. They also take in-person bookings for canal cruises and other organized **excursions**, sell theatre and concert tickets, and operate an extremely efficient **accommodation reservation service** for just €3 plus a refundable deposit which is subtracted from your final bill – especially useful in high season when finding accommodation isn't always easy.

tobacconists and VVV offices, and in several denominations, beginning at €5. The cheap-rate period for international calls is between 8pm and 8am during the week and all day at weekends.

There is good coverage for **mobile phones/cell phones** all over the Netherlands. You need to use a mobile with 900 and 1800 MHz bands. Prepaid SIM cards are available in telephone shops (on the Rokin and around Kalverstraat) and in some supermarkets.

To speak to the **Operator** (domestic and international), call ℡0800 0410; for **Directory Enquiries**, dial ℡0900 8008 (domestic), ℡0900 8418 (international).

The **Dutch phone directory** is available (in Dutch) at ⓦwww.detelefoongids.nl.

Time

Amsterdam, and indeed the whole of the Netherlands, is on **Central European Time** (CET) – one hour ahead of London, six hours ahead of New York, nine hours ahead of Los Angeles and eight hours behind Sydney. **Daylight saving** operates from the end of March to the end of October.

Tipping

Tipping isn't quite as routine a matter as it is in the US or even in the UK. However, you are expected to leave something if you have enjoyed good service – up to around ten percent of the bill should suffice in most restaurants, while hotel porters and taxi drivers may expect a euro or two on top of the fare.

Tourist information

Information on Amsterdam is easy to get hold of, either before you leave from the **Netherlands Board of Tourism**, by phone or post or via the internet – the NBT's all-encompassing website, ⓦwww.holland.com, highlights upcoming events and is strong on practical information.

For information about **what's on**, there's either the VVV (see box above) or the Amsterdam Uitburo, the cultural office of the city council, housed in a corner of the Stadsschouwburg theatre on Leidseplein (Mon–Sat 10am–7.30pm, Sun noon–7.30pm; ℡020/795 9950). You can get advice here on anything remotely cultural, as well as tickets and copies of listings magazines. Among the latter, there's a choice between the AUB's own monthly *Uitkrant*, which is comprehensive and free but in Dutch, and the VVV's *Day by Day in Amsterdam*. Alternatively, the free *NL20* magazine (in Dutch) is one of the most up-to-date and complete reference sources and can be found in many supermarkets, cafés and shops. The Wednesday entertainment supplement of the newspaper *Het Parool* also gives a good overview of most cultural activities and *Amsterdam Weekly* is a free cultural newspaper in English, published every Wednesday, with information on film, music and the arts.

Various **tourist passes** are available. The VVV's much-touted **Amsterdam Card** provides unlimited use of the city's public transport network, a complimentary canal cruise and free admission to the bulk of the city's museums and attractions. It costs €38 for one day, €48 for two consecutive days and €58 for three consecutive days. Altogether it's not a bad deal, but you have to work fairly hard to make it worthwhile. It's available from any branch of the VVV. An alternative if you're staying for more than a couple of days is the **Museumkaart** (museum card), which gives free entry to most museums in the whole of the Netherlands for a year; it costs €40 (less if you're 24 or under). Full details, including online ordering, are at ⓦwww.museumkaart.nl, or you can purchase one at any participating museum.

The **I Amsterdam** card (ⓦwww.iamsterdamcard.com) serves as a public transport pass and an entrance ticket to all the major museums; it also offers discounts at restaurants and attractions. It's available in 24hr, 48hr and 72hr versions, costing €38, €48 and €58 respectively. A free canal boat ride is included in the price. You can buy it online, or at any VVV.

Concessionary rates are applied at every city sight and attraction as well as on the public transport system. Rates vary, but usually seniors (65+) get in free or for a discounted price, while children of 5 and under get in for free; family tickets are common too.

Guided tours

No one could say the Amsterdam tourist industry doesn't make the most of its **canals**, with a veritable armada of glass-topped **cruise boats** shuttling along the city's waterways, offering everything from quick hour-long excursions to fully-fledged dinner cruises. There are several major operators which occupy the prime pitches – the jetties near Centraal Station on Stationsplein, beside the Damrak and on Prins Hendrikkade. **Prices** are fairly uniform, with a one-hour tour costing around €12 per adult, €6 per child (4–12 years old), and around €25 (€15) for a two-hour cruise at night. The big companies also offer more **specialized boat trips** – dinner cruises from around €59, literary cruises, and most notably the weekly Architecture Cruise run by Lovers (☏020/530 1090, ⓦwww.lovers.nl; €22.50/17.50). All these cruises – and especially the shorter and less expensive ones – are extremely popular, and long queues are common throughout the summer. There are also plenty of tours on dry land, from guided **cycle rides** to a meander around the city **on foot**. A selection is given below, but if you have a specific interest – Dutch art, for example – it's well worth asking at the **VVV** to see what's on offer.

Tour operators

Mee in Mokum Keizersgracht 346 ☏020/625 1390, ⓦwww.gildeamsterdam.nl. Guided walking tours of the old centre and the Jordaan provided by long-time Amsterdam residents. Tours run four or five times weekly; €5 per person. Advance reservations required.

Reederij P. Kooij on the Rokin, beside the Queen Wilhelmina statue ☏020/623 3810, ⓦwww.rederijkooij.nl. One way of avoiding the tour queues is to head for the first-rate Reederij P. Kooij, which offers a standard range of day and night cruises at competitive prices. Also has a (more crowded) jetty opposite Centraal Station on Stationsplein, and by Leidseplein.

Urban Home & Garden Tours ☏020/688 1243, ⓦwww.uhgt.nl. Three-hour tours (April–Oct) that explore a number of the city's canal houses and gardens, guided by landscape gardeners and art historians. Tours are held Fri, Sat and Sun, and cost €28.50 (the fee includes refreshments). Cash only, no credit cards.

Yellow Bike Tours Nieuwezijds Kolk 29, off Nieuwezijds Voorburgwal ☏020/620 6940, ⓦwww.yellowbike.nl. Three-hour guided cycling tours around the city (two daily April to mid-Oct) that cost €21.50 per person, including the bike. Other tours – of the Jordaan, Red Light District, etc – available. Advance reservations required.

Netherlands Board of Tourism offices

UK PO Box 30783, London WC2B 6DH ☎020/7539 7950, ⓔinfo-uk@holland.com.
US 355 Lexington Ave, New York, NY 10017
☎1-212-370-7360, ⓔinformation@holland.com.
  There are no offices in Australia or New Zealand.

Tourist offices and government sites

Australian Department of Foreign Affairs ⓦwww.dfat.gov.au, ⓦwww.smartraveller.gov.au.
British Foreign & Commonwealth Office ⓦwww.fco.gov.uk.
Canadian Department of Foreign Affairs ⓦwww.dfait-maeci.gc.ca.
Irish Department of Foreign Affairs ⓦwww.foreignaffairs.gov.ie.
New Zealand Ministry of Foreign Affairs ⓦwww.mft.govt.nz.
South African Department of Foreign Affairs ⓦwww.dfa.gov.za.
US State Department ⓦwww.travel.state.gov.

Travellers with disabilities

Despite its general social progressiveness, the Netherlands is only just getting to grips with the requirements of people with **mobility problems**. In Amsterdam and most of the other major cities, the most obvious difficulty you'll face is in negotiating the cobbled streets and narrow, often broken pavements of the older districts, where the key sights are often located. Similarly, provision for people with disabilities on **public transport** is only average, although improving – many new buses, for instance, are now wheelchair-accessible. And yet, while it can be difficult simply to get around, practically all public buildings, including museums, theatres, cinemas, concert halls and hotels, are obliged to provide access, and do.

Places that have been certified **wheelchair-accessible** now bear an International Accessibility Symbol (IAS). Bear in mind, however, that a lot of the older, narrower hotels are not allowed to install lifts, so check first. If you're planning to use the **Dutch train network** during your stay and would appreciate assistance on the platform, phone the Bureau Assistentieverlening Gehandicapten (Disabled Assistance Office) on ☎030/235 7822 at least three hours before your train departs, and there will be someone to meet and help you at the station (office open daily 7am–11pm). NS, the Netherlands Railways association, publishes information about train travel for people with disabilities online at ⓦwww.ns.nl and in various leaflets, stocked at main stations.

Travellers with a pre-existing medical condition are sometimes excluded from **insurance policies**; read the small print carefully. Ask your doctor for a medical certificate of your fitness to travel as some insurance companies insist on it.

The City

The City

The Old Centre

A msterdam's most vivacious and arguably most touristy district, the **Old Centre** is an oval-shaped tangle of narrow streets and picturesque canals, confined in the north by the River IJ and to the west and south by the Singel, the first of several canals that once girdled the entire city. Given the dominance of **Centraal Station** on most transport routes, this is almost certainly where you'll arrive. Immediately outside, **Stationsplein** is home to the main tourist and transport information offices, a busy maelstrom of buskers and bicycles, trams and tourists – and, for the past few years, construction works, as slow progress on the city's new metro line continues. From here, a stroll across the bridge will take you onto the **Damrak**, which once divided the **Oude Zijde** (Old Side) of the medieval city to the east from the smaller **Nieuwe Zijde** (New Side) to the west. It also led – and leads – to the heart of the Old Centre, **Dam Square**, which is overseen by two of the city's most impressive buildings, the **Koninklijk Paleis** (Royal Palace) and the **Nieuwe Kerk** (New Church). **Rokin** runs south from Dam Square, parallel to pedestrianized **Kalverstraat**, which is the city's prime mainstream shopping street. Sights-wise, the main targets in this area are the secluded **Begijnhof**, a circle of dignified old houses originally built for a semi-religious community in the 1340s, and the museum of city history, the **Amsterdams Historisch Museum**.

Nowadays, much of the Oude Zijde is taken up by the city's notorious **Red Light District**, which stretches across Warmoesstraat and the two canals – **Oudezijds Voorburgwal** and **Oudezijds Achterburgwal** – that formed the heart of medieval Amsterdam. There's a prevailing seediness in the Red Light District that inevitably dulls its many charms, but there are still one or two signs that you are in the city's most historic quarter: the delightful **Amstelkring**, a clandestine Catholic church dating from the seventeenth century, and the charming Gothic architecture of the **Oude Kerk**, not to mention the relatively unpretentious beauty of the **canals** themselves (if you can block out the prevailing neon). The sleazy atmosphere decreases the further east you go towards **Nieuwmarkt**, a large and unassuming square where **Kloveniersburgwal** begins, a large and stately canal that effectively marks the border of the Red Light District. Further east, another canal, **Groenburgwal**, is one of the most beguiling parts of the Old Centre, with a medley of handsome old houses lining what is one of its prettiest stretches of water.

THE OLD CENTRE

River IJ

Passenger Ferries

Centraal Station

CENTRAAL STATION

GVB

St Nicolaaskerk

Schreierstoren

RED LIGHT DISTRICT

Amstelkring

Erotic Museum

Oude Kerk

Condomerie Het Gulden Vlies

Waag

NIEUWMARKT

Trippen-huis

NIEUWMARKT

Pintohuis

Zuiderkerk & Zuidertoren

Rembrandthuis

Zwanenburgwal

WATERLOOPLEIN

Muziektheater

WATERLOOPLEIN

Amstel

Hotel de l'Europe

Hotel Doelen

Nos 141-147

Rasphuis

Munttoren

Bloemenmarkt

Allard Pierson Museum

Huis op de Drie Grachten

Oudemanhuispoort

University of Amsterdam

Wilhelmina Statue

Begijnhof

Galerie Mokum

Agnietenkapel

No 92   No 91

Amsterdams Historisch Museum

No 83

No 69   'ome Jan'

Amsterdam Dungeon

Spinhuis

Oostindisch Huis

Kleine Trippenhuis

Hash Museum

Madame Tussaud's

War Memorial

DAM SQUARE

Koninklijk Paleis

Magna Plaza

Nieuwe Kerk

De Bijenkorf

Beurs

Prostitution Info Centre

BEURSPLEIN

Sex Museum

Crowne Plaza Hotel

Luthersekerk

Hofje Van Brienen

Brouwersgracht

STATIONSPLEIN

Open

Havenfront

Damrak

Singel

Keizersgracht

Herengracht

Raadhuisstraat

Leidseplein

0   200 m

Amsterdam's **Old Centre** follows the core of the original city, its narrow streets and canals confined to the north by the River IJ and the harbour, and to the west and south by the Singel, which used to form the boundary of the old port. Amsterdam started out as a humble **fishing village** here, at the marshy mouth of the River Amstel, before the local lord gave it some significance by building a castle in 1204. Sixty years later, the Amstel was dammed – leading to the name "Amstelredam" – and the village began to flourish as a **trading centre**. The city then developed in stages, each of which was marked by the digging of new **canals** to either side of the main canal linking the River IJ with Dam Square, along today's Damrak. The city grew at first around the canals of today's Red Light District and after that on the other side of the Damrak. Time and again the wooden buildings of medieval Amsterdam went up in smoke, until finally, after a particularly severe fire in 1452, timber was banned in favour of brick and stone – and it's these handsome **canal houses** of the seventeenth and eighteenth centuries that provide the Old Centre with most of its architectural high points.

However, it's a modern **building project** that has dominated this part of the city in recent years: the plan to redevelop the station and the area around it at the same time as building a new **metro line** linking Amsterdam's city centre with the south of the city and stations across the IJ in the resurgent North. City centre stations are to be built at Centraal Station, Rokin and the Vijzelgracht, and for the best part of six years now the area around Stationsplein especially has been a massive construction site; the chaos looks set to continue for some time, until completion of the project in 2015. There has been huge controversy over the plan: some question whether it's even possible to build a tunnel under a city centre that is mainly built on wooden stilts, and work was halted for a while in 2008 when a number of city centre buildings began to collapse. But the authorities are determined to press on, and claim they will deliver not only better connections between the city centre and its outlying districts, but also a more pleasant, pedestrian-friendly Stationsplein and inner harbour. Whatever the result, it will seem like an improvement after the upheaval of the past few years.

Damrak and the Nieuwe Zijde

Running from Centraal Station to Dam Square, the **Damrak** – a broad, rather unenticing avenue lined with tacky restaurants, bars and bureaux de change – slices south into the heart of the city, first passing an inner harbour crammed with the bobbing canal cruise boats of Amsterdam's considerable tourist industry. It was a canal until 1672, when it was filled in; up until then it had been the medieval city's main nautical artery, with boats sailing up it to discharge their goods right in the centre of town on the main square. Thereafter, with the docks moved elsewhere, the Damrak became a busy commercial drag, as it remains today, and Dam Square became the centre of municipal power.

To the west of the Damrak lies the Old Centre's **Nieuwe Zijde**, whose outer boundary was marked in the 1500s by a defensive wall, hence the name of its principal avenue, **Nieuwezijds Voorburgwal** ("In Front of the Town Wall on the New Side"). The wall disappeared as the city grew, and in the nineteenth century the canal that ran through the middle of the street was earthed in, leaving the unusually wide thoroughfare that you see today. This area was, however, badly mauled by the developers in the 1970s and – give or take a scattering of old canal houses on Nieuwezijds Voorburgwal – there's no great reason to linger.

▲ Centraal Station

Centraal Station and Stationsplein

With its high gables and cheerful brickwork, the neo-Renaissance **Centraal Station** is an imposing prelude to the city. At the time of its construction on an artifical island in the 1880s, it aroused much controversy because it effectively separated the centre from the River IJ, source of the city's wealth, for the first time in Amsterdam's long history. There was controversy about the choice of architect too; the man chosen, **Petrus J.H. Cuypers**, was Catholic, and in powerful Protestant circles there were mutterings about the vanity of his designs (he had recently completed the Rijksmuseum) and their unsuitability for Amsterdam. In the event, the station was built to Cuypers' design, but it was to be his last major commission; thereafter he spent most of his time building parish churches. Whatever you think about the building it's a nice place to arrive. Its grand arches and cavernous main hall have a suitable sense of occasion, and from here all of the city lies before you – though for the moment **Stationsplein** itself is a pretty unprepossessing introduction: a messy open space, edged by ovals of water, packed with trams and dotted with barrel organs, chip stands and street performers in summer, and currently in the throes of a massive redevelopment (see box, p.43).

St Nicolaaskerk

Across the water from Stationsplein, on Prins Hendrikkade, rise the twin towers and dome of **St Nicolaaskerk** (Mon & Sat noon–3pm, Tues–Fri 11am–4pm; free), the city's foremost Catholic church, dedicated to the patron saint of sailors – and of Amsterdam. Like the station, it dates back to the 1880s; the cavernous interior holds some pretty dire religious murals, mawkish concoctions only partly relieved by swathes of coloured brickwork. Above the high altar is the crown of the Habsburg Emperor Maximilian, very much a symbol of the city and one you'll see again and again. Amsterdam had close ties with Maximilian; in the late fifteenth century he came here as a pilgrim and stayed on to recover from an illness. The burghers funded many of his military expeditions, and in return he let the city use his crown in its coat of arms – a practice which, rather surprisingly, survived the seventeenth-century revolt against Spain.

The Schreierstoren

Just around the corner from St Nicolaaskerk, at the top of the Geldersekade canal, is the squat **Schreierstoren** (Weepers' Tower), a rare surviving chunk of the city's medieval wall. Originally, the tower overlooked the River IJ and it was here that women gathered to watch their menfolk sail away, though like many good stories this is apparently apocryphal: "Schreierstoren" refers to the sharp angle – the "schreye" – at which it was built, rather than the weeping women. Nonetheless, an old and weathered stone plaque inserted in the wall is a reminder of all those supposed sad farewells, and another much more recent plaque recalls the departure of Henry Hudson from here in 1609. On this particular voyage Hudson stumbled across the "Hudson" river and an island the locals called Manhattan. The colony that grew up there became known as New Amsterdam, a colonial possession that was only renamed New York after the English seized it in 1664. These days the Schreierstoren houses a small café with a terrace overlooking the canal.

The Sex Museum

The first real sight along Damrak, if you can call it that, is the Amsterdam **Sex Museum** (daily 9.30am–11.30pm; €3), a surprisingly large museum, and very popular given its position designed to draw in the tourist hordes in search of all the titillation the city has to offer. It's reasonably entertaining, depicting the history of pin-ups, sex and erotica through the centuries, with lots of Victorian porn photos, explicit private porn collections from the 1950s and 1960s and some genuinely antique items – nineteenth – century ivory dildos, Indian prints, ancient Roman sculpture and a room devoted to Japanese erotica. There's also an ever-running reel of grainy old movies and a (fairly hardcore) "fetish" room. Not for the prudish.

The Beurs

Just beyond the harbour at Damrak 277 is the imposing bulk of the **Beurs**, the old Stock Exchange (opening hours and admission depend on exhibitions;

guided tours can be arranged on ℡020/620 8112; ⓦwww.beursvanberlage.nl) – known as the "Beurs van Berlage" – a seminal work designed at the turn of the twentieth century by the leading light of the Dutch Modern movement, **Hendrik Petrus Berlage** (1856–1934). Berlage rerouted Dutch architecture with this building, forsaking the historicism that had dominated the nineteenth century, whose prime practitioner had been Cuypers (see p.44). Instead he opted for a style with cleaner, heavier lines, inspired by the Romanesque and the Renaissance, but with the minimum of ornamentation. In so doing, he anticipated the Expressionism that swept across northern Europe from 1905 to 1925. The Beurs has long since lost its commercial function and nowadays hosts concerts and conferences, as well as exhibitions on modern art and design. The building is still the main event, from the graceful exposed ironwork and shallow-arched arcades of the main hall through to a fanciful frieze celebrating the stockbroker's trade. Seeing a temporary exhibition is the only chance you'll get to see inside, unless you visit the convivial *Café Beurs van Berlage* that fronts onto Beursplein around the corner (see p.182). There you can have a coffee and admire the tiled scenes of the past, present and future by the twentieth-century Dutch artist Jan Toorop.

De Bijenkorf

Just southwest of the Beurs, the enormous department store **De Bijenkorf** – literally "beehive" – extends south along the Damrak. De Bijenkorf posed all sorts of problems for the Germans when they first occupied the city in World War II. The store was a Jewish concern, so the Nazis didn't really want their troops shopping here, but it was just too popular to implement a total ban. The bizarre solution was to prohibit German soldiers from shopping on the ground floor, where the store's Jewish employees were concentrated, as they always had been, in the luxury goods section. These days it's a good all-round department store, with the usual floors of designer-wear and well-known brands but none of the snootiness you usually associate with such places.

The Crowne Plaza

Nieuwezijds Voorburgwal kicks off with the **Crowne Plaza Hotel** at no. 5, formerly the Holiday Inn, built on the site of an old tenement building called **Wyers**. The 1985 clearance of squatters from Wyers ranks among the more infamous of that decade's anti-squatting campaigns, involving a great deal of protest (and some violence) throughout the city. The squatters had occupied the building in an attempt to prevent yet another slice of the city being converted from residential to business use. They were widely supported by the people of Amsterdam, but they couldn't match the clout of the American hotel company and riot police were sent in; construction of the hotel followed soon after.

The Lutherse Kerk

It's a short walk from Nieuwezijds Voorbugwal along Hekelveld and down Kattengat to the **Lutherse Kerk**, a round, seventeenth-century edifice whose copper dome gives this area its nickname, **Koepelkwartier** ("Copper quarter"). Church domes are a rarity in Amsterdam, but this one was no stylistic pecca-dillo; until the late eighteenth century, only Dutch Reformed churches were permitted the (much more fashionable) bell towers, so the Lutherans got stuck with a dome. It's a grand building, seen to best advantage from the Singel canal, but it has been dogged by bad luck; in 1882 the interior was gutted by fire and, although it was repaired, the cost of maintenance proved too high for the congregation, who decamped in 1935. After many years of neglect, the adjacent *Renaissance Hotel* bought the church, turning it into a conference centre.

Nieuwezijds Kolk

Just off Nieuwezijds Voorburgwal is the open space of **Nieuwezijds Kolk**, where the angular, glassy and ultramodern ABN-Amro bank building on the corner is testament to the recent large-scale construction work that has transformed the area. When the underground car park was being dug here, workers discovered archeological remains dating back to the thirteenth century; these turned out to be the castle of the "Lords of Amstel", which, it is thought, had occupied the site when it was open marshland, even before the Amstel was dammed. The square is anchored by a quaint, brick gabled building, but the series of pedestrianized alleys that link Nieuwezijds Voorburgwal to the Damrak to the south of Nieuwezijds Kolk are without much charm. Consequently, it's better to stay on Nieuwezijds Voorburgwal as it heads south, its trees partly concealing a series of impressive canal houses, though these fizzle out as you approach Dam Square.

Spuistraat and the Spui

Spuistraat runs parallel with Nieuwezijds Voorburgwal for much of its length, a happening street, liberally sprinkled with bars and restaurants, and the location of central Amsterdam's last **squat**, *Vrankrijk*, at number 216, which at the time of writing had been closed down after a squatter was almost beaten to death there in September 2008. There was a thriving bar and club here, which looks certain to stay closed; whether the squat will reopen remains to be seen, but as one of the city's "legal" squats its chances are good as long as there are no more violent incidents. At its top and buzziest end it opens out onto the **Spui**, a wide, tram-clanking square flanked by the appealing Athenaeum bookshop and a number of café-bars. In the middle is a cloying statue of a young boy, known as 't **Lieverdje** ("Little Darling" or "Loveable Scamp"), a gift to the city from a cigarette company in 1960. It was here in the mid-1960s, with the statue seen as a symbol of the addicted consumer, that the playful Sixties anarchist group, the **Provos**, organized some of their most successful *ludiek* (pranks).

Dam Square

Situated at the heart of the city, **Dam Square** gave Amsterdam its name – it was here, in the thirteenth century, that the River Amstel was dammed; the fishing village that grew around it became known as "Amstelredam". Boats could sail down the Damrak into the square, and unload in the middle of the village, which soon prospered by trading herring for Baltic grain. In the early fifteenth century, the building of Amsterdam's principal church, the **Nieuwe Kerk**, followed by the town hall (now the Koninklijk Paleis), formally marked Dam Square as Amsterdam's centre. Today it's an open and airy but somehow rather desultory space, despite – or perhaps partly because of – the presence of the main municipal **war memorial**, a prominent stone tusk adorned by bleak, suffering figures and decorated with the coats of arms of each of the Netherlands' provinces (plus the ex-colony of Indonesia). The memorial was designed by **Jacobus Johannes Pieter Oud** (1890–1963), a De Stijl stalwart who thought the Expressionism of Berlage much too flippant.

The Koninklijk Paleis

Dominating Dam Square is the **Koninklijk Paleis** (Ⓦ www.koninklijkhuis.nl), the Royal Palace, although the title is deceptive, given that this vast sandstone structure was built as the city's Stadhuis (Town Hall), and only had its first royal occupant when Louis Bonaparte moved in during the French occupation (1795–1813).

The **exterior** of the palace is very much to the allegorical point: twin tympani depict Amsterdam as a port and trading centre, the one at the front presided over by Neptune and a veritable herd of unicorns. Above these panels are representations of the values the city council espoused – at the front, Prudence, Justice and Peace, to the rear Temperance and Vigilance on either side of a muscular, globe-bearing Atlas. One deliberate precaution, however, was the omission of a central doorway – just in case the mob turned nasty (as they were wont to do) and stormed the place.

The **interior** also proclaims the pride and confidence of the Golden Age, principally in the lavish **Citizen's Hall**, an extraordinarily handsome, arcaded

From Town Hall to Royal Palace

At the time of the building's construction in the mid-seventeenth century, Amsterdam was at the height of its powers. The city was pre-eminent among Dutch towns, and had just resisted William of Orange's attempts to bring it to heel. Predictably, the council craved a **residence** that was a declaration of the city's municipal power and opted for a startlingly progressive design by **Jacob van Campen**, who proposed a Dutch rendering of the classical principles revived in Renaissance Italy. Initially, there was opposition to the plan from the council's Calvinist minority, who pointed out that the proposed **Stadhuis** would dwarf the neighbouring Nieuwe Kerk (see p.50), an entirely inappropriate ordering, so they suggested, of earthly and spiritual values. However, when the Calvinists were promised a new church spire (which was never built) they promptly fell into line, and in 1648 work started on what was then the largest town hall in Europe, supported by no fewer than 13,659 wooden piles driven into Dam Square's sandy soil – a number every Dutch schoolchild remembers by adding a "1" and a "9" to the number of days in the year. The poet Constantijn Huygens called the new building "The world's Eighth Wonder / With so much stone raised high and so much timber under".

The Stadhuis received its **royal designation** in 1808, when Napoleon's brother Louis, recently installed as king, commandeered it as his residence. Lonely and isolated, Louis abdicated in 1810 and hightailed it out of the country. Afterwards, possession of the palace became something of a sore point between the Royal family and the city; the initial compromise kept the building as royal property on condition that the royals stayed here for part of the year, but the Oranges almost universally failed to make much of an appearance. This irritated many Amsterdammers, and in the 1930s the Oranges offered the city fifteen million guilders to build a new city hall in return for a new agreement, which allowed them to use the Palace whenever they wanted, with ownership passing to the state (as distinct from the city); the new town hall, on Waterlooplein (see p.99), was finally completed in the 1980s. Nowadays the Dutch royals live down in the Huis ten Bosch, near the Hague, and only use the Royal Palace for state occasions.

▲ The Koninklijk Paleis (Royal Palace)

marble chamber where the enthroned figure of Amsterdam looks down on the earth and the heavens, which are laid out at her feet in three circular, inlaid marble maps, one each of the eastern and western hemispheres, the other of the northern sky. Other allegorical figures ram home the municipal point: flanking "Amsterdam" to left and right are Wisdom and Strength, and the reliefs to either side of the central group represent good governance; on the left is the god Amphion, who plays his lyre to persuade the stones to pile themselves up into a wall, and to the right Mercury attempts to lull Argos to sleep – stressing the need to be vigilant. All this is part of a good-natured and witty symbolism that pervades almost all of the building: cocks fight above the entrance to the Commissioner of Petty Affairs; **Ferdinand Bol's** painting in the **Burgomasters' Council** room depicts an unsuccessful attempt to bribe and then frighten (with the elephant trumpeting behind the curtain) a Roman consul; and a medallion above the door of the Bankruptcy Chamber shows the fall of Icarus, surrounded by marble carvings depicting hungry rats scurrying around an empty money chest and nibbling at unpaid bills. In the **Magistrates' Court** is a second Bol painting, *Moses the Lawgiver*, depicting Moses descending from Mount Sinai with the Ten Commandments, but most of the paintings displayed in the palace are of little distinction.

The decorative whimsy fizzles out in the **High Court of Justice** at the front of the building, close to the entrance. Inside the consciously intimidating chamber, the judges sat on the marble benches flanked by heavyweight representations of Righteousness, Wisdom, Mercy and so forth as they passed judgement on the hapless criminal in front of them; even worse, the crowd on Dam Square could view the proceedings through the barred windows, almost always baying for blood. They usually went home contented; as soon as the judges had passed the death sentence, the condemned were whisked up to the wooden scaffold attached to the front of the building and promptly dispatched.

Magna Plaza

Behind the Royal Palace, on Nieuwezijds Voorburgwal, you can't miss the old neo-Gothic post office of 1899, now converted into the **Magna Plaza** shopping mall (Mon 11am–7pm, Tues, Wed, Fri & Sat 10am–7pm, Thurs

10am–9pm, Sun noon–7pm; ⓦ www.magnaplaza.nl), a grand affair that makes an attractive setting for the numerous clothing chains that now inhabit its red-brick interior. It certainly was a great place to buy stamps, but the post office building was never very popular despite its whimsical embellishments, which continued the town's tradition of plonking towers on every major building, partly out of civic pride and partly to contribute to the city's spiky skyline. The architect responsible, a certain C.G. Peters, took a surprising amount of flack for his creation, which was mocked as "postal Gothic".

The Nieuwe Kerk

Vying for importance with the Royal Palace is the adjacent **Nieuwe Kerk** (daily 10am–6pm; €10; ☎020/638 6909, ⓦwww.nieuwekerk.nl). Despite its name (literally "new church"), it's an early fifteenth-century structure built in a late flourish of the Gothic style, with a forest of pinnacles and high, slender gables. Badly damaged by fire on several occasions, and unceremoniously stripped of most of its fittings by the Calvinists, the **interior** is a hangar-like affair of sombre demeanour, whose sturdy compound pillars soar up to support the wooden vaulting of the ceiling. Among a scattering of decorative highlights, look out for an extravagant, finely carved mahogany **pulpit** that was fifteen years in the making, a cleverly worked copper **chancel screen** and a flashy, Baroque **organ case**.

There's also the spectacularly vulgar **tomb** of Admiral Michiel de Ruyter (1607–76), complete with trumpeting angels, conch-blowing Neptunes and cherubs. In a long and illustrious naval career **de Ruyter** trounced, in succession, the Spaniards, the Swedes, the English and the French, and his rise from deck hand to Admiral-in-Chief is the stuff of national legend. His most famous exploit was a raid up the River Thames to Medway in 1667 and the seizure of the Royal Navy's flagship, *The Royal Charles*; the subsequent Dutch crowing almost drove Charles II to distraction. De Ruyter was buried here with full military honours and the church is still used for state occasions; the coronations of queens Wilhelmina, Juliana and, in 1980, Beatrix, were all held here. After the church, pop into the adjoining *'t Nieuwe Café* (see p.183), which occupies one of the old ecclesiastical lean-tos and serves excellent coffee and delicious lunches and snacks.

The Rokin and Kalverstraat

Sandwiched between the Singel and **Rokin**, the southern part of the Old Centre is one of Amsterdam's busiest districts, mostly on account of pedestrianized **Kalverstraat**, a hectic shopping street. Taken as a whole, it's not a particularly engaging area, but it does have its moments, most enjoyably in the cloistered tranquillity of the **Begijnhof** and among the bars and cafés of the nearby **Spui** (see p.47). There is also a brace of museums – the excellent **Amsterdams Historisch Museum** and the moderately diverting archeological collection of the **Allard Pierson Museum**.

The Rokin

The **Rokin** picks up where the Damrak leaves off, cutting south in a wide sweep that follows the former course of the River Amstel. The Rokin was the business centre of the nineteenth-century city, and although it has lost much of its prestige it is still flanked by an attractive medley of architectural styles, incorporating everything from grandiose nineteenth-century mansions to more utilitarian modern buildings.

One initial highlight as you stroll south is the handsome Art-Nouveau-meets-Art-Deco Marine Insurance building at **no. 69**; others are the much earlier canal house at **no. 83** and the attractive stone mansion at **no. 91**. Across the street, at **no. 92**, is the Hajenius cigar shop with its flashy gilt interior, while a prominent equestrian **statue** of Queen Wilhelmina marks the spot where the Rokin hits the canal system. Born in The Hague, **Wilhelmina** (1880–1962) came to the throne in 1890 and abdicated in favour of her daughter, Juliana, 58 years later – a mammoth royal stint by any standard. After her retirement she wrote a memoir, *Lonely but not Alone*, which explored her strong religious beliefs, but her popularity was based on her determined resistance to the Germans in World War II, when she was the figurehead of the government-in-exile in London. Further south, beyond the Allard Pierson museum on the other side of the canal, **nos. 141–147 Oude Turfmarkt** are classic seventeenth-century canal houses, graced by bottle- and spout-shaped gables.

The Allard Pierson Museum

Overlooking the canal, the solid Neoclassical building at Oude Turfmarkt 127 used to be the headquarters of the Dutch central bank and is now the **Allard Pierson Museum** (Tues–Fri 10am–5pm, Sat & Sun 1–5pm; €6.50; Ⓦ www .allardpiersonmuseum.nl), a good old-fashioned archeological museum spread over two floors, and labelled in Dutch and English. It's not a large museum, but it has a wide-ranging collection of finds retrieved from Egypt, Greece and Italy. The particular highlight is the museum's Greek **pottery** with fine examples of both the black- and red-figured wares produced in the sixth and fifth centuries BC. Look out also for several ornate Roman **sarcophagi**, especially a whopper made of marble and decorated with Dionysian scenes, a very unusual wooden coffin from c.150 AD, which is partly carved in the shape of the man held within, and Etruscan funerary urns and carvings, including an amazingly precise statue of a baby in swaddling clothes. Of the Egyptian artefacts on the ground floor, a model of a ship and its crew from the Middle Kingdom stands out – another funerary object, used to transport the soul of the dead to the afterlife.

Hotel Doelen

The **Hotel de l'Europe** on Nieuwe Doelenstraat is one of the city's most luxurious and well-appointed places to stay, although the **Hotel Doelen** next door is perhaps of more historic interest, incorporating as it does the Kloveniers Tower, once the headquarters and meeting place of the company Rembrandt depicted in *The Night Watch*. No one knows for sure whether he painted *The Night Watch* here, but it certainly hung in the building at one time, and if you ask nicely in reception you can stroll up to see where it was, although – despite the tour groups that regularly trundle through – there's not much to look at beyond a crumbling red-brick wall and a bad photo of the painting.

Kalverstraat

Running parallel to the Rokin to the west, the pedestrianized shopping street of **Kalverstraat** curves north to Dam Square. The street has been a commercial

centre since medieval times, when it was used as a calf market, and it was also here, in 1345, that the city witnessed the Miracle of the unburnable Host (see "The Oude Kerk" p.56), and the street became a route for pilgrims. Kalverstraat really could be any European shopping street, but if you want to shop, and you're not looking for designer labels, this is the place to come.

The Begijnhof

Just off Kalverstraat, on Gedempte Begijnensloot, the **Begijnhof** (daily 9am–5pm; free; ⓦ www.begijnhofamsterdam.nl) consists of a huddle of immaculately maintained old houses looking onto a central green, their backs to the outside world; you can also sneak in here from the gate on the Spui (see p.47). The Begijnhof was founded in the fourteenth century as a home for the Beguines – members of a Catholic sisterhood living as nuns, but without vows and with the right to return to the secular world (see box, p.53). The original medieval complex comprised a series of humble brick cottages, but these were mostly replaced by the larger, grander houses of today shortly after the Reformation, though the secretive, enclosed design survived. However, a couple of pre-Reformation buildings do remain, including the **Houten Huys**, at no. 34, whose wooden facade dates from 1477, the oldest in Amsterdam and erected before the city forbade the construction of timber houses as an essential precaution against fire. The **Engelse Kerk** (English Reformed Church), which takes up one side of the Begijnhof, is of medieval construction too, but it was taken from the Beguines and given to Amsterdam's English community during the Reformation. Plain and unadorned, the church is of interest for its carefully worked pulpit panels, several of which were designed by a youthful **Piet Mondriaan** (1872–1944), the leading De Stijl artist – although to see them you'll have to attend one of its services on Sundays at 10.30am. After they had lost their church, and in keeping with the terms of the *Alteratie* (see p.258), the Beguines were allowed to celebrate Mass inconspicuously in the clandestine Catholic **Begijnhofkapel** (Mon 1–6.30pm, Tues–Fri 9am–6.30pm, Sat & Sun 9am–6pm; free), which they established in the house opposite their old church.

▲ The Begijnhof

Beguinages

One result of the urbanization of the Low Countries from the twelfth century onwards was the establishment of **beguinages** (*begijnhoven* in Dutch, *béguinages* in French) in almost every city and town. These were semi-secluded communities, where widows and unmarried women – the **Beguines** (*Begijns*) – lived together, the better to do pious acts, especially caring for the sick. In **construction**, beguinages follow the same general plan with several streets of whitewashed, terraced, brick cottages hidden away behind walls and gates and surrounding a central garden and chapel. **Beguine communities** were different from convents in so far as the inhabitants did not have to take vows and had the right to return to the secular world if they chose. In the Netherlands, the Beguine movement pretty much died out with the Reformation.

It's still used today, a homely little place with some terribly sentimental religious paintings, one of which – to the left of the high altar – depicts the Miracle of the unburnable Host, still celebrated at the Oude Kerk (see p.56).

The Amsterdams Historisch Museum

As you emerge from the east side of the Begijnhof, turn left onto narrow Gedempte Begijnensloot and it's 100m or so to the **Schuttersgalerij** – the Civic Guard Gallery. Here, an assortment of huge group portraits of the **Amsterdam militia**, ranging from serious-minded paintings of the 1540s through to lighter affairs from the seventeenth century, is displayed for free in a glassed-in passageway. They are interesting paintings – the pick are those by **Nicolaes Pickenoy** (1588–1650) – but the finest militia painting by a long chalk, Rembrandt's *The Night Watch*, is exhibited in the Rijksmuseum (see pp.113–119).

The Schuttersgalerij is part of the **Amsterdams Historisch Museum** (entrances at Nieuwezijds Voorburgwal 357 & Kalverstraat 92, Mon–Fri 10am–5pm, Sat & Sun 11am–5pm; €10; Ⓦwww.ahm.nl), which occupies the smartly restored but rambling seventeenth-century buildings of the municipal orphanage. The museum follows the city's development with a scattering of artefacts and a host of paintings from the thirteenth century onwards; the building is full of levels and corridors, but the arrows lead you through in a reasonably coherent way, and the labelling is in English as well as Dutch.

Maps and paintings punctuate the galleries and record the growth of the city, starting with an electronic map showing the city's evolution from the draining of the Amsel in 1274 to the present day. Beyond here are a number of **old views of Amsterdam** back before the Golden Age, of which Cornelis Anthonisz's 1538 *Bird's Eye View of Amsterdam* in Room 4, the oldest surviving plan of the city, stands out. There are paintings illustrating the country's former maritime prowess in Room 5, and in Room 6 Berckheyde's "depiction" of the new town hall hangs opposite a model of the building from 1648, made by the architect and slightly different from the finished article. There are also views of Dam Square in the early seventeenth century showing both the old and new town hall, while Room 7 has a depiction of the East India Company's docks in 1696, along with a scale model of the same. Room 10 examines the paternalism of the city's merchant oligarchy, with paintings depicting the regents of several orphanages, self-contented bourgeoisie in the company of the grateful poor, notably Pickenoy's picture of the Rapshuis and Van der Voort's depiction of the Spinhuis, as well as Bartholomew van der Helst's *Governors and Governesses of the Spinhuis* in the Schuttergalerij outside, which captures both the sternness of the institution (see p.60) and its daily routine going on behind them. Across the Schuttergalerij, Room 11 is

▲ Painting at the Amsterdams Historisch Museum

distinguished by two paintings of the surgeons' guild at work – look out for **Rembrandt**'s wonderful, if gruesome, *Anatomy Lesson of Dr Jan Deijman* – and the later *Anatomy Lesson of Dr William Roëll*, from 1728.

The museum doesn't just focus on the Golden Age, but dutifully and effectively records the lives of well-to-do Amsterdammers in the eighteenth century (when the city fancied itself as among the most refined and cultured centres of Europe), the nineteenth century, and right up to the **modern era**, starting with Breitner's *Dam Square* of 1898 and Jacob Maris's view of the *Schreierstoren*. There is an inevitable focus on the war years and the Nazi occupation, including film footage of the city's liberation. Postwar material includes displays on the **CoBrA** art movement (see p.280) and Karel Appel's murals for the town hall (now decorating the city's *Grand Hotel* restaurant), the development of Schiphol Airport, the liberalization of dope and the rise of coffeeshops, and even a mock-up of an old brown café.

Heiligeweg

A little further up Kalverstraat, workaday **Heiligeweg**, or "Holy Way", was once part of a much longer route used by pilgrims heading into Amsterdam, and is still used for part of the Stille Omgang (Silent Procession, see p.249). Every other religious reference disappeared centuries ago, but there is one interesting edifice here: the fanciful gateway of the old **Rasphuis** (House of Correction) that now fronts a shopping mall at the foot of Voetboogstraat. The gateway is surmounted by a sculpture of a woman punishing two criminals chained at her sides above the single word "Castigatio" (punishment). Beneath is a carving by **Hendrick de Keyser** (1565–1621), (see box, p.72), showing wolves and lions cringing before the whip; the inscription reads: "It is a virtue to subdue those before whom all go in dread."

The Red Light District

The whole area to the east of Damrak, between Warmoesstraat, Nieuwmarkt and Damstraat, is the **Red Light District**, known locally as "De Wallen" ("The Walls") on account of the series of low brick walls that contain its canals. The district stretches across the two narrow canals that marked the eastern part of medieval Amsterdam, **Oudezijds Voorburgwal** and **Oudezijds Achterburgwal**, with the far canal of **Kloveniersburgwal** forming its eastern boundary. The area is pretty seedy, although the legalized prostitution here has long been one of the city's most distinctive draws. It wasn't always so; the handsome facades of Oudezijds Voorburgwal in partic-ular recall ritzier days, when this was one of the wealthiest parts of the city, richly earning its nickname the "Velvet Canal". The two canals, with their narrow connecting passages, are thronged with "**window brothels**" and at busy times the on-street haggling over the price of various sex acts is drowned out by a surprisingly festive atmosphere – entire families grinning more or less amiably at the women in the windows or discussing the specifications (and feasibility) of the sex toys in the shops. Another feature is the hawkers who line the streets touting the peep shows and "live sex" within, though some of the more prominent establishments have been closed down recently by a council intent on cleaning up the area (see box, p.57).

There is an undertow to the district that's not particularly pleasant, and with the added delights of the drug addicts that hang around during the day you might not want to spend any longer here than is necessary. And don't even think about taking a picture of a "window brothel" unless you're prepared for some major grief from the camera-shy prostitutes, or their pimps. However, it's certainly an interesting district to visit, and it does contain two prime attractions, the medieval **Oude Kerk** and the clandestine **Amstelkring** Catholic church.

Warmoesstraat

Soliciting hasn't always been the principal activity on sleazy **Warmoesstraat**. It was once one of the city's most fashionable streets, home to Holland's foremost poet, **Joost van den Vondel** (1587–1679), who ran his hosiery business from no. 110 in between writing and hobnobbing with the Amsterdam elite. Van den Vondel was a kind of Dutch Shakespeare; his *Gijsbrecht van Amstel*, a celebration of Amsterdam during its Golden Age, is one of the classics of Dutch literature, and he wrote regular, if ponderous, official verses, including well over a thousand lines on the inauguration of the town hall. Vondel had more than his

▲ A Red Light District canal

share of hard luck too; his son frittered away the modest family fortune and he lived out his last few years as doorkeeper of the pawnshop on Oudezijds Voorburgwal known as "Ome Jan" (see p.58), dying of hypothermia at what was then the remarkable age of 92. Witty to the end, his own suggested epitaph ran: "Here lies Vondel, your grief withhold, for he hath suffered death from cold". His name lives on most prominently in the city's largest park, the Vondelpark (see p.123), which was named after him.

The Prostitution Information Centre

Just off Warmoesstraat on Oude Kerkplein, a small bronze **statue** of a woman waiting in a window highlights the main business around here, and a number of brothels ring the square, near which is the **Prostitution Information Centre**, at Enge Kerksteeg 3, right by the Oude Kerk (Wed & Fri 6–8pm, Sat noon–7pm; ☎020/420 7328, Ⓦwww.pic-amsterdam.com). This is a legally recognized *stichting* or charitable foundation that was set up in 1994 by an ex-prostitute, Mariska Majoor, to provide prostitutes, their clients and visitors with clear, dispassionate information about prostitution. Its shop, "Wallenwinkel", sells books and pamphlets, and souvenirs of the Red Light District – postcards, fridge magnets, T-shirts and the like – and it runs hour-long **tours** of the Red Light District for €12.50 a person (Sat at 5pm). All in all, it does a decent job of ridding prostitution of its seedy mystique.

The Oude Kerk

Bang in the middle of the Red Light District is Amsterdam's most appealing church, the **Oude Kerk** (Mon–Sat 11am–5pm, Sun 1–5pm; €5; Ⓦwww .oudekerk.nl), an attractive Gothic structure with high-pitched gables and finely worked lancet windows. There's been a church on this site since the middle of the thirteenth century, but most of the present building dates from a century later, funded by the pilgrims who came here in their hundreds following a widely publicized **miracle**. The story goes that, in 1345, a dying man regurgitated the

Host he had received here at Communion, and when it was thrown on the fire afterwards, it did not burn. The unburnable Host was placed in a chest and installed in a long-lost chapel somewhere off Nieuwezijds Voorburgwal, before finally being transferred to the Oude Kerk a few years later. It disappeared during the Reformation, but to this day thousands of the faithful still come to take part in the annual **Stille Omgang**, a silent nocturnal procession terminating at the Oude Kerk and held in mid-March. The church is also regularly used for art displays and concerts.

The Protestants cleared the church of almost all its ecclesiastical tackle during the Reformation, but its largely bare **interior** does hold several interesting features. These include some folksy misericords, a few faded vault paintings recovered from beneath layers of whitewash in the 1950s, and the unadorned memorial tablet of **Rembrandt**'s first wife, Saskia van Uylenburgh, beneath the smaller of the two organs. Much more diverting, however, are the three beautifully coloured **stained-glass windows** beside the ambulatory in what was once the Chapel of Our Lady. Dating from the 1550s, all three depict religious scenes – from left to right: the Annunciation, the Adoration of the Shepherds and the Assumption of the Virgin – and each is set above its respective donors. The characters are shown in classical gear with togas and sandals and the buildings in the background are firmly classical too, reflecting both artistic fashion and a belief that Greco-Roman detail was historically accurate. A fourth, rather

Commercial sex in Amsterdam

Developed in the 1960s, the Netherlands' – and especially Amsterdam's – liberal approach to social policy has had several unforeseen consequences, the most dramatic being its international reputation as a centre for both drugs and **prostitution**. However, the tackiness of the Red Light District is just the surface sheen on what has been a serious attempt to address the reality of sex for sale, and to integrate this within a normal, ordered society. In Dutch law, prostitution has long been legal, but the state had always drawn the line at brothels and soliciting in public. The difficulties this created for the police were legion, so finally, in 1996, a special **soliciting zone** was established and a couple of years later **brothels** were legalized in the hope that together these changes would bring a degree of stability to the sex industry. The authorities were particularly keen to get a grip on the use of illegal immigrants as prostitutes and also to alleviate the problem of numbers.

This legislation is partly the result of a long and determined campaign by the prostitutes' trade union, **De Rode Draad** ("The Red Thread"), which has improved the lot of its members by setting up new health insurance and pension schemes – and generally fighting for regular employment rights for prostitutes. Whether this has happened or not is debatable: the number of "window brothels" is limited, so a significant group of women ply their trade illicitly in bars and hotels. There are still lots of illegal immigrants in the Red Light District, and lots of pimps too. The **windows**, which are rented out for upwards of €100 a day, are less easy to control than registered brothels, and at least half of the District's prostitutes hand over some of their earnings to a pimp, who will usually be Dutch and often an ex-boyfriend.

The city has taken action over the past couple of years to crack down not only on this but also on the number of outlets in the Red Light District, buying up some of the buildings itself and enouraging initiatives like Redlight Fashion Amsterdam, in which young fashion designers have exhibited their clothes in some of the windows. Some of the clubs have closed too, and despite dissent from De Rode Draad, the PIC and the pressure group Platform 1010 (named after the area postcode), it seems likely that the number of sexworkers here will diminish over the next few years, and the district may begin to take on a different, perhaps less sleazy, complexion.

different stained–glass window is located on the other side of the ambulatory. A secular piece of 1655, it features the Spanish king Philip IV ceding independence to a representative of the United Provinces (the Netherlands) under the terms of the Treaty of Munster of 1648, which wrapped up the Thirty Years' War. Like the earlier windows, the architectural backdrop is classical, but here it's to emphasize the dignity of the proceedings – and the king and the Dutch emissaries wear contemporary clothes.

Outside, the Oude Kerk **tower** is open weekends between April and September (1–5pm; €5) and offers predictably great views in a city with relatively few such opportunities.

Oudezijds Voorburgwal

The front of the Oude Kerk overlooks the northern reaches of **Oudezijds Voorburgwal**, whose imposing canalside houses are a reminder of its prosperous, seventeenth-century heyday. The bottom end of the canal and in particular its last bridge is perhaps the Red Light District's busiest – and seediest – intersection, but walk for five minutes and you leave most of this behind; indeed in its upper reaches, towards the University, it's as pretty, unspoiled and historic as anywhere in the city. Through an ornate gateway at Oudezijds Voorburgwal 231 is the **Agnietenkapel** (currently under restoration), originally part of a Catholic convent, but now owned by the university. Upstairs, the chapel has a good-looking, first-floor auditorium dating from the fifteenth century, formerly used for temporary exhibitions devoted to the university's history. Roughly opposite, just over the footbridge, the large brick and stone-trimmed building at Oudezijds Voorburgwal 302 has been known as "**Ome Jan**" ("Uncle John's") ever since the days when it was central Amsterdam's pawnshop. The poet **Vondel** (see p.55) ended his days working here, and a short verse above the fancy stone entranceway, which comes complete with the city's coat of arms, extols the virtues of the pawnshop – and the evils of usury. From "Ome Jan", it's a couple of hundred metres to the southern end of Oudezijds Voorburgwal, where the **Mokum** art shop (see p.215) uses the old Jewish nickname for the city.

The Amstelkring

Situated at the northern end of the canal, Oudezijds Voorburgwal's main sight is the **Amstelkring**, OZ Voorburgwal 40 (Mon–Sat 10am–5pm, Sun 1–5pm; €7; ⓦwww.museumamstelkring.nl), which was momentarily the city's principal Catholic place of worship and is now one of Amsterdam's most enjoyable museums. Despite the reformation of 1578, the new regime treated its Catholics well, broadly speaking – commercial pragmatism has always outweighed religious zeal here – but there was a degree of discrimination; Catholic churches were recycled for Protestant use and their members no longer allowed to practise openly. The result was an eccentric compromise; Catholics were allowed to hold services in any private building providing that the exterior revealed no sign of their activities – hence the development of the city's **clandestine churches** (*schuilkerken*), among which the Amstelkring is the only one to have survived intact. Amstelkring, meaning "Amstel Circle", is the name of the group of nineteenth-century historians who saved the building from demolition.

The Amstelkring, more properly Ons Lieve Heer Op Solder ("Our Dear Lord in the Attic"), occupies the loft of a wealthy merchant's house and is perfectly delightful, with a narrow **nave** skilfully shoehorned into the available space.

Flanked by elegant balconies, the nave has an ornately carved organ at one end and a mock-marble high altar, decorated with Jacob de Wit's mawkish *Baptism of Christ*, at the other. Even the patron of the church, one Jan Hartman, clearly had doubts about de Wit's efforts – the two spares he procured just in case are now displayed behind the altar. The rest of the house has been left untouched, its original furnishings reminiscent of interiors by Vermeer or de Hooch.

The Zeedijk

You can cut through from the top end of OZ Voorburgwal to the end of the **Zeedijk**, which was originally just that – a dyke to hold back the sea – and is now a street which girdles the northern end of the Red Light District. A couple of decades ago this narrow thoroughfare was the haunt of drug addicts, and very much a no-go area at night. But it's been spruced up and now forms a lively route from Stationsplein through to Nieuwmarkt, on the eastern edge of the Red Light District, as well as being the main hub of Amsterdam's small but vibrant Chinatown. Its seaward end is home to a couple of the oldest bars in the city, and the jazz trumpeter **Chet Baker** famously died here in 1988, when he either fell or threw himself out of the window of the *Prins Hendrik Hotel* – an event remembered by an evocative plaque of the man in full blow. Further down, there are any number of Chinese, Thai and Vietnamese foodie treats, as well as the **Fo Guang Shan He Hua Temple**, on the right at Zeedijk 106, just 100m or so short of Nieuwmarkt (Tues–Sun 10–5pm) – a Buddhist temple heavy with the smell of incense and sounds of chanting. There's not much to see here but for a small donation you can pick your own ready-made dharma out of a box.

Oudezijds Achterburgwal

A block across from OZ Voorburgwal, **Oudezijds Achterburgwal** is another pretty canal, but like its neighbour long despoiled, at least in its lower reaches, by Red Light sleaze. Those after just a taster of this should drop by the popular **Erotic Museum** (daily 11am–1am; €5), with its four floors of Victorian porn, statues and drawings, mock-ups of prostitutes' rooms, reels of cartoon porn featuring Sleeping Beauty and Snow White, and a bondage room at the top – all good fun, and in a way the perfect topic for the location, though it's debatable as to how erotic it really is.

To the south is the **Hash Marihuana Hemp Museum** at Oudezijds Achterburgwal 148 (daily 10am–10pm; €7; Ⓦ www.hashmuseum.com), the first and most established of a number of dope "museums" along this stretch. As well as featuring displays on the various types of dope and numerous ways

---

Red Light District trouble

The police estimate that there are around a thousand hard-drug users in Amsterdam, who, as they put it, "cause nuisance", and there remain a few groups of **drug addicts** who hang around on the northern edge of the Red Light District. They are unlikely to molest strangers, but can still be a threatening presence. In fairness, the police have done their best to clean things up, and have dramatically improved the situation on the Zeedijk and Nieuwmarkt, which were once notorious for hard drugs, and at the canal bridge on Oude Hoogstraat, formerly nicknamed the "Pillenbrug" ("Pill Bridge"). Nonetheless, keep a close eye on your bag and wallet – the area is notorious for petty thievery.

to smoke it, the museum has an indoor marijuana garden, samples of textiles and paper made with hemp, and pamphlets explaining the medicinal properties of cannabis. There's also a shop selling pipes, books, videos and plenty of souvenirs. Amsterdam's reliance on imported dope ended in the late 1980s with the emergence of hydroponic growing techniques, whereby marijuana – and in particular a reddish variety bred in America, called "skunk" – was able to flourish under artificial lights without water. Nowadays over half the dope sold in the city's coffeeshops is grown in the Netherlands, and this place is positively evangelical about how to join in.

Across the canal, next door to Oudezijds Achterburgwal 185, at Spinhuissteeg 1, the **Spinhuis** was once a house of correction for "fallen women", who were put to work here on the looms and spinning wheels. Curiously, workhouses like this used to figure on tourist itineraries; for a small fee the public was allowed to watch the women at work, and at carnival times admission was free and large crowds came to jeer and mock. The justification for this was that shame was supposed to be part of the reforming process, but in fact the municipality unofficially tolerated brothels and the incarcerated women had simply been singled out for exemplary punishment. The Spinhuis has been turned into offices, but the old front door has survived intact, with an inscription by the seventeenth-century Dutch poet Pieter Cornelisz Hooft: "Cry not, for I exact no vengeance for wrong but to force you to be good. My hand is stern but my heart is kind."

On the other side of the canal, the triangular parcel of land at the southern end of Oudezijds Achterburgwal is packed with university buildings, mostly modern or nineteenth-century structures built in the vernacular Dutch style. Together they form a pleasant urban ensemble, but the early seventeenth-century step-gabled **Huis op de Drie Grachten** ("House on the Three Canals"), with its red shutters and mullion windows, stands out, sitting prettily on the corner of Oudezijds Achterburgwal and Oudezijds Voorburgwal.

Nieuwmarkt and around

The eastern reaches of the Red Light District peter out at cobbled **Nieuw-markt**, a wide-open, sometimes druggy square that centres on the turreted **Waag**. Nieuwmarkt is within easy walking distance of a pleasant residential district situated between two canals – **Geldersekade** and **Oudeschans** – and lies at the end of the outermost of the three eastern canals of fifteenth-century Amsterdam, **Kloveniersburgwal**, a long, dead-straight waterway flanked by a string of dignified facades. Together, these canals make for one of the most engaging parts of the city, especially at the southern end, where a small pocket of placid waterways and handsome old canal houses spreads over to neigh-bouring **Groenburgwal** – a narrow and almost impossibly pretty waterway.

Nieuwmarkt

Nieuwmarkt was long one of the city's most important markets and the place where Gentiles and Jews from the nearby Jewish Quarter (see Chapter 4) – just southeast along St Antoniebreestraat – traded. All that came to a traumatic end during World War II, when the Germans cordoned off the Nieuwmarkt with barbed wire and turned it into a holding pen. After the war, the square's old exuberance never returned and these days all that remains of its former trading is a small organic food **market** on Saturdays (9am–5pm).

The focus of the square, the sprawling, multi-turreted **Waag**, dating from the 1480s, has had a chequered history. Built as one of the city's fortified gates, Sint Antoniespoort, Amsterdam's expansion soon made it obsolete and the ground floor was turned into a municipal weighing-house, with the rooms upstairs taken over by the surgeons' guild. It was here that the surgeons held lectures on anatomy and public dissections, the inspiration for Rembrandt's *Anatomy Lesson of Dr Tulp*, displayed in the Mauritshuis Collection in The Hague. Abandoned by the surgeons and the weigh-masters in the nineteenth century, the building served as a furniture store and a fire station before falling into disuse, though it has recently been renovated to house a good café-bar and restaurant, *In de Waag* (see p.187).

Oudeschans

The **Montelbaanstoren** is a sturdy tower dating from 1512 that overlooks the **Oudeschans**, a canal dug around the same time to improve the city's shipping facilities. The tower was built to protect the city's eastern flank but its decorative spire was added later, when the city felt more secure, by **Hendrick de Keyser**, the architect who did much to create Amsterdam's prickly skyline.

The **Scheepvaarthuis** (Shipping Building), at Prins Hendrikkade 108, is an unusual edifice on the corner of Binnenkant. Completed in 1917, this is one of the flashiest of the buildings designed by the Amsterdam School of architecture, the work of a certain **Johann Melchior van der Mey** (1878–1949). An almost neurotically decorated edifice covered with a welter of detail celebrating the city's marine connections, the entrance is shaped like a prow and surmounted by statues of Poseidon and Amphitrite, his wife. Up above them are female representations of the four points of the compass, while slender turrets and Expressionistic carvings playfully decorate the walls. It's now the five-star hotel *Amrath*, but you can pop in for a drink in its bar for a glimpse of the interior, which here at least has been well preserved.

Kloveniersburgwal

Heading south along **Kloveniersburgwal** from Nieuwmarkt, it's a short hoof to the **Trippenhuis** at no. 29, an overblown mansion complete with Corinthian pilasters and a grand frieze built for the Trip family in 1662. One of the richest families in Amsterdam, the Trips were a powerful force among the **Magnificat**, the clique of families (Six, Trip, Hooft and Pauw) who shared power during the Golden Age. One part of the Trip family dealt with the Baltic trade, another with the manufacture of munitions (in which they had the municipal monopoly), but in addition they also had trade interests in Russia and the Middle East, much like the multinationals of today. In the nineteenth century the Rijksmuseum collection was displayed here, but the house now contains the Dutch Academy of Sciences.

Almost directly opposite, on the west bank of the canal, the **Kleine Trippenhuis**, at no. 26 (now a lingerie shop), is by contrast one of the narrowest houses in Amsterdam, albeit with an attractively carved facade and a balustrade featuring centaurs and sphinxes. Legend has it that Mr Trip's coachman was so taken aback by the size of the new family mansion that he exclaimed he would be happy with a home no wider than the Trips' front door – which is exactly what he got; his reaction to his new lodgings is not recorded.

A few metres south, on the corner of Oude Hoogstraat, is the former headquarters of the Dutch East India Company, the **Oostindisch Huis**, a monumental red-brick structure with high-pitched gables and perky dormer windows, built in 1605 shortly after the founding of the company. It was from here that the Company organized and regulated its immensely lucrative trading interests in the Far East, importing shiploads of spices, perfumes and exotic woods (see box, p.107). This trade underpinned Amsterdam's Golden Age; predictably, the people of what is now Indonesia, the source of most of the raw materials, received little in return. Nevertheless, despite the building's historic significance, the interior is of no interest today, being occupied by university classrooms and offices.

Further south, Kloveniersburgwal leads into the student district, where the buildings here and along adjoining canals house the various departments of the **University of Amsterdam**. At the heart of this is the **Oudemanhuispoort** (Mon–Sat 10am–4pm), a covered passageway that leads between Kloveniersburgwal and OZ Achterburgwal. Now lined by secondhand book stalls, it was formerly part of an almshouse complex for elderly men – hence the unusual name. The buildings on either side are part of the university and their gardens provide a quiet place to rest between sights. Afterwards, you can either wander through the university's peaceful precincts or cross the south end of Kloveniersburgwal to one of the prettiest corners of the city – a pocket of placid waterways and old canal houses that extends east to **Zwanenburgwal**. If you cross the canal along **Staalstraat** and stop at the second of the two little swing bridges, you'll get one of the finest views in the city, down the slender **Groenburgwal** with the Zuiderkerk looming beyond.

The Zuiderkerk

The **Zuiderkerk** (Mon–Fri 9am–4pm, Sat noon–4pm; free), dating from 1611, was the first Amsterdam church built specifically for the Protestants. It was designed by the prolific architect and sculptor, **Hendrick de Keyser** (see box, p.72), whose distinctive – and very popular – style extrapolated elements of traditional Flemish design, with fanciful detail and frilly towers added wherever possible. The basic design of the Zuiderkerk is firmly Gothic, but the soaring tower (Zuidertoren) is a fine illustration of de Keyser's work, complete with balconies and balustrades, arches, urns and columns.

The **church** was deconsecrated in the 1930s, but it was here that the bodies of the dead were temporarily stored and piled up during the terrible winter of 1944–45. In the late 1980s, it was turned into a municipal information centre with displays on housing and the environment, plus temporary **exhibitions** revealing the city council's future plans; exhibits on roads and infrastructure changes attract considerable interest. The **tower**, which has a separate entrance, can be climbed during the summer (April–Sept Mon–Sat 1–3.30pm; €3) and from the top there are sweeping views over the city centre.

St Antoniesbreestraat

You can cut through from the Zuiderkerk to **St Antoniesbreestraat**, which once linked the city centre with the Jewish Quarter. Its huddle of shops and houses was mostly demolished in the 1980s to make way for a main road, but the plan was subsequently abandoned; the buildings that now line most of the street hardly fire the soul, even if the modern symmetries – and cubist, coloured panels – of the apartment blocks that sprawl along part of the street

▲ The Zuiderkerk

are visually arresting. One of the few survivors of all these municipal shenanigans is the **Pintohuis** (Mon & Wed 2–8pm, Fri 2–5pm, Sat 11am–4pm; free), at no. 69, which is now a public library. Easily spotted by its off-white Italianate **facade**, the mansion is named after Isaac de Pinto, a Jew who fled Portugal to escape the Inquisition and subsequently became a founder of the Dutch East India Company (see box, p.107). Pinto bought this property in 1651 and promptly had it remodelled in grand style, with a facade interrupted by six lofty pilasters which lead the eye up to the blind balustrade. The mansion was the talk of the town, even more so when de Pinto had the **interior** painted in a similar style to the exterior – pop in to look at the birds and cherubs of the original painted ceiling.

2

The Grachtengordel

The western reaches of medieval Amsterdam were once enclosed by the **Singel**, part of the city's protective moat, but this is now just the first of five canals that stretch right around the city centre, extending anticlockwise from Brouwersgracht to the River Amstel in a "girdle of canals", or **Grachtengordel**. This is without doubt the most charming part of Amsterdam, a lattice of olive-green waterways and dinky humpback bridges overlooked by street upon street of handsome seventeenth-century canal houses, almost invariably undisturbed by later development. Of the three main canals, **Herengracht** (Gentlemen's Canal) was the first to be dug, followed by **Keizersgracht** (Emperor's Canal), named after the Holy Roman Emperor and fifteenth-century patron of the city, Maximilian. Further out still is **Prinsengracht**, Princes' Canal, named in honour of the princes of the House of Orange. North of Leidsegracht, the main canals are intersected by a pattern of **cross-streets**, eminently appealing **shopping streets**, where you can buy everything from carpets and handmade chocolates to designer toothbrushes and beeswax candles – all in all Amsterdam at its creative, imaginative best.

It's also a subtle cityscape – full of surprises, with a bizarre carving here, an unusual facade stone (used to denote name and occupation) there – and one in which the **gables** overlooking the canals gradually evolved. The earliest, dating from the early seventeenth century, are **crow-stepped gables**, but these were largely superseded from the 1650s onwards by **neck gables** and **bell gables**, both named for the shape of the gable top. Some are embellished, many have decorative cornices, and the fanciest – which mostly date from the eighteenth century – sport full-scale **balustrades**. The plainest gables are those of former **warehouses**, where the deep-arched and shuttered windows line up on either side of loft doors that were once used for loading and unloading goods, winched by pulley from the street down below. Indeed, outside **pulleys** remain a common feature of houses and warehouses alike, and are often still in use as the easiest way of moving furniture into the city's myriad apartments.

The grandest Grachtengordel houses are concentrated along the so-called **De Gouden Bocht** – the Golden Bend – on Herengracht between Leidsestraat

---

This chapter covers the first four canals of the Grachtengordel – the Singel, Herengracht, Keizersgracht and Prinsengracht – as they sweep down from Brouwersgracht to the Amstel. For the purposes of this guide, the district has been split into two: **Grachtengordel west** and **Grachtengordel south** – divided at roughly the halfway point, Leidsegracht. There's no obvious walking route around the area – indeed you may prefer to wander around as the mood takes you – but the description given below goes from north to south, taking in all the highlights on the way. On all three of the main canals, **street numbers** begin at Brouwersgracht and increase as you go south.

and the Amstel. Here, the architectural decorum – and arguably the aesthetic vigour – of the seventeenth century are left behind for the overblown, French-influenced mansions that became popular with the city's richest merchants in the 1700s. Nevertheless, it is perhaps the district's laid-back, easygoing atmosphere that appeals, rather than any specific sight, with one remarkable exception – the **Anne Frank Huis**, where the young, and now internationally famous, Jewish diarist hid from the Nazis in World War II. Also of interest, though on a different level altogether, is the new **Tassenmuseum** of bags and purses plus a pair of restored merchants' mansions, the **Museum Willet-Holthuysen** and the **Museum Van Loon**.

Expanding the city

The three main **Grachtengordel canals** – Herengracht, Keizersgracht and Prinsengracht – were dug in the seventeenth century as part of a comprehensive plan to extend the boundaries of a city no longer able to accommodate its burgeoning population. The idea was that the council would buy up the land around the city, dig the canals, and lease plots back to developers, thus increasing the size of the city from two to seven square kilometres. The plan was passed by the city council in 1607 and work began six years later, against a backdrop of corruption, with Amsterdammers in the know buying up the land they thought the city would soon have to purchase.

It was a monumental task, and the conditions imposed by the council were strict. The three **main waterways** were set aside for the residences and businesses of the richer and more influential Amsterdam merchants, while the **radial cross-streets** were reserved for more modest artisans' homes; meanwhile, newly arrived immigrants set to cash in on Amsterdam's booming economy were assigned, albeit informally, to the Jodenhoek – "Jews' Corner" – (see Chapter 4) and the Jordaan (see Chapter 3).

In the Grachtengordel, everyone – even the wealthiest merchant – had to comply with a set of strict and detailed **planning regulations**. In particular, the council prescribed the size of each building plot – the frontage was set at thirty feet, the depth two hundred – and although there was a degree of tinkering, the end result was the loose conformity you can see today: tall, **narrow residences**, whose individualism is mainly restricted to the stylistic permutations among the gables. Even the colour of the front doors was once regulated, with choice restricted to a shade that has since become known as "Amsterdam Green" – still something of a rarity outside Holland. It took decades to complete the project, but by the 1690s it was all pretty much finished off – at a time, ironically, when Amsterdam was in economic decline.

In essence, the Grachtengordel is a tribute to the architectural tastes of the city's middle class, an amalgam of personal wealth and aesthetic uniformity – individuality and order – that epitomized Amsterdam's Protestant bourgeoisie in its pomp.

Grachtengordel west

Stretching south from the Brouwersgracht to the Leidsegracht, **Grachtengordel west** boasts a fine selection of seventeenth-century canal houses. These are at their prettiest along **Herengracht** between Wolvenstraat and Leidsegracht, and this is where you'll also find the **Bijbels Museum**

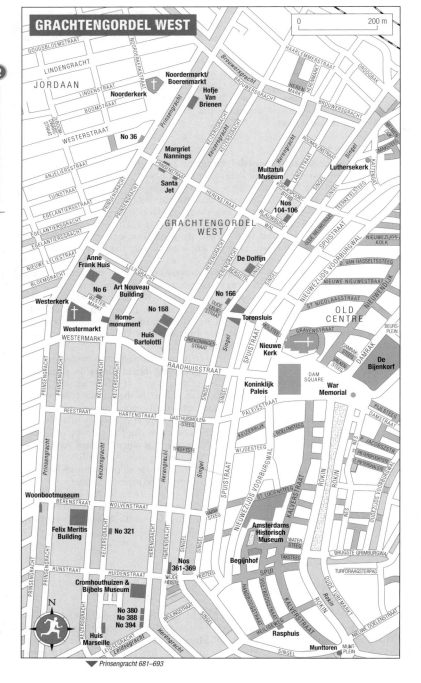

GRACHTENGORDEL WEST

0   200 m

GOUDSBLOEMSTRAAT

LINDENGRACHT

JORDAAN

LINDENSTRAAT

Noordermarkt/
Boerenmarkt

Noorderkerk

Brouwersgracht

HAARLEMMERSTRAAT

HEREN-
MARKT

BROUWERSGRACHT

DROOGBAK

Hofje
Van
Brienen

BOOMSTRAAT

WESTERSTRAAT

No 36

Margriet
Nannings

ANJELIERSSTRAAT

PRINSENSTRAAT

Santa
Jet

TUINSTRAAT

EGELANTIERSSTRAAT

EGELANTIERSGRACHT

Multatuli
Museum

Lutersekerk

HERENSTRAAT

Nos
104–106

NIEUWE LELIESTRAAT

GRACHTENGORDEL
WEST

BLAUWBURG
WAL

OUDE NIEUWSTRAAT

SPUISTRAAT

NIEUWEZIJDS VOORBURGWAL

NIEUWEZIJDS
KOLK

BLOEMGRACHT

Anne
Frank Huis

De Dolfijn

D. VAN HASSELTSSTEEG

NIEUWE NIEUWSTRAAT

No 6

Art Nouveau
Building

No 166

ST NICOLAASSTRAAT

NIEUWENDIJK

Westerkerk

No 168

Torensluis

OLD
CENTRE

Westermarkt

Homo-
monument

Huis
Bartolotti

Nieuwe
Kerk

GRAVENSTRAAT

DAMRAK

De
Bijenkorf

WESTERMARKT

RAADHUISSTRAAT

DAM
SQUARE

War
Memorial

Koninklijk
Paleis

PALEISSTRAAT

REESTRAAT

HARTENSTRAAT

GASTHUISMOLEN-
STEEG

WIJDESTEEG

PIJLSTEEG

DAMSTRAAT

Woonbootmuseum

BERENSTRAAT

WOLVENSTRAAT

Felix Meritis
Building

No 321

RUNSTRAAT

HUIDENSTRAAT

Amsterdams
Historisch
Museum

Nos
361–369

Begijnhof

Cromhouthuizen &
Bijbels Museum

No 380
No 388
No 394

Huis
Marseille

Rasphuis

Munttoren

MUNT-
PLEIN

N

▼ Prinsengracht 681–693

(Bible Museum), home to an odd assortment of models of ancient Jewish temples. Nevertheless, easily the most popular attraction here is the **Anne Frank Huis**, on Prinsengracht, which is itself just a short stroll from the soaring architecture of the **Westerkerk**.

Brouwersgracht to Prinsenstraat

Running east to west along the northern edge of the three main canals is **Brouwersgracht**, one of the most picturesque waterways in the city. Look down any of the major canals from here and you'll see the gentle interplay of water, barge, brick and stone that gives the city its distinctive allure. South of Brouwersgracht, along the west side of **Prinsengracht**, is the **Noorderkerk** (see p.88), a lugubrious pile on the edge of the Jordaan which oversees the **Noordermarkt**, the site of several markets, including the Boerenmarkt, an excellent farmers' market (Sat 9am–4pm). Just along the canal from the Noordermarkt stands **Prinsengracht 36**, which boasts an especially well-proportioned – if attenuated – facade, its neck gable, pilasters and pediment dating from 1650.

Across the canal lies the **Hofje Van Brienen** (Mon–Fri 6am–6pm & Sat 6am–2pm; free), a brown-brick courtyard complex at Prinsengracht 85–133. Originally the site of a brewery, the *hofje* (see box, p.85) was built as an almshouse in 1804 to the order of a certain Arnout van Brienen, who added a matching brick church (no entry) for good measure. A well-to-do merchant, van Brienen had locked himself in his own strongroom by accident and, in a panic, he vowed that if he were rescued he would build a *hofje* – he was and he did.

South of the Hofje Van Brienen is the first of the Grachtengordel's cross-streets, **Prinsenstraat** and its continuation **Herenstraat**, where the modest old tradesmen's houses now accommodate a string of knick-knack and clothes shops. Here you'll find a potpourri of handmade Latin American items at Santa Jet, Prinsenstraat 7, and designer clothes at Margriet Nannings, Prinsenstraat 6, 8 and 15.

Herenstraat opens out into the **Blauwburgwal**, a short and inordinately pretty slip of a canal, which had the misfortune to be hit by a bomb during the German invasion of 1940. The bomber in question had been damaged by anti-aircraft fire and dropped its load at random. This was very much a one-off: the speed of the German victory meant that central Amsterdam was hardly damaged at all, though this incident alone cost 44 lives.

The Multatuli Museum

Amsterdam's tiniest museum, the **Multatuli Museum**, is just off the Herengracht at Korsjespoortsteeg 20 (Tues 10am–5pm, Sat & Sun noon–5pm; free; Ⓦ www.multatuli-museum.nl). This was the birthplace of **Eduard Douwes Dekker** (1820–87), Holland's most celebrated nineteenth-century writer and a champion of free thinking, who wrote under the pen name Multatuli. Dekker worked as a colonial official in the Dutch East Indies for eighteen years, becoming increasingly disgusted by the graft and corruption. He returned to Amsterdam in 1856 and spent the next four years encapsulating his East Indies experiences in the elegantly written satirical novel *Max Havelaar*, which enraged the Dutch merchant class, but is now something of a Dutch literary classic (see p.286). The museum's one room is filled with letters, first editions and a small selection of his furnishings, including the **chaise longue** on which he breathed his last.

The Singel and Leliegracht

Singel 104–106 are twin mansions dating to the 1740s, equipped with the largest bell gables in the city – big but not especially attractive. Further south is the red-brick and stone-trimmed **De Dolfijn** (The Dolphin), at nos. 140–142. This was once home of Captain Banningh Cocq, one of the militiamen depicted in Rembrandt's *The Night Watch* (see p.118), but it takes its name from a late sixteenth-century Dutch grammar book written by the first owner, one Hendrick Spieghel. Nearby, **Singel 166** has the narrowest facade in the city – just 1.8m wide. It overlooks the **Torensluis**, easily the widest bridge in the Grachtengordel and decorated with a whopping bust of Multatuli (see p.67).

Just by the Torensluis is Oude Leliestraat, leading to **Leliegracht**, one of the tiny radial canals that cut across the Grachtengordel. It's a charming street, home to a number of bookshops and bars, and it also holds one of the city's finest examples of **Art Nouveau architecture** – the tall and striking building at the Leliegracht-Keizersgracht junction. Designed by Gerrit van Arkel in 1905, it was originally the headquarters of a life insurance company, hence the two mosaics with angels recommending policies to bemused earthlings.

The Anne Frank Huis

In 1960, the Anne Frank Foundation set up the **Anne Frank Huis** (daily: mid-March to mid-Sept 9am–9pm, July & Aug till 10pm; mid-Sept to mid-March 9am–7pm; closed Yom Kippur; €8.50, 10- to 17-year-olds €4, under-9s free; ☎020/556 7100, ⓦwww.annefrank.org) in the premises on Prinsengracht where the young diarist and her family hid from the Germans during World War II. Since the posthumous publication of her diaries, Anne Frank has become extraordinarily famous, in the first instance for recording the iniquities of the Holocaust, and latterly as a symbol of the fight against oppression in general and racism in particular.

▲ Anne Frank statue

The story of Anne Frank

The story of **Anne**, author of *The Diary of a Young Girl*, her sister, parents and their friends, is well known. Anne's father, **Otto Frank**, was a well-to-do Jewish businessman who fled Germany in December 1933 after Hitler came to power, moving to Amsterdam, where he established a spice-trading business on the Prinsengracht. After the German occupation of the Netherlands, Otto – along with many other Jews – felt he could avoid trouble by keeping his head down. However, by 1942 it was clear that this would not be possible; Amsterdam's Jews were isolated and conspicuous, confined to certain parts of the city and forced to wear a yellow star, and roundups were increasingly common. In desperation, Otto Frank decided to move the family into the unused back rooms of their Prinsengracht premises, first asking some of his Dutch office staff if they would help him with the subterfuge – they bravely agreed. The Franks went into hiding in July 1942, along with a Jewish business partner and his wife and son, the van Pels (renamed the van Daans in the *Diary*). Their new "home" was separated from the rest of the building by a **bookcase** that doubled as a door. As far as everyone else was concerned, they had fled to Switzerland.

So began a two-year incarceration in the **achterhuis**, or rear house, and the two families were joined in November 1942 by a dentist friend, Fritz Pfeffer (Albert Dussel in the *Diary*), bringing the number of occupants to eight. Otto's trusted office staff continued working in the front part of the building, regularly bringing supplies and news of the outside world. In her diary Anne Frank describes the **day-to-day lives** of the inhabitants of the **Secret Annex**: the quarrels, frequent in such a claustrophobic environment, the celebrations of birthdays, or a piece of good news from the Allied Front; and of her own, slightly unreal, growing up (some of which was later removed by her father prior to publication).

In 1944, the atmosphere was optimistic; the Allies were clearly winning the war and liberation seemed within reach – but it wasn't to be. One day in the summer of that year, the Franks were **betrayed** by a Dutch collaborator; the Gestapo arrived and forced open the bookcase. The occupants of the Secret Annex were arrested and dispatched to Westerbork – the transit camp in the north of the country where all Dutch Jews were processed before being moved to Belsen or Auschwitz. Of the eight from the Annex, only Otto Frank survived; Anne and her sister died of typhus within a short time of each other in **Belsen**, just one week before the German surrender.

Anne Frank's **diary** was among the few things left behind in the Annex after the Gestapo raid. It was retrieved by one of the family's Dutch helpers and handed to Otto on his return from Auschwitz. In 1947, Otto decided to publish his daughter's diary; since then, it has been translated into over sixty languages and sold literally millions of copies. Otto Frank died in 1980 at the age of 91; the identity of the collaborator who betrayed his family has never been confirmed.

A visit begins in the main body of the building, with several well-chosen displays setting the historical scene and explaining how and why the Franks took refuge here. Then you arrive at the entrance to the **Secret Annex**, or *achterhuis*, which was separated from the rest of the house by **a false bookcase**. The Secret Annex was stripped of furniture long ago, but it still bears traces of its former occupants – such as the movie-star pin-ups in Anne's bedroom and the marks on the wall recording the children's heights. The final part of the Anne Frank Huis visit is an educational section devoted to such themes as free speech, oppression and racism.

Anne Frank was only one of about 100,000 Dutch Jews who died during World War II, but this, her final home, provides one of the most enduring testaments to its horrors and, despite the number of visitors, most people find a visit very moving. Her diary has been a source of inspiration to many, including Nelson Mandela and **Primo Levi**, who wrote the following: "Perhaps it is better that way [that we can concentrate on the suffering of Anne]; if we were capable of taking in all the suffering of all those people, we would not be able to live".

Due to the popularity of the Anne Frank Huis, the queues can be on the long side; try to come early or late to avoid the crush – or book a slot online and skip the queue altogether.

The Westerkerk

Trapped in the *achterhuis*, Anne Frank liked to listen to the bells of the **Westerkerk** (Mon–Sat: April–Sept 10am–5.30pm; Oct 11am–4pm; free; Ⓦwww.westerkerk.nl), until they were taken away to be melted down for the German war effort. The church still dominates the district, its 85-metre **tower** (same hours; €5) – without question Amsterdam's finest – soaring graciously above its surroundings and offering panoramic views of the city centre from its balconies. On its top perches the crown of the Emperor Maximilian, a constantly recurring symbol of Amsterdam (see p.45) and the finishing touch to what was then only the second city church to be built expressly for the Protestants. The church was designed by **Hendrick de Keyser** (see box, p.72) and completed ten years after his death in 1631. Its construction was part of the general enlargement of the city, but whereas the exterior is all studied elegance, the interior – as required by the Calvinist congregation – is bare and plain. Apart from the soaring stone columns and long windows, which allow the light to pour in, the only feature of note is the fancy wooden pulpit, where Protestant ministers once thundered away.

The Westerkerk was also the last resting place of **Rembrandt**, though the location of his pauper's tomb is not known. Instead, a small memorial in the north aisle commemorates the artist, close to the spot where his son Titus was buried. Rembrandt adored his son – as evidenced by numerous portraits – and the boy's death dealt a final crushing blow to the ageing and embittered artist, who died just over a year later. During renovation of the church in the early 1990s, **bones** were unearthed that could have been those of Rembrandt – a possibility whose tourist potential excited the church authorities no end. Admittedly it was a long shot – paupers' tombs were usually cleared of their accumulated bodies every twenty years or so – but the obvious way to prove it was through a chemical analysis of the bones' lead content, expected to be unusually high if they were his, as lead was a major ingredient of paint. The bones were duly taken to the University of Groningen for analysis, but the tests proved inconclusive.

Westermarkt

Westermarkt, an open square in the shadow of the Westerkerk, contains two evocative **statues**. Just to the south of the church entrance, by Prinsengracht, is a small, poignant statue of **Anne Frank** by the gifted Dutch sculptor Mari Andriessen (1897–1979), also the creator of the Dokwerker (Dockworker) statue outside Amsterdam's Esnoga (see p.100). The second piece, behind the church beside Keizersgracht, consists of three pinkish granite triangles (one each for the past, present and future) which together comprise the **Homomonument**. The world's first memorial to persecuted gays and lesbians, commemorating all those who died at the hands of the Nazis, it was designed by Karin Daan and recalls

▲ The Homomonument

the pink triangles the Germans made Dutch homosexuals sew onto their clothes during World War II. The monument has become a focus for the city's gay community and the site of ceremonies and wreath-laying throughout the year, most notably on Queen's Day (April 30), Coming-Out Day (Sept 5) and World AIDS Day (Dec 1). The monument's inscription, by the Dutch writer Jacob Israel de Haan, translates as "Such an infinite desire for friendship".

The French philosopher **René Descartes** (1596–1650) once lodged at **Westermarkt 6**, a handsome building with an attractive neck gable and fancy fanlight. Apparently happy that the Dutch were indifferent to his musings – and that therefore he wasn't going to be persecuted – he wrote, "Everybody except me is in business and so absorbed by profit-making that I could spend my entire life here without being noticed by a soul". However, this declaration may itself have been subterfuge: it's quite possible that Descartes was spying on the Dutch for the Habsburg King Philip II of Spain, a possibility explored in detail in A.C. Grayling's book entitled *Descartes: The Life and Times of a Genius*. In the event, Descartes spent twenty years in the Netherlands before accepting an invitation from Queen Christina to go to Stockholm in 1649. It turned out to be a poor choice; no sooner had he got there, he caught pneumonia and died.

The Huis Bartolotti

The **Huis Bartolotti** is at Herengracht 170–172 (no public access), with a facade of red brick and stone dotted with urns, gargoyles and cherubs. The house is an excellent illustration of the Dutch Renaissance style of **Hendrick de Keyser** (see box, p.72) with a director of the West India Company, a certain Willem van den Heuvel, footing the bill. Van den Heuvel inherited a fortune from his Italian uncle and changed his name in his honour to Bartolotti – hence the name of the house. Huis Bartolotti is much more ornate than its more typical neighbour, at **Herengracht 168**, a classic canal house designed by **Philip Vingboons** (1607–78), arguably the most talented architect involved in the creation of the Grachtengordel. The house was built for Michael de Pauw,

Hendrick de Keyser

Born in Utrecht, the son of a carpenter, **Hendrick de Keyser** (1565–1621) moved to Amsterdam in 1591. Initially employed as an apprentice sculptor, de Keyser soon ventured out on his own, speedily establishing himself as one of the city's most sought-after sculptor-architects. In 1595 he was appointed the city's official stonemason, becoming city architect too in 1612. His municipal commissions included three churches – the Zuiderkerk (see p.62), the Noorderkerk (see p.88) and the Westerkerk (see p.70) – and the upper storeys of the Munttoren (see p.82). His domestic designs were, however, more playful – or at least ornate – and it was here that he pioneered what is often called the **Amsterdam Renaissance style**, in which Italianate decorative details – tympani, octagonal turrets, pilasters, pinnacles and arcades – were imposed on traditional Dutch design. The usual media were red brick and sandstone trimmings – as in the Huis Bartolotti.

a leading light in the East India Company in the 1630s, its fetching sandstone facade a suitably grand preamble to an interior that sports a riot of flamboyant stuccowork, verdant Italianate wall paintings and a splendid spiral staircase.

The Woonbootmuseum and Felix Meritis building

The **Woonbootmuseum** (Houseboat Museum; March–Oct Tues–Sun 11am–5pm; Nov–Feb Fri–Sun same hours; €3.50; ⓦwww.houseboatmuseum .nl), opposite Prinsengracht 296, is an old Dutch houseboat of 1914 that doubles as a tourist attraction with a handful of explanatory plaques about life on the water. Some three thousand barges and houseboats are connected to the city's gas and electricity networks.

One block east along Berenstraat stands the **Felix Meritis building**, at Keizersgracht 324. A Neoclassical monolith dating to 1787, the mansion was built to house a science and arts society, which was the cultural focus of the city's upper crust for nearly one hundred years. Dutch cultural aspirations did not, however, impress everyone. It's said that when Napoleon visited Amsterdam the entire building was redecorated for his reception, only to have him stalk out in disgust, claiming that the place stank of tobacco. Oddly enough, it later became the headquarters of the Dutch Communist Party, but they sold it to the council, which now leases it to the Felix Meritis Foundation (ⓦwww.felix.meritis.nl), which hosts a mix of conferences and concerts with a pan-European theme.

The Cromhouthuizen and the Bijbels Museum

A row of five houses at **Herengracht 361–369** is an excellent spot to compare and contrast the main types of **gable**: stepped at no. 361, bell at nos. 365 and 367 and neck at no. 369, and there's more handsome architecture across the canal at Herengracht 364–370, where the graceful and commanding **Cromhouthuizen** consist of four matching stone mansions. These are embellished with tendrils, garlands and scrollwork, and finessed by charming little bull's-eye windows and elegant neck gables. Built in the 1660s for one of Amsterdam's wealthy merchant families, the Cromhouts, the houses were designed by **Philip Vingboons** (1607–78), the most inventive of the architects who worked on the Grachtengordel during the city's expansion. As a Catholic, Vingboons was confined to private commissions – inconvenient no doubt, but at a time when Protestants and Catholics were at each other's throats right across Europe, hardly insufferable.

Two of the houses have been adapted to hold the **Bijbels Museum** (Bible Museum; Mon–Sat 10am–5pm, Sun 11am–5pm; €7.50; ⓦ www.bijbelsmuseum .nl) and these still exhibit several decorative flourishes from their original function as homes for the rich. The best examples are on the ground floor behind the museum entrance, and comprise a striking spiral staircase and a painted ceiling of classical gods and goddesses by Jacob de Wit. You'll spot these at the end of a visit to the museum, which begins on Floor 3 (the top floor), where there's a large and detailed nineteenth-century model of the **Tabernacle**, the portable sanctuary in which the Israelites carried their holy of holies, the Ark of the Covenant. Attempts to reconstruct biblical scenes were something of a cottage industry in the Netherlands in the late 1800s, with scores of Dutch antiquarians beavering away, Bible in one hand and modelling equipment in the other, but the creator of this particular model, a Protestant vicar by the name of **Leendert Schouten** (1828–1905), went one step further, making it his lifetime's work. It was a good move; Schouten became a well-known figure and his model proved a popular attraction, drawing hundreds of visitors to his home. Schouten also assembled an interesting assortment of Middle Eastern **archeological finds** dating from the period when the Israelites were in exile in Egypt, and these are displayed on the third floor too.

Floor 2 sticks to a similar theme, with the main exhibit being a large and detailed model of Jerusalem's Temple Mount, made at the end of the nineteenth century when Palestine was part of the Ottoman Empire. A short film explores the history of the Temple Mount too. There are yet more models of the Temple on Floor 1, one at the time of Herod, another of when Solomon was king, and a small "Aroma Cabinet" of Biblical fragrances – palm, almond and so forth. There's also an outstanding collection of **antique Bibles** in the cellar, the most important of these being the official **Statenvertaling** (literally State's Translation), published in 1637. Key to the development of Dutch Protestantism, the Statenvertaling was the result of years of study by the leading scholars of the Netherlands, who returned to the original Greek and Hebrew texts for this translation; it sold by the cartload.

Herengracht 380–394 and the Huis Marseille

The gracious symmetries of the Cromhouthuizen contrast with the grandiose pretension of **Herengracht 380**, built in the style of a French chateau for a tobacco planter in 1889. Ornately decorated, the mansion's main gable is embellished with reclining figures and the bay window by cherubs, mythical characters and an abundance of acanthus leaves. It was the first house in the city to be supplied with electricity and it now houses the Netherlands Institute for War Documentation – the Nederlands Instituut voor Oorlogsdocumentatie. Opposite, across the canal, is the only spot in Amsterdam where the houses come straight out of the water, Venice-like, without the intervention of a pavement.

Also on the west side of the canal, **Herengracht 388** is another handsome **Philip Vingboons** building, while **Herengracht 394**, the narrow house with

Han van Meegeren and the forged Vermeers

Keizersgracht 321, on the other side of the canal from the Meritis building, is in itself fairly innocuous, but this was once the home of the Dutch art forger **Han van Meegeren** (1889–1947). During the German occupation of World War II, Meegeren sold a "previously unknown" Vermeer to a German art dealer working for Herman Goering; what neither the agent nor Goering realized was that Meegeren had painted it himself. A forger *par excellence*, Meegeren had developed a sophisticated ageing technique in the early 1930s. He mixed his paints with phenol formaldehyde resin dissolved in benzene and then baked the finished painting in an oven for several hours; the end result fooled everyone, including the curators of the Rijksmuseum, who had bought another "Vermeer" from him in 1941.

The forgeries may well have never been discovered but for a strange sequence of events. In May 1945 a British captain by the name of Harry Anderson discovered Meegeren's "Vermeer" in Goering's art collection. Meegeren was promptly arrested as a collaborator and, to get himself out of a pickle, he soon confessed to this and other forgeries, arguing that he had duped and defrauded the Nazis rather than helping them – though he had, of course, pocketed the money. It was a fine argument and his reward was a short prison sentence – but in the event he died before he was locked up.

the bell gable at the corner of Leidsegracht, bears a distinctive **facade stone** illustrating the legend of the four Aymon brothers, shown astride their trusty steed. The subject of a popular medieval chanson, the legend is all about honour, loyalty and friendship, dynastic quarrels and disputes, revolving around the trials and tribulations of the horse. The long, rambling tale ends when the redoubtable beast repeatedly breaks free from the millstones tied around its neck and refuses to drown; the third time it comes to the surface, the brothers walk away, no longer able to watch the agonies of their animal. Assuming he's been abandoned, the horse cries out and promptly expires.

The **Huis Marseille**, Keizersgracht 401 (Tues–Sun 11am–6pm; €5; Ⓦ www.huismarseille.nl), is a photography museum offering a rolling programme of exhibitions mostly featuring contemporary photographers. The museum occupies a grand old mansion, but the display space is confined to just four rooms.

Leidsegracht

The **Leidsegracht** is a largely residential canal, lined with chic town houses and a medley of handsome gables. It's a tranquil scene – or at least it would be were it not for the flat-topped tour boats, which use the canal as a short cut as they shunt into and out of Prinsengracht. An eighteenth-century wine merchant by the name of Paling would have welcomed the sight of a boat when he slipped into the Leidsegracht on a dark November evening. Well known as one of the greediest men in Amsterdam, he could apparently shovel down seven pounds of beef, a leg of lamb and thirty herrings in one sitting. He also liked his wine, a weakness that prompted his early demise when he fell – or staggered – into the Leidsegracht and no one heard the splash in time.

Just off Leidsegracht on Prinsengracht are nos. 681–693, where an exquisite set of seven neck gables – one for each of the provinces that originally broke away from the Habsburgs – comprises an especially harmonious ensemble that dates back to 1715.

Grachtengordel south

Grachtengordel south holds many of the city's proudest and most touted mansions, clustered along **De Gouden Bocht** – the Golden Bend – the curve of Herengracht between Leidsestraat and the River Amstel. It's on this stretch that the merchant elite abandoned the material modesty of their Calvinist forebears, indulging themselves with lavish mansions, whose fancy facades more than hinted at the wealth within. In the late seventeenth and eighteenth centuries, this elite also forsook brick for stone and the restrained details of traditional Dutch architecture for pompous Neoclassicism, their defeat of the Spanish Habsburgs, allied with their commercial success, prompting them to compare themselves to the Greeks and Romans. In the event, it was all an illusion – the bubble burst when Napoleon's army arrived in 1793 – and, although the opulent interiors of two old mansions, the **Museum Willet-Holthuysen** and the **Van Loon Museum**, still give a flavour of those heady days, for the most part all that's left – albeit a substantial legacy – are the wonderful facades. Few of these big, old houses still act as family homes and most have been recycled as offices and flats, but one has recently been converted into the delightful purse and bag museum, the **Tassenmuseum Hendrikje**.

Grachtengordel south contains some rather less savoury areas, too, where ill-considered twentieth-century development has blemished the city, especially in the seediness of the **Rembrandtplein** and the mediocrity of both Vijzelstraat and **Leidseplein**.

Leidseplein

Lying on the edge of the Grachtengordel, **Leidseplein** is the bustling hub of Amsterdam's nightlife, a somewhat cluttered and disorderly open space that heaves with revellers each and every weekend. The square once marked the end of the road in from Leiden and, as horse-drawn traffic was banned from the

▲ Leidseplein

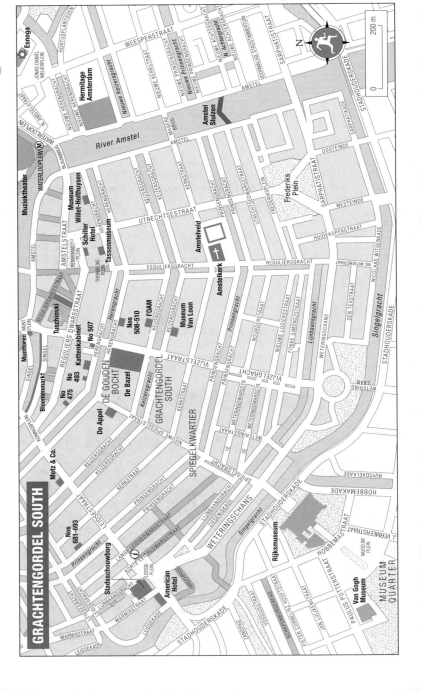

GRACHTENGORDEL SOUTH

Esnoga

Jonas Daniel Meijerplein

Hortusplantsoen

WEESPERSTRAAT

N. AMSTELSTRAAT

WATERLOOPLEIN

Muziektheater

WATERLOOPLEIN M

BLAUWBRUG

Hermitage Amsterdam

NIEUWE HERENGRACHT

NIEUWE HERENGRACHT

NIEUWE KEIZERSGRACHT

NIEUWE KEIZERSGRACHT

NIEUWE PRINSENGRACHT

Nieuwe Prinsengracht

NIEUWE PRINSENGRACHT

NIEUWE ACHTERGRACHT

N. Achtergracht

NIEUWE ACHTERGRACHT

SARPHATISTRAAT

AMSTEL

River Amstel

MAGERE BRUG

Amstel Sluizen

OOSTEINDE

Frederiks Plein

SARPHATISTRAAT

WESTEINDE

STADHOUDERSKADE

SARPHATIKADE

Museum Willet-Holthuysen

KEIZERSGRACHT

KEIZERSGRACHT

HERENGRACHT

HERENGRACHT

AMSTELSTRAAT

AMSTEL

AMSTELSTRAAT

REMBRANDTPLEIN

THORBECKEPLEIN

Schiller Hotel

Tassenmuseum

UTRECHTSESTRAAT

UTRECHTSEDWARSSTRAAT

PRINSENGRACHT

Prinsengracht

PRINSENGRACHT

FREDERIKSPLEIN

Amstelveld

HUIDEKOPERSTRAAT

NIC. WITSENSTRAAT

NICOLAAS WITSENKADE

F.EGULIERSGRACHT

Amstelkerk

REGULIERSGRACHT

Singelgracht

STADHOUDERSKADE

MUNTPLEIN

Muntoren

SINGEL

Bloemenmarkt

SINGEL

KONINGSPLEIN

Tuschinski

REGULIERSBREESTRAAT

REGULIERS DWARSSTRAAT

Kattenkabinet

No 507

Nos 508-510

FOAM

HERENGRACHT

HERENGRACHT

Herengracht

KEIZERSGRACHT

KEIZERSGRACHT

Museum Van Loon

PRINSENGRACHT

NOORDERSTRAAT

NIEUWE LOOIERSSTRAAT

FOKKE SIMONSZSTRAAT

WETERINGSCHANS

DEN TEXSTRAAT

LIJNBAANSGRACHT

No 493

No 475

DE GOUDEN BOCHT

De Bazel

Keizersgracht

KERKSTRAAT

GRACHTENGORDEL SOUTH

NIEUWE SPIEGELSTRAAT

VIJZELSTRAAT

VIJZELGRACHT

PRINSENGRACHT

PRINSENGRACHT

WETERINGDWARSSTR

WETERINGDWARSSTR

WETERINGSTRAAT

1E

WETERINGLAAN

WETERING

De Appel

Metz & Co.

KEIZERSGRACHT

KEIZERSGRACHT

KERKSTRAAT

PRINSENGRACHT

SPIEGELKWARTIER

SPIEGELGRACHT

LIJNBAANSGRACHT

ZIESENISKADE

WETERINGSCHANS

Singelgracht

STADHOUDERSKADE

RUYSDAELKADE

HOBBEMAKADE

Nos 681-683

LEIDSESTRAAT

Prinsengracht

LANGE LEIDSEDWARSSTRAAT

KORTE LEIDSEDWARSSTRAAT

Stadsschouwburg

LEIDSEPLEIN

LEIDSEGRACHT

LIJNBAANSGRACHT

MARNIXSTRAAT

American Hotel

SINGELGRACHT

LEIDSEKADE

MARNIXSTRAAT

MARNIXKADE

LEIDSEKADE

LEIDSEKADE

Rijksmuseum

STADHOUDERSKADE

HOBBEMASTRAAT

J. VERMEERSTRAAT

MUSEUM PLEIN

Van Gogh Museum

MUSEUM QUARTER

PAULUS POTTERSTRAAT

JAN LUIJKENSTRAAT

PIETER CORNELISZ HOOFTSTRAAT

SCHERPENZEELSTRAAT

VOSSIUSSTRAAT

ZANDPAD

N

0   200 m

centre at the time, it was here that the Dutch left their horses and carts – a sort of equine car park. Today, it's quite the opposite; relentless traffic made up of trams, bikes, cars and pedestrians gives the place a frenetic feel, and the surrounding side streets are jammed with bars, restaurants and clubs in a bright jumble of jutting signs and neon lights. It's not surprising, therefore, that on a good night Leidseplein can be Amsterdam at its carefree, exuberant best.

Leidseplein also contains two buildings of some architectural merit. The first is the grandiose **Stadsschouwburg**, a neo-Renaissance edifice dating back to 1894 that was so widely criticized for its clumsy vulgarity that the city council of the day temporarily withheld the money for decorating the exterior. Home to the National Ballet and Opera until the Muziektheater (see p.99) was completed on Waterlooplein in 1986, it is now used for theatre, dance and music performances (see p.208). However, its most popular function is as the place where the Ajax football team gathers on the balcony to wave to the crowds whenever they win anything – as they often do.

Across the street, just off the square on Leidsekade, is one of the city's oddest buildings, the **American Hotel**, whose monumental and slightly disconcerting rendering of Art Nouveau comes complete with angular turrets, chunky dormer windows and fancy brickwork. Completed in 1902, the present structure takes its name from its demolished predecessor, which was – as the stylistic peccadillo of its architect, one W. Steinigeweg – adorned with statues and murals of North American scenes. Inside the present hotel is the *Café Americain* (see p.184), once the fashionable haunt of Amsterdam's literati, but now a mainstream location for coffee and lunch. The Art Nouveau decor is still worth a peek – an artful combination of stained glass, shallow arches and geometric patterned brickwork.

Leidsestraat and the Spiegelkwartier

Northeast of Leidseplein is **Leidsestraat**, one of Amsterdam's principal shopping streets, comprising a long, slender gauntlet of fast food, fashion and shoe shops of little distinction. That said, the department store **Metz & Co**, at the junction with Keizersgracht, occupies a good-looking stone building of 1891, its facade adorned by caryatids and topped by a distinctive corner dome. At the time of its construction, it was the tallest commercial building in the city – one reason why the owners were able to entice **Gerrit Rietveld** (1888–1964), the leading architectural light of the artistic movement De Stijl, to add a rooftop glass and metal showroom in 1933. The showroom has survived and is now a café (see p.184) offering a fine view over the city centre; perhaps surprisingly, Rietveld designed just one other building in Amsterdam – the Van Gogh Museum (see pp.119–121).

One block east of Metz & Co is Nieuwe Spiegelstraat, an appealing mix of shops and boutiques, which extends south into Spiegelgracht to form the **Spiegelkwartier**. The district is home to the pricey end of Amsterdam's antiques trade as well as **De Appel**, a lively centre for contemporary art with well-presented, temporary exhibitions, at Nieuwe Spiegelstraat 10 (times vary with exhibitions, but normally Tues–Sun 10am–6pm; €4; ⓦwww.deappel.nl).

De Gouden Bocht

Nieuwe Spiegelstraat meets the elegant sweep of Herengracht near the west end of **De Gouden Bocht** where the canal is overlooked by a long sequence of double-fronted mansions, some of the most opulent dwellings in the city. Most of the houses here were extensively remodelled in the late seventeenth and eighteenth centuries. Characteristically, they have double stairways leading to the entrance, with small doors underneath (originally for servants' use), and large doors above; the majority are topped off with the ornamental cornices that were fashionable at the time. Classical references are common, both in form – pediments, columns and pilasters – and decoration, from scrolls and vases through to geometric patterns inspired by ancient Greece.

One of the first buildings to look out for on the north side of the canal – just across from (and to the west of) Nieuwe Spiegelstraat – is **Herengracht 475**, an extravagant stone mansion decorated with allegorical figures and surmounted by a slender balustrade. Typically, the original building was a much more modest affair, dating from the 1660s, but eighty years later the new owner took matters in hand to create the ornate facade of today. Just along the canal to the east, **Herengracht 493** is similarly grand, though here the building is polished off with an extravagantly carved pediment. A couple of doors down, Herengracht 497 is, by comparison, rather restrained, but the interior has been turned into the idiosyncratic **Kattenkabinet** (Cat Cabinet; Tues–Fri 10am–4pm, Sat & Sun 12–5pm; €5; ⓦ www.kattenkabinet.nl), a substantial collection of art and artefacts relating to cats. They were installed by a Dutch financier, whose cherished moggy, John Pierpont Morgan (named after the American financier), died in 1984; feline fanatics will be delighted by the exhibits.

A short distance away, **Herengracht 507** is an especially handsome house, though not too grand, its Neoclassical pilasters, pediment, mini-balcony and double-stairway nicely balanced by the slender windows. This was once the home of Jacob Boreel (1630–97), one-time mayor, whose attempt to impose a burial tax started a riot during which the mob ransacked his house.

The Stadsarchief – De Bazel

Opposite **Herengracht 507**, stretching down Vijzelstraat as far as Keizersgracht, is one of Amsterdam's weirdest and most monumentally incongruous buildings – you can't possibly miss its looming, geometrical brickwork. Now home to a conference centre and the **Stadsarchief**, the state archives, it started out as the headquarters of a Dutch shipping company, the **Nederlandsche Handelsmaatschappij**, before falling into the hands of the ABN-AMRO bank, which was itself swallowed by a consortium led by the Royal Bank of Scotland in 2007 – just before the worldwide banking crisis. Dating to the 1920s, the building is commonly known as **De Bazel** (ⓦ www.debazelamsterdam.nl) after the architect Karel de Bazel (1869–1923), whose devotion to theosophy formed and framed his design. Founded in the late nineteenth century, **theosophy** combined metaphysics and religious philosophy, arguing that there was an over-arching spiritual order with reincarnation for all as an added bonus. Every facet of de Bazel's building reflects this desire – or search – for order and balance from the pink and yellow brickwork of the exterior (representing male and female respectively) to the repeated use of motifs drawn from the Middle East, the source of much of the cult's spiritual inspiration. At the heart of the building is the magnificent **Schatkamer** (Treasury; Tues–Sat 10am–5pm & Sun 11am–5pm; free), a richly decorated, Art Deco extravagance that feels rather like a royal crypt. Exhibited here is an intriguing selection of photographs and documents drawn from the city's archives – anything from 1970s squatters occupying City Hall to hagiographic tracts on the virtues of the Dutch naval hero, Admiral de Ruyter and, perhaps best of the lot, photos of miscreants (or rather the poor and the desperate) drawn from police archives. The exhibits are changed regularly and in the basement there's a small film studio showing documentaries about the city, both past and present.

The Tassenmuseum Hendrikje

The delightful **Tassenmuseum Hendrikje**, Herengracht 573 (Purse & Bag Museum; daily 10am–5pm; €6.50; Ⓦ www.tassenmuseum.nl), holds a simply superb collection of handbags, pouches, wallets, bags and purses from medieval times onwards, exhibited on three floors of a sympathetically refurbished grand old mansion. The collection begins on the top floor with a curious miscellany of items from the sixteenth to the nineteenth centuries. Here you'll find examples of several types of bag that preceded the purse – portefeuilles, chatelaines, frame-bags, reticules and stocking purses to name but five. The next floor down focuses on the twentieth century with several beautiful Art Nouveau handbags and a whole cabinet of 1950s specimens made of "hard plastic", an early form of perspex. Another display features handbags made from animals – the eel, crocodile, python and lizard bags look attractive, as long as you don't pause to think about how they were made, but the armadillo bag is really rather gruesome. The final floor is given over to temporary displays with contemporary bags and purses the favourite theme. The museum also has a pleasant café.

Close by, the facades of Herengracht 508–510 are worth close inspection: both have neck gables dating from the 1690s, and both sport sea gods straddling dolphins, while tritons – half-men, half-fish – trumpet through conch shells to pacify the oceans.

The Museum Willet-Holthuysen

The **Museum Willet-Holthuysen** (Mon–Fri 10am–5pm, Sat & Sun 11am–5pm; €6; Ⓦ www.museumwilletholthuysen.nl), near the Amstel at Herengracht 605, is billed as "the only fully furnished patrician house open to the public", which just about sums it up. The house dates from 1685, but the

▲ The Museum Willet-Holthuysen

interior was remodelled by successive members of the coal-trading Holthuysen family until the last of the line, Sandra Willet-Holthuysen, donated her home and its contents to the city in 1895.

The museum **entrance** is through the old servants' door, leading into the basement, which holds a small collection of **porcelain and earthenware**. Up above are the family rooms, most memorably the **Blue Room**, which has been returned to its original, eighteenth-century Rococo splendour, a flashy and ornate style copied from France and held to be the epitome of refinement and good taste by local merchants. The **Ballroom**, all creams and gilt, is similarly opulent and the **Dining Room** is laid out for dinner as of 1805, complete with the family's original Meissen dinner set.

The top floor displays the fine and applied art collection assembled by Sandra's husband, Abraham Willet. There are Dutch ceramics, pewter and silverware as well as four finely carved ivory pieces depicting the elements, made in Germany in the eighteenth century. Among the paintings, look out for a landscape by Willem Maris (1844–1910) and a distinctly smug self-portrait of Abraham at the age of 28. The exhibits are regularly moved around, however, to make way for temporary exhibitions.

At the back of the house lie the formal **gardens**, a neat pattern of miniature hedges graced by the occasional stone statue, and framed by the old coach house.

The Amstel and the Magere Brug

Just east of Willet-Holthuysen, Herengracht comes to an abrupt halt beside the wide and windy **River Amstel**, which was long the main trade route into the Dutch interior – goods arriving by barge and boat were traded for the imported materials held in Amsterdam's many warehouses. To the left is the Blauwbrug (Blue Bridge) and the Old Jewish Quarter (see Chapter 4), whilst in the opposite direction is the **Magere Brug** (Skinny Bridge), the most famous and arguably the cutest of the city's many swing bridges. Legend has it that the current bridge, which dates back to about 1670, replaced an even older and skinnier version, originally built by two sisters who lived on opposite sides of the river and were fed up with having to walk so far to see each other.

South of the bridge are the **Amstel sluizen**, the river's locks. Every night, the municipal water department closes these locks to begin the process of **sluicing** out the canals. A huge pumping station on an island out to the east of the city then pumps fresh water from the IJsselmeer into the canal system; similar locks on the west side of the city are left open for the surplus to flow into the IJ and, from there, out to sea via the North Sea Canal. The city's canal water is thus refreshed every three nights – though, what with three centuries of shopping trolleys, rusty bikes and general detritus, the water is only appealing as long as you're not actually in it.

Reguliersgracht and FOAM

On the north side of Prinsengracht is the small open space of the **Amstelveld**, popular for impromptu football games, with the squat, seventeenth-century **Amstelkerk**, made of plain white wood, occupying one of its corners. It's here also that Prinsengracht intersects with **Reguliersgracht**, perhaps the prettiest of the three surviving radial canals that cut across the Grachtengordel – its dainty humpback bridges and green waters overlooked by charming seventeenth- and eighteenth-century canal houses.

One of the busiest attractions in this part of the city is **FOAM**, Keizersgracht 609 (Fotografiemuseum; Sat–Wed 10am–6pm, Thurs & Fri 10am–9pm; €7.50; Ⓦwww.foam.nl), which offers an inventive programme of photographic exhibitions, many of which have a local (and very modish) theme. The work of local ad agencies has provided the source materials for several exhibitions and there's been international stuff, too – for example, the American photographer Richard Avedon was featured in 2009.

The Museum Van Loon

Across the canal from FOAM, the **Museum Van Loon**, at Keizersgracht 672 (Wed–Mon 11am–5pm; €6; Ⓦwww.museumvanloon.nl), boasts the grandest canal house interior open to the public in Amsterdam. The first tenant of the property, which was built in 1672, was the artist Ferdinand Bol, who married an exceedingly wealthy widow and promptly hung up his easel for the rest of his days. The last owners were the van Loons, co-founders of the East India Company and long one of the city's leading families, though they came something of a cropper at the end of World War II. In 1884 a member of the family, Hendrik, purchased this house for his son Willem, on the occasion of his marriage to Thora Egidius. Thora had friends and relatives in Germany and during the occupation she entertained them – unwisely, considering that several of her guests were high-ranking Nazi officials. After the war, allegations of collaboration besmirched Thora's reputation and an embarrassed Queen Wilhelmina fired her as her *dame du palais*, a position she had held since 1898; Thora died two months later.

The **interior** of the house has been returned to something akin to its eighteenth-century appearance, with wood panelling and fancy stuccowork, plus ancestral portraits of stern men and sober women in their be-ruffed Sunday best. Highlights include the ornate copper **balustrade** on the staircase, into which is worked the name "Van Hagen-Trip" (after the former owners of the house); the van Loons filled the spaces between the letters with fresh iron curlicues to prevent their children falling through. The top-floor landing has several pleasant grisaille **paintings** of classical figures – including Alexander the Great and Julius Caesar – and one of the bedrooms, the "painted room", is decorated with a Romantic painting of Italy, depicting a coastal scene with overgrown classical ruins and diligent peasants. Such artistic conceits were a favourite motif with Amsterdam's bourgeoisie from around 1750 to 1820. The oddest items are the **fake bedroom doors**; the eighteenth-century owners were so keen to avoid any lack of symmetry that they camouflaged the real doors and created imitation, decorative replacements in the "correct" position instead. The other oddity is at the bottom of the garden, where the old **coach house** has *trompe l'oeil* windows; again, symmetry dictated that the building must have windows, but no self-respecting plutocrat wanted to be watched by his servants – hence the illusion.

Thorbeckeplein, Rembrandtplein and Reguliersbreestraat

Short and stumpy **Thorbeckeplein** hosts an assortment of unexciting bars and restaurants, flanking a statue of **Rudolf Thorbecke** (1798–1872), a far-sighted liberal politician and three-times Dutch premier whose reforms served to democratize the country in the aftermath of the European-wide turmoil of 1848.

Thorbeckeplein leads into **Rembrandtplein**, a dishevelled patch of greenery that was formerly Amsterdam's butter market. The square took its present name in 1876, and is today one of the city's nightlife centres, although its crowded restaurants and bars are firmly geared towards tourists. Rembrandt's **statue** stands in the middle, his back wisely turned against the square's worst excesses. Of the prodigious number of cafés and bars here, only the café of the *Schiller Hotel* at no. 26 stands out, with an original Art Deco interior lit by geometrical chandeliers and decorated with stained-glass windows.

The crumbling alleys to the north of Rembrandtplein contain several of the city's raunchier gay bars, while **Reguliersbreestraat** is just supremely tacky. Nevertheless, tucked in among the slot-machine arcades, fast-food joints and sex shops is the city's most extraordinary cinema – the **Tuschinski**, at Reguliersbreestraat 26–28. Opened in 1921 by a Polish Jew, Abram Tuschinski, the cinema boasts a marvellously well-preserved Art Deco facade and interior, which features coloured marble and a wonderful carpet, handwoven in Marrakesh to an original design. Tuschinski himself died in Auschwitz in 1942. The network of alleys behind the cinema was once known as **Duivelshoek** (Devil's Corner), and, although it's been tidied up and sanitized, enough backstreet seediness remains to make it a spot to be avoided late at night.

The Munttoren and Bloemenmarkt

Muntplein is overlooked by the sturdy, late-medieval **Munttoren**, originally part of the old city wall. Later, it was adopted as the municipal mint – hence its name – a plain brick structure to which Hendrick de Keyser (see box, p.72), in one of his last commissions, added a flashy **spire** in 1620. Metres away, on the southern bank of the Singel, lies the floating **Bloemenmarkt** (flower market; Mon–Sat 8.30am–5pm, though some stalls open on Sun), which is popular with locals and tourists alike. The market is one of the main suppliers of flowers to central Amsterdam, but its blooms and bulbs now share stall space with souvenir clogs, garden gnomes and delftware.

The Jordaan and Western docklands

L ying to the west of the city centre, the **Jordaan** (pronounced "your-darn") is a likeable and easily explored area of slender canals and narrow streets flanked by an agreeable mix of architectural styles, from modest modern terraces to handsome seventeenth-century canal houses. Traditionally the home of Amsterdam's working class, with its boundaries clearly defined by the Prinsengracht to the east and the Lijnbaansgracht in the west, the Jordaan's character has been transformed in recent years by a middle-class influx, and the district is now one of the city's most sought-after residential neighbourhoods. Before then, and indeed until the late 1970s, the Jordaan's inhabitants were primarily stevedores and factory workers, earning a crust among the docks, warehouses, factories and boat yards that extended beyond **Brouwersgracht**, the Jordaan's north-eastern boundary and nowadays one of Amsterdam's prettiest canals. Specific sights are few and far between, but nonetheless it's still a pleasant area to wander around.

The pint-sized **Scheepvaartsbuurt** (Shipping Quarter), part of the city's old industrial belt and now a mixed shopping and residential quarter, edges the Jordaan to the north, bisected by Haarlemmerstraat and its continuation Haarlemmerdijk. Just to the north lie the **Western docklands**, or Westerdok, the oldest part of the sprawling complex of artificial islands that today sweeps along the south side of the River IJ, containing many of the city's maritime facilities. This patch of land was dredged out of the river to provide extra warehousing and dock space in the seventeenth century. The maritime bustle has pretty much disappeared here, but after a long period of neglect the area is rapidly finding new life as a chichi residential quarter, with smart apartments installed in its warehouses and its clutch of elegant canal houses revamped and reinvigorated, especially on **Zandhoek**. Finally, the working-class neighbour-hood to the west of the Westerkanaal, which marks the limit of the Western docklands, is of interest for the **Het Schip** complex, a wonderful example of the Amsterdam School of Architecture and, perhaps more importantly, an example of social housing at its most optimistic.

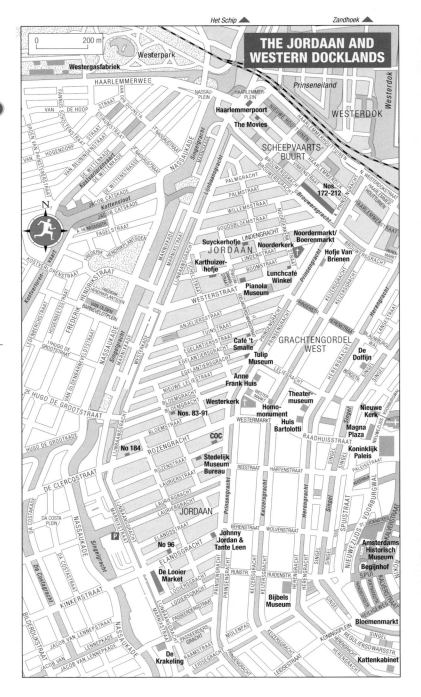

The Jordaan

In all probability the **Jordaan** takes its name from the French word *jardin* ("garden"), since the area's earliest settlers were Protestant Huguenots, who fled here to escape persecution in the sixteenth and seventeenth centuries. Another possibility is that it's a corruption of the Dutch word for Jews, *joden*, who also sought refuge here. Whatever the truth, the Jordaan developed from open country – hence the number of streets and canals named after flowers and plants – into a refugee enclave, a teeming, cosmopolitan quarter beyond the pale of bourgeois respectability. Indeed, when the city fathers planned the expansion of the city in 1610, they made sure the Jordaan was kept outside the city boundaries. Consequently, the area was not subject to the rigorous planning restrictions of the main *grachten* – Herengracht, Keizersgracht and Prinsengracht – and its lattice of narrow streets followed the lines of the original polder drainage ditches, rather than any municipal plan. This gives the district its distinctive, mazy layout, and much of its present appeal.

By the late nineteenth century, the Jordaan had become one of Amsterdam's toughest neighbourhoods, a stronghold of the city's industrial **working class**, mostly crowded together in cramped and unsanitary housing. Unsurprisingly, it was a highly politicized area, where protests against poor conditions were frequent, often coordinated by an influential and well-organized Communist Party. In the postwar period the slums were either cleared or renovated, but rocketing property prices in the wealthier parts of the city pushed middle-class professionals into the Jordaan from the early 1980s. This process of gentrification was at first much resented, but today the area is home to many young and affluent "alternative" Amsterdammers, who rub shoulders more or less affably with working-class Jordaaners with long-standing local roots.

Leidsegracht and Elandsgracht

The southern boundary of the Jordaan is generally deemed to be the **Leidsegracht**, though this is open to debate; according to dyed-in-the-wool locals the true Jordaaner is born within earshot of the Westerkerk bells, and you'd be hard-pushed to hear the chimes this far south. The narrow streets and canals just to the north of the Leidsegracht are routinely modern, but **Elandsgracht** does hold, at no. 109, the enjoyable indoor **De Looier antiques market** (daily 11am–5pm; closed Fri), which is good for picking up mainly Dutch bygones, including tiles and ceramics, with a few stalls dealing in specialist wares such as silver trinkets or delftware. There are a couple of cafés inside too, and on Elandsgracht itself you might pause to look at the statues of **Johnny Jordaan** and **Tante Leen**, accompanied by musicians – two twentieth-century singers who

---

The Jordaan's hofjes

One feature of the Jordaan's varied architectural pleasures is its **hofjes** – almshouses built around a central courtyard and originally occupied by the city's elderly and needy. There were – and are – *hofjes* all over the city (most famously the Begijnhof – see p.52), but there's a real concentration here in the Jordaan. Most date back to the seventeenth or eighteenth centuries, but the majority have been rebuilt or at least overhauled – and all are still lived in, often by those people they were originally built for. The Jordaan's most diverting *hofjes* are the **Karthuizerhofje**, on Karthuizersstraat (see p.88), and the **Suyckerhofje** on Lindengracht (see p.89).

▲ De Looier antiques market

were for years the sound of the working-class Jordaan, and whose songs are still remembered and sung in some of the more raucous cafés in the area. Football fanatics will also want to take a peek at the sports shop at Elandsgracht 96, where **Johan Cruyff** – star of Ajax in the 1970s and one of the greatest players of all time – bought his first pair of football boots.

Lijnbaansgracht and Rozengracht

The narrow **Lijnbaansgracht** (Ropewalk Canal) threads its way round most of the city centre, and in between Elandsgracht and Rozenstraat its lapping waters are flanked by cobbled, leafy streets lined with old brick buildings. On **Rozenstraat** itself, at no. 59, is an annex of the Stedelijk Museum (see p.121), the **Stedelijk Museum Bureau** (Tues–Sun 11am–5pm; free; ⓦ www.smba.nl), which provides space for up-and-coming Amsterdam artists, with small-scale exhibitions, installations and occasional lectures and readings.

One block further north, **Rozengracht** lost its canal years ago and is now a busy and somewhat unattractive main road, though it was here at **no. 184** that **Rembrandt** spent the last ten years of his life – a scrolled plaque set high into the wall distinguishes his old home. Rembrandt's last years were scarred by the death of his partner Hendrickje in 1663 and his son Titus five years later, but nevertheless it was in this period that he produced some of his finest work. Also dated to these years is *The Jewish Bride*, a touchingly warm and heartfelt portrait of a bride and her husband, completed in 1668 and now in the Rijksmuseum (see pp.113–119). From Rozengracht, it's the shortest of walks to the Westerkerk and the Anne Frank Huis.

Bloemgracht

The streets and canals extending north from Rozengracht to Westerstraat form the heart of the Jordaan and provide the district's prettiest moments. Beyond Rozengracht, the first canal is the **Bloemgracht** (Flower Canal), a leafy waterway dotted with houseboats and traversed by dinky little bridges, its network of cross-streets sprinkled with cafés, bars and quirky shops. There's a warm, relaxed community atmosphere here which is really rather beguiling, not to mention a clutch of fine old canal houses. Pride of architectural place goes to **nos. 87–91**, a sterling Renaissance building of 1642 complete with mullion windows, three crowstep gables, brightly painted shutters and distinctive facade stones, representing a *steeman* (city-dweller), a *landman* (farmer) and a *seeman* (sailor). **Nos. 83–85** next door were built a few decades later – two immaculately maintained canal houses adorned by the bottleneck gables typical of the period.

Egelantiersgracht

On picturesque **Egelantiersgracht** (Rose-Hip Canal) at no. 12 is 't **Smalle**, one of Amsterdam's oldest cafés, opened in 1786 as a *proeflokaal* – a tasting house for the (long-gone) gin distillery next door. In the eighteenth century, when quality control was erratic to say the least, each batch of *jenever* (Dutch gin) could turn out very differently, so customers insisted on a taster before they splashed out. As a result, each distillery ran a *proeflokaal* offering free samples, and this is a rare survivor. The café's waterside terrace remains an especially pleasant and popular spot to take a tipple (see p.180).

Right on the corner of Egelantiersgracht, the Amsterdam **Tulip Museum** (daily 10am–6pm; €3) is truly more of a shop than a museum, and sells all sorts of flower-related items in its upstairs shop. But it does sell bulbs too, and the downstairs exhibition space gives a brief but moderately interesting introduction to this very Dutch phenomenon, with lots of detail on the speculative bubble in tulip prices during the Golden Age.

Westerstraat

A narrow cross-street – 1e Egelantiersdwarsstraat and its continuation 1e Tuind-warsstraat and 1e Anjeliersdwarsstraat – runs north from **Egelantiersgracht** to

▲ Bloemgracht

workaday **Westerstraat**, a busy thoroughfare, which is home to the small but charming **Pianola Museum** (Sun 2–5pm; €5; ⓦ www.pianola.nl), at no. 106, whose collection of pianolas and automatic music-machines dates from the beginning of the twentieth century. Fifteen have been restored to working order, and there are usually one or two playing throughout the afternoon, which are a delight to watch. These machines, which work on rolls of perforated paper, were the jukeboxes of their day, and the museum has a vast archive of over 15,000 rolls of music, some of which were "recorded" by famous pianists and composers – Gershwin, Debussy, Scott Joplin, Art Tatum and others. The museum runs a programme of pianola music concerts throughout the year (except July/Aug), where the rolls are played back on restored machines (exact times are listed on their website). Nearby, hidden behind a white doorway, is the largest of the Jordaan's *hofjes* (see box, p.85), the **Karthuizerhofje**, Karthuizersstraat 89–171, a substantial courtyard complex established as a widows' hospice in the middle of the seventeenth century, though the present buildings are much more recent. With its picket-fenced gardens and old ornate water-pumps, it makes an appealing, peaceful diversion.

The Noorderkerk

At the east end of Westerstraat, overlooking the Prinsengracht, is Hendrick de Keyser's **Noorderkerk** (Mon, Thurs & Sat 11am–1pm; free), the architect's last creation and probably his least successful, finished two years after his death in 1623. A bulky, overbearing brick building, it represented a radical departure from the conventional church designs of the time, having a symmetrical Greek cross floor plan, with four equally proportioned arms radiating out from a steepled centre. Uncompromisingly dour, it proclaimed the serious intent of the Calvinists who worshipped here in so far as the pulpit – and therefore the preacher – was at the centre and not at the front of the church, a symbolic break with the Catholic past. Nevertheless, it's still hard to understand quite how de Keyser, who designed such elegant structures as the Westerkerk, could have ended up creating this.

The Noordermarkt

The **Noordermarkt**, the somewhat unimpressive square outside the church, contains a **statue** of three figures bound to each other, a poignant tribute to the bloody Jordaanoproer riot of 1934, part of a successful campaign to stop the government cutting unemployment benefits during the Depression; you'll find the statue just in front of the church's west door. The inscription reads "The strongest chains are those of unity". The church also boasts a **plaque** honouring those Communists and Jews who were rounded up here by the Germans in February 1941. The square hosts two of Amsterdam's best open-air **markets**. There's a general household goods and flea market on Mondays (9am–1pm), plus a popular Saturday farmers' market, the **Boerenmarkt** (9am–4pm), a lively affair with organic fruit and vegetables, freshly baked breads and a plethora of oils and spices for sale. Cross an unmarked border, though, and you'll find yourself in the middle of a bird market, which operates on an adjacent patch at much the same time, and, if you're at all squeamish, is best avoided – the brightly coloured birds squeezed into tiny cages are not for everyone. Incidentally, the bustling *Lunchcafé Winkel* (see p.183), beside the Noordermarkt at the corner with Westerstraat, sells huge wedges of home-made **apple pie**, which many Jordaaners swear is the best in town.

Lindengracht

Just to the north of the Noorderkerk, the **Lindengracht** ("Canal of Limes") lost its waterway decades ago, and is a fairly nondescript thoroughfare, though home to the **Suyckerhofje** of 1667 – easy to miss through a small gateway at no. 94, and with a lovely enclosed garden that is a typical example of the Jordaan's many *hofjes*. Lindengracht has also played a prominent role in local folklore since the day in 1886 when a policeman made an ill-advised attempt to stop an eel-pulling contest. Horrible as it sounds, **eel-pulling** was a popular pastime hereabouts: a live eel, preferably smeared in soap to make the entertainment last a little longer, was suspended from a rope strung across a canal. Teams took to their boats and tried to pull the poor creature off the rope, the fun being to see who would end up in the water; the winner came away with the eel – or at least a good piece of it. In 1886 the crowd unceremoniously bundled the policeman away, but when reinforcements arrived, the whole thing got out of hand and there was a full-scale **riot** – the Paling-Oproer ("Eel Uprising") – which lasted for three days and cost 26 lives.

Brouwersgracht

The east end of the Lindengracht intersects with **Brouwersgracht**, which marks the northerly limit of both the Jordaan and the Grachtengordel (see Chapter 2). In the seventeenth century, Brouwersgracht lay at the edge of Amsterdam's great harbour, one of the major arteries linking the open sea with the city centre. Thronged by vessels returning from – or heading off to – every corner of the globe, it was lined with storage depots and warehouses. Breweries flourished here too – hence its name – capitalizing on their ready access to shipments of fresh water. Today, the harbour bustle has moved way out of the centre to the northwest, and the **warehouses**, with their distinctive spout-neck gables and shuttered windows, have been converted into some of the most expensive apartments in the city. There's an especially fine uninterrupted row of these warehouses at **Brouwersgracht 172–212**, across the canal from the

▲ Brouwersgracht

Lindengracht. You'll also find some handsome merchants' houses on the Brouwersgracht, as well as moored houseboats and a string of quaint little swing bridges, making it altogether one of the most classically picturesque canals in the whole of the city and a pleasant area for a stroll.

③ The Scheepvaartsbuurt and the Western docklands

The **Scheepvaartsbuurt** – the Shipping Quarter – is an unassuming neighbourhood which focuses on **Haarlemmerstraat** and its continuation **Haarlemmerdijk**, a long, rather ordinary thoroughfare lined with cafés and food shops, which once bustled with stevedores and working ships bound to and from Haarlem. In the eighteenth and nineteenth centuries, this district boomed thanks to its location between Brouwersgracht and the **Western docklands**, a narrow parcel of land dredged out of the River IJ immediately to the north and equipped with docks, warehouses and shipyards. The construction of these artificial islands took the pressure off Amsterdam's congested maritime facilities and was necessary to sustain the city's economic success. Stretching from the Western to the Eastern docklands, these riverside wharves functioned as Amsterdam's heartbeat until the city's shipping facilities began to move away from the centre, a process accelerated by the construction of Centraal Station, slap in the middle of the old quayside in the 1880s. The Western docklands hung on to some of the marine trade until the 1960s, but today – bar the odd small boatyard – industry has to all intents and purposes disappeared and the area is busy reinventing itself. There is still a vague air of faded grittiness here, but the old, forgotten warehouses – within walking distance of the centre – are rapidly being turned into bijou studios, and dozens of plant-filled houseboats are moored alongside the narrow streets.

Haarlemmerdijk

Before World War II the **Haarlemmerstraat** and its westerly extension, **Haarlemmerdijk**, were congested thoroughfares, but the trams that once ran here were rerouted and this is now a pleasant if unremarkable pedestrianized strip with bars, shops and cafés. The only architectural high point is the meticulously restored Art Deco interior of **The Movies** cinema (see p.212), near the west end of the street at Haarlemmerdijk 161. Just metres away, the busy Haarlemmerplein traffic junction sports the grandiose Neoclassical gateway, **Haarlemmerpoort**, built on the site of a medieval entrance to the city in 1840 for the new king William II's triumphal entry into the city. The euphoria didn't last long. William was a distinguished general who had been wounded at Waterloo, but as a king he proved much too crusty and reactionary to be popular, only agreeing to mild liberal reforms after extensive rioting in Amsterdam and elsewhere.

The Western docklands

To visit the Western docklands, proceed north from the near (east) side of the Haarlemmerpoort. Walk through the tunnel beneath the railway lines and then turn right along Sloterdijkstraat, which soon crosses the canal over onto

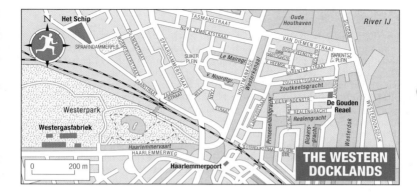

Galgenstraat (Gallows St), once the site of the municipal gallows which were made clearly visible to passing ships to discourage potential law-breakers. Galgenstraat bisects the smallest of the Western docklands islands, diminutive **Prinseneiland**, a pleasing mix of houseboats, former warehouses and old canal houses, guarded by a pair of dainty little bridges.

Continue straight along Galgenstraat, over the next canal, and then turn north up Grote Bickersstraat for the bridge over to another Western docklands island, **Realeneiland**, whose houseboats, ex-warehouses and mini-boatyards give it a distinctly nautical flavour. On the island, tiny, waterside **Zandhoek** once offered an uninterrupted view over the harbour and was long a favourite with the city's sea captains, who constructed a clutch of fine old canal houses along here in the seventeenth and eighteenth centuries. A number of them have survived and several are decorated with distinctive facade stones, including **De Gouden Reael**, at no. 14, whose stone sports a gold coin. Before Napoleon introduced a system of house numbers, these stones were the principal way for visitors to distinguish one house from another, and many homeowners went to considerable lengths to make theirs unique. Jacob Real, the Catholic tradesman who owned this particular house, also used the image of a *real* – a Spanish coin – to discreetly advertise his sympathies for the Catholic Habsburgs. The building now houses a very good café-restaurant (see p.192).

At the top of Zandhoek, cross over the canal and then turn left along Zoutkeetsgracht; another left turn, this time onto Planciusstraat, returns you to the pedestrian tunnel near the Haarlemmerpoort.

The Westerpark and Westergasfabriek

Beyond the Haarlemmerpoort, off to the right, the **Westerpark** is a small park running alongside a narrow sliver of canal with a small lake and some formally planted areas. At its far end, the **Westergasfabriek** is a complex of red-brick nineteenth-century buildings that was formerly a gasworks, then a venue for acid house raves in the 1990s, and has since been renovated and is finding its feet as an arts and entertainment complex. There are a number of arts and media related businesses here, several galleries, a cinema and a number of places to eat and drink, as well as the **Huis van Aristoteles** – a giant play area for kids (see p.238). You can get in from the park but the Westergasfabriek's main entrance is on Haarlemmerweg.

Het Schip

On the north side of the park, before you reach the Westergasfabriek, a pedestrian tunnel leads under the railway lines to **Zaanstraat**, the southern edge of a working-class neighbourhood that stretches north to the busy Spaarndammer Dijk boulevard. Taken as a whole, this part of the city is really rather glum, but hang a left on Zaanstraat and you soon reach Spaarndammerplantsoen, the site of **Het Schip**, a municipal housing block which is a splendid – and pristine – example of the Expressionistic Amsterdam School of architecture. Seven years in the making, from 1913 to 1920, the complex takes its name from its ship-like shape and is graced by all manner of fetching decorative details – from the intriguing mix-and-match windows to the wavy brick facades and ornamental sculptures of which the bulging "cigar" turret is its most self-indulgent. The architect responsible was **Michael de Klerk** (1884–1923), who also designed the two other housing blocks on Spaarndammerplantsoen, though Het Schip is easily the most striking. De Klerk reacted strongly against the influence of Berlage, whose style – exemplified by the Beurs – favoured clean lines and functionality, opting instead for much more playful motifs.

De Klerk installed a post office in Het Schip and the interior, with its superb multicoloured tiling, has been restored and now serves as the small **Museum Het Schip** (Wed–Sun 1–5pm; €5; Ⓦ www.hetschip.nl; bus #22 from Centraal Station). Through the use of multimedia, short films and leaflets, the museum looks at the living conditions of the city's proletariat at the start of the twentieth century, in relation to the history of the Amsterdam School. The museum sells a pamphlet for self-guided tours explaining the architectural highlights of the complex, still used as social housing today. Half-hour guided tours (on request; €2.50) take you inside one of the restored residences and up to the turret, which serves no purpose other than being an aesthetic touch by de Klerk. Politically motivated, de Klerk and his architectural allies were eager to provide high-quality homes for the working class, though their laudable aims were often undermined – or at least diluted – by a tendency to overelaborate. For details of de Klerk's other major commission in Amsterdam, the De Dageraad housing project, see p.130. Across the road from the museum, the pleasant *Lunchroom Het Schip* serves tasty light meals and often gets packed with tour groups.

The Old Jewish Quarter and Eastern docklands

Once one of the marshiest parts of Amsterdam, the narrow slab of land between the curve of the River Amstel, Oudeschans and Nieuwe Herengracht was the home of **Amsterdam's Jews** from the sixteenth century up until World War II. By the 1920s, this Old Jewish Quarter, aka the **Jodenhoek** ("Jews' Corner"), had become one of the busiest parts of town, crowded with tenement buildings and smoking factories, its main streets holding scores of open-air stalls, selling everything from pickled herrings to pots and pans. Sadly, the war put paid to all this and in 1945 the district lay derelict – and postwar redevelopment has not treated it kindly either. Its focal point, **Waterlooplein**, has been overwhelmed by a domineering town and concert hall, the Stadhuis en Muziektheater, which caused much controversy at the time of its construction, and the once-bustling Jodenbreestraat is now bleak and very ordinary, with **Mr Visserplein**, at its east end, little more than a busy traffic junction.

Picking your way round these obstacles is not much fun, but persevere – among all the cars and concrete are several moving reminders of the Jewish community that perished in World War II, most memorably the late seventeenth-century **Esnoga** (Portuguese synagogue), one of the city's finest buildings. Close by, four other synagogues have been merged into the fascinating **Joods Historisch Museum** (Jewish Historical Museum), celebrating Jewish culture and custom. There's a Rembrandt connection here too: in 1639 the artist moved into a house on the Jodenbreestraat and this has been restored as the **Rembrandthuis**, which, in addition to several period rooms, has a fine collection of the great man's etchings and features temporary displays on him and his contemporaries. From the Rembrandthuis, it's a brief stroll south to **Hermitage Amsterdam**, an art gallery used for lavish temporary exhibitions of fine and applied art on loan from the Hermitage Museum in St Petersburg.

Immediately to the east of the Old Jewish Quarter lies the **Plantagebuurt**, a well-heeled residential area that's home to the city's botanical gardens, the **Hortus Botanicus**, as well as the **Artis Zoo** (see p.240) and the excellent **Verzetsmuseum** (Dutch Resistance Museum).

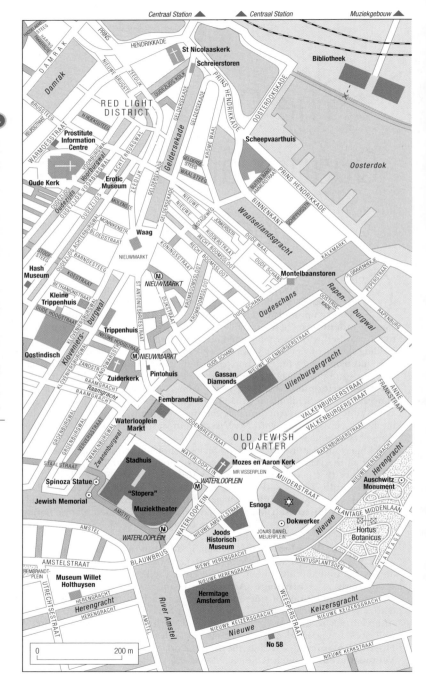

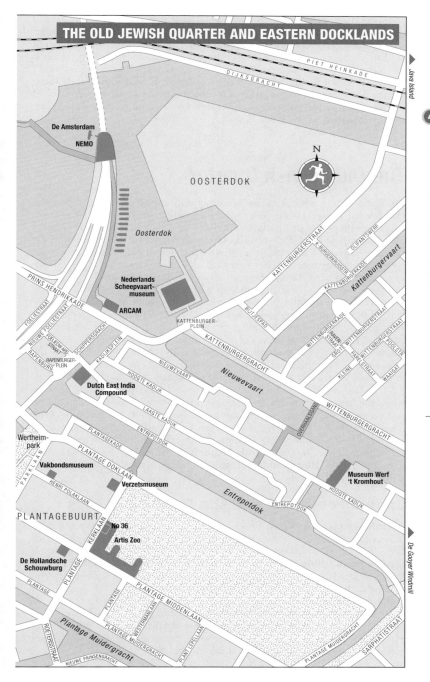

THE OLD JEWISH QUARTER AND EASTERN DOCKLANDS

PIET HEINKADE

DIJKSGRACHT

▶ Java Island

De Amsterdam
NEMO

OOSTERDOK

N

Oosterdok

PRINS HENDRIKKADE

Nederlands
Scheepvaart-
museum

ARCAM

KATTENBURGERPLEIN

KATTENBURGERSTRAAT

K. BURGERKRUISSTR.

OLIFANTSWERF

KATTENBURGERKADE

Kattenburgervaart

KATTENBURGERKADE

BUITESPAD

FOELIESTRAAT
NIEUWE FOELIEWLS
STRAAT
RAPENBURG
RAPENBURGER-
PLEIN

SCHIPPERSGRACHT

KADIJKSPLEIN

KATTENBURGERGRACHT

NIEUWEVAART

Nieuwevaart

WITTENBURGERKADE
RAVEN-
STRAAT
GROTE WITTENBURGERSTRAAT
POOLSTR.
KLEINE WITTENBURGERSTRAAT
PLANC
WAAGAT

HOOGTE KADIJK

Dutch East India
Compound

LAAGTE KADIJK

ENTREPOTDOK

WITTENBURGERGRACHT

OVERHAALSGANG

Wertheim-
park

PARKLAAN

Vakbondsmuseum

PLANTAGEKADE

PLANTAGE DOKLAAN

HENRI POLAKLAAN

Verzetsmuseum

Entrepotdok

ENTREPOTDOK

Museum Werf
't Kromhout

HOOGTE KADIJK

PLANTAGEBUURT

KERKLAAN

No 36

Artis Zoo

▶ De Gooyer Windmill

De Hollandsche
Schouwburg

PLANTAGE

PLANTAGE

PLANTAGE MIDDENLAAN

Plantage Muidergracht

PLANTAGE MUIDERGRACHT

PLANTAGE WESTERMANLAAN

PLANT. LEPELLAAN

NIEUWE PRINSENGRACHT

ROETERSSTRAAT

PLANTAGE MUIDERGRACHT

SARPHATISTRAAT

Moving on from the Plantagebuurt, it's a short hop north to the reclaimed islands of the **Oosterdok**, dredged out of the River IJ to accommodate warehouses and docks in the seventeenth century. The Oosterdok is one part of the Eastern docklands, a vast maritime complex which once spread right along the River IJ to link with the Western docklands (see Chapter 3). Industrial decline set in during the 1880s, but the assorted artificial islands of the eastern docklands – often lumped together as Zeeburg – are currently being redefined as a residential and leisure district, featuring some startling modern architecture and several award-winning buildings.

The Old Jewish Quarter

Throughout the nineteenth century and up until the German occupation, the **Old Jewish Quarter** – the Jodenhoek – was a hive of activity, its main streets lined with shops and jam-packed with open-air stalls, where Jews and Gentiles traded in earnest. Fatefully, it was also surrounded by canals and it was these the Germans exploited to create the **ghetto** that foreshadowed their policy of starvation and deportation. They restricted movement in and out of the quarter by raising most of the swing bridges (over the Nieuwe Herengracht, the Amstel and the Oudeschans) and imposing stringent controls on every other access route. The Jews, readily identifiable by the yellow Stars of David they were obliged to wear from May 1942, were not allowed to use public transport, ride bicycles or own telephones, and were placed under a rigorously imposed curfew. Meanwhile, roundups and deportations had begun shortly after the Germans arrived, and continued into 1945. By the end of the war, the Jodenhoek was deserted, and as the need for wood and raw materials intensified in the cold winter that followed, many of the houses were dismantled for fuel.

The Jodenhoek remained a neglected corner of the city well into the 1970s, when the battered remnants took another hit with the large-scale demolition that preceded the construction of the metro beneath Waterlooplein. By these means, the prewar Jodenhoek disappeared almost without trace, the notable exception being the imposing **Esnoga** and the four connected synagogues of the Ashkenazi Jews, now the **Joods Historisch Museum**. The district's other main sight is the **Rembrandthuis**, which features special exhibitions on the artist's work, life and times.

Jodenbreestraat and the Rembrandthuis

Jodenbreestraat, the "Broad Street of the Jews", was once the hub of Jewish activity in the city. Badly served by postwar development, this ancient thorough-fare is now short on charm, but in these unlikely surroundings, at no. 6, stands the **Rembrandthuis** (daily 10am–5pm; €8; ⓦ www.rembrandthuis.nl), whose intricate facade is decorated by pretty wooden shutters and a graceful pediment. Rembrandt bought this house at the height of his fame and popularity, living here for almost twenty years and spending a fortune on its furnishings – an expense that ultimately contributed to his bankruptcy (see box, p.118). An inventory made at the time details the huge collection of paintings, sculptures and art treasures he had amassed, almost all of which were confiscated after he was declared insolvent and forced to move to a more modest house on Rozengracht in the Jordaan in 1658. The city council bought the Jodenbreestraat house in 1907 and has revamped the premises on several occasions, most recently in 1999.

Entry is via the modern annex, but you're soon into Rembrandt's old house, where a string of **period rooms** has been restored to something resembling their appearance when the artist lived here – the reconstruction being based on the inventory. The period furniture is appealing enough, especially the dinky box-beds, and the great man's studio is surprisingly large and well lit, but pride of place goes to the "Art Cabinet", which is jam-packed with *objets d'art* and miscellaneous rarities reassembled here in line with the original inventory. There are African spears and shields, Pacific seashells, Venetian glassware and even busts of Roman emperors, all of which were meant to demonstrate Rembrandt's wide interests and eclectic taste. The period rooms are also decorated with **seventeenth-century Dutch paintings**, but most are distinctly second-rate and none of them is actually a Rembrandt. The most interesting paintings are those by Rembrandt's master in Amsterdam, Pieter Lastman (1583–1633) – not because of their quality, but rather because their sheer mawkishness demonstrates just how far Rembrandt soared above his artistic milieu.

Beyond the Art Cabinet, the rest of the Rembrandthuis is usually given over to temporary exhibitions on the artist and his contemporaries. Here also, space permitting, is the museum's own collection of **Rembrandt's etchings**, as well as several of the original copper plates on which he worked. It's a large and varied collection, with the biblical illustrations usually attracting the most attention, though the studies of tramps and vagabonds are equally appealing.

Gassan Diamonds

From the Rembrandthuis, it's a couple of minutes' walk to the **Gassan Diamonds** factory (frequent guided tours daily 9am–5pm; 45min; free; ☎020/622-5333, Ⓦwww.gassandiamonds.com), which occupies a large and imposing brick building dating from 1897 on Nieuwe Uilenburgerstraat.

▲ The Rembrandthuis

The Jews in Amsterdam

From the late sixteenth century onwards, Amsterdam was a haven for refugee Jews escaping persecution throughout the rest of Europe. The **Union of Utrecht**, ratified in 1579, signalled the start of the influx. Drawn up by the largely Protestant northern Dutch provinces in response to the invading Spanish army, the treaty combined the United Provinces (later to become the Netherlands) in a loose federation, whose wheels could only be greased by a degree of religious toleration then unknown elsewhere across the Continent. Whatever the Protestants may have wanted, they knew that the Catholic minority (around 35 percent) would only continue to support the rebellion against the Spanish Habsburgs if they were treated well – the Jews benefited by osmosis and consequently immigrated here in their hundreds.

This **toleration** did, however, have its limits: Jewish immigrants were forced to buy citizenship; Christian-Jewish marriages were illegal; and, as with the Catholics, they were only allowed to practise their religion discreetly behind closed doors. A proclamation in 1632 also excluded them from most guilds – effectively withdrawing their right to own and run most types of business. This forced them either to excel in those trades not governed by the guilds or introduce new non-guild trades into the city. Nonetheless, by the middle of the eighteenth century the city's Jewish community was active in almost every aspect of the economy, especially in bookselling, tobacco, banking and commodity futures.

The first major Jewish influx was of **Sephardic Jews** from Spain and Portugal, where persecution had begun in earnest in 1492 and continued throughout the sixteenth century. In the 1630s the Sephardim were joined in Amsterdam by hundreds of (much poorer) **Ashkenazi** Jews from German-speaking central Europe. The two groups established separate synagogues and, although there was no ghetto as such, the vast majority settled on and around what is now Waterlooplein, then a distinctly unhealthy tract of low-lying land that was subject to regular flooding by the River Amstel. Initially known as **Vlooyenburg**, this district was usually referred to as the **Jodenhoek**, or "Jews' Corner", though this was not, generally speaking, a pejorative term and neither did the Dutch eschew living here; Rembrandt, for instance, was quite happy to take up residence and frequently painted his Jewish neighbours. Indeed, given the time, the most extraordinary feature of Jewish settlement in Amsterdam was that it occasioned mild curiosity rather than outright hate, as evinced by surviving prints of Jewish religious customs, where there is neither any hint of stereotype nor discernible demonization.

The restrictions affecting both Jews and Catholics were removed during **Napoleon**'s occupation of the United Provinces, when the country was temporarily renamed the Batavian Republic (1795–1806). Freed from official discrimination, Amsterdam's Jewish community flourished and the Jewish Quarter expanded, nudging northwest towards Nieuwmarkt and east across Nieuwe Herengracht, though this was just the focus of a community whose members lived in every part of the city. In 1882, the dilapidated houses of the Jodenhoek were razed and several minor canals filled in to make way for **Waterlooplein**, which became a largely Jewish marketplace, a bustling affair that sprawled out along St Antoniesbreestraat and Jodenbreestraat.

At the turn of the twentieth century, there were around 60,000 Jews living in Amsterdam, but **refugees** from Hitler's Germany swelled this figure to around 120,000 in the 1930s. The disaster that befell this community during the **German occupation** is hard to conceive, but the bald facts speak for themselves; when Amsterdam was liberated, there were only 5000 Jews left and the Jodenhoek was, to all intents and purposes, a ghost town. At present, there are about 25,000 Jews resident in – and spread out across – the city, but while Jewish life in Amsterdam has survived, its heyday is gone forever.

Before World War II, many local Jews worked as diamond cutters and polishers, though there's little sign of the industry in the area today – Gassan being the main exception. Traditionally, the city's diamond workers were poorly paid and endured foul working conditions, but all this changed after the creation of the Diamond Workers' Union, the ANDB (Algemene Nederlandse Diamantbewerkersbond), at the end of the nineteenth century. Unionised, the diamond workers transformed their pay and conditions, becoming the vanguard of the working class under the leadership of the socialist rabbi **Henri Polak** (1868–1943). The ANDB also pushed education and did more to integrate the city's Jews into the mainstream than any other organization; predictably, the Germans made short work of the union during the occupation. **Tours** of the Gassan factory include a visit to the cutting and polishing areas as well as a gambol round the diamond jewellery showroom.

Waterlooplein

Jodenbreestraat runs just parallel to the **Stadhuis en Muziektheater** (town and concert hall), a sprawling complex whose indeterminate modernity dominates **Waterlooplein**, a rectangular parcel of land that was originally swampy marsh. This was the site of the first Jewish Quarter, but by the late nineteenth century it had become an insanitary slum, home to the poorest of the Ashkenazi Jews. The slums were cleared in the 1880s and thereafter the Waterlooplein and its open-air market became the centre of Jewish life in the city. During the war, the Germans used the square to round up their victims, but despite these ugly connotations the Waterlooplein was revived in the 1950s as the site of the city's main **flea market** – and remains so to this day (Mon–Sat 9am–5pm), albeit on a much smaller scale. As far as the city council was concerned, the market's reappearance was only a stopgap while they mulled over plans to entirely reinvent the depopulated Jodenhoek; for starters, whole streets were demolished to make way for the motorist – with Mr Visserplein, for example, becoming little more than a traffic intersection – and then, warming to their theme in the late 1970s, the council announced the building of the massive new Waterlooplein town and concert hall complex that stands today. Opposition was immediate and widespread as it was feared the end result would be an eyesore, but attempts to prevent the building failed, and the **Muziektheater** opened in 1986. Since then it has established an international reputation for the quality of its performances (see p.208). One of the story's abiding ironies is that the title of the protest campaign – "**Stopera**" – has passed into common usage to describe the whole complex.

Inside the "Stopera", amid all the jaded concrete, there are a couple of minor attractions, beginning with the **glass columns** in the glass-roofed public passageway towards the rear of the complex. These give a salutary lesson on the fragility of the Netherlands; two contain water indicating the sea levels in the Dutch towns of Vlissingen and IJmuiden (below knee level), while another records the levels recorded during the 1953 flood disaster (way above head height). Down the stairs, a display indicates what is known as "Normal Amsterdam Level" (NAP), originally calculated in 1684 as the average water level in the River IJ and still the basis for measuring altitude above sea level across Europe. Metres away, in the Muziektheater's foyer, is a forceful and inventive **memorial** to the district's Jews, in which a bronze violinist bursts through the floor tiles.

Outside, at the very tip of Waterlooplein, where the River Amstel meets the Zwanenburgwal canal, there is a second memorial – a black stone **tribute** to

Mr Visserplein

Mr Visserplein is a busy junction for traffic speeding towards the IJ tunnel. It takes its name from **Lodewijk Ernst Visser** (1871–1942), President of the Supreme Court of the Netherlands in 1939. He was dismissed the following year when the Germans occupied the country, and became an active member of the Jewish resistance, working for the illegal underground newspaper *Het Parool* ("The Password") and refusing to wear the yellow Star of David. He vehemently opposed the Nazi-appointed Judenrat (Jewish Council), publicly denouncing all forms of collaboration and arguing that the Dutch government should take responsibility for all Dutch citizens, Jew and Gentile alike. Visser died from a heart attack shortly after he was threatened with deportation to a concentration camp.

the dead of the Jewish resistance; the inscription from Jeremiah translates "If my eyes were a well of tears, I would cry day and night for the fallen fighters of my beloved people." Metres away, a third sculpture honours **Spinoza** (see below), who looks suitably serene above an inscription that reads "The aim of the state is freedom".

Mozes en Aaron Kerk

Just behind the Muziektheater, on the corner of Mr Visserplein, is the **Mozes en Aaron Kerk**, a rather glum Neoclassical structure built on the site of a clandestine Catholic church in the 1840s. It takes its unusual name from a pair of facade stones bearing effigies of the two prophets that adorned the earlier building. Earlier still, the site was occupied by the house where the philosopher and theologian **Baruch Spinoza** was born in 1632. Of Sephardic descent, Spinoza's pantheistic views soon brought him into conflict with the elders of the Jewish community. At the age of 23, he was excommunicated and forced out of the city, moving into a small village where he survived by grinding lenses. After an attempt on his life, Spinoza moved again, eventually ending up in The Hague, where his free-thinking ways proved more acceptable.

The Esnoga

Unmissable on the corner of Mr Visserplein is the brown and bulky brickwork of the **Esnoga** (Portuguese Synagogue; Sun–Fri 10am–4pm; closed Yom Kippur; €6.50; Ⓦ www.esnoga.com), completed in 1675 for the city's Sephardic Jews. One of Amsterdam's most imposing buildings, the central structure, with its grand pilasters and blind balustrade, was built in the broadly Neoclassical style that was then fashionable in Holland. It is surrounded by a courtyard complex of small outhouses, where the city's Sephardim have fraternized for centuries. Barely altered since its construction, the synagogue's lofty interior follows the Sephardic tradition in having the Hechal (the Ark of the Covenant) and *tebah* (from where services are led) at opposite ends. Also traditional is the **seating**, with two sets of wooden benches (for the men) facing each other across the central aisle – the women have separate galleries up above. A set of superb brass chandeliers holds the candles that remain the only source of artificial light. When it was completed, the synagogue was one of the largest in the world, its congregation almost certainly the richest; today, the Sephardic community has dwindled to just 250 families, most of whom live outside the city centre.

In one of the outhouses, a short film sheds light on the history of the synagogue and of Amsterdam's Sephardim; the mystery is why the Germans left the building alone – no one knows for sure, but it seems likely that they intended to turn it into a museum once all of the Jews had been slaughtered.

Jonas Daniel Meijerplein

Next to the Esnoga, on the south side of its retaining outhouses, is **Jonas Daniel Meijerplein**, a scrawny triangle of gravel named after the eponymous lawyer, who in 1796, at the age of just 16, was the first Jew to be admitted to the Amsterdam Bar. It was here in February 1941 that around four hundred Jewish men were forcibly loaded up on trucks and taken to their deaths at Mauthausen concentration camp, in reprisal for the killing of a Dutch Nazi during a street fight. The arrests sparked off the **February Strike** (Februaristaking), a general strike in protest against the Germans' treatment of the Jews. It was organized by the outlawed Communist Party and spearheaded by Amsterdam's transport workers and dockers – a rare demonstration of solidarity with the Jews whose fate was usually accepted without visible protest in all of occupied Europe. The strike was quickly suppressed, but is still commemorated by an annual wreath-laying ceremony on February 25, as well as by Mari Andriessen's statue of the **Dokwerker** (Dockworker), here on the square.

▲ Scroll in the Joods Historisch Museum

The Joods Historisch Museum

Across the square from the Esnoga, on the far side of the main road, the **Joods Historisch Museum** (Jewish Historical Museum; daily 11am–5pm; closed Yom Kippur; €10; Ⓦ www.jhm.nl) is cleverly shoehorned into four adjacent Ashkenazi synagogues dating from the late seventeenth century. For years after World War II these buildings lay abandoned, but they were finally refurbished – and connected by walkways – in the 1980s, to accommodate a Jewish resource and exhibition centre. The first major display area, just beyond the reception desk on the ground floor of the Nieuwe Synagoge, features temporary exhibitions on Jewish life and culture with vintage photographs usually to the fore. Close by, also in the Nieuwe Synagoge, the Print Room concentrates on the many Jewish-Dutch musicians who kept Amsterdammers entertained before World War II. There are potted biographies of the leading performers and an audioguide offers a chance to listen to them in full voice and throttle.

Moving on, the ground floor of the capacious **Grote Synagoge**, which dates from 1671, holds an engaging display on Jewish life. There is a fine collection of religious silverware here, plus all manner of antique artefacts illustrating religious customs and practices, alongside a scattering of paintings and portraits. The gallery up above, reached via a spiral staircase, holds a finely judged social history of the country's Jewish population from 1600 to 1900, with an assortment of bygones, documents and paintings tracing their prominent role in a wide variety of industries, both as employers and employees. A complementary history of the Jews in the Netherlands from 1900 onwards occupies the upper level of the neighbouring **Nieuwe Synagoge**. Inevitably, attention is given to the trauma of World War II, but there is also a biting display on the indifferent/hostile reaction of many Dutch men and women to liberated Jews in 1945.

For more on Amsterdam during the German occupation, visit the Dutch Resistance Museum (see p.106).

The Plantagebuurt

Laid out in the middle of the nineteenth century, the pleasant, leafy streets of the **Plantagebuurt**, falling to either side of **Plantage Middenlaan** boulevard, were developed as part of a concerted attempt to provide good-quality housing for the city's expanding middle classes. Although it was never as fashionable as the older residential parts of the Grachtengordel, the new district did contain elegant villas and spacious terraces, making it the first suburban port of call for many upwardly mobile Jews. Nowadays, the Plantagebuurt is still one of the more prosperous parts of the city, in a modest sort of way, and boasts two especially enjoyable attractions – the **Hortus Botanicus** (Botanical Gardens) and the **Verzetsmuseum** (Dutch Resistance Museum). Nearby, just over the **Plantage Muidergracht** canal, and stretching west to the River Amstel, is a small parcel of old Amsterdam, dating back to the late seventeenth century. The main attraction here is **Hermitage Amsterdam**, which showcases temporary exhibitions of fine and applied art loaned from St Petersburg's Hermitage Museum.

Starting at Centraal Station, **trams** #9 and #14 run along Plantage Middenlaan, passing by – or near – all the district's main attractions.

The Amstelhof and Hermitage Amsterdam

During the second phase of the digging of the Grachtengordel, the three main canals that ringed the city centre were extended beyond the River Amstel up towards the Oosterdok – hence "Nieuwe" Herengracht, Keizersgracht and Prinsengracht. At first, takers for the new land were few and far between and the city had no option but to offer it to charities at discount prices. One result was the establishment of the **Amstelhof**, a large *hofje* (almshouse) built for the care of elderly women (and ultimately men too) in the 1680s on behalf of the Dutch Reformed Church. In time, the Amstelhof, a singularly stern-looking structure, grew to fill most of the chunk of land between Nieuwe Herengracht and Nieuwe Keizersgracht, becoming a fully fledged hospital in the process, but in the 1980s it became clear that its medical facilities were out of date and it went up for sale. Much municipal huffing and puffing ensued until the director of the Hermitage Museum in St Petersburg and his Dutch contacts dreamed up a real cultural wheeze: they proposed that the Amstelhof be turned into a museum, **Hermitage Amsterdam**, at Nieuwe Herengracht 14 (daily 10am–5pm; €10; ⓦwww.hermitage.nl), for the display of items loaned from the original Hermitage. It was – and is – a very ambitious scheme, with a substantial number of galleries now displaying prime pieces. Exhibitions, which usually last about five months, have included "Nicholas & Alexandra" and "Palace Protocol in the Nineteenth Century".

Nieuwe Keizersgracht

In the nineteenth century, many wealthier Jews escaped the crowded conditions of the Old Jewish Quarter to live along Nieuwe Keizersgracht and Nieuwe Prinsensgracht, but this community did not survive World War II. One painful reminder of the occupation still stands at **Nieuwe Keizersgracht 58**, across the canal behind the Amstelhof. From 1940, this house, with its luxurious Neoclassical double doorway set beneath twin caryatids, was the headquarters of the **Judenrat** (Jewish Council), through which the Germans managed the ghetto and organized the deportations. The role of the Judenrat is extremely controversial. Many have argued that they were tainted collaborators, who hoped to save their own necks by working with the Germans and duping their fellow Jews into thinking that the deportations were indeed – as Nazi propaganda insisted – about the transfer of personnel to new employment in Germany. Just how much the council leaders knew about the gas chambers remains unclear, but after the war the surviving members of the Jewish Council successfully defended themselves against charges of collaboration, claiming that they had been a buffer against the Germans rather than their instruments.

Hortus Botanicus

The lush **Hortus Botanicus** (Mon–Fri 9am–5pm, Sat & Sun 10am–5pm; closes 4pm Dec & Jan; closes 7pm July & Aug; €7; ⓦwww.dehortus.nl) is an appealing – if smallish – botanical garden whose entrance is on Plantage Middenlaan. The Hortus was founded in 1682 as **medicinal** gardens for the city's physicians and apothecaries after an especially bad outbreak of the plague. Thereafter, many of the city's merchants made a point of bringing back exotic species from the East, the result being the six-thousand-odd plant species exhibited today – both outside and in a series of hothouses. Botanical

▲ Hortus Botanicus

specimens also went the other way; in 1848, for instance, two oil palms left the gardens for Java, where they were used to establish the first of that island's many oil palm plantations.

The gardens are divided into several distinct sections, each clearly labelled, its location pinpointed on a map available at the entrance kiosk. Most of the outdoor sections are covered by plants, trees and shrubs from temperate and Arctic zones, with many of the more established trees dating back to a major replanting in 1895. The largest of the hothouses is the **Three–Climate Glass-house**, partitioned into separate climate zones: subtropical, tropical and desert. The gardens also hold a **butterfly house** and a capacious **palm house** with a substantial collection of cycad palms. It's all very low-key – and none the worse for that – and the gardens make a relaxing break on any tour of central Amsterdam, especially as the **café**, *De Hortus* (see p.184), in the old orangery serves tasty lunches and snacks.

Wertheimpark and De Hollandsche Schouwburg

Across the street from the botanical gardens, beside the canal, is the pocket-sized **Wertheimpark**, where the **Auschwitz monument** is a simple affair with symbolically broken mirrors and an inscription that reads *Nooit meer Auschwitz* ("Auschwitz – Never Again"). It was designed by the Dutch author and artist Jan Wolkers, who first came to prominence in the 1960s with a string of barbed novels – *Candyfloss, Oegstgeest Revisited* – railing against his Calvinist upbringing.

Further east down Plantage Middenlaan is another sad relic of the war, **De Hollandsche Schouwburg**, at no. 24 (daily 11am–4pm; closed Yom Kippur; free; Ⓦwww.hollandscheschouwburg.nl). Originally a theatre where Jewish artists could perform without let or hindrance, the Germans turned it into a Jews-only theatre in October 1941, and the main assembly point for Amsterdam Jews prior to their deportation in the summer of the following year. Inside, there was no daylight and families were interned in conditions that foreshadowed those of the camps they would soon be transported to. The front of the building has been refurbished, with the ground floor now holding a list of the dead and an eternal flame; a fifteen-minute film tells the story of the theatre before the German occupation, complete with examples of the songs of various key performers. On the floor above, there's also an excellent small **exhibition** on the plight of the city's Jews, with lots of occupation photographs labelled in Dutch, with an English translation available at reception. By contrast, the old **auditorium** at the back of the building has been left as an empty, roofless shell. A memorial **column** of basalt on a Star of David base stands where the stage once was, an intensely mournful monument to suffering of unfathomable proportions.

As a counter to this record of remorseless suffering, have a look at the commemorative plaque across the street on the wall of Plantage Kerklaan 36. This building once housed the municipal register of births and deaths, records which were extremely helpful to the Germans and their Dutch collaborators in tracking down Jews and young men they wanted to conscript as forced labour. In March 1943 twelve members of the Resistance, dressed as policemen, entered the building, sedated the guards – who were taken to the zoo next door – then blew the place up; almost all of the twelve were caught and executed – their names are on the plaque.

Vakbondsmuseum

The **Vakbondsmuseum** (Trade Union Museum; Tues–Fri 11am–5pm, Sun 1–5pm; closed for refurbishment till 2011) at Henri Polaklaan 9 is a handsome structure. It was erected for the Diamond Workers' Union in 1900 to a distinctive design by **Hendrik Petrus Berlage** (1856–1934), who incorporated Romanesque features – such as the castellated balustrade and the deeply recessed main door – within an Expressionist framework. From the outside, it looks very much like a fortified mansion, hence its nickname **De Burcht** ("Stronghold"), but this design was not just about Berlage's architectural whims. Acting on behalf of the employers, the police – and sometimes armed scabs – were regularly used to break strikes, and the union believed members could, in an emergency, retreat here to hold out in relative safety.

The museum's striking, brightly coloured **interior** develops these stylistic themes with a beautiful mixture of stained-glass windows, stone arches, painted brickwork and patterned tiles. In the foyer is a bust of the remarkable

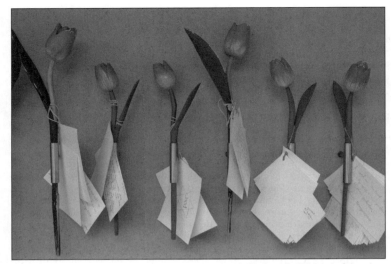

▲ Display at De Hollandsche Schouwburg

Henri Polak, both a part-time rabbi and founder of the ANDB, the Diamond Workers' Union, which became the city's most powerful union. A Socialist who was committed to change via constitutional means, Polak organized the diamond workers as never before and was evangelical about members' self-improvement, arranging all manner of reading and discussion groups. Up the stairs from the foyer, Floor 1 holds the handsome, wood-panelled **Bestuurskamer** (union boardroom), which is kitted out in classic Arts and Crafts style. The room sports three paintings on asbestos cement – one each for sleep, work and relaxation – which celebrate the introduction of the eight-hour working day in 1911, the union's most famous victory.

When the museum reopens, there will be several other exhibition areas devoted to the trade union movement.

Verzetsmuseum

The excellent **Verzetsmuseum**, at Plantage Kerklaan 61 (Dutch Resistance Museum; Tues–Fri 10am–5pm; Mon, Sat & Sun 11am–5pm; €6.50; Ⓦ www .verzetsmuseum.org), relates the story of the **German occupation** of the Netherlands and the progress of the Resistance in World War II, from the invasion of May 1940 to the liberation of 1945. Thoughtfully presented, the display along the central gangway examines the main themes of the occupation, dealing honestly with the fine balance between cooperation and collaboration. On either side, smaller display areas are devoted to different aspects of the **Resistance**, like the coordinated transport strike towards the end of the war and more ad hoc responses, like the so-called **Melkstaking** (Milk Strike) in the spring of 1943, when hundreds of milk producers refused to deliver, in protest at the Germans' threatened deportation of 300,000 former (demobilized) Dutch soldiers to labour camps in Germany. There is also a particularly interesting section on the Jews, outlining the way in which the Germans gradually isolated them, breaking their connections with the rest of the Dutch population before moving in for the kill.

Interestingly, the Dutch Resistance proved especially adept at forgery, forcing the Germans to make the identity cards they issued more and more complicated – but without much success. A further sub-section focuses on the Dutch East Indies, modern-day Indonesia, where many of the inhabitants initially welcomed the Japanese when they brushed the Dutch aside during the Japanese invasion of the islands in 1942. The Indonesians soon learnt that the Japanese were not to be preferred to their old masters, but when the Dutch tried to reassert their control at the end of World War II in a shoddy and shameful colonial war, the Indonesians fought back, eventually winning independence in 1949.

Throughout the museum, a first-rate range of old **photographs** illustrates the (English and Dutch) text along with a host of original **artefacts**, from examples of illegal newsletters to signed German death warrants and, perhaps most moving of all, farewell letters thrown from the Auschwitz train. Apart from the treatment of the Jews, perhaps the most chilling feature of the occupation was the use of indiscriminate **reprisals** to terrify the population. Adopted in 1944, when the Dutch Resistance became a major irritant, this policy of mass reprisals cowed most of the population most of the time, though there was always a minority courageous enough to resist. Some of these brave men and women are commemorated by little metal sheets, which provide potted biographical notes – and it's this mixture of the general and the personal that is the museum's particular strength.

The Oosterdok

Just to the north of the Plantagebuurt lies the **Oosterdok**, whose network of artificial islands was dredged out of the River IJ to increase Amsterdam's shipping facilities in the seventeenth century. By the 1980s, this mosaic of docks, jetties and islands had become something of a post-industrial eyesore, but since then an ambitious redevelopment programme has turned things around and parts of the area are now occupied by some of the city's most popular housing. The only obvious sights here are the **Nederlands Scheepvaartmuseum**

The Dutch East India Company

Founded in 1602, the **Dutch East India Company** (the VOC – Verenigde Oostindische Compagnie) was the chief pillar of Amsterdam's wealth for nearly two hundred years. Its high-percentage profits came from importing spices into Europe, and to secure its supplies the company's ships ventured far and wide, establishing trading links with India, Sri Lanka, Indo-China, Malaya, China and Japan, though modern-day Indonesia was always the main event. Predictably, the company had a cosy relationship with the merchants who steered the Dutch government; the company was granted a trading monopoly in all the lands east of the Cape of Good Hope and could rely on the warships of the powerful Dutch Navy if they got into difficulty. Neither was their business purely mercantile; the East India Company exercised unlimited military, judicial and political powers in those trading posts it established, the first of which was Batavia in Java in 1619.

In the 1750s, the Dutch East India Company went into decline, partly because the British expelled them from most of the best trading stations, but mainly because the company had borrowed too heavily. The French army of occupation had little time for the privileges and pretensions of the VOC, abolishing its ruling council and ultimately dissolving the company in 1799.

(Netherlands Maritime Museum), though the interior is closed for a major refit until 2012, maybe later, and the NEMO science and technology centre, which is primarily geared towards kids.

Entrepotdok

At the northern end of Plantage Kerklaan, just beyond the Verzetsmuseum (see p.106), a footbridge leads over to **Entrepotdok**, on the nearest – and most interesting – of the Oosterdok islands. Old brick **warehouses** stretch along much of the quayside, distinguished by their spout gables, multiple doorways and overhead pulleys. Built by the **Dutch East India Company** (see box, p.107) in the eighteenth century, they were once part of the largest warehouse complex in continental Europe, a gigantic customs-free zone established for goods in transit. On the ground floor, above each main entrance, every warehouse sports the name of a town or island; goods for onward transportation were stored in the appropriate warehouse until there were enough to fill a boat or barge. The warehouses have been tastefully converted into offices and apartments, a fate they share with the central Dutch East India Company compound, whose modest brickwork culminates in a chunky Neoclassical entrance at the west end of Entrepotdok on Kadijksplein.

The Nederlands Scheepvaartmuseum

The **Nederlands Scheepvaartmuseum** (Netherlands Maritime Museum; closed until further notice; ⓦ www.scheepvaartmuseum.nl) occupies the old arsenal of the Dutch Navy, a vast sandstone structure built on the Oosterdok beside Kattenburgerplein in the 1650s. It's underpinned by no fewer than 18,000 wooden piles driven deep into the riverbed at enormous expense, a testament to the nautical ambitions of the Dutch elite. The building's four symmetrical facades are dour and imposing despite the odd stylistic flourish, principally some quaint dormer windows and Neoclassical pediments, and they surround a central, cobbled courtyard under which was kept a copious supply of freshwater to supply the ships. It's the perfect location for a Maritime Museum and when it reopens, probably in 2012, it promises to be one of the city's key attractions.

ARCAM, NEMO and the Bibliotheek

Set on the Prins Hendrikkade waterfront is **ARCAM** (Tues–Sat 1–5pm; free; ⓦ www.arcam.nl), the Amsterdam Centre for Architecture, housed in a distinctive

Onward routes from the Nederlands Scheepvaartmuseum

From the Maritime Museum, there's a choice of several routes: if you're heading west, both the Canal Bus (see p.25) and the Museumboot (see p.25) will speedily return you to Centraal Station from the neighbouring NEMO centre (see p.240). Alternatively, you can walk back to Centraal Station in about fifteen minutes, either along Prins Hendrikkade or rather more appealingly via the footbridge spanning the water between NEMO and the Oosterdokskade, the location of the new city library, the Bibliotheek. Finally, diligent sightseers can either venture southeast to the De Gooyer windmill (see p.110) or northeast – preferably by tram from Centraal Station – to the tangle of River IJ islands that comprise Zeeburg (see pp.110–112).

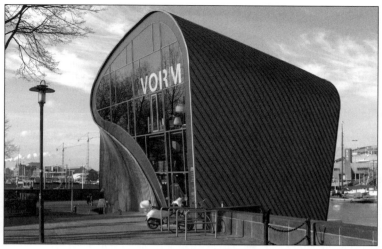
▲ ARCAM (Amsterdam Centre for Architecture)

aluminium and glass structure designed by the Dutch architect **René van Zuuk**. The design was much praised at the time of its construction, but the building does look rather disconcertingly like the head of a golf club. Inside, a small gallery area is used for an imaginative programme of temporary exhibitions on contemporary architecture in general and building plans for Amsterdam in particular.

Moored behind ARCAM are all sorts of antique **boats and barges**, which together make an informal record of the development of local shipping; the earliest boats date from the middle of the nineteenth century, and plaques, in English and Dutch, give the historical lowdown on the more important vessels. The boats lead towards the massive elevated hood that rears up above the entrance to the River IJ tunnel. A good part of this hood is now occupied by **NEMO** (Tues–Sun 10am–5pm; Mon open same hours during school holidays and in July & Aug; €11.50, under-4s free; ⓦ www.e-nemo .nl), a (pre-teenage) kids' attraction *par excellence*, with all sorts of interactive science and technological exhibits spread over six decks. For more on NEMO, see p.240.

Outside, moored at the NEMO jetty, is a full-scale replica of an East Indiaman, the 78-metre **De Amsterdam** (same times; €2 with NEMO ticket, otherwise €5). The ship has been temporarily relocated here while the Maritime Museum, which owns it, is closed. The original ship first set sail in 1748, but came to an ignominious end, getting stuck on the British coast near Hastings. Visitors can wander its decks and galleys, storerooms and gun bays at their leisure.

From NEMO a footbridge leads over the harbour to the brand-new city library, the **Bibliotheek**, which occupies a large and well-appointed modern block on Oosterdokskade (daily 10am–10pm; free internet access; ⓦ www.oba .nl). From here, a second, even longer nautical walkway leads along the edge of the harbour back to Centraal Station. Alternatively, you can take Prins Hendrikkade for the short walk west to the Oudeschans canal (see p.61), which serves as an attractive introduction to the Old Centre.

Museum Werf 't Kromhout and De Gooyer windmill

At no. 147 on Hoogte Kadijk is the **Museum Werf 't Kromhout** (Tues 10am–3pm; €5; **ⓦ**www.machinekamer.nl), one of the city's few remaining **shipyards**. In their heyday, the Eastern docklands were strewn with shipyards just like this one. The first major contraction came at the end of the nineteenth century when steel and steam replaced timber and few of the existing yards were big enough to make the switch successfully. A number, including 't Kromhout, struggled on, by concentrating on the repair and construction of smaller inshore and canal boats. Even so, 't Kromhout almost went bust in 1969 and was only saved by turning into a combination of working shipyard and tourist attraction, its yard full of old boats, its museum littered with ancient engines and shipyard tools.

Continuing southeast along Hoogte Kadijk from 't Kromhout, it's about 500m to **De Gooyer windmill**, standing tall between two canals at Funenkade 5. Amsterdam was once dotted with windmills, used for pumping water and grinding corn, but most were demolished years ago and this is a rare survivor. If you have come this far, you'll be pleased to discover that the bar and mini-brewery in the old public baths adjoining the windmill – the **Brouwerij Het IJ** (daily 3–8pm) – sells an excellent range of beers and ales. They brew an alarmingly strong amber ale called Columbus (9 percent), as well as less frightening stuff, such as the creamy Natte (6.5 percent).

It takes about twenty minutes to walk back from the windmill to the Nederlands Scheepvaartmuseum, or take bus #22 from neighbouring Zeeburgerstraat.

Zeeburg

To the north and east of the Oosterdok, **Zeeburg** – basically the old docklands between the city library (see p.109) and KNSM Island – has become one of the city's most up-and-coming districts. Actually a series of artificial islands and peninsulas connected by bridges, the docks here date back to the end of the nineteenth century, but like dockland areas all over Europe they fell into disuse and disrepair during the 1970s with the advent of large container ships, which couldn't travel this far upriver. By the early 1990s the area was virtually derelict, but it was then that the city council began a massive renovation, which has been going on for the past twenty years or so. As a result, this is the fastest-developing part of Amsterdam, with a mixture of renovated dockside structures and new landmark buildings that give it a modern (and very watery) feel that's markedly different from the city centre – despite being just a ten-minute walk from Centraal Station. It's the general appearance of the district, rather than any specific sight, which provides its main appeal, so you're best off exploring by bike, especially as distances are – at least in Amsterdam terms – comparatively large: from the library to the east end of KNSM Island is about 4km. Alternatively, there are two useful transport connections from Centraal Station: tram #26 to Sporenburg island via Piet Heinkade and bus #42 to Java Island and KNSM Island.

Java and KNSM islands

From the library on Oosterdokskade, it's a signed five- to ten-minute walk underneath the rail and over the tram lines to two of the Eastern docklands'

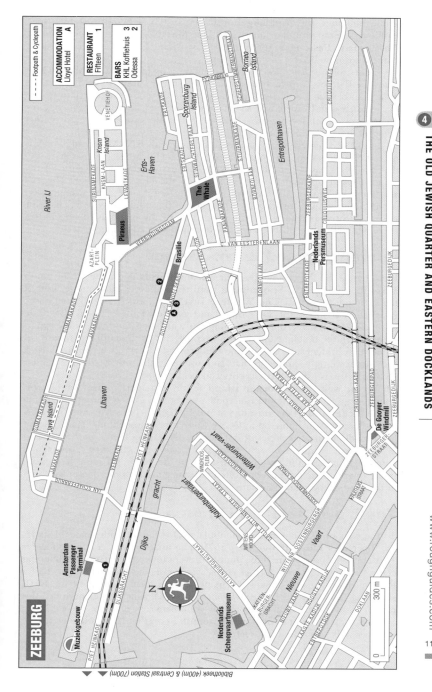

ZEEBURG

- - - - Footpath & Cyclepath

ACCOMMODATION
Lloyd Hotel   A

RESTAURANT
Fifteen   1

BARS
KHL Koffiehuis   3
Odessa   2

River IJ

Knsm Island
Borneo Island
Sporenburg Island
Java Island

Erts-Haven

The Whale

Piraeus

Brasilie

Entrepothaven

Nederlands Persmuseum

Amsterdam Passenger Terminal

Muziekgebouw

IJhaven

Piet Heinkade

Dijks gracht

Wittenburger-vaart

Kattenburgervaart

Nieuwe Vaart

De Gooyer Windmill

Nederlands Scheepvaartmuseum

N

300 m

0

prime buildings, the **Muziekgebouw** (see p.208), a brand-new, high-spec, multipurpose music auditorium overlooking the River IJ, and the neighbouring **Amsterdam Passenger Terminal**, a glass-walled behemoth, where visiting cruise ships now berth.

A short stroll east leads you to the 200-metre-long **Jan Schaeferbrug**, which spans the IJ across to **Java Island**, a long and narrow sliver of land, where tall residential blocks, mostly five storeys high, line up along the four mini-canals that cut across it. In form and layout these high-rises are a successful contemporary take on the seventeenth-century canal houses of the city centre, with a string of quirky, wrought-iron bridges adding extra style and panache.

The east end of Java Island merges seamlessly with **KNSM Island**, which is named after the shipping company (the Royal Dutch Steamboat Company) that was once based here. Leafy **KNSM-Laan** runs down the centre of the island, flanked by modern blocks, of which the German-designed **Piraeus** apartment building, at the west end of the street, gives the clearest impression of the clumsily monumental nature of much of the architecture here. That said, waterside **Surinamekade**, on the north side of the island, is much prettier, decorated with houseboats, barges and decommissioned fishing smacks.

Sporenburg and Borneo island

From beside the Piraeus building, the **Verbindingsdam** causeway leads south across the water to the **Sporenburg peninsula** and the blunt modernism of the structure known as **The Whale**, a large and distinctive residential block designed by architect Frits van Dongen and completed in 1995. It takes its name from its size and shape, the sharp outlines of which apparently allow the sun to better warm the building. On the southern edge of Sporenburg is Panamakade, where two bridges lead over to the modern, cubic terraces of Borneo island: the more westerly bridge is flat and ordinary, the other, the precipitous **Pythonbrug**, is named after its curvy, snakelike shape.

From the west end of **Borneo island**, C van Eesterenlaan slices south across a wide strip of water, the old Entrepothaven, bound for Zeeburgerkade, home to the **Nederlands Persmuseum** at no. 10 (Dutch Press Museum; Tues–Fri 10am–5pm & Sun noon–5pm; €4.50; Ⓦwww.persmuseum.nl). The museum has a mildly interesting series of displays on the leading Dutch newspapermen of yesteryear, beginning with Abraham Casteleyn, who first published a combined business and political newssheet in the 1650s. Of more immediate interest perhaps are the cartoons, often vitriolic attacks on those in power both in the Netherlands and elsewhere.

The Lloyd Hotel and around

To the west of the Sporenburg peninsula at Oostelijke Handelskade 34 stands the super-slick **Lloyd Hotel** (see p.167), in an imaginatively revamped former 1920s prison. Close by are three minor points of interest: the **Brasilie** shopping centre, which occupies a former cocoa warehouse, the **Odessa**, a replica of a Russian merchant ship, now a restaurant, and the former offices of the **KHL shipping line**, now the *KHL Koffiehuis* (see p.181), which once controlled this part of the dockland until the company went bankrupt in 1935.

To get back to Centraal Station, take tram #26 on Piet Heinkade, a couple of minutes' walk from the *Lloyd Hotel*.

Amsterdam on the water

If Amsterdammers hadn't had the ingenuity to build their city on marsh and reclaimed land, sitting their buildings on wooden piles sunk into the sand, then the city wouldn't exist at all. Like the surrounding countryside, it is made out of – and defined by – water, and its buildings complement their watery surroundings everywhere you look, whether it's in the classic canal vistas of the seventeenth-century city or the contemporary developments in the former docks and the outskirts of the city centre.

Here are ten things you can see or do to make the most of Amsterdam's unique watery environment:

Canal boat tours

What the hell, there are worse ways of spending your time than taking on the glass-topped **tourist boats** that chunter round the city's canals to cheesy canned commentary – you can even take a tour by candlelight. ⓦwww.rederijkooij .nl. See p.25.

Canal boats ▲

Queen's Day celebrations on the water ▼

Queen's Day

There is no better time to explore the city's canals than on **Queen's Day** as it's the one day of the year when everyone takes to the water, on all sorts of craft, complete with pounding sound systems and free-flowing booze. Watch the fun from bridges and intersections or try to grab a place on one of the boats yourself. See p.35.

Blijburg

Right out on the eastern end of the city at IJburg, "**Blijburg aan Zee**" is the ultimate urban beach, a slim crescent of sand that's home to a buzzy summer vibe with bands and DJs, plus a bar and beach café which serves organic food. Take tram #26 to the end of the line. ⓦwww .blijburg.nl. See p.184.

Zeeburg ▼

Zeeburg

The old squatter areas of the **eastern docklands** are home to some of the city's most audacious architecture and, increasingly, some of its greatest nightlife. You can get here by ferry on Sundays, at two-hourly intervals from behind Centraal Station – it takes half an hour to KNSM island. See p.110.

Bareboat exploration

The best way to get around Amsterdam's canals is, of course, to do it yourself, either by hiring a **pedalboat** – Ⓦwww.canal.nl – or better still a **motorboat** – Ⓦwww.rentaboatamsterdam.com. Private boats start at €50 an hour, €200 per day, for up to six people. See p.25.

Oosterdok

Wandering around the artificial islands of the **Oosterdok** gives one of the most authentic insights into Amsterdam's seafaring past, whether it's inspecting the old boats and barges moored near the Nemo science museum, or strolling past the eighteenth-century quays and warehouses of the Entrepotdok. See p.107.

▲ Boating on the canal

▼ Marken

Marken

Taking the bus to Volendam and then jumping on the ferry to the ex-island of **Marken** doesn't take long, but the town feels a long way from Amsterdam's centre and gives some idea of how the place would have been when it was a stormy coast on an inland sea. Ⓦwww.markenexpress.nl. See p.148.

Amsterdam NAP

Normal Amsterdam Water level, or Normaal Amsterdams Peil (NAP), is the **Dutch benchmark water level** – more or less the same as sea level on the Dutch coast. You can view the brass bolt that shows NAP in the Muziektheater, although it's worth bearing in mind that it isn't the most reliable measure, because Amsterdam is sinking by around 2cm a year. See p.99.

▼ Amsterdam NAP

Woonbootmuseum

The **Houseboat Museum** on Prinsengracht is the one place where you can poke around a houseboat and see what it's really like to live on Amsterdam's waterways without invading anyone's privacy. The museum is set in a traditional Dutch houseboat dating from 1914. See p.72.

NDSM Shipyard

Take a ferry from behind Centraal Station to Amsterdam Noord, where the buildings and slipways of the **NDSM Shipyard** have been resurrected as exhibition space and artists' studios, fast becoming some of the city's most happening cultural hangouts, and also firmly rooted in the city's maritime past. See p.137.

The Woonbootmuseum ▲

Wildlife on the canal ▼

What's in the water?

The one activity that really isn't recommended in Amsterdam's canals is swimming. People do end up in the drink from time to time, after which they are fished out and sent straight to hospital for a stomach pump and tetanus shot. Having said that, the water is in fact much cleaner than it used to be, and the canals are no longer channels for the city's raw sewage, although they are full of rubbish – car wrecks, old bikes, you name it. There is even a reasonable level of marine life down in the depths – indigenous fish such as carp and pike, as well as more recent arrivals like Chinese mitten crabs and corbicula clams, said to favour the car wrecks on the bottom.

5

The Museum Quarter and the Vondelpark

During the nineteenth century, Amsterdam burst out of its restraining canals, gobbling up the surrounding countryside with a slew of new, residential **suburbs**. These neighbourhoods are mostly described in Chapter 6, but Amsterdam's two leading **museums**, packed into a relatively small area around the edge of Museumplein, deserve their own chapter. The larger of the two, the **Rijksmuseum**, is in the throes of a major and extraordinarily long-winded revamp (scheduled to end in 2013), but the kernel of the collection – a superb sample of **Dutch paintings** from the seventeenth century, Amsterdam's Golden Age – is still on display in the Philips Wing, the only part of the museum to remain open during the refurbishment. Similarly impressive is the nearby **Van Gogh Museum**, which boasts the most satisfying collection of van Gogh paintings in the world, with important works representative of all his artistic periods. Together, the two museums form one of Amsterdam's biggest draws – to be supplemented by the contemporary art of the neighbouring **Stedelijk Museum**, due to reopen in 2010 after a complete refit. And, after all this art, you can head off into the expansive **Vondelpark** for a stroll.

Museumplein

Pancake-flat **Museumplein** is a large open space extending south from the Rijksmuseum to Van Baerlestraat, its wide lawns and gravelled spaces used for a variety of outdoor activities, from visiting circuses to political demonstrations. Other than being the location of the three museums described in this chapter, there's not a great deal to it, though the group of slim steel blocks about three-quarters of the way down on the left-hand side forms a **war memorial**, commemorating the men, women and children who perished in the concentration camp at Ravensbruck.

The Rijksmuseum

Facing out towards the Singelgracht canal, at the head of Museumplein, the **Rijksmuseum** (daily 9am–6pm, Friday until 8.30pm; €11; audio guide €5; ⓦ www.rijksmuseum.nl) occupies an imposing pile designed by **Petrus J.H. Cuypers** (1827–1921) – also the creator of Centraal Station – in the early

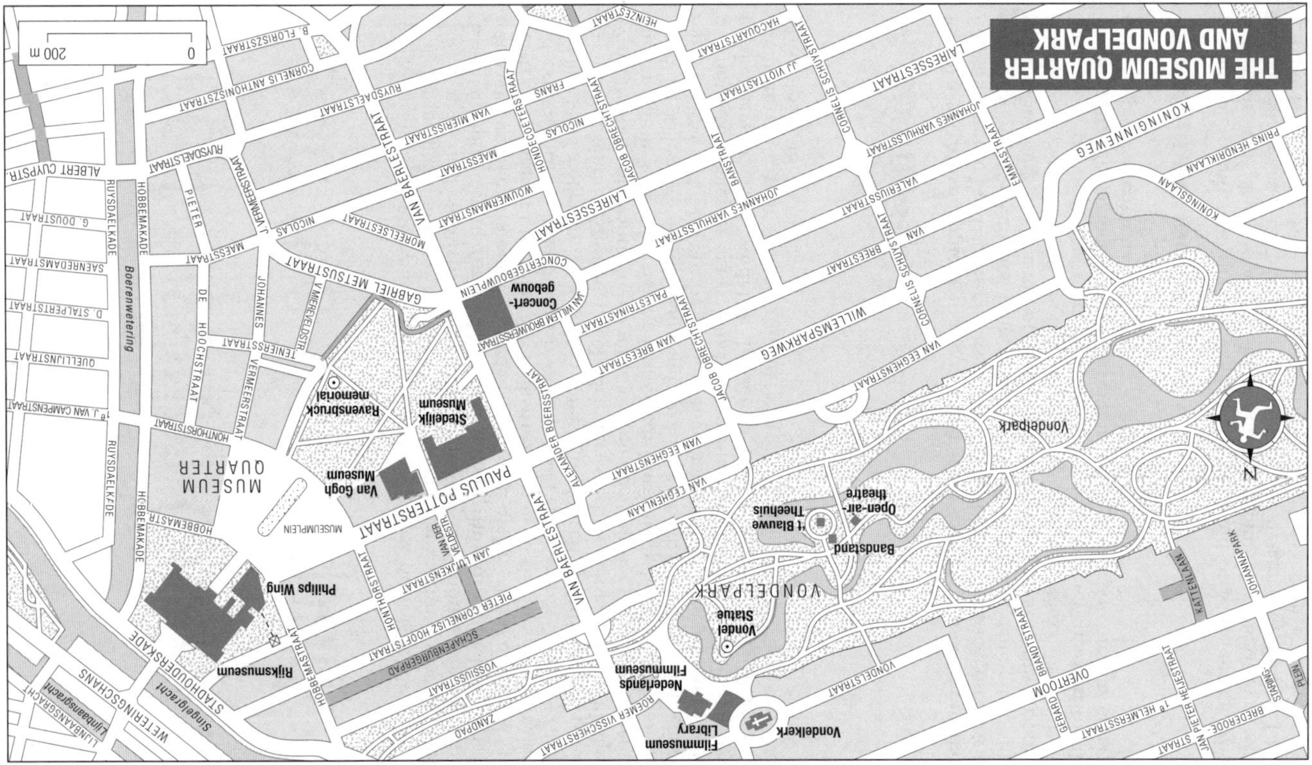

THE MUSEUM QUARTER AND VONDELPARK

200 m

N

Museum Quarter labels:
Rijksmuseum
Philips Wing
MUSEUM QUARTER
Van Gogh Museum
Ravensbruck memorial
Stedelijk Museum
Concert-gebouw
MUSEUMPLEIN

Vondelpark labels:
Vondelkerk
Filmmuseum Library
Nederlands Filmmuseum
Vondel Statue
Bandstand
't Blauwe Theehuis
Open-air theatre
VONDELPARK
Vondelpark

Street names:
WETERINGSCHANS
Singelgracht
STADHOUDERSKADE
HOBBEMAKADE
Boerenwetering
RUYSDAELKADE
LIJNBAANSGRACHT
Lijnbaansgracht
HOBBEMASTR.
HOBBEMASTRAAT
HONTHORSTRAAT
PIETER CORNELISZ HOOFTSTR.
J. VAN CAMPENSTRAAT
QUELLIJNSTRAAT
D. STALPERTSTRAAT
SAENREDAMSTRAAT
G. DOUSTRAAT
ALBERT CUYPSTR.
PIETER
DE HOOCHSTRAAT
JOHANNES VERMEERSTRAAT
J. VERMEERSTRAAT
GABRIEL METSUSTRAAT
VAN BAERLESTRAAT
NICOLAS MAESSTRAAT
RUYSDAELSTRAAT
CORNELIS ANTHONISZSTRAAT
B. FLORISZSTRAAT
PAULUS POTTERSTRAAT
VAN DER VELDESTR.
JAN LUYKENSTRAAT
TEN VELDESTR.
SCHAPENBURGERPAD
ZANDPAD
VOSSIUSSTRAAT
PIETER CORNELISZ HOOFTSTR.
VONDELSTRAAT
ROEMER VISSCHERSTRAAT
VAN BAERLESTRAAT
ALEXANDER BOERSSTRAAT
VAN EEGHENLAAN
VAN EEGHENSTRAAT
P.C. HOOFTSTRAAT
VAN MIEREVELDSTR.
JAN WILLEM BROUWERSSTRAAT
CONCERTGEBOUWPLEIN
ROELOF HARTSTRAAT
MOREELSESTRAAT
MOUWERMANSTRAAT
NICOLAS MAESSTRAAT
FRANS
HONDECOETERSTRAAT
LAIRESSESTRAAT
JACOB OBRECHTSTRAAT
MOUWERMANSTRAAT
VAN BREESTRAAT
PALESTRINASTRAAT
PALESTRINASTRAAT
WILLEMSPARKWEG
VAN EEGHENSTRAAT
JACOB OBRECHTSTRAAT
JOHANNES VERHULSTSTRAAT
BANSTRAAT
CORNELIS SCHUYTSTRAAT
CORNELIS SCHUYTSTRAAT
VALERIUSSTRAAT
VAN
J.J. VIOTTASTRAAT
JACOB OBRECHTSTRAAT
FRANS
HEINZESTRAAT
EMMASTRAAT
JOHANNES VERHULSTSTRAAT
LAIRESSESTRAAT
KONINGINNEWEG
PRINS HENDRIKLAAN
KONINGSLAAN
OVERTOOM
BRANDTSTRAAT
GERARD
KATTENLAAN
JAN PIETER HEIJESTRAAT
P. HELMERSSTRAAT
BREDERODE
STADING
JOHANNAPARK
PLEIN

▲ The Rijksmuseum

1880s. The leading Dutch architect of his day, Cuypers specialized in neo-Gothic churches, but this commission called for something more ambitious, the result being a reworking of the neo-Renaissance style then popular in the Netherlands, complete with towers and turrets, galleries, dormer windows and medallions. More importantly, the museum possesses an extravagant collection of **paintings** from every pre-twentieth-century period of Dutch art, together with a vast hoard of **applied art and sculpture**. Until the rest of the museum reopens in 2013, the **Philips Wing** is the only section receiving visitors, its entrance tucked away along Jan Luijkenstraat. The positive news is that the wing's thirteen rooms are used to good effect to display the essence of the permanent collection under the title "The Masterpieces" – a splendid selection of seventeenth-century Dutch paintings from the *Gouden Eeuw* (Golden Age), as well as **delftware**, **silverware** and various other resonant items from Dutch history. There is some rotation, but you can count on seeing all the leading Rembrandts plus a healthy sample of canvases by Steen, Hals, Vermeer and their leading contemporaries.

Bear in mind that the relatively small size of the exhibition space means that **queues** can be long, especially in summer and at weekends – it's a good idea to book online first or come early in the day.

Rooms 1 to 5

The Philips Wing begins in style with two large galleries – Rooms 1 and 2 – which give the historical background to the **Dutch Golden Age** with features on the country's success as a trading nation and its naval prowess. Among the paintings on display here is the breezily self-confident *The Celebration of the Treaty of Münster*, by **Bartholomeus van der Helst** (1613–70) – he became one of Amsterdam's most popular portraitists after Rembrandt abandoned the normal protocols of portraiture to adopt an introspective, religious style that did not impress the city's burghers one bit. For the Dutch at least, the treaty was well worth celebrating: signed in 1648, it ended the Thirty Years' War and recognized the United Provinces (now the Netherlands) as an independent state, free

Delftware

Named after the Dutch city of **Delft**, where it was manufactured, **delftware** traces its origins to fifteenth-century Mallorca, where craftsmen developed **majolica**, a kind of porous pottery that was glazed with metallic oxides. During the Renaissance, these techniques were exported to Italy from where they spread north, first to Antwerp and then to the United Provinces (aka the Netherlands). Initially, delft pottery **designs** featured landscapes, portraits and Bible stories, while the top end of the market was dominated by more ornate Chinese porcelain imported by the Dutch East India Company. However, when a prolonged civil war in China broke the supply line, Delft's factories quickly took over the luxury side of the market by copying Chinese designs. By the 1670s, Delft was churning out blue-and-white tiles, plates, panels, jars and vases of all descriptions by the thousand, even exporting to China, where they undercut Chinese producers. The delft factories were themselves undercut by the British and the Germans from the 1760s on, and by the time Napoleon arrived they had all but closed down. There was a modest revival of the delft industry in the 1870s and there are several Dutch producers today, but it's mostly cheap, mass-produced stuff of little originality.

of Habsburg control. Opposite van der Helst's painting a smaller work, by **Gerard ter Borch**, witnesses the event itself. The Thirty Years' War had convulsed most of western Europe by pitting Catholic against Protestant. **Adriaen van de Venne** (1589–1662) was quite clear which side he was on; his curious *Fishing for Souls*, in Room 2, has the disorganized Catholics on the right river bank – and the Protestants merrily heaving in souls on the left.

Room 3 contains several antique **dolls' houses**, Room 4 is mostly **silverware**, and Room 5 showcases a large assortment of **delftware**, from plates and tiles through to vases, chargers and flower holders. Dating from the late sixteenth century, the earlier pieces are comparatively plain, typically decorated with rural, classical or biblical scenes, whereas the later porcelain is more elaborate and often copied from – or in imitation of – Chinese ceramics (see box above).

Rooms 6, 7 and 8

Upstairs, Room 6 holds early seventeenth-century paintings by **Thomas de Keyser**, **Gerard Honthorst** and **Hendrik Avercamp** that together introduce several different genres – portraiture, still life and nature. Room 7 contains several superb canvases by **Frans Hals** (1582–1666), most notably his *Merry Drinker* and the expansive *Marriage Portrait of Isaac Massa and Beatrix Laen*. Relaxing beneath a tree, a portly Isaac glows with contentment as his new wife sits beside him in a suitably demure manner. An intimate scene, the painting also carries a detailed iconography; the ivy at Beatrix's feet symbolizes her devotion to her husband, the thistle faithfulness, the vine togetherness and in the fantasy garden behind them the peacock is a classical allusion to Juno, the guardian of marriage. In the same room, look out for the cool church interiors of **Pieter Saenredam** (1597–1665), whose *Old Town Hall of Amsterdam* is a characteristically precise work in which the tumbledown predecessor of the current building (now the Royal Palace) witnesses the comings and goings of blackhatted townsmen in the stilted manner of a Lowry.

In Room 8, examples of the work of **Salomon van Ruysdael** (1602–70) – a Haarlem artist with a penchant for soft, tonal river scenes – share space with the brightly coloured canvases of **Pieter Lastman** (1583–1633). Lastman's most famous apprentice was **Rembrandt** and there are examples of the great man's early work here in this room too, most notably his portrait of Maria Trip, an Amsterdam oligarch kitted out in her pearls and gold lace finery. Room 8 also features some of the work of Rembrandt's better-known pupils, including **Nicholas Maes** (1632–93), whose caring *Young Woman by the Cradle* is not so much a didactic tableau as an idealization of motherhood. Another pupil, **Ferdinand Bol** (1616–80), painted *Portrait of Elizabeth Bas* in a style so close to that of his master that it was regarded as a Rembrandt until the director of the museum proved otherwise in 1911. Perhaps the most talented of Rembrandt's pupils was **Carel Fabritius**, who was killed in 1654 at the age of 32, when Delft's gunpowder magazine exploded. His *Portrait of Abraham Potter*, a restrained, skilful work of soft, delicate hues, contrasts with the same artist's earlier *The Beheading of St John the Baptist*, in which the head is served on a platter in chillingly grisly style.

Room 9

Room 9 has several fine examples of **Rembrandt's later work**, notably the celebrated *Members of the Clothmakers Guild* and a late *Self-Portrait*, with the artist caught in mid-shrug as the Apostle Paul, a self-aware and defeated old man. Also here are the artist's touching depiction of his cowled son, *Titus*, and *The Jewish Bride*, one of his very last pictures, finished in 1667. No one knows who the couple are, nor whether they are actually married (the title came later), but the painting is one of Rembrandt's most telling, the paint dashed on freely and the hands touching lovingly – as the art historian Kenneth Clark wrote, in "a marvellous amalgam of richness, tenderness and trust". In marked contrast to these paintings are a number of landscapes by **Jan van Goyen** and **Jacob van Ruisdael**.

Rooms 10 and 11

Room 10 holds some examples of the small, finely realized works of **Gerard Dou** (1613–75) and **Gabriel Metsu** (1625–67), flashes of everyday life that sit well with the work of **Johannes Vermeer** (1632–75). The latter is well represented; *The Love Letter* reveals a tension between servant and mistress – the lute on the woman's lap was a well-known sexual symbol – while *The Kitchen Maid* is an exquisitely observed domestic scene, right down to the nail – and its shadow – on the background wall. Similarly, in the precise *Young Woman Reading a Letter*, the map behind her hints at the far-flung places her loved one is writing from. What you won't get, however, is Vermeer's *Girl with a Pearl Earring* – this is on display in the Mauritshuis gallery in The Hague. **Gerard ter Borch** (1617–81) also depicted apparently innocent scenes, both in subject and title, but his *Woman at a Mirror* glances in a meaningfully anxious manner at her servants, who look on with delicate irony from behind dutiful exteriors. There are yet more sub-texts in ter Borch's *Paternal Admonition* – just what exactly is the young woman being told off for?

The paintings of **Pieter de Hooch** (1629–84) are less symbolic – more exercises in lighting – but they're as good a visual guide to the everyday life and habits of the seventeenth-century Dutch bourgeoisie as you'll find – as evidenced by his *Interior with Women beside a Linen Basket*, showing the women of the house changing the linen while a series of doorways reveals the canal bank in the background; and his curious *A Mother's Duty* in which the mother is delousing the child's head.

Room 10 also exhibits several works by **Jan Steen** (1625–79). Steen's *Feast of St Nicholas*, with its squabbling children, makes the festival a celebration of

Rembrandt's progress

Born in Leiden to a family of millers, **Rembrandt Harmenszoon van Rijn** (1606–69) picked up his first artistic tips as an apprentice to Pieter Lastman in Amsterdam in the early 1620s. It was here that the artist developed a penchant for mythological and religious subjects. After his apprenticeship, in around 1625, Rembrandt went back to Leiden to establish himself as an independent master painter and, this achieved, some six years later he returned to Amsterdam, where he was to stay for the rest of his life.

In the early 1630s Rembrandt concentrated on **portrait painting**, churning out dozens of pictures of the burghers of his day, a profitable business that made him both well-to-do and well known. In 1634 he married **Saskia van Uylenburgh** and five years later the couple moved into a smart house on Jodenbreestraat, now the Rembrandthuis museum (see p.96). All seemed well, and certainly Rembrandt's portraits of his wife are tender and loving, but these years were marred by the death of all but one of his children in infancy, the sole survivor being his much-loved **Titus** (1641–68).

In 1642 Rembrandt produced what has become his most celebrated painting, **The Night Watch**, but thereafter his career went into decline, essentially because he forsook portraiture to focus on increasingly sombre and introspective **religious works**. Traditionally, Rembrandt's change of artistic direction has been linked to the death of Saskia in 1642, but although it is certainly true that the artist was grief-stricken, he was also facing increased competition from a new batch of portrait artists, primarily Bartholomeus van der Helst, Ferdinand Bol and Govert Flinck. Whatever the reason, there were few takers for Rembrandt's religious works and he made matters worse by refusing to adjust his spending. The crunch came in 1656, when he was formally declared insolvent, and four years later he was obliged to sell his house and goods, moving to much humbler premises in the Jordaan (see p.86). By this time, he had a new cohabitee, **Hendrickje Stoffels** (a clause in Saskia's will prevented them from ever marrying), and in the early 1660s, she and Titus took Rembrandt in hand, sorting out his finances and his work schedule. With his money problems solved, a relieved Rembrandt then produced some of his finest paintings – for example *The Jewish Bride* – emotionally deep and contemplative works with a rough finish, the paint often daubed with an almost trowel-like heaviness. Hendrickje died in 1663 and Titus in 1668, a year before his father.

disorderly greed, while the drunken waywardness of his *Merry Family* and *Family Scene* verge on the anarchic. Steen knew his bourgeois audience well; his caricatures of the proletariat blend humour with moral condemnation – or at least condescension – a mixture perfectly designed to suit their tastes. The artist was also capable of more subtle works, a famous example being his *Woman at her Toilet*, which is full of associations, referring to sexual pleasures just had or about to be taken; for example, the woman is shown putting on a stocking in a conspicuous manner, the point being that the Dutch word for stocking, *kous*, is also a slang word for a woman's genitalia.

By contrast, in Room 11, **Willem van de Velde II**'s (1633–1707) preoccupations were nautical, his canvases celebrating either the might of the Dutch navy or the seaworthiness of the merchant marine, as in the churning seas of the superbly executed *Gust of Wind*, whose counterpoint is to be found in the calm waters and gunfire of *The Cannon Shot*.

Room 12

Dominating Room 12, Rembrandt's **The Night Watch** (*De Nachtwacht*) of 1642 is the most famous of all the artist's paintings. Restored after being slashed in 1975, the scene is of a **militia company**, the Kloveniersdoelen, one of the companies formed in the sixteenth century to defend the United Provinces (later the Netherlands) against Spain. As the Habsburg threat receded, so the militias became social clubs for the well heeled, who were eager to commission their own group portraits as signs of their prestige. Rembrandt charged the princely sum of one hundred guilders for each member of the company who wanted to be in the picture; sixteen – out of a possible two hundred – stumped up the cash, including the company's moneyed captain, **Frans Banningh Cocq**, whose disapproval of Rembrandt's live-in relationship with Hendrickje Stoffels (see box, p.118) was ultimately to polish off their friendship. Curiously, *The Night Watch* is, in fact, a misnomer – the painting got the tag in the eighteenth century when the background darkness was misinterpreted. There were other misconceptions about the painting too, most notably that it was this work that led to the downward shift in Rembrandt's standing with the Amsterdam elite; in fact, there's no evidence that the militiamen weren't pleased with the picture, or that Rembrandt's commissions dwindled after it was completed.

Though not as subtle as much of the artist's later work, *The Night Watch* is an adept piece, full of movement and carefully arranged. Paintings of this kind were collections of individual portraits as much as group pictures, and for the artist their difficulty lay in doing justice to every single face while simultaneously producing a coherent group scene. Abandoning convention in vigorous style, Rembrandt opted to show the company preparing to march off – a snapshot of military activity in which banners are unfurled, muskets primed and drums rolled. There are a couple of **allegorical figures** as well, most prominently a young, spotlit woman with a bird hanging from her belt, a reference to the Kloveniersdoelen's traditional emblem of a claw. Militia portraits commonly included cameo portraits of the artist involved, but in this case it seems that Rembrandt didn't insert his likeness, though some art historians insist that the pudgy-faced figure peering out from the back between the gesticulating militiamen is indeed the artist himself.

Opposite *The Night Watch* is another Civic Guard portrait, *The Meagre Company*, started by **Frans Hals** and finished by **Pieter Codde** due to a dispute. It's a great painting, full of sensitively realized, individual portraits, but not only are the wildly differing painting styles of Hals and Rembrandt immediately apparent, but the more conservative arrangement of Hals's figures forms a striking contrast with Rembrandt's more fluid, dynamic work.

The Van Gogh Museum

Vincent van Gogh (1853–90) is arguably the most popular, most reproduced and most talked-about of all modern artists, so it's not surprising that the **Van Gogh Museum** (daily 10am–6pm, Friday until 10pm; €12.50, children 13–17 years €2.50; audioguide €4; @www.vangoghmuseum.nl), comprising a fabulous collection of the artist's work, is one of Amsterdam's top attractions.

The museum occupies two modern buildings on the north edge of Museumplein, with the key paintings housed in an angular building designed by a leading light of the De Stijl movement, **Gerrit Rietveld** (1888–1964), and opened to the public in 1973. Well conceived and beautifully presented, this part of the museum provides an introduction to the man and his art based on paintings that were mostly inherited from Vincent's art-dealer brother Theo. To the rear of Rietveld's building, connected by a ground-floor escalator, is the ultramodern annex. This aesthetically controversial structure – financed by the same Japanese insurance company that paid $35 million for one of van Gogh's *Sunflowers* canvases in 1987, and completed in 1998 – provides temporary exhibition space. Most of the **exhibitions** held here focus on one aspect or another of van Gogh's art and draw heavily on the **permanent collection**, which means that the paintings displayed in the older building are regularly rotated.

As you might expect, the museum can get very crowded, and the **queues** can be long, so come early to avoid the crush or book online.

The collection

Just beyond the museum entrance, a flight of stairs leads to the **first floor**, where the paintings of van Gogh are presented in chronological order. The first go back to the artist's **early years** (1880–85) in Holland and Belgium: dark, sombre works in the main, ranging from an assortment of drab grey and brown still lifes to the gnarled faces and haunting, flickering light of *The Potato Eaters* – one of van Gogh's best-known paintings, and the culmination of hundreds of studies of the local peasantry.

Further along, the sobriety of these early works is easily transposed onto the urban landscape of **Paris** (1886–88), particularly in the *View of Paris*, where the city's domes and rooftops hover below Montmartre under a glowering, blustery sky. But before long, under the sway of fellow painters and the sheer colour of the city itself, van Gogh's approach began to change. This is most noticeable in two of his many self-portraits and in the pictures from **Asnières**, just outside Paris, where the artist used to go regularly to paint. In particular, look out for the surprisingly soft hues and gentle tones of his *Courting Couples*, and the disturbing yellows of *Still Life with Quinces and Lemons*. There's also a rare **photograph** of van Gogh in **Asnières** (though it's only of his back), which shows him in conversation with the artist Emile Bernard.

In February 1888 van Gogh moved to **Arles**, inviting Gauguin to join him a little later (see box, p.121). With the change of scenery came a heightened interest in colour, and the predominance of **yellow** as a recurring motif; it's represented best in such paintings as *The Harvest*, and most vividly in the disconcerting juxtapositions of *Bedroom in Arles*. Also from this period comes a striking canvas from the artist's *Sunflowers* series, justly one of his most lauded works, and intensely – almost obsessively – rendered in the deepest oranges, golds and ochres he could find. Gauguin told of van Gogh painting these flowers in a near-trance; there were usually sunflowers in jars all over their house – in fact, they can be seen in Gauguin's portrait of van Gogh from the same period, also displayed in this section.

During his time at the asylum in **St Rémy**, van Gogh's approach to nature became more abstract, as evidenced by his unsettling *Wheatfield with a Reaper*, the dense, knotty *Undergrowth* and his palpable *Irises*. Van Gogh is at his most expressionistic here, the paint applied thickly, often with a palette knife, a practice he continued in his final, tortured works painted at **Auvers-sur-Oise**, where he lodged for the last three months of his life. It was at Auvers that he painted the frantic *Wheatfield with Crows*, in which the fields swirl and writhe under weird and dark skies, as well as the organized chaos of *Tree Roots* and the glowering *Wheatfield under Thunderclouds*.

The second and third floors provide a backup to the lead collection. The **second floor** has temporary displays on themes related to van Gogh as well as a study area with PC access to a detailed account of the artist's life and times. The **third floor** features other paintings from the museum's permanent collection, including van Gogh sketches and some of his less familiar paintings. It's here that you're likely to find *A Pair of Shoes*, an

Van Gogh's ear

In February 1888, **Vincent van Gogh** (1853–90) left Paris for **Arles**, a small town in the south of France. At first the move went well, with van Gogh warming to the open vistas and bright colours of the Provençal countryside. In September he moved into the dwelling he called the Yellow House, where he hoped to establish an artists' colony, gathering together painters of like mind. Unfortunately for van Gogh, his letters of invitation were ignored by most, and only **Gauguin**, who arrived in Arles in late October, stayed for long. Initially the two artists got on well, hunkering down together in the Yellow House and sometimes painting side by side, but the bonhomie didn't last. They argued long and hard about art, an especially tiring business for van Gogh, who complained: "Sometimes we come out of our arguments with our heads as exhausted as a used electric battery". Later, Gauguin would claim that van Gogh threatened him during several of these arguments; true or not, it is certainly the case that Gauguin had decided to return to Paris by the time the two had a ferocious quarrel on the night of December 23. The argument was so bad that Gauguin hotfooted it off to the local hotel, and when he returned in the morning he was faced by the police. After Gauguin's exit, a deeply disturbed van Gogh had taken a razor to his **ear**, severing part of it before presenting the selected slice to a prostitute at the local brothel. Presumably, this was not an especially welcome gift, but in van Gogh's addled state he may well have forged some sort of connection with bullfighting, where the dead bull's ears are cut off and given as a prize to the bullfighter. Hours after Gauguin's return, van Gogh was admitted to hospital, the first of several extended stays before, fearing for his sanity, he committed himself to the asylum of **St Rémy** in May 1889. Here, the doctor's initial assessment described him as suffering from "acute mania, with hallucinations of sight and hearing"; van Gogh attributed his parlous state to excessive drinking and smoking, though he gave up neither during his year-long stay.

In May 1890, feeling lonely and homesick, van Gogh discharged himself from St Rémy and headed north to Paris before proceeding to the village of **Auvers-sur-Oise**. At first, van Gogh's health improved and he even began to garner critical recognition for his work. However, his twin ogres of depression and loneliness soon returned to haunt him and, in despair, van Gogh shot himself in the chest. This wasn't, however, the end; he took two days to die, even enduring a police visit when he refused to answer any questions, pronouncing: "I am free to do what I like with my own body".

idiosyncratic painting that used to hang in the house van Gogh shared with Gauguin in Arles. There is also a display entitled "Predecessors, contemporaries and followers (1840–1890)". The paintings are rotated regularly, but you can expect to see a seminal early painting of the *Route de Versailles* by **Pissarro**, views of Amsterdam and Zaandam windmills by **Monet**, and various pieces by Toulouse-Lautrec, Cézanne, Bernard, Seurat, Gauguin, Anton Mauve and Charles Daubigny.

Stedelijk Museum

The **Stedelijk Museum** (reopens 2010; ⓦ www.stedelijk.nl), just along the street from the Van Gogh Museum, has long been Amsterdam's number one venue for modern and contemporary art. It's housed in a big old building, undergoing a complete refurbishment for a scheduled reopening in the spring of 2010. The museum will focus on cutting-edge, temporary exhibitions of **modern art** – from photography and film through to sculpture and collage – and these will be supplemented by the museum's large and wide-ranging

permanent collection. Among many highlights, the latter includes a particularly large sample of the work of **Mondriaan** (1872–1944), from his early, muddy abstracts to the boldly coloured rectangular blocks for which he's most famous. The Stedelijk is also strong on **Kasimir Malevich** (1878–1935), whose dense attempts at Cubism lead to the dynamism and bold primary tones of his "Suprematist" paintings – slices, blocks and bolts of colour that shift around as if about to resolve themselves into some complex computer graphic. Other high spots include several **Marc Chagall** paintings and a number of pictures by American abstract Expressionists Mark Rothko, Ellsworth Kelly and Barnett Newman, plus the odd work by Lichtenstein, Warhol, Robert Ryman, Kooning and Jean Dubuffet.

The Concertgebouw

Across Van Baerlestraat just to the southwest of the Stedelijk Museum is the **Concertgebouw** (Concert Hall; ☎020/671 8345, ⓦwww.concertgebouw.nl), home of the famed – and much recorded – Royal Concertgebouw Orchestra (*Koninklijk Concertgebouworkest*). When the German composer Brahms visited Amsterdam in the 1870s he was scathing about the locals' lack of culture and, in particular, their lack of an even halfway suitable venue for his music. In the face of such ridicule, a consortium of Amsterdam businessmen got together to fund the construction of a brand-new concert hall and the result was the Concertgebouw, completed in 1888. An attractive structure with a pleasingly grand Neoclassical facade, the Concertgebouw has become renowned among musicians and concertgoers for its marvellous acoustics. Thanks to a facelift and the replacement of its crumbling foundations in the early 1990s, it's looking better than ever, with a glass gallery that contrasts nicely with the red brick and stone of the rest of the building.

The Concertgebouw showcases an ambitious programme of classical music with the offerings of the Royal Concertgebouw Orchestra supplemented by

▲ Main hall of the Concertgebouw

the regular appearance of the **Netherlands Philharmonic Orchestra** (Nederlands Philharmonisch Orkest) as well as all manner of visiting orchestras. Ticket **prices** are reasonable (€30–50) and there are regular free – or heavily subsidized – lunchtime concerts throughout the year. **Guided tours** of the Concertgebouw take place on Sundays (noon–1pm) and Mondays (5–6pm) and cost €10. The tour takes in the Grote Zaal and Kleine Zaal auditoria, as well as various behind-the-scenes activities – control rooms, piano stores, artistes' dressing rooms and the like.

The Vondelpark

Amsterdam is short of green spaces, which makes the leafy expanse of the **Vondelpark**, a short distance from both Museumplein and the Concertgebouw, doubly welcome. This is easily the largest and most popular of the city's parks, its network of footpaths used by a healthy slice of the city's population.

The park dates back to 1864, when a group of leading Amsterdammers clubbed together to transform the soggy marshland that lay beyond the old Leidsepoort gateway, on the western edge of Leidseplein, into a landscaped park. The group were impressed by the contemporary English fashion for natural (as distinct from formal) landscaping. They gave the task of developing the new style of park to the Zocher family, big-time gardeners who set about their task with gusto, completing the project in 1865. Named after the seventeenth-century poet **Joost van den Vondel** (see p.55), the park proved an immediate success. It now possesses over a hundred tree species, a wide variety of local and imported plants, and – among many incidental features – a dinky little **bandstand** and a grand statue of a pensive Vondel, shown seated with quill in hand, near the park's main entrance. Neither did the Zochers forget their Dutch roots: the park is latticed with narrow waterways crossed by pretty bridges and ponds that are home to many types of **wildfowl**, including numerous heron, though it's the large colony of (very noisy) bright-green parakeets which grab the attention. The Vondelpark has several children's **play areas**, and during the summer regularly hosts free **concerts** and theatrical performances, mostly in its tiny **open-air theatre** (Openluchttheater), right in the centre of the park.

The Nederlands Filmmuseum and the Vondelkerk

Housed in a grand nineteenth-century building at the northeast corner of the Vondelpark, the **Nederlands Filmmuseum** (☏020/589 1400, ⓦwww .filmmuseum.nl) is really more an art-house **cinema** than a museum – a showcase for films of all kinds, most of which are shown in their original language, with subtitles in Dutch or sometimes English. There are several screenings nightly, as well as regular matinees, and the programme often follows a prescribed theme. Look out also for the free screenings of classic movies in the summer.

The Filmmuseum also possesses a large **archive** of old films and is a dab hand at celluloid restoration. In the large building next door, at Vondelstraat 69, the museum's **film library** (Mon, Tues & Thurs 1–5pm) has a well-catalogued

▲ The Nederlands Filmmuseum

collection of books, magazines and journals (some in English), though they are for reference only and not loaned out.

Across the street is the lugubrious, brown-brick hull and whopping spire of the **Vondelkerk**, which has had more than its share of bad luck. Work on the church, which was designed by **Cuypers** (see p.113), began in 1872, but finances ran out the following year and the building was not completed until the 1880s. Twenty years later, it was struck by lightning and in the ensuing fire its tower was burnt to a cinder – the present one was added much later. The church always struggled to find a decent-sized congregation, but limped on until it was finally deconsecrated in 1979, and turned into offices thereafter.

The outer districts

Amsterdam is a comparatively small city, and the majority of its residential **outer districts** are easily reached from the city centre by public transport or, at a pinch, by bike. The **south** holds most interest, including the **Oud Zuid** (Old South), at the heart of which is the lively, cosmopolitan **De Pijp** quarter, home to the **Heineken Experience**, sited in the company's old brewery. Also in the Oud Zuid is the striking architecture of the **De Dageraad** housing project and there are yet more handsome buildings in the adjoining **Nieuw Zuid** (New South), which itself is near the enjoyable woodland of the **Amsterdamse Bos**. As for the other districts, you'll find a good deal less reason to make the trek, though multicultural influences in the **east** give this part of the city some diversity, and this is also the location of the excellent **Tropenmuseum**, and further south, the **Amsterdam ArenA**, home of Ajax football club. Finally, the **north** of the city, on the other side of the IJ, reachable by way of a short (free) ferry ride from behind Centraal Station, is again almost entirely residential, but it's pleasant enough if you're cycling through on the way to open country.

The Oud Zuid

Amsterdam's city centre is ringed by the Singelgracht, just beyond which lies the **Oud Zuid** and its most authentic district, **De Pijp** ("The Pipe"), Amsterdam's first real suburb. New development beyond the Singelgracht began around 1870, but after laying down the street plans of De Pijp, the city council left the actual house-building to private developers, who constructed the long rows of largely featureless five- and six-storey buildings that still dominate the area today. It is these sombre canyons of brick tenements that gave the district its name as the apartments were said to resemble pipe-drawers: each had a tiny street frontage but extended deep into the building. De Pijp remains a largely working-class neighbourhood and, despite some gentrification, it is still one of the city's more closely-knit communities, and a cosmopolitan one to boot, with many new immigrants – Surinamese, Moroccan, Turkish and Asian – finding a home here. Nevertheless, specific attractions in De Pijp are thin on the ground, being principally confined to the **Heineken Experience** and the **Albert Cuypstraat open-air market**. The same applies to the Oud Zuid as a whole, though the handsome architecture of the **De Dageraad housing project** is well worth seeking out.

To get to De Pijp by **public transport** from Centraal Station, take tram #16 or #24 as far as Albert Cuypstraat; or take tram #25, which heads along

THE OUTER DISTRICTS

N

ZAANSTAD
ZAANDAM
Het Twiske
Noordhollandskanaal
A8
N203
Noordzee kanaal
Amerikahaven
RIJGOORDWEG
Westhaven
NIEUWE HEMWEG
A10
KLAPROZENWEG
A10 E35
River IJ
N. LEEUWARDERWEG
N247
RINGWEG NORD
WATERLAND
NOORD
NOORDZEEWEG
BASISWEG
HAARLEMMERWEG
River IJ
NASSAUKADE
ZUIDERZEEWEG
A10 E35
BURGEMEESTER ROELSTR
Centraal Station
Molen de Gooyer
OSDORPERWEG
Sloterplas
Rembrandtpark
Artis Zoo
JOHAN HUIZINGALAAN
OOKMEERWEG
HEEMSTE VAART
OUD WEST
Heineken Experience
MAURITSKADE
Amstel
OOST Flevo-park
Tropen-museum
A1
PLESMANLANN
Vondelpark
DE PIJP
Ooster-park
EINSTEINWEG
A9
SLOTERWEG
NIEUWE HAAGSEWEGZ
OUD ZUID
Olympisch Stadion
NIEUW ZUID
Beatrix-park
RIVIERENBUURT
RINGWEG OOST
Amsterdam RAI
A10
RINGWEG ZUID
Amstelpark
River Nieuwe Meer
NIEUWE MEERDIJK
BUITENVELDERTSELAAN
AMSTELVEENSEWEG
Bosbaan
A2
DAALWIJKDREEF
GOOISEWEG
Amsterdamse Bos
BURGEM STRAMANWEG
BIJLMERMEER
A9
Amsterdam Schiphol International Airport
SCHIPOLWEG
AMSTELVEEN
CoBrA Museum of Modern Art
K. KARELWEG
Amsterdam ArenA & Ajax Museum
BURGEM STRAMANWEG
ROZENBURG
De Poel
A9
BOVENKERK

0   2 km

Weteringschans, threads round the Sarphatipark and then continues down (the southern reaches of) De Pijp's main drag, Ferdinand Bolstraat. For De Dageraad, take tram #4, also from Centraal Station.

The Wetering circuit

At the southern end of Vijzelgracht, on the city-centre side of the Singelgracht, is the **Wetering circuit** roundabout, which has two low-key **memorials** to World War II. On the southwestern corner of the roundabout, by the canal, is a sculpture of a wounded man holding a bugle; it was here, on March 12, 1945, that thirty people were shot by the Germans in reprisal for acts of sabotage by the Dutch Resistance – given that the war was all but over, it's hard to imagine a crueller or more futile action. Across the main street, the second memorial in

▲ De Pijp shop

the form of a brick wall commemorates H.M. van Randwijk, a Resistance leader. The restrained wording on the monument translates as:

**When to the will of tyrants,
A nation's head is bowed,
It loses more than life and goods –
Its very light goes out.**

The Heineken Experience

On the far side of the Singelgracht, on the northern edge of De Pijp at Stadhouderskade 78, the **Heineken Experience** (daily 11am–7pm; €15; Ⓦ www.heinekenexperience.com; tram #16 or #24 from Centraal Station) is housed in the former Heineken brewery, a whopping building that was the company's headquarters from 1864 to 1988, at which time the firm restructured and its brewing moved out of town. Since then, Heineken has developed the site as a tourist attraction, with displays on the history of beer-making in general and Heineken in particular. The old brewing hall is included on the

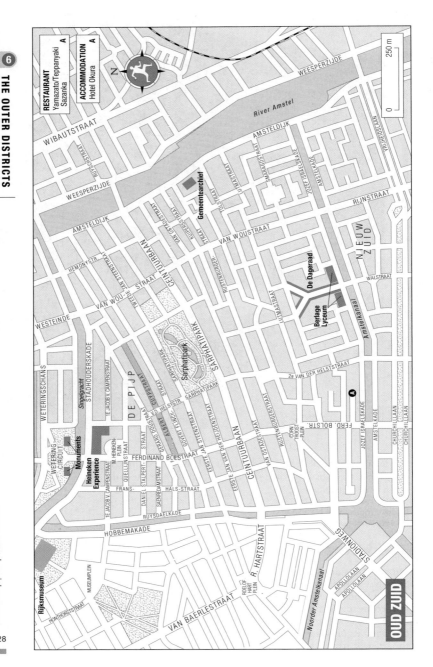

▲ The Heineken Experience

tour, but for many the main draw is the beer itself – although the days when you could quaff unlimited quantities are long gone. Considering it's not a real brewery any more (you won't see any brewing taking place), Heineken make a decent stab at both entertaining and informing – as well as promoting the brand, of course. There are lots of gimmicky but fun attractions, including a whole gallery devoted to Heineken's various advertising campaigns and a weird show on what it's like to be a bottle of Heineken, from bottling plant to delivery. You can also order a bottle of Heineken with your name on it, visit the stables to see the brewer's Shire horses, and star in your own Heineken music video, which you can email to your friends. You also get a free drink at two bar stops along the way. The second stop – at The World Bar – makes a convivial end to the proceedings and they throw in a Heineken glass as a souvenir on the way out.

Freddy Heineken

Heineken may not be the finest lager in the world, but no other brewer, Guinness apart, has thought up such catchy advertising slogans – "Heineken refreshes the parts other beers cannot reach", for one, is well-nigh impossible to beat. **Alfred** (**"Freddy"**) **Heineken** (1923–2002) was the mastermind behind the company's rise to alcoholic success, but his route was far from straightforward. The company was founded in 1864 by Alfred's grandfather, Gerard, but his son and successor, Henry Pierre, sold the family's majority stake in 1942. Freddy didn't like this at all, but he bided his time, working his way up through the company ranks before skilfully amassing a majority shareholding in the 1950s. Chairman from 1979, Freddy ran the company with a beady eye for the main chance, increasing its sales dramatically both at home and abroad, while simultaneously developing a reputation as a playboy, or, more cordially, "bon vivant". Whatever the term, Freddy was hardly subtle; allegedly, the bedroom suite at the back of his office had a four-poster bed, a Jacuzzi and a painting of a naked woman stroking a cat entitled *The Woman with Two Pussies*.

In 1983 Freddy was **kidnapped** by three masked men and held for three weeks, before the police finally rescued him. Thereafter, he withdrew from the public eye, but maintained close relations with many of the country's richest and most powerful citizens until his death.

Albert Cuypstraat and the Sarphatipark

Running south from the Heineken Experience, **Ferdinand Bolstraat** is De Pijp's main drag, but the long, slim, east–west thoroughfare of **Albert Cuypstraat** (pronouced "cowp-straat") is its heart. The general **market** held here – which stretches for over 1km between Ferdinand Bolstraat and Van Woustraat – is the largest in the city (in fact it claims to be the largest in Europe), with a huge range of stalls selling everything from cut-price carrots and raw herring sandwiches to saucepans and Day-Glo thongs. The market is open every day except Sunday, 10am until 5pm. Check out, too, the shops flanking the market on both sides, as they're often cheaper than their equivalents in the city centre.

A couple of blocks south of the Albert Cuypstraat market is the leafy **Sarphatipark**, a welcome splash of greenery amongst the surrounding brick and concrete. The park, complete with footpaths and a slender lake, was laid out before the construction of De Pijp got under way, initially intended as a place for the bourgeoisie to stroll.

Heading east from the Sarphatipark, the main **Ceintuurbaan** artery crosses **Van Woustraat**, a long, if unremarkable shopping street that stretches south to the Amstelkanaal with the Nieuw Zuid (see p.131) beckoning just beyond. Turn right along the northern side of the Amstel canal for De Dageraad; tram #4 runs the length of **Van Woustraat**.

De Dageraad

Best approached along Jozef Israelskade, which runs along the north side of the Amstelkanaal, the **De Dageraad** housing project is a superb and immaculately maintained example of the work of Michael de Klerk and Piet Kramer. Built between 1919 and 1922 on behalf of the ANDB, the Diamond Workers Union, this was – indeed is – public housing inspired by socialist utopianism, a grand vision built to elevate (and educate) the working class, hence its name

– "The Dawn". Overlooking the canal, the handsome brick and stone work of the **Berlage Lyceum** marks the start of De Dageraad with 350 workers' houses stretching beyond to either side of Pieter Lodewijk Takstraat and Burgemeester Tellegenstraat. The architects used a reinforced concrete frame as an underlay to each house, thus permitting folds, tucks and curves in the brick exteriors – a technique known as "apron architecture" (*Schortjesarchitectuur*). Strong, angular doors, sloping roofs and turrets punctute the facades and you'll find a corner tower at the end of every block – it's simply stunning.

From Centraal Station **tram #4** runs along **Van Woustraat**; get off at Jozef Israelskade and it's a five-minute walk to De Dageraad. To get to Apollolaan in the Nieuw Zuid (see below) from De Dageraad, walk south across the canal to Churchilllaan and take tram #12 or #25 west to Ferdinand Bolstraat and walk the remaining 500m.

The Nieuw Zuid

Beyond De Pijp and the Oud Zuid lies the **Nieuw Zuid** (New South), which runs south from the Amstel and Noorder Amstel canals as far as the railway tracks and west from the River Amstel to the old Olympic stadium. By contrast with most of the Oud Zuid, this was the first properly planned extension to the city since the concentric canals of the seventeenth century. The Dutch architect **Hendrik Petrus Berlage** (1856–1934) was responsible for the grand overall plan, but after his death much of the implementation passed to a pair of prominent architects of the **Amsterdam School**, Michael de Klerk (1884–1923) and Piet Kramer (1881–1961), who added a playfulness to the scheme – turrets and bulging windows, sloping roofs and frilly balustrades – that you can still see in some of the buildings today. Neither was this architectural virtuosity confined to the houses of the well-to-do. In 1901 a reforming Housing Act forced the city council into a concerted effort to clear Amsterdam's slums, the principal result being the high-quality public housing that still characterizes parts of the Nieuw Zuid, though the prime examples are elsewhere – one in the Western docklands (see p.92) and another, De Dageraad, in the Oud Zuid (see p.130). Later, cutbacks in the city's subsidy meant that the more imaginative aspects of Berlage's original scheme for the Nieuw Zuid were toned down, but the area's wide boulevards and narrow side streets were completed as conceived. In this, Berlage wanted to reinterpret the most lauded features of the city's seventeenth-century canals – their combination of the grand and spacious with the homely and communal, all in a crisp symmetrical frame.

Nowadays the Nieuw Zuid is one of Amsterdam's most sought-after addresses. **Apollolaan** and its immediate environs are especially favoured, with a string of well-maintained apartment blocks intercepted by the occasional larger house designed in a sort of Arts-and-Crafts-meets-Expressionist style. As with almost any residential area, specific attractions are rare, but there is the **Amsterdam Hilton**, on Apollolaan, where John and Yoko bedded down in 1969, as well as the sprawling parkland of the **Amsterdamse Bos**, just to the southwest of the Nieuw Zuid.

Trams #5 and #24 from Centraal Station run along **Beethovenstraat**, which hits Apollolaan about halfway along. For the Amsterdamse Bos, take tram #16 or #24.

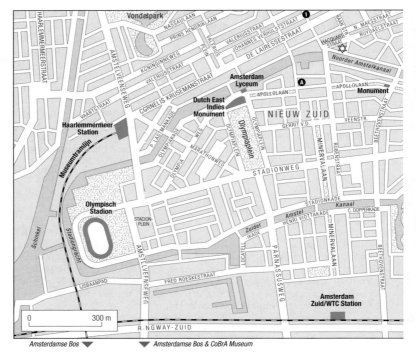

Amsterdamse Bos ▼ ▼ Amsterdamse Bos & CoBrA Museum

Apollolaan and around

Apollolaan, a wide residential boulevard just south of the Noorder Amstel-kanaal, is representative of Berlage's intended grand design, with locals popping to the shops on **Beethovenstraat**, the main commercial drag. Nonetheless, despite its obvious charms the Nieuw Zuid was far from an instant success with the Dutch bourgeoisie. Indeed, in the late 1930s the district became something of a Jewish enclave – the family of Anne Frank, for example, lived for a time on Merwedeplein just off Churchilllaan. This embryonic community was swept away during the German occupation, their sufferings retold in Grete Weil's (Dutch-language) novel *Tramhalte Beethoven-straat*. A reminder of those terrible times is to be found at the intersection of Apollolaan and Beethovenstraat, where a **monument**, built in 1954, commemorates the shooting of 29 resistance fighters here in 1944 in retribution for the killing of a German security officer – a striking monument showing three somberly determined victims.

On a different note, Apollolaan is also known for the canalside **Amsterdam Hilton** at no. 138 (see p.130), a modern high-rise hotel where John Lennon and Yoko Ono staged their famous week-long "Bed-In" for peace in 1969. Part celebrity farce, part skilful publicity stunt – "Hair, Peace; Bed, Peace" signs were plastered all over the place – the couple's anti-war proclamations were certainly heard far and wide, but in Britain the press focused on the supposed evil influence of Yoko on John, which satisfied at least three subtexts – racism, sexism and anti-Americanism. The two megastars stayed in Suite 902/4 – as visitors can still do today.

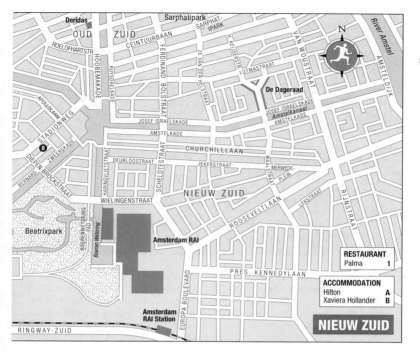

At the west end of Apollolaan is the **Amsterdam Lyceum**, another excellent example of the Amsterdam School of architecture, and in front is a large and bold brick monument of 1955 celebrating the **Dutch East Indies**, an unrepentant tribute to several hundred years of colonialism.

The Amsterdamse Bos

Comprising a substantial chunk of wooded parkland, the **Amsterdamse Bos** (Ⓦ www.amsterdamsebos.nl) is the city's largest open space. Planted during the 1930s, the park was a laudable, large-scale attempt to provide gainful work for the city's unemployed, whose numbers had risen alarmingly following the Wall Street Crash of 1929. Originally a bleak area of flat, marshy fields, it's now a mixture of well-tended city park, leafy waterways, deep woodland and grassy meadows, intersected by foot and cycle paths.

The Museumtramlijn

It's a little more convoluted, but you can also get to the Amsterdamse Bos on the vintage trams of the **Museumtramlijn** (Easter–Oct daily 11am–5pm; every 20–30min; ☏020/673 7538, Ⓦ www.museumtramlijn.org; €4 return). The trams depart from Haarlemmermeer Station, about 500m south of the western tip of the Vondelpark. The Museumtramlijn trams, imported from as far away as Vienna and Prague, clank south along the eastern edge of the Bos to the suburb of Bovenkerk on its southeast corner – a thirty-minute (7km) journey in all, although you can get off earlier at the main entrance to the park or at other stops along the way.

▲ The Amsterdamse Bos

The main **entrance** to the Bos is in the northeast corner of the park, just off Amstelveenseweg at its junction with Van Nijenrodeweg – and around 500m south of the main southern ring road. To get there by public transport from Centraal Station, take **tram** #16 or #24 and get off one stop before the terminus, which is at the hospital. Walking into the park from Amstelveenseweg, it's a couple of minutes to the visitor centre, the **Bezoekerscentrum het Bosmuseum**, at Bosbaanweg 5 (daily noon–5pm; ☎020/545 6100). They have exhibitions on the park's flora and fauna; sell maps and dispense advice on walking and cycling trails; and will tell you where to rent **bikes, canoes and pedaloes** (April–Nov only) – there are outlets close by. From the visitor centre, it's also the briefest of walks to the *Grand Café Bosbaan* (daily 10am till late), which serves drinks, snacks and full meals, and whose terrace overlooks the **Bosbaan** – a dead-straight canal, over 2km long and popular for boating and swimming. Elsewhere in the park there are children's playgrounds and spaces for various sports, including ice-skating, as well as an animal reserve, where a small herd of Scottish Highland cows is allowed to roam in relative solitude.

The CoBrA Museum of Modern Art

The **CoBrA Museum of Modern Art** (Tues–Sun 11am–5pm; €9.50; ☎020/547 5050, ⓦwww.cobra-museum.nl), located well to the south of the Amsterdamse Bos entrance, close to the Amstelveen bus station at Sandbergplein 1, can be reached from the centre by bus #170, #171 or #172. This soothing white gallery, its glass walls giving a view of the canal behind, displays the works of the artists of the **CoBrA movement**, founded in 1948. The movement grew out of comparative artistic developments in the cities of Copenhagen, Brussels and Amsterdam – hence the name. CoBrA's first exhibition, held at Amsterdam's Stedelijk Museum, showcased the big, colourful canvases, with bold lines and forms, for which the movement became famous. Their work displayed a spontaneity and inclusivity that was unusual for the art world of the time and it stirred a veritable hornet's nest of artistic controversy.

You'll only find a scattering of their work here in the gallery, but there's enough to get an idea of what CoBrA were about, not least in Karel Appel's (1921–2006) weird, junky bird sculpture outside, and his brash, childlike paintings inside – in many ways Appel was the movement's leading light. Upstairs, the museum hosts regular temporary exhibitions of works by contemporary artists. There's a good shop, too, with plenty of prints and books on the movement, plus a bright café where you can gaze upon Appel's sculpture at length.

Amsterdam Oost

Next door to Amsterdam's Oud Zuid (Old South), **Amsterdam Oost** (East) is a rough-and-ready working-class quarter that also stretches out beyond the Singelgracht. The area begins with Amsterdam's old eastern gate, the **Muiderpoort** (pronounced "mao-der-port"), overlooking the canal at the end of Plantage Middenlaan. In the 1770s the gate was revamped in pompous style, a Neoclassical refit complete with a flashy cupola and grandiosely carved pediment. Napoleon staged a triumphal entry into the city through the Muiderpoort in 1811, but his arrival was tempered by the behaviour of his half-starved troops, who were so dazzled by a city of (what was to them) amazing luxury that they could barely be restrained from looting. The Oost district has one obvious attraction – the **Tropenmuseum**, near the Muiderpoort and located on the corner of another of the city's municipal parks, the **Oosterpark**.

The Tropenmuseum

Across the Singelgracht canal on Mauritskade rises the gabled and turreted **Royal Tropeninstituut** – formerly the Royal Colonial Institute – a sprawling complex containing the **Tropenmuseum** (daily 10am–5pm; €7.50, 6- to 17-year-olds €4; ☎020/568 8200, ⓦwww.tropenmuseum.nl; tram #9 from Centraal Station), whose entrance is around the side at Linnaeusstraat 2. With its cavernous central hall and three floors of gallery space, this is Amsterdam's ethnographic museum, focusing on all the world's tropical and subtropical zones – which it does incredibly well, with a spectacular collection of art, applied art and other exhibits, displayed in an engaging, modern, yet largely gimmick-free way. Among the many artefacts there are Javanese stone friezes, elaborate carved wooden boats from Papua and New Guinea, a gamelan orchestra, a whole room of ancestral and death masks, and some incredible ritual poles cut from giant New Guinea mangroves. The collection is explained in English and imaginatively presented through a variety of media – slides, DVDs and audio clips – and you can watch everything from Dutch colonials meeting the natives over a hundred years ago to nomads of the Central Asian steppes huddling inside a traditional tent. There are also fun, creative displays devoted to such subjects as music-making, puppetry and traditional storytelling. Perhaps best of all are the museum's studiously authentic reconstructions of contemporary life around the world – a mock-up of a Nigerian bar and residential compound, a Middle Eastern teahouse, a south American café, a Filipino jeepney bus – plus its candid expositions on the problems besetting the developing world, both urban and rural, such as the destruction of the tropical rainforests. The permanent collection is enhanced by an ambitious programme of temporary exhibitions, such as one dealing with Haitian voodoo. There's also a **shop**, with crafts and music

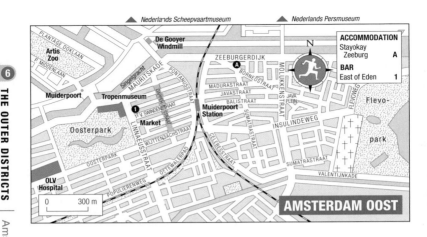

from and books about the developing world, and downstairs, the **Tropentheater** (see p.205) specializes in Third World cinema, music and dance.

The Oosterpark and beyond

Behind the Royal Tropeninstituut, the manicured greenery of the **Oosterpark** is a pleasant introduction to the massed housing that extends south and east. A working-class district for the most part, particularly on the far side of Linnaeusstraat, the area also has a high immigrant presence, and the street names – Javastraat, Balistraat, Borneostraat – recall Holland's colonial past. This is one of the city's poorer neighbourhoods, with a sea of ageing terraced houses, though whole streets have been torn down to make way for new and better public housing. If you find yourself with some time to fill after the Tropenmuseum you might consider a stroll along **Dapperstraat market** (Mon–Sat 9am–5pm), one block east of Linnaeusstraat, the eastern equivalent to the Albert Cuypstraat market (see p.228), though slightly less atmospheric.

Amsterdam ArenA

Not strictly in Amsterdam Oost, but nonetheless on this side of town, the home ground of Ajax, the **Amsterdam ArenA** (museum & stadium tours: April–Sept 5–7 daily 11am–4.30pm; Oct–March Mon–Sat & last Sun of the month 4 daily 11am–4.30pm; €10.50; 1hr 30min; ☎020/311 1336, ⊛www.amsterdamarena.nl) is well worth the fifteen-minute metro trip, both to visit the **Ajax Museum** and to take a tour of the stadium itself. Either take the metro to Strandvliet and walk around the stadium to the main entrance on the far side, or go a stop further on to Bijlmer station, from which the ArenA Boulevard, lined with new shops and cafés, leads to the main entrance. Much as you would expect, the museum is a historical homage to Holland's most successful football club, Ajax, charting its origins at the turn of the twentieth century – lots of photos of men in big shorts in muddy fields – through its various stadia and the evolution of the famous red-and-white strip. There are special shrines to two of the club's most illustrious players – Cruyff and van Basten – as well as a rather sentimental short film depicting the rise to stardom of its leading players. The centrepiece, true to the club's obvious self-image as one of the big hitters of European football (there's relatively little on the domestic league), is a display devoted to Ajax's European campaigns, with tickets, programmes, shirts and footage of the key moments from each final, from their first victory – in 1971 against Panathinaikos – to their most recent. As for the stadium, hour-long walk-in tours are conducted throughout the day in Dutch and English between 11am and 4.30pm, which will impress even the most fair-weather fan, especially if you happen to time it right and get there during training (the Ajax training ground is adjacent to the stadium). Tours take in the main concourses, the press room – where you can snap yourself in front of the sponsors' logos – and the view from up in the security box; you're also allowed onto a strip of the hallowed turf. In fact, the pitch is perhaps the most remarkable thing about the Amsterdam ArenA: the stadium is built in such a way that the grass receives hardly any sunlight and no wind, which means it doesn't drain or grow very well and has to be relaid at least two or three times a year. See p.244, "Sports and activities", for information on seeing a game at the ArenA.

Amsterdam Noord

Amsterdam Noord (North), on the far side of the River IJ, has flourished since the construction of the IJ tunnel linked it with the city centre in the 1960s. A modern suburban sprawl, the district is short on obvious charm, but a more cultured aspect is evolving in the redevelopment of the **NDSM Shipyard**. Reachable by ferry from behind Centraal Station, the former shipyard's cavernous structures now provide studio and exhibition space for artists, and there are plans to develop the area into an arts and events centre. Further out into the countryside the area to head for is the **Waterland**, an expanse of peat meadows, lakes and marshland to the northeast of the built-up area. Until the turn of the twentieth century, this parcel of land was a marshy fen; it was made more tractable by the digging of drainage canals, prompting wealthy Amsterdammers to build their summer residences here. These myriad waterways are home to a wide range of **waterfowl**, as are the many lakes, the largest of which – abutting the Markermeer, formerly part of the Zuider Zee – is the **Kinselmeer**. The best way to explore the Waterland is by **bike**, and the VVV (plus larger bookshops) sells a detailed map – the *Plattegrond van Amsterdam-Noord* (€2.95) – marked with the area's cycle paths. One good trip of about 40km begins at the **IJpleinveer ferry dock** (see box below) on the north side of the IJ, from where you follow Meeuwenlaan to the large roundabout at the start of Nieuwendammerdijk. This long lane leads east, running parallel to the river, before meeting Schellingwoudedijk and then Durger Dammerdijke, at the southern tip of the long dyke that stretches up the coast. You can return to the dock the same way or travel back a little inland.

Ferries across the IJ

There are five GVB public transport **ferries** across the IJ and three of them depart from De Ruyterkade, behind Centraal Station. None of the three takes cars, but all carry foot passengers, bicycles and motorbikes for free. Of the three, the **Buiksloterwegveer** (Mon–Sat 6.30am–10.54pm, till 9pm from Buiksloterweg, Sun 11.06am–6.54pm) shuttles back and forth every twelve minutes or so, running to the foot of Buiksloterweg. The smaller **IJpleinveer** (Mon–Sat 6.27am–11.57pm, Sun 9.12am–11.57pm) connects with the **IJplein** at the southern end of Meeuwenlaan, the starting point of the Waterland bike tour described above; it runs roughly every ten to fifteen minutes.

Day-trips from the city

Amsterdammers always try to persuade you that there's nothing remotely worth seeing outside their city, but the truth is very much the opposite – indeed, you're spoilt for choice. The fast and efficient Dutch railway network puts a whole swathe of the Netherlands within easy reach, including all of the **Randstad** (literally "Ring City"), a sprawling conurbation that stretches south of Amsterdam to encompass the country's other big cities, primarily The Hague, Utrecht and Rotterdam. Amid the urban sprawl, and very close to Amsterdam, is one especially appealing medium-sized town, **Haarlem**, whose attractive centre is home to the outstanding Frans Hals Museum. Further south – about 40km from Amsterdam and 15km from Haarlem – is another enticing attraction, the world–famous **Keukenhof Gardens**, the springtime showcase for the country's flower growers, the land striped by long lines of brilliant blooms. To the north of Amsterdam, there's more countryside and less city. The most obvious targets are the old seaports bordering the freshwater **Markermeer**, comprising the southern part of the IJsselmeer, created when the Afsluitdijk dam cut the former Zuider Zee off from the North Sea in 1932. No trains venture out along this coast, but it's an easy bus ride from Amsterdam to the nearest three places of interest: the former fishing village of **Marken**, the port of **Volendam** and – best of the lot – the beguiling, one-time shipbuilding centre of **Edam**. Edam is, of course, famous for its cheese, but its open-air cheese market is not a patch on that of **Alkmaar**, itself an amiable and attractive small town forty minutes by train north of Amsterdam.

Haarlem

Though only fifteen minutes from Amsterdam by train, **HAARLEM** has a very different pace and feel from its big-city neighbour. It is an easy-going, medium-sized town of around 15,000 souls, benefiting from an old, attractive centre that's easily absorbed in a few hours or an overnight stay. Founded on the banks of the River Spaarne in the tenth century, the town first prospered when the counts of Holland decided to levy shipping tolls here, but later it developed as a cloth-making centre. In 1572 the townsfolk sided with the Protestant rebels against the Habsburgs, a decision they must have regretted when a large Spanish army led by

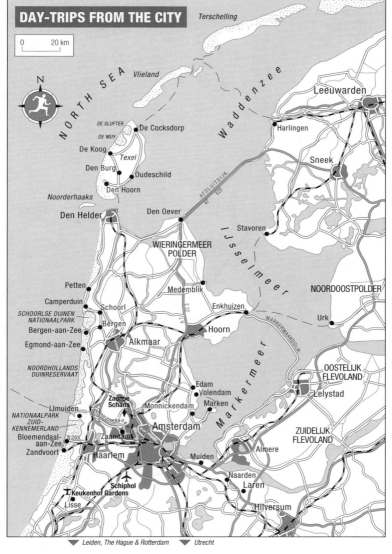

DAY-TRIPS FROM THE CITY

Terschelling

0   20 km

N

NORTH SEA

Vlieland

Waddenzee

Leeuwarden

DE SLUFTER
De Cocksdorp
DE MUY
De Koog
Texel
Den Burg
Oudeschild
Den Hoorn
Noorderhaaks

Harlingen

Sneek

AFSLUITDIJK   A7 E22

Den Helder   *Den Oever*

Stavoren

**WIERINGERMEER
POLDER**

IJsselmeer

NOORDOOSTPOLDER

Petten
Medemblik

Camperduin
Schoorl
SCHOORLSE DUINEN
NATIONAALPARK
Bergen
Enkhuizen
Urk

MARKERWAARDDIJK

Bergen-aan-Zee
Egmond-aan-Zee
Alkmaar   *Hoorn*

NOORDHOLLANDS
DUINRESERVAAT

Markermeer

**OOSTELIJK
FLEVOLAND**

Edam
Volendam
Lelystad
IJmuiden
**Zaanse
Schans**   *Monnickendam*   *Marken*

NATIONAALPARK
ZUID-
KENNEMERLAND
*Bloemendaal-
aan-Zee*
Zaandam
Amsterdam

**ZUIDELIJK
FLEVOLAND**

Zandvoort
Haarlem   *Muiden*

Almere

Naarden
Schiphol   *Laren*
†*Keukenhof Gardens*
Lisse   *Hilversum*

▼ *Leiden, The Hague & Rotterdam*   ▼ *Utrecht*

Frederick of Toledo besieged them later in the same year. The siege was a desperate affair that lasted for eight months, but finally the town surrendered after receiving various assurances of good treatment – assurances which Frederick promptly broke, massacring over two thousand of the Protestant garrison and all their Calvinist ministers. Recaptured in 1577 by the Protestant army of William the Silent, Haarlem went on to enjoy its greatest prosperity in the seventeenth century, becoming a centre for the arts and home to a flourishing school of

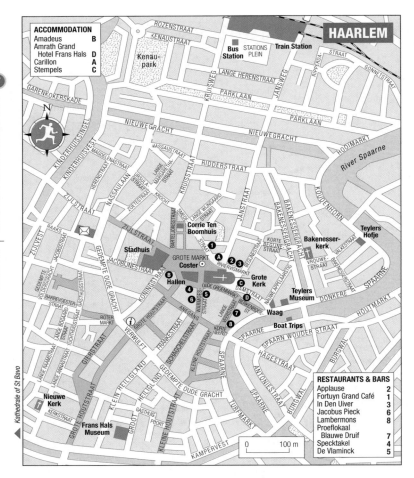

ACCOMMODATION
Amadeus	**B**
Amrath Grand	
Hotel Frans Hals	**D**
Carillon	**A**
Stempels	**C**

RESTAURANTS & BARS
Applause	2
Fortuyn Grand Café	1
In Den Uiver	3
Jacobus Pieck	6
Lambermons	8
Proeflokaal	
Blauwe Druif	7
Specktakel	4
De Vlaminck	5

painters, whose canvases are displayed at the first-rate **Frans Hals Museum**, located in the almshouse where the artist spent his last – and, for some, his most brilliant – years.

Arrival and information

There are fast and very frequent train services between Amsterdam and Haarlem; trains leave every ten minutes or so and take about fifteen minutes. The city's **train station** is just north of the city centre, about ten minutes' walk from the main square, the Grote Markt; **buses** stop just in front. The **VVV** is on the other side of the centre, at Verwulft 11 (April–Sept Mon–Fri 9.30am–5.30pm, Sat 10am–5pm, Sun 11am–3pm; Oct–March same hours, closed Sun; ☎0900/61 61 600, ⊛www.vvvhaarlem.nl), and issues free **city maps** and brochures. **Bike rental** is available at the train station.

Accommodation

The VVV has details of a small number of **rooms in private houses**, mostly on the outskirts of town and costing in the region of €45 per double per night, and can provide hotel information.

Amadeus Grote Markt 10 ☎ 023/532 4530, ⓦ www.amadeus-hotel.com. This homely, medium-sized hotel has plain but perfectly comfortable en-suite rooms for around €80 a double including breakfast. The front bedrooms have pleasant views over the main square.

Amrath Grand Hotel Frans Hals Damstraat 10 ☎ 023/518 1818, ⓦ www.bestwestern.com. Right in the town centre, this modern chain hotel has 79 smart and well-appointed modern rooms for around €100 most of the time, breakfast not included.

Carillon Grote Markt 27 ☎ 023/531 0591, ⓦ www.hotelcarillon.com. Bang on the Grote Markt, this couldn't be more central. Rooms are fine if a little Spartan, but they're well equipped and good value at €80 a double. Triples and quads for around €100.

Stempels Klokhuisplein 9 ☎ 023/512 3910. Housed in a former printworks right behind the Grote Kerk, this is a complex of boutique hotel, bar and restaurant that does its best to be Haarlem's most desirable place to stay. The staff could be friendlier but its doubles for €100–140 are reasonable value.

The Town

At the heart of Haarlem is the **Grote Markt**, a wide and attractive open space flanked by an appealing ensemble of neo-Gothic, Gothic and Renaissance architecture, including an intriguing, if exceptionally garbled, **Stadhuis**, whose turrets and towers, balconies, gables and galleries were put together in piecemeal fashion between the fourteenth and seventeenth centuries. At the other end of the Grote Markt stands a **statue** of a certain **Laurens Coster** (1370–1440), who, Haarlemmers insist, is the true inventor of printing. Legend tells of Coster cutting a letter "A" from the bark of a tree, dropping it into the sand by accident, and, hey presto, he realized how to create the printed word. The statue shows him earnestly holding up the letter concerned, though actually most historians agree that it was the German Johannes Gutenberg who invented printing in the 1440s.

Haarlem's hofjes

You could do worse than spend a day exploring Haarlem's **hofjes** – small, unpretentious complexes of public housing built for the old and infirm in the seventeenth century. The best known and perhaps most accessible is the one that was home to Frans Hals in the last years of his life and is now the museum dedicated to him and his contemporaries. But there are others dotted around town, most of them still serving their original purpose but with their gardens at least open to the public. The most grandiose is the riverside **Teylers Hofje**, a little way east of the museum of the same name around the bend of the Spaarne at Koudenhorn 64. Unlike most of the other *hofjes*, which are decidedly cosy, this is a Neoclassical edifice dating from 1787 and featuring solid columns and cupolas. To the west, the elegant fifteenth-century tower of the **Bakenesserkerk** on Vrouwestraat is a flamboyant, onion-domed affair soaring high above the Haarlem skyline, and marks the nearby **Bakenes Hofje**, Haarlem's oldest, with a delightful enclosed garden. On the other side of the city centre, the **Brouweshofje**, just off Botermarkt, is a small, peaceful rectangle of housing, with windows framed by brightly painted red and white shutters, while the nearby **Hofje Van Loo**, on nearby Barrevoetstraat, is unlike the rest, open to view from the road.

The Grote Kerk

The Coster statue stands in the shadow of the **Grote Kerk**, or Sint Bavokerk (Mon–Sat 10am–4pm; €2), a soaring Gothic structure supported by mighty buttresses, which dwarfs the surrounding clutter of ecclesiastical outhouses. If you've been to the Rijksmuseum in Amsterdam (see pp.113–119), the church may seem familiar, at least from the outside, since it turns up in several paintings of Haarlem by the seventeenth-century artists Berckheyde and Saenredam – only the black-coated burghers are missing. Finished in 1538, and 150 years in the making, the church is surmounted by a handsome lantern tower, which perches above the transept crossing; the tower is made of wood clad in lead, a replacement for a much grander stone tower that had to be dismantled in 1514 when its supports began to buckle.

Entry to the church is at the back, on Oude Groenmarkt, with a humble passageway leading to the southeast end of the **nave**, whose towering beauty is enhanced by the creaminess of the stone and the bright simplicity of the white-washed walls. The Protestants cleared the church of most of its decoration during the Reformation, but the splendid wrought-iron **choir screen** has survived, as have the choir's wooden stalls with their folksy misericords, carved with expressive faces, each one different. In front of the screen is the conspicuous Neoclassical **tomb** of Haarlem's own Christiaan Brunings (1736–1805), a much-lauded hydraulic engineer and director of Holland's water board, who devised a strategy for controlling the waters of the lower Rhine.

Close by, next to the south transept, is the **Brewers' Chapel**, where the central pillar bears two black markers – one showing the height of a local giant, the 2.64-metre-tall Daniel Cajanus, who died in 1749, the other the 0.84-metre-high dwarf Simon Paap from Zandvoort (1789–1828). In the middle of the nave, the pulpit's banisters are in the form of snakes – fleeing from the word of God – while across the other side is the pocket-sized **Dog Whippers' Chapel**, built for the men employed to keep dogs under control in the church, as evidenced by the rings to tether them to, now separated from the nave by an iron grille.

▲ The Grote Kerk, Haarlem

At the west end of the church, the mighty Christian Müller **organ** was manufactured in Amsterdam in the 1730s. It is said to have been played by Handel and Mozart (the latter on his tour of the country in 1766, at the age of ten) and is one of the biggest in the world, with over five thousand pipes and lots of snazzy Baroque embellishment. Hear it at work at one of the free organ recitals held in the summer (mid-May to mid-Oct Tues 8.15pm, July & Aug also Thurs 3pm; free). Beneath the organ, Jan Baptist Xavery's lovely group of draped marble figures represents Poetry and Music offering thanks to Haarlem, which is depicted as a patroness of the arts – in return for its generous support in the purchase of the organ.

The Hallen

Back outside, just beyond the western end of the church, the rambling **Hallen** divides into two; first up is the old meat market, the **Vleeshal**, which boasts a flashy Dutch Renaissance facade and a basement given over to the modest **Archeologisch Museum** (Wed–Sun 1–5pm; free). A couple of doors along is the **Kunstcentrum De Hallen** (Tues–Sat 11am–5pm, Sun noon–5pm; €5), an art gallery where the emphasis is on temporary exhibitions of modern and contemporary art and photography.

The Corrie Ten Boomhuis

After these modest attractions, you'll probably want to push on south to Haarlem's star turn, the Frans Hals Museum (see below), but you might consider a brief detour north from the Grote Markt to the **Corrie Ten Boomhuis**, Barteljorisstraat 19 (April–Oct Tues–Sat 10am–4pm; Nov–March Tues–Sat 11am–3pm; 1hr guided tours only; free; ⓦ www.corrietenboom.com), where a Dutch family – the Ten Booms – hid fugitives, resistance fighters and Jews alike, above their jewellers shop during World War II. There isn't actually much to look at, but the guided tour is instructive and moving, if a tad drawn-out. The family, whose bravery sprang from their Christian faith, was betrayed to the Gestapo in 1944, and only one, Corrie Ten Boom, survived – as does the jewellers itself, still doing business at street level.

The Frans Hals Museum

Haarlem's biggest draw, the **Frans Hals Museum** (Tues–Sat 11am–5pm, Sun noon–5pm; €7.50; ⓦ www.franshalsmuseum.nl), is a five-minute stroll south of the Grote Markt at Groot Heiligland 62; to get there, take pedestrianized Warmoesstraat and keep going. The museum occupies an old almshouse complex, a much-modified red-brick *hofje* with a central courtyard, where the aged Hals lived out his last destitute years on public funds. The collection comprises a handful of prime works by Hals along with a sample of Flemish and Dutch paintings from the fifteenth century onwards, all immaculately presented and labelled in English and Dutch.

The museum begins with a small group of early **sixteenth-century paintings**, the most prominent of which is a triptych from the **School of Hans Memling**. Next door are two works by **Jan van Scorel** (1495–1562): a polished *Adam and Eve* and *Pilgrims to Jerusalem*, one of the country's earliest group portraits, and, beyond that, **Cornelis Cornelisz van Haarlem's** (1562–1638) giant *Wedding of Peleus and Thetis*, an appealing rendition of what was then a popular subject, though Cornelisz gives as much attention to the arrangement of his elegant nudes as to the subject. This marriage precipitated civil war among the gods and was used by the Dutch as an emblem of warning against

Frans Hals

Little is known about **Frans Hals** (c.1580–1666). Born in Antwerp, the son of Flemish refugees who settled in Haarlem in the late 1580s, he has relatively few surviving works – some two hundred paintings, and nothing like the number of sketches and studies left behind by his contemporary, Rembrandt. His outstanding gift was as a portraitist, showing a sympathy with his subjects and an ability to capture fleeting expression that some say even Rembrandt lacked. Seemingly quick and careless flashes of colour characterize his work, but they are always blended into a coherent and marvellously animated whole.

discord, a call for unity during the long war with Spain. Similarly, and in the same room, the same artist's *Massacre of the Innocents* connects the biblical story with the Spanish siege of Haarlem in 1572, while three accomplished pictures by **Hendrik Goltzius** (1558–1617) hang opposite – depictions of Hercules, Mercury and Minerva. Look out also for *Adam and Eve* by the Haarlem painter **Marten van Heemskerck** (1498–1574), whose work dominates the next room, in particular a brutal and realistic *Christ Crowned with Thorns* and a painting of St Luke with the Virgin and infant Jesus, a gift to the Haarlem St Luke's guild. Moving on, the next rooms hold several paintings by the **Haarlem Mannerists**, including two tiny and precise works by **Karel van Mander** (1548–1606), leading light of the Haarlem School and mentor of many of the city's most celebrated painters, including Hals, and depictions of the Grote Kerk by **Gerrit Berckheyde** (1638–98) and others. Look out also for **Pieter Brueghel the Younger**'s (1564–1638) berserk *Dutch Proverbs*, illustrating a whole raft of contemporary proverbs – a detailed key next to the painting gives the lowdown.

The **Hals paintings** begin in earnest in Room 14 with a set of five "Civic Guard" portraits – group portraits of the militia companies initially formed to defend the country from the Spanish, but which later became social clubs for the gentry. With great flair and originality, Hals made the group portrait a unified whole instead of a static collection of individual portraits, his figures carefully arranged, but so cleverly as not to appear contrived. For a time, Hals himself was a member of the Company of St George, and in his *Officers of the Militia Company of St George* he appears second from left in the top left-hand corner – one of his few self-portraits. See also Hals's Haarlem contemporary Johannes Verspronck's (1600–62) *Regentesses of the Holy Ghost Orphanage* – one of the most accomplished pictures in the gallery.

Hals's **later paintings** are darker, more contemplative works, closer to Rembrandt in their lighting and increasingly sombre in their outlook. The artist's *Regents of St Elizabeth Gasthuis* has a palpable sense of optimism, whereas his twin *Regents and Regentesses of the Oudemannenhuis* are quite the opposite – commissioned when Hals was in his eighties, a poor man despite a successful painting career, hounded for money by the town's tradesmen and by the mothers of his illegitimate children. As a result he was dependent on the charity of people like those depicted here: their cold, self-satisfied faces staring out of the gloom, the women reproachful, the men only marginally more affable. There are those who claim Hals had lost his touch by the time he painted these pictures, yet their sinister, almost ghostly power suggests quite the opposite. Van Gogh's remark that "Frans Hals had no fewer than 27 blacks" suddenly makes perfect sense.

The Teylers Museum

It's a short stroll from the Grote Markt to the **River Spaarne**, whose wandering curves mark the eastern periphery of the town centre, home to the surly stone facade of the **Waag** (Weigh House) and the country's oldest museum, the **Teylers Museum**, located in a grand Neoclassical building at Spaarne 16 (Tues–Sat 10am–5pm, Sun noon–5pm; €7; Ⓦ www.teylersmuseum.nl). Founded in 1774 by a wealthy local philanthropist, one **Pieter Teyler van der Hulst**, the museum is delightfully old-fashioned, its wooden cabinets crammed with fossils and bones, crystals and rocks, medals and coins, all displayed alongside dozens of antique scientific instruments of lugubrious appearance and uncertain purpose. The finest room is the **rotunda** – De Ovale Zaal – a handsome, galleried affair with splendid wooden panelling, and there is also a room of nineteenth-century and early twentieth-century Dutch paintings, featuring the likes of Breitner, Israëls, Weissenbruch and Wijbrand Hendriks (1774–1831), who was once the keeper of the art collection here.

Eating and drinking

For a fairly small town, Haarlem has a surprisingly good range of bars, cafés and restaurants, all within easy walking distance of each other.

Applause Grote Markt 23a ☎023/531 1425. A chic little bistro serving Italian food with excellent main courses hovering at around €15. Wed–Sun noon–3pm & 5.30–9.30pm.

Fortuyn Grand Café Grote Markt 21. A popular café-bar with charming 1930s decor, including a tiled entrance and quaint glass cabinets preserved from its days as a shop. Decent food, otherwise a nice place for a coffee or hot chocolate.

In Den Uiver Riviervismarkt 13. Just off the Grote Markt, this lively and extremely appealing brown café is decked out in traditional Dutch café style; it has occasional live music too.

Jacobus Pieck Warmeosstraat 18 ☎023/532 6144. Welcoming café-restaurant that's a good bet for either lunch or dinner, with sandwiches, burgers and salads for €5–8 at lunchtime and a more substantial menu served in the evening. Mon 11am–4pm, Tues–Sat 11am–4.15pm & 5.30–10pm.

Lambermons Korte Veerstraat 51 ☎023/542 7804. Large and comfortable restaurant and brasserie serving both classic Dutch and French food – everything from *bouillabaisse* to *pot au feu*, to oysters and seafood – or just cheese and charcuterie plates if you prefer. Brasserie Tues–Sat noon–10pm, restaurant 6–10pm.

Proeflokaal Blauwe Druif Lange Veerstraat 7. Just off the main square, this is an intimate, typically Dutch bar.

Specktakel Spekstraat 4 ☎023/532 3841. Inventive little restaurant that tries its hand at an international menu – everything from kangaroo through to antelope. For the most part, the main courses are very successful and cost around €17. Daily from 5pm, Sat also noon–4pm.

De Vlaminck Warmoesstraat 3. Decent and very central *friterie* and snack bar if you fancy a lunch on the go. Tues 11.30am–6pm, Sat 11.30am–5pm, Sun noon–5pm.

The Dutch bulbfields

The pancake-flat fields extending south from Haarlem towards Leiden are the heart of the **Dutch bulbfields**, whose bulbs and blooms support a billion-euro industry and some ten thousand growers, as well as attracting tourists in their droves. Bulbs have flourished here since the late sixteenth century, when a certain **Carolus Clusius**, a Dutch botanist and one-time gardener to the

Habsburg emperor, brought the first **tulip bulb** over from Vienna, where it had – in its turn – been brought from modern-day Turkey by an Austrian aristocrat. The tulip flourished in Holland's sandy soil and was so highly prized that it created a massive speculative bubble. At the height of the boom – in the mid-1630s – bulbs were commanding extraordinary prices; the artist Jan van Goyen, for instance, paid 1900 guilders and two paintings for ten rare bulbs, while another set of one hundred bulbs was swapped for a coach and pair of horses. The bubble burst in 1636, thanks to the intervention of the government, and the bulb industry returned to normal, though it left hundreds of investors ruined, much to the satisfaction of the country's Calvinist ministers, who had railed against the excesses.

Other types of bulb were introduced after the tulip, and today the **spring flowering sequence** begins in mid-March with crocuses, followed by daffodils and yellow narcissi in late March, hyacinths and tulips in mid- and late April through to May, and gladicli in August.

The Keukenhof Gardens

The **views** of the bulbfields from any of the trains heading towards Leiden from the north and northeast can often be sufficient in themselves, with the fields divided into stark geometric blocks of pure colour, but with your own transport you can take in their full beauty by way of special **routes** marked by hexagonal signposts; local VVVs (tourist offices) sell pamphlets describing the routes in detail. Alternatively, if you're after bulbs, then make a beeline for bulb growers' showcase, the **Keukenhof Gardens** (late March to late May daily 8am–7.30pm; €13.50; ⓦ www.keukenhof.nl), located on the edge of the little town of **LISSE**, beside the N208 about 15km north of Leiden. The largest flower gardens in the world, dating back to 1949, the Keukenhof was designed by a group of prominent bulb growers to convert people to the joys of growing flowers from bulbs in their own gardens. Literally the "kitchen garden", its site is the former estate of a fifteenth-century countess, who used to grow herbs and vegetables for her dining table. Several million flowers are on show for their full flowering period, complemented – in case of especially harsh winters – by thousands of square metres of glasshouse holding indoor displays. You could easily spend a whole day here, swooning with the sheer abundance of it all, but to get the best of it you need to come early, before the tour buses pack the place. There are several restaurants in the grounds and a network of well-marked footpaths explore every horticultural nook and cranny.

To get to the Keukenhof by **public transport** from Amsterdam, take the train from Centraal Station to Leiden Centraal (every 30min; 40min journey) and then catch **bus #54** (every 30min; 30min journey) from the main bus station next door.

Volendam, Marken and Edam

The turbulent waters of the **Zuider Zee** were once busy with Dutch trading ships shuttling to and from the Baltic. This trade was the linchpin of Holland's prosperity in the Golden Age, revolving around the import of huge quantities of grain, the supply of which was municipally controlled to safeguard against famine. The business was immensely profitable and its proceeds built a string of prosperous seaports – including **Volendam** – and nourished market towns like **Edam**, while the Zuider Zee itself supported a batch of fishing villages such as **Marken**. In the eighteenth century, the Baltic trade declined and the harbours silted up, leaving the ports economically stranded, and, with the rapid increase in the Dutch population during the nineteenth century, plans were made to reclaim the Zuider Zee and turn it into farmland. In the event, the Zuider Zee was only partly reclaimed, creating a pair of freshwater lakes – the **Markermeer** and the **IJsselmeer**.

These placid, steel-grey **lakes** are popular with day-tripping Amsterdammers, who come here in their droves to sail boats, observe the waterfowl, and visit a string of attractive small towns and villages. These begin on the coast just a few kilometres north of Amsterdam with the picturesque old fishing village of Marken and the former seaport of Volendam just up along the coast. From Volendam, it's three kilometres further up the coast to Edam, the pick of the local bunch, a small and infinitely pretty little town of narrow canals and handsome old houses.

There are fast and frequent **buses** from Amsterdam's Centraal Station to Marken, Volendam and Edam, but more poetically, there's a seasonal **passenger ferry**, the Marken Express (see p.148), which skittles along the coast between Marken and Volendam, giving a taste of the pond-like Markermeer. At a bit of a push, all three places can be visited in a day.

Volendam

The former fishing village of **VOLENDAM** is the largest of the Markermeer towns and has had, by comparison with its neighbours, some rip-roaring cosmopolitan times. In the early years of the twentieth century it became something of an artists' retreat, with both Picasso and Renoir spending time here, along with their assorted acolytes. The artists are, however, long gone and nowadays Volendam is, in season, crammed with day-trippers running the gauntlet of the souvenir stalls that run the length of the cobbled main street, whose perky gables line up behind the harbour. The **Volendams Museum**, by the bus stop at Zeestraat 41 (mid-March to mid-Nov daily 10am–5pm; €2.50), has displays of paintings by the artists who have come here over the years, along with mannekins in local costumes and several interiors – a shop, school and living room – as well as the museum's crowning glory – a series of mosaics made from 11 million cigar bands: the bizarre lifetime project of a local Volendam artist. You can see more paintings in the antique-filled public rooms of the *Hotel Spaander*, on the waterfront, whose creaking wooden floors, low ceilings, paintings and sketches are pleasant reminders of more artistic times. The hotel was opened in 1881 and its first owner, Leendert Spaander, was lucky enough to have seven daughters, quite enough to keep a whole bevy of artists in lust for a decade or two. Some of the artists paid for their lodgings by giving Spaander paintings – hence today's collection.

Practicalities

In Volendam, **buses** #110 and #118 from Amsterdam and Monnickendam drop passengers on Zeestraat, just across the street from the **VVV**, at Zeestraat 37 (mid-March to Oct Mon–Sat 10am–5pm; Nov to mid-March Mon–Sat 10am–3pm; ☎0299/363 747, ⓦwww.vvvvolendam.nl). From the VVV, it's a five-minute walk to the waterfront, from where there is a regular **passenger ferry** to Marken (see p.148). If you want to **stay** there's no better place than the *Hotel Spaander*, Haven 15–19 (☎0299/363 595, ⓦwww.hotelspaander.com;

from €120, not including breakfast). The *Spaander*'s bar and restaurant are also good places to **eat**.

Marken

Once an island in the Zuider Zee, **Marken** was, until its road connection to the mainland in 1957, pretty much a closed community, supported by a small fishing industry, but now it welcomes many tourists, whose numbers can reach alarming proportions on summer weekends. That said, there's no denying the picturesque charms of the island's one and only village – also called **MARKEN** – where the immaculately maintained houses, mostly painted in deep green with white trimmings, cluster on top of artificial mounds raised to protect them from the sea.

There are two main parts to the village. **Havenbuurt**, around and behind the harbour, is the bit you see in most of the photographs, where many of the waterfront houses are raised on stilts. Although these are now panelled in, they were once open, allowing the sea to roll under the floors in bad weather, enough to terrify most people half to death. One or two of the houses are open to visitors as typical of Marken, and the waterfront is lined with snack bars and souvenir shops, often staffed by locals in traditional costume, but you do get a hint of how hard life used to be – both here and in **Kerkbuurt**, five minutes' walk from the harbour around the **church**, an ugly 1904 replacement for its sea-battered predecessor. Kerkbuurt is quieter and less touristy than Haven-buurt, its narrow lanes lined by ancient dwellings and a row of old eel-smoking houses, one of which is now the **Marker Museum**, Kerkbuurt 44 (April–Oct Mon–Sat 10am–4.30pm, Sun noon–4pm; Oct Mon–Sat 11am–4pm; €2.50; Ⓦwww.markermuseum.nl), furnished as an old fishermen's cottage and devoted to the history of the former island and its fishing industry.

Practicalities

Marken is accessible direct from Amsterdam by **bus** #111, departing from outside Centraal Station (every 30min); the journey takes forty minutes. The bus drops passengers beside the car park on the edge of Marken village, from where it's a five-minute walk to the lakeshore. Marken does not have a VVV. A **passenger ferry**, the Marken Express (Ⓣ029/936 3331, Ⓦwww.markenexpress .nl; March–Oct daily 11am–5pm, every 30–45min; 25-min journey; €7 return, bikes €2 return), links Marken with Volendam (see p.147), but otherwise travelling between the two means a fiddly bus trip involving a change of buses – and bus stops – at **Monnickendam**, itself a former Zuider Zee port, but now a busy sailing centre. The Amsterdam–Marken bus #111 stops on the southern edge of Monnickendam at the Swaensborch stop, from where it's a ten-minute walk across Monnickendam to the Bernhardbrug stop for bus #110 or #118 north to Volendam and Edam. Just back from the main harbour, the *Hof van Marken* hotel, Buurt II, 15 (Ⓣ0299/601 300), has very comfortable rooms, furnished in a bright contemporary style from €95, and a simple but elegant restaurant, open Wed–Sun for dinner, and lunch and dinner at weekends. The *Land en Zeezicht* restaurant on the harbour at Havenbuurt 6 (Ⓣ0299/601 302) does a decent smoked eel sandwich as well as more substantial meals.

Edam

Just 3km from Volendam, you might expect **EDAM** to be jammed with tourists, considering the international fame of the rubbery red balls of cheese

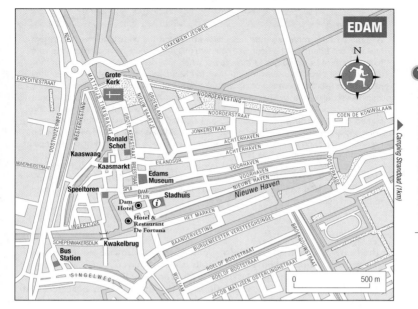

that carry its name. In fact, Edam usually lacks the crowds of Volendam and Marken and remains a delightful, good-looking and prosperous little town of neat brick houses, high gables, swing bridges and slender canals. Founded by farmers in the twelfth century, it experienced a temporary boom in the seventeenth as a shipbuilding centre with river access to the Zuider Zee. Thereafter, it was back to the farm – and the excellent pasture land surrounding the town is still grazed by large herds of cows, though nowadays most **Edam cheese** is produced elsewhere – in Germany, among other places ("Edam" is the name of a type of cheese and not its place of origin). This does, of course, rather undermine the authenticity of Edam's open-air **cheese market**, held every Wednesday morning in July and August on the Kaasmarkt (see p.150), but it's still a popular attraction and the only time the town heaves with tourists.

Arrival and information

Every thirty minutes or so, **buses** #110, #116 and #118 leave from outside Amsterdam's Centraal Station bound for Edam; the journey takes forty minutes. Edam's **bus station** is on the southwest edge of town, on Singelweg, a five- to ten-minute walk from Damplein, where the **VVV**, in the Stadhuis (mid-March to Oct Mon–Sat 10am–5pm, also Sun 1–4.30pm in July & Aug; Nov to mid-March Mon–Sat 10am–3pm; ☎0299/315 125, ⓦwww.vvv-edam .nl), issues town maps and brochures. The VVV also has details of – and takes bookings for – local **boat trips**, both along the town's canals and out into the Markermeer. **Bike rental** is available at Ronald Schot, in the town centre at Grote Kerkstraat 7 (Tues–Fri 8.30am–6pm & Sat 8.30am–5pm; ☎0299/372 155, ⓦwww.ronaldschot.nl); one-day bike rental costs €6.50.

The Edam mermaid

A number of **mermaid legends** have evolved around the coastal towns of northern Holland, but Edam's is the best. In 1403, two milkmaids were rowing across the lake to the north of Edam to get to their cows, when they spied a mermaid, whom they agreed must have been washed up over the sea dyke during a storm. Later, they returned to fish the mermaid out of the lake and, in the way of such things, blushes were saved all round by the layer of seaweed and moss protecting the creature's modesty. Back in town, the mermaid slipped into a dress willingly enough and soon picked up all the necessary domestic and devotional skills, learning how to spin, cook and kiss the crucifix, though some versions of the legend feature a less obliging mermaid who didn't take kindly to her chores and was forever trying to escape. The mermaid is supposed to have lived in Edam for fifteen years and one of the now-demolished town gates was decorated with a mermaid statue in her memory. More important was the municipal subtext; as the legend confirmed, the women of Edam were so kind and the town so pleasant that even a slippery siren was prepared to hole up here.

The Town

At the heart of Edam is **Damplein**, a pint-sized main square alongside which an elongated, humpbacked bridge vaults the Voorhaven canal, which now connects the town with the Markermeer and formerly linked it to the Zuider Zee. The bridge stopped the canal flooding the town, which occurred with depressing regularity, but local shipbuilders hated the thing as it restricted navigation, and on several occasions they launched night-time raids to break it down, though eventually they bowed to the will of the local council.

Facing the bridge is the **Edams Museum** (April–Oct Tues–Sun 10am–4.30pm; €3; ⓦ www.edamsmuseum.nl), which occupies an attractive old house whose crow-stepped gables date back to 1530. Inside, a series of cramped and narrow rooms holds a modest display on the history of the town as well as an assortment of local bygones, including a couple of splendid box-beds. The museum's pride and joy is, however, its **floating cellar**, supposedly built by a retired sea captain who couldn't bear the thought of sleeping on dry land, but actually it was constructed to stop the house from flooding.

Edam's eighteenth-century **Stadhuis** stands on Damplein, a severe Louis XIV-style structure whose plain symmetries culminate in a squat little tower. The ground floor of the Stadhuis is home to the VVV (see p.149). Upstairs is the second part of the Edams Museum (same times & ticket), comprising a handful of old Dutch paintings; the most curious is the portrait of **Trijntje Kever** (1616–33), a local girl who grew to over 2.5m tall – displayed in front of the portrait is a pair of her specially made shoes.

From Damplein, it's a short walk to the rambling **Grote Kerk** (April–Oct daily 2–4.30pm; free), on the edge of the fields to the north of town. This is the largest three-ridged church in Europe, a handsome, largely Gothic structure whose strong lines are disturbed by the almost comically stubby spire, which was shortened to its present height after lightning started a fire in 1602. The church interior is distinguished by its magnificent stained-glass windows – which date from the early seventeenth century and sport both heraldic designs and historical scenes – and by its whopping **organ**.

Stroll back from the church along Matthijs Tinxgracht, just to the west of Grote Kerkstraat, and you soon reach the **Kaasmarkt**, site of the summer **cheese market** (July to mid-Aug Wed 10.30am–12.30pm). It's a good deal humbler than Alkmaar's (see p.154), but follows the same format, with the cheeses laid out in rows before buyers sample them. Once a cheese has been purchased, the cheese porters, dressed in traditional white costumes and straw boaters, spring into action, carrying them off on their gondola-like trays. Overlooking the market is the **Kaaswaag** (Cheese Weighing House), whose decorative panels feature the town's coat of arms, a bull on a red field with three stars. From the Kaasmarkt, it's a couple of hundred metres south to the fifteenth-century **Speeltoren**, an elegant, pinnacled tower that is all that remains of Edam's second most important medieval church, and roughly the same distance again – south along Lingerzijde – to the impossibly picturesque **Kwakelbrug** bridge.

Accommodation, eating and drinking

As regards accommodation, the VVV has a small supply of **rooms in private houses** (averaging €40–50 for a double), which they will book on your behalf for no extra charge. **Hotels** are scarce in Edam, but the charming ⚑ *De Fortuna*, just round the corner from the Damplein at Spuistraat 3 (☎0299/371 671, ⓦ www.fortuna-edam.nl; from €95), is an attractive option. Abutting a narrow canal, this three-star hotel is the epitome of cosiness, its 23 guest rooms distributed among two immaculately restored old houses and three cottage-like buildings round the back. The *Dam Hotel*, Keizersgracht 1 (☎0299/371 766), is also a good option, with a cosy bar and comfortable, attractively furnished rooms from €125. The nearest **campsite**, *Camping Strandbad*, is east of town on the way to the lakeshore at Zeevangszeedijk 7A (April–Sept; ☎0299/371 994, ⓦ www.campingstrandbad.nl;) – a twenty-minute walk east along the canal from Damplein.

For **food**, ⚑ *De Fortuna* also has a first-rate **restaurant**, a lively and eminently agreeable spot decorated in traditional style and with an imaginative, modern menu featuring local ingredients; main courses average around €20. Reservations, especially at the weekend, are essential. The *Dam Hotel* has a nice bar just for a drink or lunch, as well as a decent upscale restaurant and an outside terrace.

▲ Edam waterfront houses

Alkmaar

Forty minutes north of Amsterdam by train, the amenable little town of **ALKMAAR** has preserved much of its medieval street plan, its compact centre surrounded by what was once the town moat and laced with spindly canals. The town is also dotted with fine old buildings, but is best known for its much-touted **cheese market**, an ancient affair that these days ranks as one of the most extravagant tourist spectacles in the province of Noord-Holland. Alkmaar was founded in the tenth century in the middle of a marsh – hence its name, which is taken from the auk, a diving bird which once hung around here in numbers – as in *alkeen meer*, or auk lake. Just like Haarlem, the town was besieged by Frederick of Toledo, but heavy rain flooded its surroundings and forced the Spaniards to withdraw in 1573, an early Dutch success in their long war of independence. At the time, Alkmaar was small and comparatively unimportant, but the town prospered when the surrounding marshland was drained in the 1700s, and it received a boost more recently when the northern part of the old moat was incorporated into the Noordholland-skanaal, itself part of a longer network of waterways running north from Amsterdam to the open sea.

Arrival and information

From Alkmaar's train and bus station, it's a ten-minute walk to the centre of town; outside the station head straight along Spoorstraat, turn left at the end onto Geestersingel and then turn right over the bridge to get to Kanaalkade; keep going along here until you reach Houttil Pieterstraat. This leads straight to the main square, Waagplein, where you'll find the **VVV** (Mon–Fri 10am–5.30pm, Sat 9.30am–5pm; ☎072/511 4284, ⓦ www.vvvalkmaar.nl). They sell a useful town brochure, have details of the area's walking and cycling routes, and can give advice on bike rental. Among several places, **bike rental** is available at the train station and at De Kraak, Verdronkenoord 54 (June–Aug daily 10am–9pm, May Wed–Fri 11am–6pm, Sat & Sun 10am–8pm; ☎072/512 5840, ⓦ www.dekraak.nl), where they also hire canoes and rowing boats. **Rondvaarttocht canal trips** leave the Mient for a quick zip round the town's central waterways – an enjoyable way to spend forty minutes (May–Sept daily, hourly 11am–5pm; April & Oct Mon–Sat, hourly 11am–5pm; 45min; €5.30); tickets are on sale at the VVV.

Accommodation

Alkmaar only takes an hour or two to explore, but if you decide to stay, the VVV has plenty of **rooms in private houses** for around €40 per double per night, including breakfast, though most places are on the outskirts of town. As for **hotels**, the new boutiquey *Grand Hotel Alkmaar*, Gedempte Nieuwesloot 36 (☎072/576 0970), ⓦ www.grandhotelalkmaar.nl), has been stylishly converted from a former post office and has sleek modern rooms from €112.50, including breakfast and free internet access. The *Hotel Pakhuys*, just off Waagplein at Peperstraat 1 (☎072/520 2500, ⓦ www.inonshuys.nl), has lovely canalside doubles from €99, not including breakfast – slightly less in the annex down the street – some with Jacuzzis and kitchenettes, and with free wi-fi.

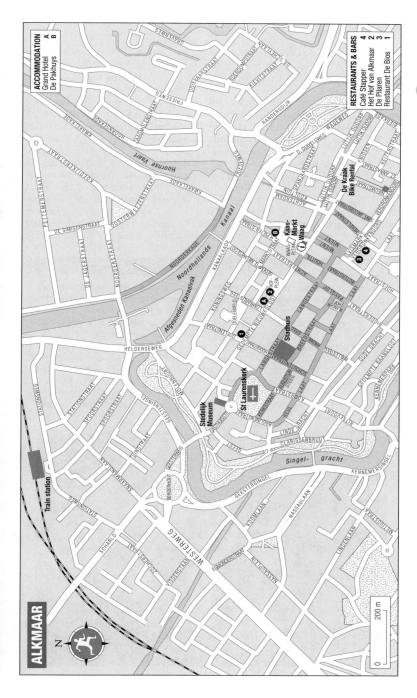

ALKMAAR

N

ACCOMMODATION
Grand Hotel   A
De Pakhuys   B

RESTAURANTS & BARS
Café Stapper   4
Het Hof van Alkmaar 2
De Pilaren   3
Restaurant De Bios   1

Train station

GRAVENWEG

KWAALKADE

De SCHELFHOUT

OUDE VAARTSTRAAT

FRIESEWEG

BOERENSTRAAT

KILVITSSTRAAT

HOORNSE MOLENSTRAAT

HOORNSE KADE

Hoornse Vaart

KOEDIJKERSTRAAT

PETTEMERSTRAAT

De SIMISONSTRAAT

OOSTERWELTERLIJKSTRAAT

De JAGERSTRAAT

NOORDERSTRAAT

Kanaal

Noordhollands

Kanaalvaak

KANAALKADE

Algesneden Kanaalvak

HELDERSEWEG

KONINGSWEG

DOELENVELD

DOELENSTRAAT

GEESTERSINGEL

STATIONSWEG

STATIONSTRAAT

SPOORSTRAAT

SPOORDIJK

SNAARMANSLAAN

LIJNSTRAAT

SCHARLO

ZOCHERSTRAAT

VISSERSTRAAT

BERGERHOF

GEESTERSINGEL

WESTERWEG

KOORLAAN

EGMONDERSTRAAT

NASSAULAAN

NASSAULAAN

LINDENLAAN

MEUSSTRAAT

Singel-gracht

KENNEMERSINGEL

GEESTERSINGEL

KOOMLAAN

CLARISSENBRUU

LINDE GRACHT

GEEST

OUDE GRACHT

GEDEMPTE BAANSLOOT

KENNEMERPARK

RIDDERSTRAAT

HOFSTRAAT

PAULOOG

LAAT

SINT JACOBSTRAAT

VERDRONKENOORD

LUTTIK OUDORP

D. DUIVELSWEG

WAGEWEG

RANDERSDIJK

GROOT NIEUWLAND

DOELENSTRAAT

De Kraak
Bike Rental

LAAT

MIENT

HOUTTIL

St Laurenskerk

Stedelijk
Museum

OOSTERBURG

Stadhuis

LANGESTRAAT

KOORSTRAAT

BREEDSTRAAT

LANGESTRAAT

SCHOUTENSTRAAT

BAGIJNENSTRAAT

HEUL
GRACHT

Kaas-
Markt

Waag

WAAG
PLEIN

HOF
PLEIN

A 2

1

B

www.roughguides.com

153

0   200 m

The Town

Even if you've only come here for the cheese market, it's well worth seeing something of the rest of the town before you leave. On the main square, the **Waag** (Weighing House) was originally a chapel – hence the imposing tower – dedicated to the Holy Ghost, but was converted and given its delightful east gable shortly after the town's famous victory against the Spanish. The **gable** is an ostentatious Dutch Renaissance affair bedecked with allegorical figures and decorated with the town's militant coat of arms. The Waag holds the **VVV** (see p.152) and the **Hollands Kaasmuseum** (April–Oct Mon–Sat 10am–4pm; €3; ⓦ www.kaasmuseum.nl), with displays on – predictably enough – the history of cheese, cheese-making equipment and the like. At the far end of the Waagplein, the **Biermuseum de Boom** (Mon–Sat 1–4pm; €3.50), above the De Boom bar, has three floors devoted to the art of making and distributing beer – no great shakes, but no worse than the cheese museum. In the other direction, at the south end of Mient, the open-air **Vismarkt** (Fish Market) marks the start of the **Verdronkenoord** canal, whose attractive medley of facades and gables leads east to the spindly

Alkmaar's cheese market

Cheese has been sold on Alkmaar's main square since the 1300s, and although it's no longer a serious commercial concern, the **kaasmarkt** (cheese market; Friday 10am–12.30pm, from the first Friday in April to the first Friday in Sept) continues to pull in the crowds – so get there early if you want a good view. The ceremony starts with the buyers sniffing, crumbling, and finally tasting each cheese, followed by intensive bartering. Once a deal has been concluded, the cheeses – golden discs of Gouda mainly, laid out in rows and piles on the square – are borne away on ornamental carriers by groups of four **porters** (*kaasdragers*) for weighing. The porters wear white trousers and shirt plus a black hat whose **coloured bands** – green, blue, red or yellow – represent the four companies that comprise the cheese porters' guild. Payment for the cheeses, tradition has it, takes place in the cafés around the square.

Accijenstoren (Excise Tower), part harbour master's office, part fortification, built in 1622 during the long struggle with Spain. Turn left at the tower along Bierkade and you'll soon reach **Luttik Oudorp**, another attractive corner of the old centre, its slender canal jammed with antique barges.

One block south of the Waag, pedestrianized **Langestraat** is Alkmaar's main and mundane shopping street, whose only notable building is the **Stadhuis**, a florid edifice, half of which (the Langestraat side) dates from the early sixteenth century. At the west end of Langestraat lurks **St Laurenskerk** (early April to early Sept Fri 10am–5pm; June–Aug also Tues–Sat 10am–5pm, Sun noon–5pm; €3), a de-sanctified Gothic church of the late fifteenth century whose pride and joy is its **organ**, commissioned at the suggestion of the diplomat and political bigwig Constantijn Huygens in 1645. The case was designed by Jacob van Campen, the architect who was later to design Amsterdam's town hall (see p.48), and decorated with paintings by **Caesar van Everdingen** (1617–78). The artist's seamless brushstrokes – not to mention his willingness to kowtow to the tastes of the burgeoning middle class – were to make Everdingen a wealthy man. In the apse is the **tomb** containing the intestines of the energetic Count Floris V of Holland (1254–96), who improved the region's sea defences, succoured the poor and did much to establish the independence of the towns hereabouts, until his untimely demise at the hands of his own nobles; the rest of him ended up in Rijnsburg, near Leiden. Nowadays the church hosts exhibitions and Friday lunchtime and Wednesday evening organ concerts during summer.

Across from the church, Alkmaar's cultural centre holds a theatre, offices and a mildly diverting local museum, the **Stedelijk Museum** (Tues–Sun 10am–5pm; €6; ⓦwww.stedelijkmuseumalkmaar.nl), whose three floors focus on the history of the town. Well displayed, but almost entirely labelled in Dutch only, the collection has a short film on the history of the town (in English), and paintings, maps and models of Alkmaar during its glory years in the sixteenth and seventeenth centuries. The many paintings include a typically precise interior of Alkmaar's **St Laurenskerk** by Pieter Saenredam (1597–1665), a striking *Holy Family* by the Mannerist Gerard van Honthorst (1590–1656) and a huge canvas depicting the bloody siege of 1573 by the medievalist Jacobus Hilverdink (1809–64). The top floor explores the history of the town during the twentieth century and hosts a large and well-displayed collection of antique toys along with pictures by local artist Charley Toorop, daughter of the Dutch impressionist Jan Toorop.

Eating and drinking

Alkmaar has a generous scattering of **cafés and restaurants**, and it's not hard to find somewhere decent to eat. *Het Hof van Alkmaar* is pretty good for both lunch and dinner, a delightfully restored medieval nunnery just off Gedempte Nieuwesloot at Hof van Sonoy 1 (daily noon–10pm; ⓣ072/512 1222), with inexpensive omelettes, sandwiches and pancakes for lunch, and at night tasty Dutch cuisine with main courses averaging €15–20; there's an outside terrace too. Just along the street, a good second choice is *Restaurant De Bios*, in modern premises at Gedempte Nieuwesloot 54 (Tues–Wed noon–10pm, Thurs–Sat 10am–1am, Sun noon–10pm; ⓣ072/512 4422), whose menu has a French slant. The *Pakhuys Hotel* has a cool wine bar with a nice selection of bar snacks, as well as a restaurant.

Alkmaar has two main groups of **bars**, one on Waagplein, the other just a couple of minutes' walk away around the Vismarkt. Among the former there's *De Notario*, a big, bustling café that does good lunches and evening meals, and nearby *De Boom*, Houtil 1, a small unpretentious bar with a museum of beer upstairs (see p.154). On the Vismarkt, there's *De Pilaren*, a livelier, more youthful spot catering to a cooler crowd, some of whom take refuge in *Café Stapper* next door if the music gets too much.

Listings

Listings

www.roughguides.com

8

Accommodation

msterdam is one of the most popular tourist destinations in Europe and has the range of hotels you might expect, from handsomely converted old canal houses through to plain and simple places that provide a bed and little more. Given the city's popularity, prices tend to be higher than in most other European cities, especially at peak times of the year – July and August, Easter and Christmas – but whenever you visit it's advisable to book well ahead as vacant rooms can get very thin on the ground. More positively, **prices** are very sensitive to demand, so special **deals and discounts** are commonplace, especially during the week (or on weekends at business-focused hotels), and the city's compactness means that you'll almost inevitably end up somewhere central or within easy reach of the centre. Note also that many of Amsterdam's buildings have narrow, very steep **staircases**, and no lifts; indeed, in the older houses the installing of lifts is actually illegal. If this is a consideration for you, check before you book. Most of the places listed in this chapter have websites and can be booked online, or through the major hotel booking sites – try ⓦwww.hotels.nl. You can also compare prices and availability through the reservation department of the **Amsterdam Tourism & Convention Board** (☎020/551 2525, ⓦwww.iamsterdam.com or www.bookings.nl). Two other useful websites (in Dutch) are ⓦwww.weekendcompany.nl and ⓦwww.weekendjeweg.nl. Once you've arrived, the city's **VVVs** (tourist offices) will make hotel reservations on your behalf, either in advance or on the same day for a nominal fee, but note that during peak periods and weekends they get extremely busy with long and exhausting queues. VVVs also sell an accommodation guide detailing most of the city's hotels; for VVV locations and opening hours, see p.36.

Finally, note that all **directions** given in the listings, including trams, are from Centraal Station (usually abbreviated as "CS"), unless otherwise indicated.

Where to stay

To help you choose a place to stay, the **listings** in this chapter are **divided by area**, using the same headings as in the guide chapters. All of the hostels, hotels and B&Bs are marked on the **colour maps** at the end of the book. For **gay accommodation** listings, see Chapter 12.

If you choose to stay in the **Old Centre**, you'll never have to search for nightlife. Cheap hotels abound in the Red Light District and this is the first place to start looking if money is tight, although women travellers may find it more than a little intimidating. The rest of the Old Centre chips in with many more hotels and all are within easy walking distance of the main sights and principal shopping areas.

Grachtengordel west is only a few minutes' walk from the bustle of Dam Square, but it has a number of quiet canalside hotels, though the least expensive places are concentrated along Raadhuisstraat, one of the city's busiest streets. **Grachtengordel south** is not as appealing a district as its neighbour, but it is ideally positioned for the plethora of nightclubs, bars and restaurants on and around Leidseplein and Rembrandtplein. There are plenty of hotels for all budgets here, including a number of very appealing – and occasionally stylish – options along the surrounding canals.

Staying in the **Jordaan** puts you in among the locals, well away from the prime tourist zones. There's no shortage of bars and restaurants here either, as well as some of the city's prettiest canals, but you'll be at least fifteen minutes' walk from the bright lights. Be aware when looking for a place to stay that Marnixstraat and Rozengracht are busy traffic streets.

Very few tourists stay in the **Old Jewish Quarter**; the streets and canals off the main traffic arteries of Weesperstraat and Plantage Middenlaan are largely residential, with very few bars or restaurants. Consequently, although you're pretty much guaranteed a quiet night's sleep here, you'll be a tram ride away from any of the leading sights.

The main reason for staying out of the centre in the **Museum Quarter** is to be close to the city's two premier museums – the Van Gogh and the Rijksmuseum – although the nightlife around Leidseplein is also within easy striking distance. There are no canals in the area, and two of the main drags, Overtoom and 1e Constantijn Huygensstraat, constantly rumble with traffic, but there are several particularly good hotels on quiet, leafy side streets, as well as two of the city's best hostels on the edge of the leafy Vondelpark.

There's not too much reason to venture out into the city's far-flung suburbs, but the **outer districts** do possess two noteworthy hotels (see p.169).

Hotels and B&Bs

The Amsterdam Tourism & Convention Board classifies all of the city's recognized hotels into five categories, with five stars the most luxurious, one star the most basic. The stars are allocated according to set criteria – if reception is open 24hrs for example – and this relates to the price, but location and aesthetics are not, indeed cannot be, graded. Amsterdam's **hotels** start at around €80 but at the lower end of the market you have to be careful – some of the least expensive rooms can be very grim, though at least some form of **breakfast** – "Dutch" (ham, bread and jam) or "English" (eggs, ham, bread and jam) – is normally included in the price. Consequently, it's advisable to ask to see the room before you slap down any money, and if you don't like it, refuse it. Note too that with some of the independently run hotels the cheapest rooms often have **shared facilities**, and en-suite rooms, if available, could be an extra €10–20. A significant number of hotels in Amsterdam have large three- or four-bed family rooms available from €180. **B&Bs** are on the increase; those listed are among the best.

Prices given below are, unless otherwise indicated, for the high (summer) season, though Amsterdam is such a popular spot that you can't assume you'll pay much less in the winter.

Old Centre

Bellevue Martelaarsgracht 10 ☎020/707 4500, ⊛www.bellevuehotel.nl. **Two-minute walk from CS.** All rooms are decorated in a modern style and the location couldn't be more convenient. Prices start at around €160 for a double, not including breakfast.

Botel Amstel Moored at Oosterdokskade 2 ☎020/626 4247, ⊛www.amstelbotel.com. **Five-minute walk from CS.** The idea of a floating hotel may seem romantic – especially in houseboat-heaven Amsterdam – but the 175 identically decorated rooms here are poky and connected by claustro-phobic corridors. Something a bit different certainly, but you might find staying here is a bit like spending your holiday on a cross-Channel ferry. The well-equipped bar has internet access and stays open until 12.45am. Prices depend on whether you want a view of the water or not, but rooms are at least cheap, at €90–100 for a double, and around €120 for a triple (with bunk bed).

Convent NZ Voorburgwal 67 ☎020/627 5900, ⊛www.theconventamsterdam.com. Not quite as atmospheric as the name suggests, but it's very well placed, 5min from Centraal Station and Dam Square, and occupies a historic building, formerly home to a newspaper and a number of medieval residences. Its 148 rooms admittedly don't exude a lot of character, but they're comfortable and well equipped and there are frequently deals on offer, and not just on weekdays. There's a nice downstairs bar too.

The Crown Oudezijds Voorburgwal 21 ☎020/626 9664, ⊛www.hotelthecrown.com. **Five-minute walk from CS.** This is really a hotel for single people, and its pricing policy – €40–70 per person – reflects that. The rooms at the back are dark and a bit austere; the ones at the front are nicer, but prone to noise from the busy canal outside. Very safe despite its location right in the middle of the Red Light District. The 24-hour bar has a pool table and amiable staff. Triples, quads and six-person rooms are also available.

Doelen Nieuwe Doelenstraat 24 ☎020/554 0600, ⊛www.nh-hotels.com. **Tram #4, #9, #16, #24 or #25 to Muntplein.** Famous as the hotel where Rembrandt painted *The Night Watch* (see p.118), and with a stately elegance about it that might appeal if your budget won't stretch to the *Hotel de l'Europe* along the water. It's smaller than it looks from the outside, and has a nice breakfast room overlooking the water. Doubles €220–300, not including breakfast – though deals abound, especially at weekends.

France Oudezijds Kolk 11 ☎020/535 3777, ⊛www.florishotels.com. **Five-minute walk from CS.** A friendly hotel located on a tiny and little-trafficked canal just off the burgeoning Zeedijk; both the lobby and the rooms have been redone in a brisk Ikea style. Its decent-sized doubles range between €95 and €195, with bath and breakfast; wi-fi access is free in every room.

De Gerstekorrel Damstraat 22–24 ☎020/624 9771, ⊛www.gerstekorrel.com. **Tram #4, #9,**

Accommodation prices

The hotel and guesthouse prices in this book are given for the cheapest double room available during the high season, and, unless indicated otherwise, include breakfast. Single rooms, where available, usually cost between sixty and eighty percent of the price of a double. For hostel accommodation, the price per person for a dorm bed is given. Hotel prices vary enormously with availability. For example, the official rack rate for a double room at the *Hotel Arena* (see p.167) is €289, but when booked at least 21 days in advance the price can go down as low as €99, so doing a bit of research before you go is well worthwhile.

#16, #24 or #25 to Dam Square. Pretty functional rooms, and at €169 for a double, not really cheap. Still, much of the time you will pay less than this, and as there are no common areas you get to eat the inclusive breakfast in bed whether you like it or not. No lift.

Grand Oudezijds Voorburgwal 197 ⊕020/555 3111, ⊛ www.thegrand.nl. Tram #4, #9, #16, #24 or #25 to Dam Square. Originally a Royal Inn dating from 1578, and after that the Amsterdam Town Hall, this fine classical building is one of the city's architectural high points, and now part of the Sofitel chain. The rooms are large, well appointed and boldly decorated in crisp, modern style. There are all the usual facilities you would expect from a five-star hotel, including a spa with indoor pool and Turkish bath and a Roux brothers restaurant on site. Official rates start at €420, excluding five percent tax and breakfast, which is a whopping €30 extra, but special deals are abundant.

Grand Hotel Krasnapolsky Dam 9 ⊕020/554 9111, ⊛ www.nh-hotels.com. Tram #4, #9, #16, #24 or #25 to Dam Square. Located in a huge, striking mid-nineteenth-century building, this four-star hotel occupies virtually an entire side of Dam Square. Its rooms are attractively decorated, if unspectacular, and doubles go for €200–250 (no breakfast), though bargains are sometimes available.

Hotel de l'Europe Nieuwe Doelenstraat 2–8 ⊕020/531 1777, ⊛ www.leurope.nl. Tram #4, #9, #16, #24 or #25 to Muntplein. One of the

▲ Hotel de l'Europe

city's top hotels, it retains a wonderful *fin-de-siècle* charm, with large, well-furnished rooms, an attractive riverside terrace and a great central location. Standard doubles are €445, and an extra €50 for a river Amstel view, but this is about as luxurious as the city gets and last-minute bargains are plentiful. At the time of writing they had a major renovation and expansion coming up.

Hotel des Arts Rokin 154–156 ⊕020/620 1558, ⊛ www.hoteldesarts.nl. Tram #4, #9, #16, #24 or #25 to Muntplein. This hotel's 22 rooms are cosy and well furnished and the welcome is friendly. Prices start at around €138 including breakfast, though the larger canal-facing rooms are around €158.

Le Coin Nieuwe Doelenstraat 5 ⊕020/524 6800, ⊛ www.lecoin.nl. Tram #4, #9, #16, #24 or #25 to Muntplein. In a good location opposite the swanky *Hotel de l'Europe*, but a quarter of the price, with doubles starting at €139, and breakfast an extra €11.50. All rooms have kitchenettes and are kitted out in contemporary style.

Misc Kloveniersburgwal 20 ⊕020/330 6241, ⊛ www.hotelmisc.com. Metro Nieuwmarkt or a 10min walk from CS. Very friendly hotel on the edge of the Red Light District with six good-sized rooms, each elegantly decorated in a different theme. The bright breakfast area overlooks the canal and is great for people-watching. Wi-fi connection. Rates start at €145, including an excellent breakfast – great value.

Nes Kloveniersburgwal 137–139 ⊕020/624 4773, ⊛ www.hotelnes.nl. Tram #4, #9, #16, #24 or #25 to Muntplein. Pleasant and quiet hotel with helpful staff. Well positioned away from noise but close to shops and nightlife. The size and quality of the rooms can vary quite a bit, so don't be afraid to ask to see other rooms if you're disappointed. Prices vary too: they start at €80, but you can reckon on paying €130–150 for a double room, and triples and quads are available at €80–135.

NH City Centre Spuistraat 288 ⊕020/420 4545, ⊛ www.nh-hotels.com. Tram #1, #2 or #5 from CS to Spui. This appealing chain hotel occupies a sympathetically renovated 1920s Art Deco former textile factory, and is well situated for the cafés and bars of the Spui, and the Museum Quarter. Rooms vary in size, some have canal views, and all boast extremely comfy beds and good showers.

There are often deals available, but doubles generally go for around €150 in high season. The buffet breakfast is extra (€18), but will set you up for the day.

Rho Nes 5 ☎020/620 7371, ✺www.rhohotel .com. Tram #4, #9, #16, #24 or #25 to Dam Square. Built as a theatre in 1908, the lovely, high-ceilinged, *fin-de-siècle* lobby gives a slightly misleading impression: the rooms are on the small side and have been unimaginatively modernized. Still, it's pleasant enough, and in a good central location just off Dam Square. Doubles from €115, including buffet breakfast. Daily bike rental available.

Rokin Rokin 73 ☎020/626 7456, ✺www .rokinhotel.com. Tram #4, #9, #16, #24 or #25 to Rokin. This conveniently located three-star family hotel has small, modern doubles with exposed beams, some singles, and two triples. Breakfast (included) is served in the pleasant basement room and free wireless is available. Lift access to three of the four floors. The private car park is a handy bonus. €115–155.

Sint Nicolaas Spuistraat 1a ☎020/626 1384, ✺www.hotelnicolaas.nl. Five-minute walk from CS. With more character than many of the other budget hotels in the area, the *Sint Nicolaas's* cosy downstairs bar-reception gives way to around thirty smartly refurbished rooms, all with baths and flatscreen TVs, which are around €180 in high season. Very conveniently located, too.

Victoria Damrak 1–5 ☎020/623 4255, ✺www .parkplaza.com. Two-minute walk from CS. This tall, elegant building opposite Centraal Station has been one of the city's best hotels for years, but really needed its recent renovation to revamp the fusty decor. The bar has been done up and the rooms are well on their way, all to be able to compete with the crop of sleek options that has appeared in recent years. Its location couldn't be more convenient, and there are often bargains to be had in its nicely decorated rooms; amenities include a fitness centre and pool. The cheapest doubles are about €200–300, not including breakfast.

Vijaya Oudezijds Voorburgwal 44 ☎020/626 9406, ✺www.hotelvijaya.com. Ten-minute walk from CS. Right in the heart of the Red Light District, next door but one to the Amstelkring (see p.58), this is a warren of rooms spread over a couple of old canal houses. It's rather threadbare, but not bad for the €85–110 price for a double. No lift.

Winston Warmoesstraat 129 ☎020/623 1380, ✺www.winston.nl. Ten-minute walk from CS. This self-consciously young and cool hotel has funky rooms individually decorated with wacko art, and a busy ground-floor bar that has occasional live music. It's a formula that works a treat; the Winston is popular and often full – though this is probably also due to its low prices: €80–100 for a double, with breakfast, for the cheapest rooms during the week and €120–160 for triples and quads. Rooms are light and airy, some en suite, some with a communal bathroom. Erotic images abound in some, so if you're travelling as a family you might want to check first to prevent any embarrassing questions. Also dorm beds from €29. Lift and full disabled access.

Grachtengordel west

Agora Singel 462 ☎020/627 2200, ✺www .hotelagora.nl. Tram #1, #2 or #5 to Koningsplein. Handily located, small and amiable hotel near the flower market and close to the Spui. The guest rooms here, of which there are just sixteen, are kitted out in simple, basic style and vary greatly in size. As well as doubles, three- and four-bed rooms are available, and there's a large breakfast room too. Rooms cost upwards of €132, €145 with a canal view and breakfast included.

Ambassade Herengracht 341 ☎020/555 0222, ✺www.ambassade-hotel.nl. Tram #1, #2 or #5 from CS to Spui. Elegant canalside hotel made up of ten seventeenth-century houses, with smartly furnished lounges, a well-stocked library and comfortable recently revamped en-suite rooms from €195 and suites from €275. Friendly staff and free 24-hour internet access. Breakfast is an extra €16, but well worth it.

Chic & Basic Herengracht 13 ☎020/522 2345, ✺www.chicandbasic.com. Ten-minute walk from CS. Dutch branch of this spunky Spanish concept, offering 26 basic but cool rooms, some of them overlooking the canal. The changeable lighting system allows you to adjust the colouring of the room according to your mood. Rates start at €125, breakfast an extra €7.50.

Clemens Raadhuisstraat 39 ☎020/624 6089, ✺www.clemenshotel.com. Tram #13 or #17 from CS to Westermarkt. Friendly, well-run

▲ Dylan

budget hotel, with knowledgeable owner, close to the Anne Frank Huis, this is one of the better options along this busy main road. Individually decorated doubles without shower from €75, with shower from €120; breakfast included. All rooms offer free internet connection, and you can rent laptops for just a few euros.

Dylan Keizersgracht 384 ☏ 020/530 2010, ⓦ www.dylanamsterdam.com. **Tram #1, #2 or #5 from CS to Leidsestraat/Keizersgracht.** This stylish hotel is housed in a seventeenth-century building that centres on a beautiful courtyard and terrace. Its 41 sumptuous rooms range in style from opulent reds or greens to minimal white and oatmeal shades, and have flat-screen TVs and stereos. The restaurant offers modern French cuisine and the bar is open to non-guests. The ambiance is hip without being pretentious, and that goes for the staff too, making it popular with many guests returning. Luxury suites overlooking the Keizersgracht canal will set you back €1700; standard doubles from €475. Breakfast €28 extra.

Estherea Singel 303–309 ☏ 020/624 5146, ⓦ www.estherea.nl. **Tram #1, #2 or #5 from CS to Spui.** This enjoyable and very comfortable four-star hotel occupies a pair of sympathetically modernized old canal houses in a great location, a brief stroll from the Spui. There's no hankering after minimalism here – the carpets are thick and plush, the public areas rich in browns and reds. The guest rooms are similar in style, with beds that you can literally sink into, and

the pick of them overlook the canal. Free internet access. Official rates are around €260 excluding tax and breakfast (an extra €16), but when booked well in advance you can find a room as low as €130.

Hegra Herengracht 269 ☏ 020/623 7877, ⓦ www.hegrahotel.nl. **Tram #1, #2 or #5 from CS to Spui.** Welcoming atmosphere and relatively inexpensive for the location, on a handsome stretch of canal near the Spui. Rooms are small but comfortable, either en suite or with shared facilities. Doubles from €84 with breakfast, with private shower but shared toilet.

Hoksbergen Singel 301 ☏ 020/626 6043, ⓦ www .hotelhoksbergen.nl. **Tram #1, #2 or #5 from CS to Spui.** Standard-issue hotel, with a light and open breakfast room overlooking the Singel canal. Basic and rather charmless en-suite rooms, all with telephone and TV, from €98 for the smallest room to larger doubles for €125; breakfast and tax included. Self-catering apartments too from €120.

't Hotel Leliegracht 18 ☏ 020/422 2741, ⓦ www.thotel.nl. **Tram #13 or #17 to Westermarkt.** Extremely appealing, low-key hotel located in an old high-gabled house along a quiet stretch of canal. The eight spacious rooms – three with canal views – are decked out in a pleasant and unassuming modern style with large beds, TV, fridge and either bath or shower. Minimum three-night stay at the weekend (Thurs–Mon). Extremely friendly and helpful staff/owners. Doubles from €145.

Pax Raadhuisstraat 37 ☏ 020/624 9735. **Tram #13 or #17 to Westermarkt.** Straightforward, city-centre cheapie with a mixture of fair-sized rooms sleeping one to four people; all finished in a minimalist style. As with most of the hotels along this busy stretch, ask for a room at the back. Doubles from €70, free wireless but no breakfast.

Pulitzer Prinsengracht 315 ☏ 020/523 5235, ⓦ www.starwood.com. **Tram #13 or #17 to Westermarkt.** An entire row of seventeenth-century canal houses creatively converted into a prestigious, five-star hotel. The recently renovated rooms are all done up in soft tones, some overlooking the inner courtyard, others with canal views. Very popular with visiting business folk. Luxury doesn't come cheap though, with doubles starting at €300.

Singel Hotel Singel 13 ☏ 020/626 3108, ⓦ www.singelhotel.nl. **Five-minute walk from CS.** Pleasant hotel located in three charming canal houses right next to the old Lutheran church. The rooms are rather small, but well equipped, some overlooking the Singel. Rates from €139, breakfast included.

The Times Hotel Herengracht 135 ☎020/330 6030, ⊚www.thetimeshotel.nl. Tram #1, #2 or #5 from CS to Spui. Colourful design hotel with a wink to old Dutch masters – each room contains gigantic paintings of Vermeer, Rembrandt or Van Gogh. Doubles around €159, excluding breakfast (an extra €10).

Toren Keizersgracht 164 ☎020/622 6033, ⊚www.hoteltoren.nl. Tram #13 or #17 from CS to Westermarkt. Cosy, retro-chic boutique hotel, converted from two elegant canal houses (one of which was once the home of the Dutch prime minister), where the emphasis is on intimacy and comfort. All rooms have been recently renovated, and there's an annex if the main building is full. There's also a nice bar/breakfast room downstairs and they offer a specially adapted menu from nearby *Christophe* if you want to eat in the evening. Very attentive and friendly staff too. Doubles €160–260, depending on season and canal views.

Wiechmann Prinsengracht 328–332 ☎020/626 3321, ⊚www.hotelwiechmann.nl. Tram #13 or #17 to Westermarkt. Family-run for over fifty years, this medium-sized hotel occupies an attractively restored canal house, close to the Anne Frank Huis, with dark wooden beams and restrained style throughout. Large, bright rooms are in perfect condition – be it a bit old-fashioned – with TV and shower, and cost €140, €20 more for a canal view. Prices stay the same throughout the year.

Grachtengordel south

Backstage Hotel Leidsegracht 114 ☎020/624 4044, ⊚www.backstagehotel.com. Tram #1, #2 or #5 to Prinsengracht. Hotel aimed to accommodate musicians playing at the nearby Melkweg or Paradiso. Furnishings such as theatre mirrors, PA spotlights and flight cases in the 22 newly decorated rooms are bound to make them feel at home, but non-musicians are also welcome. Facilities include free internet, a 24-hour bar and pool table. Rooms from €100.

Carlton Amsterdam Vijzelstraat 4 ☎020/622 2266, ⊚www.nh-hotels.com. Tram #4, #9, #16, #24 or #25 to the Muntplein. Next door to the flower market, this large, four-star chain

hotel has over two hundred well-appointed bedrooms equipped with standard modern fittings and furnishings. Some of the "deluxe" rooms on the top floor have balconies and grand views over the city centre. Prices vary enormously, but you can reckon on paying between €150 and €250 for a double.

Dikker & Thijs Fenice Prinsengracht 444 ☎020/620 1212, ⊚www.dtfh.nl. Tram #1, #2 or #5 to the corner of Prinsengracht and Leidsestraat. Small and stylish hotel not far from Leidseplein. The modern rooms vary in decor but all include minibars, telephones and TVs; those on the top floor offer a good view of the city. Standard doubles from €160, breakfast excluded.

Eden Amsterdam American Leidsekade 97 ☎020/556 3000, ⊚www.amsterdamamerican .com. Tram #1, #2 or #5 to Leidseplein. This landmark Art Deco hotel, dating from 1902, was once the height of chic; the high rollers have since moved on, and the bedrooms are now standard-issue modern affairs, but they are large and comfortable, with double-glazed windows (a useful addition, since the hotel is just off Leidseplein). Doubles from as little as €150 if booked well in advance.

Marcel van Woerkom Leidsestraat 87 ☎020/622 9834, ⊚www.marcelamsterdam .com. Tram #1, #2 or #5 to Prinsengracht. Popular guesthouse run by an English-speaking graphic designer and artist, who attracts like-minded people to this stylishly restored house. This is a relaxing and

▲ Toren

▲ Marcel van Woerkom

peaceful haven from the buzz of the city, with regulars returning year after year, so you'll need to book well in advance in high season. Four en-suite doubles, including one with private patio garden, available for two, three or four people sharing. No breakfast, but there are tea- and coffee-making facilities. Rates start at €130 for a double, with a minimum of two nights.
Prinsenhof Prinsengracht 810 ☎020/623 1772, ⓦwww.hotelprinsenhof.com. **Tram #4 from CS to Prinsengracht.** Tastefully decorated, this is one of the city's top budget options with doubles for €69 without shower, €89 with. With only eleven spacious rooms, booking ahead is essential.
Rembrandt Square Hotel Amstelstraat 17 ☎020/890 4740, ⓦwww.edenhotelgroup.com. **Tram #4 or #9 to Rembrandtplein.** Minimalist four-star hotel with an urban feel, located just off the busy Rembrandtplein. The 166 rooms are all well equipped and tastefully decorated in grey shades. Room rates from €175. Alternatively, the *Eden Hotel Amsterdam*, a slightly less expensive branch of the Eden group, is just around the corner on the river Amstel.
Schiller Rembrandtplein 26–36 ☎020/554 0700, ⓦwww.nh-hotels.com. **Tram #4 or #9 to Rembrandtplein.** Once something of a hangout for Amsterdam's intellectuals, the *Schiller*, named after the painter and

architect, still has one of the city's better-known brasseries on its ground floor decorated in fetching Art Deco style. The drawback is its location – on tacky Rembrandtplein – but if you're here to sample a few of the city's nightclubs, the Muziektheater or the shops along Leidsestraat, you couldn't be better situated. Rates without breakfast begin at around €200 although discounts are available.
Seven Bridges Reguliersgracht 31 ☎020/623 1329, ⓦwww.sevenbridgeshotel.nl. **Tram #16, #24 or #25 to Keizersgracht.** One of the city's most charming hotels – and excellent value for money too. Takes its name from its canalside location, which affords a view of no fewer than seven quaint little bridges. Beautifully decorated in antique style, its spotless rooms are regularly revamped, and it's small and popular, so advance reservations are pretty much essential. Breakfast is served in your room. Rates start at €110 per double, and vary with the view.
Weber Marnixstraat 397 ☎020/627 2327, ⓦwww.hotelweber.nl. **Tram #1, #2 or #5 from CS to Leidseplein.** Seven spacious rooms decorated in a brisk, modern style above a popular bar, mainly attracting a youthful clientele. Rooms from €125, with a small in-room breakfast included.

The Jordaan and Western docklands

Acacia Lindengracht 251 ☎020/622 1460, ⓦwww.hotelacacia.nl. **Bus #18 to Willemstraat, or a 15min walk from CS.** This small hotel, situated in the heart of the Jordaan, is on a corner, so some of the rooms have sweeping views of the canal and its adjoining streets. The pastel-pink rooms, which sleep two to four people, are rather nondescript with small beds and a shower room. Doubles from €90, including breakfast; there are also self-catering studios (€100).
Van Onna Bloemgracht 102 ☎020/626 5801, ⓦwww.hotelvanonna.nl. **Tram #13 or #17 from CS to Westermarkt.** A quiet, well-maintained place on a tranquil canal. The building dates back over three hundred years and still retains some of its original fixtures, though the rooms themselves are rather modest, with basic furniture and blankets on beds. Simple set-up – no TV, no smoking and cash payment only. Booking advised.

Rooms sleeping up to four people for €45 per person, including breakfast.

The Old Jewish Quarter and Eastern docklands

Adolesce Nieuwe Keizersgracht 26 ☎020/626 3959, ⓦ www.adolesce.nl. **Tram #9 from CS to Waterlooplein.** Popular and welcoming hotel in an old canal house not far from Waterlooplein. There are ten neat and trim modern rooms and a large dining room. Doubles €100; triples also available for €120. Closed Nov–March. No breakfast but all day coffee and tea facilities.

Hotel Arena 's Gravesandestraat 51 ☎020/850 2400, ⓦ www.hotelarena.nl. **Metro to Weesperplein, then an 8min walk.** A little way east of the centre, in a renovated old convent on the edge of the Oosterpark, this place, formerly a popular hostel, is a hip three-star hotel, complete with split-level rooms and minimalist decor. Despite the odd pretentious flourish, it manages to retain a relaxed vibe attracting both businesspeople and travellers alike. Lively bar, intimate restaurant, and late-night club (Fri & Sat) located within the former chapel. Official rates start at €289 but you will usually pay half, sometimes even less when booked well in advance or very last minute. Breakfast is an extra €16.

InterContinental Amstel Professor Tulpplein 1 ☎020/622 6060, ⓦ www.intercontinental.com. **Metro Weesperplein.** The absolute top of the range – one of the best and most luxurious hotels in the country, occupying a grand, chateau-style, nineteenth-century mansion beside the Singelgracht canal, and favoured by visiting celebrities. If you have the means, splash out; cheapest doubles from €450.

Lloyd Hotel Oostelijke Handelskade 34 ☎020/561 3636, ⓦ www.lloydhotel.com. **Tram #26 from CS; three-minute walk from the Rietlandsparken stop. See map, p.111.** Situated in the up-and-coming Oosterdok (Eastern Docklands) district, this ex-prison and migrant workers' hostel has been renovated to become one of Amsterdam's slickest hotels. Rather pretentiously subtitled a "cultural embassy", it has an arts centre too, with regular exhibitions, readings and performances, an art library, and a nice, bustling feel that revolves around its airy central restaurant and lobby area on the ground floor. Uniquely, it serves all kinds of travellers, with rooms ranging from one-star

affairs for €100 to €340 offerings. Some rooms are great, others not, so don't be afraid to ask to change. The location is better than you might think – just 5min by tram from Centraal Station – but at these prices you still might prefer to be in the centre.

The Museum Quarter and Vondelpark

Acro Jan Luyckenstraat 44 ☎020/662 5538, ⓦ www.acro-hotel.nl. **Tram #2 or #5 to Hobbemastraat.** This hotel has small and fairly functional rooms, but a friendly welcome and a nice bar on the ground floor mean that it gets booked up a long way in advance. Doubles €110–140 with breakfast.

Bema Concertgebouwplein 19b ☎020/679 1396, ⓦ www.bemahotel.com. **Tram #5 or #24 to Van Baerlestraat.** Large, clean rooms within a huge house under the canny eye of the friendly manager-owner. The eight rooms aren't modern but they're full of character, and the hotel is handy for the Concertgebouw and the main museums. Minimum two-night stay at weekends. En-suite doubles €90, including breakfast delivered to your room. Triples and quads also available, and a couple of apartments too.

Bilderberg Hotel Jan Luyken Jan Luykenstraat 58 ☎020/573 0730, ⓦ www.janluyken.nl. **Tram #2 or #5 from CS.** Nicely refurbished, good-sized rooms mark out this decent stab at a mini four-star, full-service hotel, with prices starting at €150 for one of the smaller

▲ Lloyd Hotel

standard rooms. There's a nice lounge and bar downstairs too.

College Roelof Hartstraat 1 ☏020/571 1511, ⓦwww.collegehotelamsterdam .com. Tram #5 or #24 to junction of Roelof Hartstraat and Van Baerlestraat. Converted from an old schoolhouse, the *College* is one of the most original and elegant recent additions to Amsterdam's accommodation scene. Original, because it's largely run by students of the city's catering school; elegant, because of the sheer class of the refurbishment. The cheapest doubles start at €235 (less when booked in advance) – and are well worth it.

Filosoof Anna van den Vondelstraat 6 ☏020/683 3013, ⓦwww.hotelfilosoof.nl. Tram #1 from CS to Jan Pieter Heijestraat. A lovely, small hotel, with each room decorated according to a different philosophical theme. It's all beautifully kept, nothing is too much trouble, and the garden outside is a rare Amsterdam treat. A bit out of the way but handy for the Vondelpark. A really good choice in this part of town. Doubles cost €100–150, with an extra €15 for breakfast.

Fita Jan Luykenstraat 37 ☏020/679 0976, ⓦwww.fita.nl. Tram #2 or #5 to Van Baerlestraat. Mid-sized, friendly, family-run hotel in a quiet spot between the Vondelpark and the museums. Comfortable en-suite doubles, all non-smoking, cost €135–165. Free phone calls within Europe and to America, and free use of the hotel's wi-fi (and laptop if you need it).

▲ College

Karen McCusker Zeilstraat ☏020/679 2753 (mornings), ⓦwww.bedandbreakfastamsterdam .net. Tram #2 to Amstelveenseweg. This small B&B, run by an Englishwoman who moved to Amsterdam in 1979, comprises two cosy and clean, Laura Ashley-style (non-smoking) double rooms in her home, close to the Vondelpark. There's also a suite available, with bathroom, kitchen and private balcony, suitable for longer stays. Ring first, because the owner isn't always around and you'll also need to reserve well in advance. Double with shared bathroom costs around €80, €105 with en-suite bathroom – and there's a minimum stay of two nights during the week and three nights at weekends.

NL Hotel Nassaukade 368 ☏020/689 0030, ⓦwww.nl-hotel.com. Tram #1, #2 or #5 from CS to Leidseplein and then a 5min walk. Pick of the lot in the area, with thirteen design rooms decorated with funky wallpaper and plenty of Buddhas and tulips. Some rooms have access to a small private patio. The hospitable owners are a good source of advice for the trendy spots in the area. Rates from €125, breakfast an extra €10.

Owl Hotel Roemer Visscherstraat 1 ☏020/618 9484, ⓦwww.owl-hotel.nl. Tram #1, #2 or #5 from CS to Leidseplein. The reasonably priced doubles are relatively bland, but the location is nice and quiet, with a downstairs lounge opening onto a lovely garden, and – run by the same family for nearly forty years – the staff are a welcoming bunch. Doubles from €130.

Parkzicht Roemer Visscherstraat 33 ☏020/618 1954, ⓦwww.parkzicht.nl. Tram #1 from CS to Leidseplein. This quiet, unassuming hotel, on a pretty backstreet near the Vondelpark and museums, has been going since the 1930s and has an appealing lived-in look. It's clean and full of character, if a bit old-fashioned; some rooms have fireplaces and each is furnished with old Dutch wood furniture. Singles, doubles and triples available, with a mixture of shared and en-suite facilities; prices are €84–96 for a double, €130 for a triple.

Patou PC Hooftstraat 63 ☏020/676 0232, ⓦwww.hotelpatou.nl. Tram #2 or #5 from CS to Van Baerlestraat. Small but stylish boutique hotel named after the well-known French couturier, located on the expensive PC Hooftstraat above the brasserie sharing the same name. Minimalist design – with an eye for detail and comfort – make this a pleasant place to stay. Rates start at €195, excluding breakfast.

Piet Hein Vossiusstraat 53 ☎020/662 7205, ⓦwww.hotelpiethein.nl. Tram #1, #2 or #5 from CS to Leidseplein. Five minutes' walk from Leidseplein, this sleek three-star has large rooms with views over the entrance to the Vondelpark and slightly more expensive rooms in the modern annex overlooking its peaceful back garden. There's also a comfy bar (with internet access) that's normally open until 1am. Rates start at €165. Lift access.

Prinsen Vondelstraat 36–38 ☎020/616 2323, ⓦwww.prinsenhotel.nl. Tram #1 from CS to Leidseplein. Family-run hotel built in the nineteenth century by Dutch architect P.J.H. Cuypers (of Centraal Station fame) on the edge of the Vondelpark. It's not especially pretty, but it is quiet and has a large, secluded back garden. En-suite doubles with all mod cons go for around €125–135, triples and quads for €150–200.

Toro Koningslaan 64 ☎020/673 7223, ⓦwww .hoteltoro.nl. Tram #2 from CS to Valeriusplein. Housed in a grand old villa overlooking the Vondelpark's westerly reaches, this hotel is like a small country house, with a welcoming downstairs sitting room and tastefully furnished rooms from €150, some of which overlook the park. There's also a private garden and terrace with views of a lake in the Vondelpark. It's a good choice if you don't mind being slightly out of the action.

🏃 **Vondel** Vondelstraat 18–30 ☎020/616 4075, ⓦwww.hotelvondel.com. Tram #1 from CS to Leidseplein. This hotel tries hard to be cool and sleek, and mostly succeeds, with black paint and light, natural wood characterizing the lovely rooms, which have flat-screen TVs. There's a pleasant bar and breakfast room and modern art decorates the common areas. Doubles vary in size and start at around €160, breakfast excluded.

Zandbergen Willemsparkweg 205 ☎020/676 9321, ⓦwww.hotel-zandbergen.com. Tram #2 to Emmastraat. This light, airy, family-run hotel on a busy street near the Vondelpark has eighteen clean, spacious and tastefully decorated rooms, with minibars and free wi-fi. Doubles go for €125–160 depending on the type of room, and triples and quads are available too for €165–215, as well as a bright and spacious penthouse suite for €235 a night.

The outer districts

Amsterdam Hilton Apollolaan 138 ☎020/710 6000, ⓦwww.amsterdam.hilton.com. Tram #5 or #24 to Apollolaan. See map, pp.132–133. Way outside the centre by a canal in the distinctly upmarket Nieuw Zuid district, this hotel has all the facilities you could hope for, from lounge bar, café and health club through to an Italian restaurant. Mainly attracting business-oriented clientele, it's only really worth considering if you can afford to soak up a bit of 1960s nostalgia in its (admittedly stunning) Lennon and Ono suite, where the couple held their famous 1969 "Bed-In" for peace; one night here will set you back €1750, otherwise doubles hover around the €260 mark.

Okura Ferdinand Bolstraat 333 ☎020/678 7111, ⓦwww.okura.nl. Tram #25 to Cornelis Troost-plein. See map, p.128. Don't be fooled by its concrete, purpose-built facade: this deluxe hotel, situated close to the RAI Conference Centre, comes equipped with all the usual facilities you would expect, plus a shopping arcade with a Japanese food store. Its 315 rooms boast huge marble bathrooms, and in its suites mod cons include mood lighting and remote-controlled curtains. Two of its four restaurants (see p.195) have Michelin stars. If you're feeling particularly flush you could book "The Suite", set over two floors with a suspended glass staircase, cinema and private butler; a night here will set you back a cool €10,000. Doubles from €295.

Van Ostade Van Ostadestraat 123 ☎020/679 3452, ⓦwww.bicyclehotel.com. Tram #25 to Van de Helststraat. Friendly, youthful place down a quiet residential street, not far from Albert Cuypmarkt in De Pijp. It bills itself as the "bicycle hotel", renting out bikes for €7.50 per day and giving advice on routes and suchlike. There's also garage space for two cars (€20 per car; book in advance). Two-, three- and four-bed rooms, plus one with bunk beds, are basic but clean. Doubles start from €80 with shared facilities, €115 for en-suite rooms, including breakfast.

Xaviera Hollander B&B Stadionweg 17 ☎020/673 3934, ⓦwww.xavierahollander .com. Tram #5 or #24 to Stadionweg. See map, pp.132–133. Spending a night at the home of illustrious former madam, Xaviera Hollander, better known as the "Happy Hooker", may sound dubious but the experience is a whole lot more respectable than you'd imagine. Situated in the chichi Nieuw Zuid, this spacious, homely villa has two kitschy rooms, the larger of which has a terrace, though it suffers a little from traffic noise. Prudish it ain't, with semi-clad photos of Xaviera and friends dotted about and shelves of well-thumbed sex-help books, but it's certainly memorable. Parking available. No credit cards. Both rooms have shared facilities. Rates from €110.

Hostels

If you're on a tight budget, the least expensive central option is to take a dorm bed in a **hostel**, and there are plenty to choose from: Hostelling International places, unofficial private hostels, even Christian hostels. Most hostels will either provide (relatively) clean bed linen or charge a few euros for it – your own sleeping bag might be a better option. Many places also lock guests out for a short period each day to clean; some also set a nightly curfew, though these are usually late enough not to cause too much of a problem. Some hostels don't accept reservations from June to August.

The cheapest **dorms** you'll find are in the "Shelter" Christian-run hostels, at €17–23 per person per night; the average elsewhere is closer to €25. A few otherwise good-value places have a policy of charging more at **weekends** than during the week – a price hike of as much as €5 that can come as an unpleasant surprise. Note that you can pay the same rate for a bed in a sixteen-person dorm as you'd pay to be in a four-person dorm elsewhere, and that any place which won't allow you to see where you'll be sleeping before you pay is worth avoiding. If you want a little extra privacy, many hostels also offer triples, doubles and singles for much less than you'd pay in a regular hotel – though the quality and size of rooms can leave a lot to be desired.

Old Centre

Bob's Youth Hostel Nieuwezijds Voorburgwal 92 ☎020/623 0063, ⊛www.bobshostel.nl. **Ten-minute walk from CS.** An old favourite with backpackers, *Bob's* is a lively place with small, basic dorm beds for €18–25 per person, including breakfast in the coffeeshop on the ground floor. They also let four apartments (€70 for two people, €90 for three). However, they kick everyone out at 10.30am to clean, which is not so good if you want a lie-in. Walk-in policy only.

Bulldog Low-Budget Hotel Oudezijds Voorburgwal 220 ☎020/620 3822, ⊛www .bulldoghotel.com. **Tram #4, #9, #16 or #24 from CS to Dam Square, then a three-minute walk.** Part of the *Bulldog* coffeeshop chain, with a bar and DVD lounge downstairs complete with leather couches and soft lighting. Dorm beds with shower range between €24 and €32, a bit more at weekends, including breakfast, and there are also double rooms from €105 to €120, as well as fully equipped apartments from €150 – all with bathrooms and TVs. Great terrace in summer.

Flying Pig Downtown Nieuwendijk 100 ☎020/420 6822, ⊛www.flyingpig.nl. **Five-minute walk from CS.** Clean, large and well run by ex-travellers familiar with the needs of backpackers. Free use of kitchen facilities, no curfew, and the hostel bar is open all night. It's justifiably popular, and a very good deal, with mixed dorm beds from about €25 depending on the size of the dorm; queen-size bunks sleeping two also available. During the peak season you'll need to book well in advance. See also the *Flying Pig Uptown*, p.171.

The Globe Oudezijds Voorburgwal 3 ☎020/421 7424, ⊛www.hostel-theglobe.nl. **Tram #4, #9, #16 or #24 to Dam Square.** A popular hostel that's a favourite with those on all-day drinking binges, partly due to its 24-hour sports bar with screen. It's not a palace by anyone's standards, but may do the trick if you're not in Amsterdam to sleep much. Spartan but clean dorm beds from €18 (weekends €35), twins for a steep €80–135. €5 key deposit. Breakfast is an extra €6.

Meeting Point Warmoesstraat 14 ☎020/627 7499, ⊛www.hostel-meetingpoint.nl. **Ten-minute walk from CS.** Warm and cosy central hostel with space in eight- to eighteen-bed dorms. Private bar with pool table for guests is open 24 hours. Cash payment only. Breakfast €2.50. Prices range between €18 and €30.

Shelter City Barndesteeg 21 ☏020/625 3230, Ⓦ www.shelter.nl. Metro Nieuwmarkt. A non-evangelical Christian youth hostel smack in the middle of the Red Light District. Beds in large dorms from €22.50, including a sizeable breakfast, which makes this one of the city's best deals (from €24.50 for a bed in a smaller dorm). Dorms are single-sex; lockers require a €5 deposit and there's a curfew (2am). You might be handed a booklet on Jesus when you check in, but you'll get a quiet night's sleep and the sheets are clean. See also *The Shelter Jordan*, opposite.

Stay Okay Stadsdoelen Kloveniersburgwal 97 ☏020/624 6832, Ⓦ www.stayokay.com /stadsdoelen. Metro Nieuwmarkt or Waterlooplein, or tram #4, #9, #16, #24 or #25 from CS to Muntplein. The closest to Centraal Station of the three official hostels, with clean, semi-private dorms at €21.50 for members, who get priority in high season; non-members pay €24. Price includes linen, breakfast and locker, plus use of communal kitchen. Guests get a range of discounts on activities in the city too. See also the city's other HI hostels, the *Stay Okay Vondelpark* (see below), which has a greater choice of rooms, and the brand new *Stay Okay Zeeburg* (see opposite).

Grachtengordel south

Hans Brinker Budget Hotel Kerkstraat 136 ☏020/622 0687, Ⓦ www.hans-brinker.com. Tram #1, #2 or #5 from CS to Prinsengracht. Well-established and raucously popular Amsterdam hostel, with around 500 beds. Dorms are basic and clean and beds go for around €22–25, and singles, doubles and triples are also available. All rooms are en suite. The facilities are good: free internet after 10pm, disco every night, and it's near to the buzz of Leidseplein, too. A hostel to head for if you're out for a good time (and not too bothered about getting a solid night's sleep), though be prepared to change dorms during your stay. Walk-in policy only in high season.

International Budget Hostel Leidsegracht 76 ☏020/624 2784, Ⓦ www.internationalbudgethostel .com. Tram #1, #2 or #5 to Prinsengracht. An excellent budget option on a peaceful little canal in the heart of the city. Small, simple rooms sleeping up to four with shared bathroom; breakfast in the café is extra. Young, friendly staff. Singles and twin rooms with private facilities (€80), dorm beds between €22 and €32 per person.

The Jordaan and Western docklands

The Shelter Jordan Bloemstraat 179 ☏020/624 4717, Ⓦ www.shelter.nl. Tram #13 or #17 to Marnixstraat. The second of Amsterdam's two Christian hostels (the other is *Shelter City*, see opposite) is situated in a particularly attractive and quiet part of the Jordaan, close to the Lijnbaansgracht canal. Great-value beds start at €22.50 (down to €16.50 in low season) including breakfast. Fri & Sat €3–5 supplement. Dorms sleeping 14–20 are single-sex and non-smoking; downstairs there's a decent café.

The Old Jewish Quarter and Eastern Docklands

Stay Okay Zeeburg Timorplein 21 ☏020/551 3190, Ⓦ www.stayokay.com/zeeburg. Closest train station: Amsterdam Muiderpoort. A brand spanking new hostel located in a former school in a residential area on the eastern outskirts of the city. Large dorms from €22.50 for non-members (up to €33.50 if you're unlucky), breakfast included. Located in the same building is Studio K, which shows arthouse films and has a decent restaurant. In high season a minimum of two nights is required when you want to stay a Saturday.

The Museum Quarter and Vondelpark

Flying Pig Uptown Vossiusstraat 46 ☏020/400 4187, Ⓦ www.flyingpig.nl. Tram #1, #2 or #5 to Leidseplein, then a short walk. The better of the two *Flying Pig* hostels, facing the Vondelpark and close to the city's most important museums. Immaculately clean and well maintained by a staff of travellers. Free use of kitchen facilities, no curfew and good tourist information. Fourteen-bed dorms start at €21.90 per person and there are a few two-person queen-size bunks, as well as double rooms – great value.

Stay Okay Vondelpark Zandpad 5 ☏020/589 8996, Ⓦ www.stayokay.com /vondelpark. Tram #1, #2 or #5 to Leidseplein, then a 5min walk. Well located with good facilities such as a bar, restaurant,

TV lounge, internet access and bicycle shed, plus various discount deals on tours and museums. Rates vary enormously, but in high season you can expect to pay as much as €33.50 for non-members (€31 for members), including use of all facilities,

shower (though no towels), sheets and breakfast. Secure lockers and no curfew. To be sure of a place in high season you'll need to book at least two months ahead. In high season, there is a minimum stay of two nights if you want to book on a Saturday.

Apartments and houseboats

For groups or families, short-term **apartment** rentals can work out cheaper than staying in a hotel, with the further advantages of privacy and the convenience (or at least relative cheapness) of self-catering. Apartments sleeping four or five can often be found for the same price as a double room in a hotel. **Houseboats** tend to be significantly more luxurious and expensive. Both are often organized through local hotels. **City Mundo** (Ⓦ www.citymundo.com) is a booking service for private accommodation, including rooms, apartments and houseboats. Bookings of three to 21 days start at €25–33 per person per night (for up to four people). The website lists a hundred properties at any one time, taken from a database of a couple of hundred, and changes according to availability. They do charge a whopping €20 reservation cost though. Alternatively, the following are reliable city-centre options.

Acacia Lindengracht 251 ☎ 020/622 1460, Ⓦ www.hotelacacia.nl. Studios sleeping two people at €100 per night in the heart of the Jordaan.

Amsterdam House 's Gravelandseveer 7, 1011 KN Amsterdam ☎ 020/626 2577, Ⓦ www.amsterdamhouse.com. Two-room apartments start at €135 per night; houseboats €165.

Hoksbergen Apartments Singel 301 ☎ 020/626 6043, Ⓦ www.hotelhoksbergen.nl. Apartments sleeping up to five from €120.

Camping

There are a number of **campsites** on the peripheries of Amsterdam, most of them readily accessible by car or public transport. Those listed are two of the more established and central options.

Campsites

Vliegenbos Meeuwenlaan 138 ☎ 020/636 8855, Ⓦ www.vliegenbos.com. Bus #32 or #33 from CS or take the ferry to Buiksloterweg and allow a 15min walk; drivers take Exit S116 off the A10. A relaxed and friendly site, just a ten-minute bus ride into Amsterdam North from Centraal Station. Facilities include a general shop, bar and restaurant. Rates start at €8.30 per night per person with hot showers included. There are also huts with bunk beds and basic cooking facilities for €72.50 per night for four people; phone

ahead to check availability. Car parking is €8.30. Under-16s need to be accompanied by an adult; no pets. Open April–Sept.

Zeeburg Zuider IJdijk 20 ☎ 020/694 4430, Ⓦ www.campingzeeburg.nl. Tram #26 from CS to Zuiderzeeweg, then a 10min walk; drivers take Exit S114 off the A10. Well-equipped campsite in the Eastern docklands with a bar, restaurant, laundry, kayak and bicycle rental, plus lots of green fields. Tent pitches cost €5 in addition to a €5.50 charge per person per night, and €5 for a car. Two-berth cabins cost €40 and four-berth €80, including bed linen. Open all year.

Eating and drinking

Amsterdam may not be Europe's gastronomic centre, but the **food** in the average Dutch restaurant has improved by leaps and bounds in recent years, and there are a great number of places serving good, often inventive, home-grown cuisine. The city also boasts a wide range of ethnic restaurants, especially Indonesian, Chinese and Thai, as well as numerous cafés and bars – often known as *eetcafés* – that serve adventurous, reasonably priced food in a relaxed and unpretentious setting. Amsterdam is also, of course, a great place for a **drink**; the Netherlands' proximity to the great beer-drinking nation of Belgium – the birthplace of modern beer – helps explain the variety on offer.

The city is filled to the gunnels with dining and drinking options, and you should have no trouble finding somewhere convenient and enjoyable to suit your budget. On Thursday, Friday and Saturday nights it's advisable to start early (between 6pm & 7pm), or make a reservation, if you want to get a table at any of the more popular **restaurants**. If you just want lunch, or a bite between sights, there are plenty of places throughout the city – **cafés and tearooms** – where you can just grab a cup of coffee and a sandwich or light lunch. **Bars** almost always serve sandwiches, and usually something more substantial as well; those that serve good-quality food are indicated in the listings.

Dutch meal times are a little idiosyncratic; breakfast tends to be later than you might expect, and other meals tend to be eaten earlier. If you choose to eat **breakfast** away from your hotel, you'll find very few cafés open before 8am or 8.30am. The standard Dutch **lunch** hour is from noon to 1pm; most restaurants are at their busiest at **dinner**, between 7pm and 8pm, and mostly stop serving by 10 or 10.30pm.

Dutch food tends to be higher in protein content than in variety; steak, chicken and fish, along with filling soups and stews, are staples, usually served up in substantial quantities. At its best, though, it can be excellent, with many restaurants, and even bars and *eetcafés*, offering increasingly adventurous crossovers with French and Mediterranean cuisine, at reasonable prices.

With Amsterdam's singular approach to the sale and consumption of cannabis, you might choose to enjoy a joint after your meal, rather than a beer; included in this chapter is a selection of "**coffeeshops**" where you can buy grass or hash. Be aware that, due to recent legislation, smoking tobacco inside bars and coffeeshops is no longer permitted, although tobacco substitutes and pure joints are still available.

Bars, cafés and restaurants are marked on the colour maps and listed in the index at the back of the book.

Breakfast

In all but the cheapest and the most expensive of hotels, **breakfast** (*ontbijt*) will be included in the price of the room. Though usually nothing fancy, it's always substantial; rolls, cheese, ham, hard-boiled eggs, jam and honey or peanut butter are the principal ingredients. Many bars and cafés serve rolls and sandwiches in similar mode, although few open much before 8am or 8.30am.

Dutch **coffee** is normally good and strong, served with a little tub of *koffiemelk* (evaporated milk); ordinary milk is rarely used. If you want coffee with warm milk, ask for a *koffie verkeerd*. Tea generally comes with lemon – if anything; if you want milk you have to ask for it. Chocolate (*chocomel*) is also popular, hot or cold; for a real treat, drink it hot with a layer of fresh whipped cream (*slagroom*) on top. Some cafés also sell aniseed-flavoured warm milk (*anijsmelk*).

Snacks and sandwiches

Dutch **fast food** has its own peculiarities. Chips/fries (*friet* or *patat*) are the most common standby. *Vlaamse* or "Flemish-style", sprinkled with salt and smothered with lashings of mayonnaise (*frietsaus*), are the best, and other accompaniments include curry, goulash, tomato or *saté* (peanut) sauce. If you just want salt, ask for *patat zonder*; fries with salt and mayonnaise are *patat met*. You'll also come across *krokketen* – spiced minced meat (usually either veal or beef), covered with breadcrumbs and deep-fried – and *fricandel*, a frankfurter-like sausage. All these are available over the counter at pungent fast-food places, or, for a euro or so, from coin-op heated glass compartments on the street and in train stations.

Much tastier are the **fish** specialities sold by street vendors, which are good as a snack or a light lunch – see box, p.185. Another snack you'll see everywhere is **shwarma** or *shoarma* – another name for a doner kebab: shavings of lamb pressed into a pitta bread – sold in numerous Middle Eastern restaurants and

Dutch cheese

Dutch **cheeses** have a somewhat unjustified reputation abroad for being bland and rubbery, but in fact they can be delicious, even if there isn't the variety you find in, say, France or Britain. Most Dutch cheeses vary little from the familiar pale yellow, semi-soft **Gouda**, within which differences in taste come from the varying stages of maturity: *jonge* (young) cheese has a mild flavour, *belegen* (mature) has a fuller flavour, while *oude* (old) can be pungent and strong, with a grainy, flaky texture. Generally, the older they get, the saltier they are. Best-known among the other cheeses is **Edam**, also semi-soft in texture but slightly creamier than Gouda; it's usually shaped into balls and coated in red wax ready for export – it's not eaten much in the Netherlands. **Leidse** is simply a bland Gouda laced with cumin or caraway seeds, with most of its flavour coming from the seeds; **Maasdam** is a Dutch version of Emmental or Jarlsberg: strong, creamy and full of holes, sold under brand names such as Leerdammer and Maasdammer; you'll also come across Dutch-made Emmental and Gruyère. The Dutch like their cheese in thin slices, cut with a cheese slicer rather than in large chunks.

Amsterdam has several specialist **cheese shops** (see p.224) and there's also a good range of cheeses on sale at the Saturday farmers' market on the Noordermarkt (9am–1pm). Finally, Amsterdam is within easy striking distance of two world-famous cheese markets, one at Edam (see p.149), the other at Alkmaar (see p.154).

takeaways for about €4. Other, less common, street foods include **pancakes** (*pannenkoeken*), sweet or spicy, also widely available at restaurants; waffles (*stroop-wafels*), doused with syrup; and, in November and December, *oliebollen*, greasy doughnuts sometimes filled with fruit (often apple) or custard (known as a *Berliner*) and traditionally eaten on New Year's Eve.

Bars often serve **sandwiches and rolls** (*boterham* and *broodjes*) – mostly open, and varying from a slice of tired cheese on old bread to something so embellished it's almost a complete meal – as well as more substantial dishes. A sandwich made with French bread is known as a *stokbrood*. In the winter, *erwtensoep* (or *snert*) – thick pea soup with smoked sausage, served with smoked bacon on pumpernickel – is available in many bars, and for about €5 a bowl makes a cheap but hearty lunch. Alternatively, there's the *uitsmijter* (a "kicker-out", derived from the practice of serving it at dawn after an all-night party to prompt guests to depart); now widely available at all times of day, it comprises one, two, or three fried eggs on buttered bread, topped with a choice of ham, cheese or roast beef; at about €5–6, it's another good budget lunch option.

Cakes and biscuits

Dutch **cakes and biscuits** are always good, best eaten in a *banketbakkerij* (patis-serie) with a small serving area; alternatively buy to take away and munch them on the hoof. Top of the list is the ubiquitous Dutch speciality *appelgebak* – chunky, memorably fragrant apple-and-cinnamon pie, served hot in huge wedges, often with whipped cream (*met slagroom*). Other sweet nibbles include *speculaas*, a crunchy cinnamon cookie with a gingerbread-like texture; *stroopwafels*, butter wafers sandwiched together with runny syrup; and *amandelkoek*, cakes with a crisp biscuit outside and melt-in-the-mouth almond paste inside.

Full meals

The majority of bars serve food – everything from sandwiches to a full menu – in which case they may be known as **eetcafés**. This type of place is usually open all day, serving both lunch and evening meals. Full-blown **restaurants**, on the other hand, tend to open in the evening only, usually from around 5.30pm or 6pm until 10pm.

If you're on a budget, stick to the **dagschotel** (dish of the day) wherever possible, for which you pay around €12 for a meat or fish dish, with a generous serving of potatoes and other vegetables or salad; note that it's often only served at lunchtime or between 6 and 8pm. Otherwise, you can pay up to €20–25 for a meat or fish main course in an average restaurant. **Vegetarian** dining isn't a problem: many *eetcafés* and restaurants have at least one meat-free dish on the menu, and the city has a scattering of veggie restaurants, offering three-course set meals from about €10.

As for foreign cuisines, the Dutch are particularly partial to **Indonesian** food; *Nasi goreng* and *Bami goreng* (rice or noodles with meat) are good basic dishes, though there are normally more exciting items on the menu, some very spicy; chicken or beef in peanut sauce (*saté*) is always available. Or you could ask for a **rijsttafel** – a sampler meal, comprising boiled rice and/or noodles served with perhaps ten or twelve small, often spicy dishes and hot *sambal* sauce on the side. Usually ordered for two or more people, you can reckon on paying around €20–25 per person. Surinamese restaurants are much rarer, but they offer a distinctive, essentially Creole cuisine – try *roti*, flat pancake-like bread served with a spicy curry, hardboiled egg and vegetables. **Italian** food is ubiquitous, with pizzas and pasta dishes starting at a fairly uniform €10 or so in most places.

Drinks

Amsterdam's favourite tipple is **beer**, mostly Pilsener-style lager, usually served in a relatively small measure (just under a half-pint, with a foaming head) – ask for *een pils*. The three leading Dutch brands – Amstel, Grolsch and Heineken – are worldwide bestsellers, but are available here in considerably more potent formats than the insipid varieties shunted out for export. Different beers come in different glasses – white beer (*witbier*), which is light, cloudy and served with lemon, has its own tumbler; and most of the speciality Belgian beers have their own distinctive glasses with stems of different shapes and sizes.

    Wine is reasonably priced – expect to pay around €7 or so for an average bottle of French white or red in a supermarket, €17 in a restaurant. Most restaurants also stock a large selection of new world wines: mainly Australian, South African and Chilean. As for spirits, **jenever**, Dutch gin, is not unlike English gin but a bit weaker and a little oilier, made from molasses and flavoured with juniper berries. It's served in a small glass and is traditionally drunk straight, often knocked back in one gulp with much hearty back-slapping. There are a number of varieties, principally *oude* (old), which is smooth and mellow, and *jong* (young), which packs more of a punch – though neither is terribly alcoholic. The older *jenevers* (including *zeer oude*, very old) are a little more expensive but stronger and less oily. Ask for a *borreltje* (straight *jenever*), a *bittertje* (with Angostura bitters) or, if you've a sweeter tooth, try a *bessenjenever* – blackcurrant-flavoured gin. A glass of beer with a *jenever* chaser is a *kopstoot*.

    Other drinks you'll come across include numerous Dutch **liqueurs**, notably *advocaat* (eggnog), and the sweet blue *curaçao*, and an assortment of lurid **fruit brandies**, which are best left for experimentation at the end of an evening. There's also the Dutch-produced **brandy**, *Vieux*, which tastes as if it's made from prunes but is in fact grape-based.

Bars

With every justification, Amsterdam is famous for its traditional, old-style bars or **brown cafés** – a *bruin café* or *bruine kroeg* – cosy, intimate places so called because of the dingy colour of their walls, stained by years of tobacco smoke, and their antique-verging-on-rickety furnishings and fittings, again mostly brown. At the other extreme are the slick, pan-European **designer bars**, sometimes known as "grand cafés", which tend to be as un-brown as possible and geared towards a largely young crowd, though many students are loyal to the brown cafés. In between are a host of bars that pick and mix the old and the new. Bars, of every kind, **open** daily at around 10am or 5pm; those that open in the morning do not close at lunchtime, and all stay open until around 1am during the week, 2am at weekends (sometimes until 3am). Another type of drinking spot – though there are very few of them left – is the tasting house (*proeflokalen*), originally the sampling rooms of small private distillers, now tiny, stand-up places that sell only spirits – *jenever* – and often close early, from around 8pm. For listings of **gay bars** see Chapter 12.

Architecture in **Amsterdam**

Amsterdam has one of the best-preserved city centres in the world, free of the high-rises and cluttered, modern development that characterize so many other European capitals. Despite that, it is not a monumental city – there are no triumphal thoroughfares and few memorable palaces and churches. This was not a royal or an aristocratic city but a merchant one, with a tolerant attitude to religion, and the character of the architecture reflects this; it is Amsterdam's private, low-key dwellings, rather than its grand monuments, that give the city its distinctive charm.

Beginnings

Amsterdam was a great site for a trading city, bang on the confluence of two rivers. But in other respects it was a terrible choice – like many Dutch towns, a flat and waterlogged plain, in which buildings needed to be supported by thousands of wooden piles bashed into the sandy soil. Just across from Centraal Station, the wooden house at **Zeedijk 1** – now home to the *In 't Aepjen* bar – is one of very few timber buildings still left, dating back to around 1550, while not far from here, one of Amsterdam's oldest surviving buildings is the **Oude Kerk**, dating from the 1300s. Deeper into the city centre, the **Houten Huys** in the **Begijnhof** dates from 1477, and still boasts its original Gothic timber frontage.

The Begijnhof ▲

Herengracht ▼

The Golden Age

Brick became the building material of choice from the late sixteenth century onwards, and buildings began to acquire the distinctive **gables** that adorn houses all over the city. The earliest type was the step-gable; the house at **Oudezijds Voorburgwal 14** is a good example of this early Renaissance style, with its stone embellishments on red brick. The gable soon developed – most notably under the greatest Dutch architect of the period, **Hendrick de Keyser** (1565–1621) – into a more distinctive "Amsterdam" form, in which the previously plain step-gables were decorated with stonework and sculpture. One of the most lavish examples is the double-step-gabled residence at **Singel 140–142** – where Captain Banning Cocq (the principal figure in Rembrandt's *The Night Watch*) lived – built in 1600 by de Keyser.

The seventeenth century saw a surge in the city's population, and a major **expansion** was required to successfully absorb its newcomers. This exercise in city planning was way ahead of its time, using the expansion to create the graceful sweep of canals you see today. It was also the heyday of Dutch architecture, and Hendrick de Keyser, and others, left their mark with a series of trailblazing works, such as the **Huis Bartolotti** at Herengracht 170–172, with its ornate step-gables, as well as two of the city's most characteristic seventeenth-century churches: the **Westerkerk** and the **Zuiderkerk**.

De Keyser's distinctive Westerkerk tower was finished by his successor as the leading city architect, **Jacob van Campen** (1595–1657), who brought overseas influences to his work. He is best known for building Amsterdam's new town hall in 1665, now the **Royal Palace** – a more restrained building than its predecessors, exhibiting the Palladian proportions that the architect had absorbed in Italy. Van Campen's contemporary, **Philip Vingboons** (1607–78), was responsible for a number of the private houses on the by now burgeoning city extension, many of them sporting the fashionable neck-gable – a slimmed-down version of the step-gable; some appealing examples can be seen at **Herengracht 168** and the Cromhouthuizen at **Herengracht 364–370**.

The nineteenth century

The eighteenth century was relatively uneventful, but in the nineteenth century the city developed a distinctive new style, partially spearheaded by **Petrus J.H. Cuypers** (1827–1921), famed for his neo-Gothic creations. Cuypers not only built the monumental **Centraal Station**, but

▲ Huis Bartolotti

▼ The Royal Palace (Koninklijk Paleis)

The Rijksmuseum ▲

Eastern docklands architecture ▼

The Muziekgebouw ▼

also contributed a series of buildings in the outskirts – not least the **Rijksmuseum**, which was purpose-built as the country's national museum, and shouts from its gabled rooftops the importance of tradition and the legacy of Dutch art.

The turn of the century ushered in further changes with the international, modern style of **Hendrik Petrus Berlage** (1856–1934), exemplified in his **Beurs** on the Damrak, exhibiting the attributes of a restrained yet highly decorative vision. Berlage's work inspired the **Amsterdam School**, a group of architects working in the city in the early twentieth century, led by **Piet Kramer** (1881–1961) and **Michael de Klerk** (1884–1923). The movement's keynote building was de Klerk's **Het Schip** housing complex of 1920, on the western edge of the centre.

Contemporary Amsterdam

Modern Amsterdam is changing fast, with new developments constantly adding to the city's architectural variety. The largest, perhaps most influential of these are the **docklands** schemes to the west and east of the city centre, where some of the city's long-neglected waterways are being transformed into a modern-day version of the seventeenth-century master plan. The docklands to the east, and **Zeeburg** in particular, are home to some of the city's most exciting new architecture – a mixture of renovated warehouses and assertive new structures, the most notable being the avant-garde **Muziekgebouw**. There are also some clever, contemporary takes on the traditional Dutch waterfront on **Java Island**, whose modern terraces and curvy bridges evoke the canal houses of the city centre – and as such bring the city's architectural story full circle.

Many bars – often designated **eetcafés** – offer a complete food menu, and most will make you a sandwich or a bowl of soup; at the very least you can snack on hard-boiled eggs from the counter. Those bars that specialize more in food than drink are listed in our "Restaurants" section (see pp.185–196).

Prices are fairly standard everywhere, and the only time you'll pay through the nose is when there's music, or if you're desperate enough to step into the obvious tourist traps around Leidseplein and along the Damrak. Reckon on paying roughly €1.80–2.20 for a standard-measure small draught beer, €3–4 or so for wheat and bottled beer, and €3 for a glass of wine or a shot of *jenever*.

Locations are marked on the colour **maps** at the back of this book.

The Old Centre

Absinthe Nieuwezijds Voorburgwal 171. Small, late-night basement lounge bar, slightly hidden from the street, but in a prime position close to the area's bars and clubs. Not surprisingly, it specializes in absinthe – or at least the turn-of-the-twentieth-century decadence that's associated with it. DJs at the weekend. Daily from 10pm.

In 't Aepjen Zeedijk 1. This building has been a bar since the days when Zeedijk was a haunt for sailors gambling away their last few guilder and having to pay by barter rather than cash. Its name – literally "In the Monkeys" – refers to the fact that monkeys were once the stock in trade here. There are no monkeys now, but not much else has changed.

De Bekeerde Suster Kloveniersburgwal 6. Don't waste your time in the unappealing bars of the Red Light District proper; this place is a few steps away and offers home-brewed beer, a good bar menu and a very convivial atmosphere, just off the top end of Nieuwmarkt. Mon–Thurs 3pm–1am, Fri & Sat noon–2am, Sun noon–midnight.

Belgique Gravenstraat 2. Tiny and very appealing bar behind the Nieuwe Kerk that specializes in brews from Belgium. Sample them with plates of Dutch and Trappist cheese. Daily 3pm–1am.

Blincker St Barberenstraat 7. Squeezed between the top end of Nes and Oudezijds Voorburgwal, this hi-tech theatre bar, all exposed steel and hanging plants, is very nicely done – and more comfortable than it looks. Also serves food. Mon–Thurs 11am–1am, Fri & Sat 11am–3am.

Bubbles & Wines Nes 37. Over 50 wines available by the glass in this intimate and elegant wine and champagne bar. The knowledgeable staff will advise you on drinks to suit your taste. Mon–Sat from 3.30pm, Sun from 2pm.

De Buurvrouw St Pieterspoortsteeg 29. Dark, noisy bar with a wildly eclectic crowd; a great alternative place to head for in the centre. Mon–Thurs 9pm–3am, Fri–Sun 9pm–4am.

Dante Spuistraat 320. A wannabe trendy bar-cum-art gallery right in the heart of the city's densest concentration of watering holes. There are cosier places, but to peruse the art – and the people perusing the art – it's decent enough.

Diep Nieuwezijds Voorburgwal 256. Not much more than an ordinary brown café during the day, but a hip hangout with DJs at night. Mon–Thurs 5pm–1am, Fri–Sun 5am–3am.

Het Doktertje Roozenboomsteeg 4. Small, dark, brown café with stained glass to keep you from being ogled by the world outside. Liqueurs fill the shelves behind the tiny bar. Tues–Sat 4pm–1am.

De Drie Fleschjes Gravenstraat 16. Long-standing tasting house for spirits and liqueurs. No beer, and no seats either; its clients tend to be well heeled or well soused (often both). Mon–Sat noon–8.30pm, Sun 3–8pm.

De Engelbewaarder Kloveniersburgwal 59. Once the meeting place of Amsterdam's bookish types, this is still known as a literary café. It's relaxed and informal, with live jazz on Sunday afternoons. Mon–Thurs 11am–1am, Fri & Sat 11am–3am, Sun 2pm–1am.

De Engelse Reet Begijnensteeg 4. Also known as the *Pilsener Club*, this place is more like someone's living room than a bar – indeed, all drinks mysteriously appear from a back room. Photographs on the wall record generations of drinking, which has been going on here since 1893.

Gaeper Staalstraat 4. Convivial brown café packed during term time with students from the university across the canal. Tasty food, plus outdoor seating good for people-watching.

't Gasthuis Grimburgwal 7. Another brown café popular with students. Both this place and *Gaeper* are run by brothers, and they're done up in more or less the same style. Here, some of Amsterdam's cheapest hot food is served, both at lunchtime and in the evenings.

Gollem Raamsteeg 4. Small, cosy, split-level bar with rickety furniture, wood panelling and a comprehensive selection of Belgian beers, plus a few Dutch brews for variety – and with the correct glasses to drink them from. The genial barman will help you choose. Mon–Fri 4pm–1am, Sat & Sun 2pm–2am.

Hoppe Spui 18. One of Amsterdam's longest-established and best-known bars, and a likeable, scruffy joint, popular with the city's business folk. Especially good in summer, when the throng spills out onto the street. Daily 8am–1am (Fri & Sat till 2am).

Kapitein Zeppos Gebed Zonder End 5. This hangout is tucked away down a tiny street off Grimburgwal and is very easy to miss. It's a bar and a restaurant and boasts a theatricality worthy of its place at the top end of Amsterdam's small theatre district; regular live music too.

De Koningshut Spuistraat 269. In the early evening, at least, it's standing room only in this small, spit-and-sawdust bar, popular

with office workers on their way home or to dinner.

Lime Zeedijk 104. Right in the middle of Chinatown, this cool yet comfy hangout is the ideal place for a post-dinner cocktail or pre-club livener.

Lokaal 't Loosje Nieuwmarkt 32. Quiet, old-style brown café that's been here for two hundred years and looks it, with an attractive old tiled interior. A pleasant atmosphere, and always busy. Daily 9am–1am (Fri & Sat till 3am).

De Ooievaar Stolofspoort 1. Old *proeflokaal* that's a civilized escape from the nearby sleaze of the Red Light District – and handily situated for Centraal Station. Boiled eggs at the bar go down well with the gin, and there's beer, too.

Het Paleis Paleisstraat 16. This bar is a favourite with students from the adjoining university buildings. Trendily refurbished, it also serves food – focaccia sandwiches, salads and suchlike.

Poco Loco Nieuwmarkt 24. One of the liveliest cafés on the Nieuwmarkt, with a cheerful retro interior attracting a matching clientele. Also a good selection of tapas and daily specials from €11. Daily 10am–1am (Fri & Sat till 3am).

Scheltema Nieuwezijds Voorburgwal 242. Formerly a journalists' bar, but since all the newspaper headquarters along here moved to the suburbs, its faded early twentieth-century interior, including reading tables, isn't quite the hub of activity it once was. It's cosy and atmospheric, though, with an outdoor terrace in summer.

Schuim Spuistraat 189. Popular and spacious bar-café with retro furniture and a young and unpretentiously boho crowd, popular with students from the nearby university.

The Tara Rokin 85–89. Amsterdam has quite a few Irish pubs these days, but this is one of the best on several levels: decent food (including a great all-day breakfast), regular football and other sports on TV and live music from 10.30pm on Saturdays during the winter. It's very central too.

In de Wildeman Kolksteeg 3. This lovely old-fashioned bar has a barely changed wood and tile interior that still boasts its original low bar and shelving: a peaceful escape from the loud, tacky shops of nearby Nieuwendijk. One of the centre's most appealing watering holes. Daily noon–1am (Fri & Sat till 2am).

▲ Gollem

Wynand Fockink Pijlsteeg 31. This small, intimate bar, hidden just behind the *Krasnapolsky* hotel off Dam Square, is one of the city's older *proeflokaalen*, and it offers a vast range of its own flavoured *jenevers* that were once distilled down the street. It's standing-room only here – you bend down at the counter and sip your *jenever* from a glass filled to the brim. Daily 3–9pm.

Grachtengordel west

Brix Wolvenstraat 16 ☏020/639 0351, ⊛www .cafebrix.nl. Chic, basement bar-café featuring jam and jazz sessions twice weekly, plus Asian fusion cuisine (starters only) for around €8. Daily from 5pm.

Café 't Arendsnest Herengracht 90. In a handsome old canal house, this bar boasts impressive wooden decor – from the longest of bars to the tall wood-and-glass cabinets – and specializes in Dutch beers, of which it has 130 varieties, twelve on tap. Attracts an older clientele. Daily 4pm–midnight, 2am at the weekend.

Hegeraad Noordermarkt 34. Lovingly maintained, old-fashioned brown café-bar with a fiercely loyal, older clientele. The back room, furnished with paintings and red plush seats, is the perfect place to relax with a hot chocolate.

Het Molenpad Prinsengracht 653. Recently revamped café which hasn't lost its laidback atmosphere. Fills up with a young, professional crowd after 6pm. Daily noon–1am (Fri & Sat till 2am).

Het Papeneiland Prinsengracht 2. With its wood panelling, antique Delft tiles and ancient stove, this rabbit warren of a place is one of the cosiest bars in the Grachtengordel. Jam-packed late at night with a garrulous crew of locals and tourists alike. Daily 10am–1am (Fri & Sat till 3am).

De Pieper Prinsengracht 424. Laid-back neighbourhood brown bar, at the corner of Leidsegracht, with rickety old furniture and a mini-terrace beside the canal. Has a surprisingly large selection of liqueurs plus a genial, sometimes very drunk, atmosphere. Mon–Thurs 11am–1am (Fri & Sat till 2am).

De Prins Prinsengracht 124. With its well-worn decor and chatty atmosphere, this popular and lively bar offers a wide range of drinks and a well-priced bar menu with food served from 10am to 9pm. Large – at least in Amsterdam terms – and airy,

it's popular with twenty-somethings. Daily 10am–1am.

Van Puffelen Prinsengracht 375/7. This long-established and popular spot is divided into two, with a brown café-bar on one side and an *eetcafe* on the other. The café-bar is an appealing place to drink, with a good choice of international beers, while the restaurant side concentrates on Dutch(ish) dishes with lots of organic frills, but the results are variable. Main courses average around €18, but the daily specials are much more economical. Mon–Wed from 3pm, Thurs–Sun from noon.

Grachtengordel south

Café van Leeuwen Keizersgracht 711. Convivial café, jam-packed with the local in-crowd after a day at the office. Also a good selection of small bites, like tasty *crostinis*, and many wines by the glass. Occasional live jazz on Sunday. Mon–Thurs 9am–1am, Fri 9am–3am, Sat 10am–3am, Sun 11am–1am.

De Duivel Reguliersdwarsstraat 87. Tucked away on a street of bars and coffeeshops, this is the best hip-hop bar in Amsterdam, with non-stop beats and a faithful clientele. Daily 8pm–3/4am.

Herengracht Herengracht 34. Posh and up-to-the-minute spot, popular with the Amsterdam jet set. DJs on weekends. Daily 11am–1am (Fri & Sat till 3am).

Lux Marnixstraat 403. Designer bar geared for the pre-club scene with a good line in full-volume house and regular DJs, attracting a young, alternative crowd. Daily 8pm–3am (Fri & Sat till 4am).

Morlang Keizersgracht 451. Lively, split-level bar-cum-restaurant decorated in soft, modern style and attracting a prosperous clientele. Good bar and occasional live music too. Next door to the *Walem* (see below). Daily 11am–1am.

Oosterling Utrechtsestraat 140. Intimate neighbourhood bar that's been plying its trade for donkeys' years. Kitted out in attractive traditional style, it specializes in *jenever*, with dozens of brands and varieties. No mobile phones. Mon–Sat noon–1am, Sun 1–8pm.

Walem Keizersgracht 449. A chic bar-restaurant – cool, light and vehemently un-brown; eat in or chill out at the bar with a Mojito. The clientele is stylish, and the food a hybrid of French- and Dutch-inspired dishes; mains start at €14.50. Breakfast in the garden during the summer is a highlight. Daily 10am–1am, Fri & Sat until 2am.

Weber Marnixstraat 397. Popular local hangout, just off the Leidseplein, attracting musicians, students and young professionals. Crowded and noisy on weekends. Daily 8pm–3am (Fri & Sat till 4am).

De Zotte Proeflokaal Raamstraat 29. Down a grubby alley not far from the Leidseplein, this laid-back bar specializes in Belgian beer, of which it has dozens of varieties. Daily 4pm–1am, bar food served 6–9.30pm.

The Jordaan and Western docklands

De Blaffende Vis Westerstraat 118. Somewhat of an institution, this is a typical neighbourhood bar at the corner of the 2e Boomdwarsstraat. Nothing pretentious, but oodles of atmosphere and a well-priced bar menu. Daily 9am–1am, Mon from 7am, Fri & Sat till 3am.

Chris Bloemstraat 42. Very proud of being the Jordaan's (and Amsterdam's) oldest bar, dating from 1624, this place has a comfortable, homely atmosphere. Daily 3pm–1am, Fri & Sat until 2am, Sun till 9pm

Dulac Haarlemmerstraat 118. Very appealing Art Deco grand café, with lots of nooks to sit in, housed in what was an old city bank – the metal doors remain but nowadays the only money changing hands is at the bar, especially at weekends when it stays open till 3am. DJs from Thursday to Sunday play

▲ Finch

a mixture of funk, disco and pop. Mon & Tues from 4pm, Wed–Sun from noon.

Finch Noordermarkt 5. This smart café-lounge bar situated near the Noorderkerk attracts a stylish, relaxed crowd, drawn by the design-school ambience, good tunes and superb location overlooking the Prinsengracht. Daily 10am–1am (Fri & Sat till 3am).

De Kat in de Wijngaert Lindengracht 160. With the enticing name "The Cat in the Vineyard", this small bar is the epitome of the Jordaan local, and quiet enough for conversation. Sun–Thurs 10am–1am, Fri 10am–3am, Sat 9am–3am.

Nol Westerstraat 109. Raucous but jolly Jordaan singing bar, this luridly lit dive closes late, especially at weekends, when the back-slapping joviality and drunken sing-alongs keep you rooted until the small hours. Daily except Tues 9pm–3am, Fri & Sat until 4am.

Pacific Parc Haarlemmerweg 6 Ⓦwww .pacificparc.nl. Part of the Westergasfabriek redevelopment, this bar-restaurant has lots of outdoor seating looking onto the canal and is a cool summer hangout for food or just drinks. Live music and DJs on weekends. Mon–Thurs 10am–1am, Fri & Sat 10am–3am, Sun 11am–11pm.

Proust Noordermarkt 4. Trendy design bar, but the laidback Jordaan atmosphere attracts students and young urban professionals. The focal point is the giant lamp in the shape of a revolver. Reasonably priced bar menu. Mon 9am–1am, Tues–Thurs 5pm–1am, Fri noon–3am, Sat 9.30am–3am, Sun 11am–1am.

De Reiger Nieuwe Leliestraat 34. Situated in the thick of the Jordaan, this is one of the area's many meeting places, an old-style café-bar filled with modish Amsterdammers, and with faded portraits on the walls. Mains around €19. Sun–Tues 5pm–midnight, Wed–Fri 5pm–1am, Sat 3pm–1am.

't Smalle Egelantiersgracht 12. Candlelit and comfortable café-bar, with a pontoon on the canal out front for relaxed summer afternoons. Daily 10am–1am, Fri & Sat until 2am.

Thijssen Brouwersgracht 107. An old-time favourite with neighbourhood locals. Nothing fancy, but perfect for lingering over coffee or fresh mint tea with a magazine. The tiny terrace gives good views of the bustling market. Mon–Thurs 8am–1am, Fri 8am–3am, Sat 7.30am–3am, Sun 9am–1am.

De Tuin 2e Tuindwarsstraat 13. The Jordaan has some marvellously unpretentious bars, and this is one of the best: agreeably unkempt and always full of locals. Daily 10am–1am, Fri & Sat until 3am, Sun from 11am.

Old Jewish Quarter and Eastern docklands

Brouwerij Het IJ Funenkade 7. Long-established, really rather rudimentary bar and mini-brewery in the old public baths adjoining the De Gooyer windmill. Serves up an excellent range of beers and ales, from the thunderously strong (9 percent) Columbus amber ale to the creamier, more soothing Natte (6.5 percent). Daily 3–8pm.

De Druif Rapenburgerplein 83. Possibly the city's oldest bar, and one of its most beguiling, this is a resolutely brown establishment with barrel-ends on one wall and old photos on another. Attracts a local crew, who give it a village pub feel. Daily 3pm–1am (Fri & Sat till 2am).

De Groene Olifant Sarphatistraat 510. Metres from the Muiderpoort, this is an old, wood-panelled brown *eetcafe*, rich in character, with floor-to-ceiling windows and an excellent varied menu of international (but Dutch-based) dishes; mains from €13. Daily from 11am, but kitchen daily noon–4pm & 6–10.30pm.

KHL Koffiehuis Oostelijke Handelskade 44, ⓦwww.khl.nl. See map, p.111. Old-fashioned coffeehouse (not to be confused with coffeeshop) with wooden panelling and heavy red curtains, located in a 1917 state monument. Small but varied menu and live music in the back room on Saturday and Sunday. Tues–Thurs 11am–1am, Fri 11am–2am, Sat noon–3am, Sun noon–1am.

Odessa Veemkade 259 ☎020/419 3010. This bar-restaurant in a replica of an old Russian boat serves up middling Dutch and international food, good cocktails, and turns into a club after 10pm. A watery place to hang out on a summer's evening. Wed & Thurs 4pm–1am, Fri & Sat 4pm–3am.

De Sluyswacht Jodenbreestraat 1. This pleasant little bar occupies an old and now solitary gabled house that stands sentry by the lock gates opposite the Rembrandthuis. A great spot to nurse a beer on a warm summer's night, with a lovely view down the canal towards the Montelbaanstoren.

▲ De Tuin

The Museum Quarter and Vondelpark

Ebeling Overtoom 52. Dark and cosy lounge bar converted from an old bank. The toilets are in the vaults, and the whole thing is a pretty far cry from the traditional brown café vibe. There's Guinness on tap, decent music and a modern, comfortable environment. Mon–Sat from 11am (from noon on Sun) till late.

Welling J.W. Brouwersstraat 32. Situated right behind the Concertgebouw, this traditional haunt of gloomy Amsterdam intellectuals is usually packed solid with performers and visitors alike before and after evening performances.

Wildschut Roelof Hartplein 1. Five-minute walk from the Concertgebouw. Just around the corner from the *College Hotel*, this busy bar-café is famous for its congenial, spacious Art Deco interior and outdoor seating in summer. By far the nicest place to drink in the area, with a decent menu too.

The outer districts

Bazar Albert Cuypstraat 182. This cavernous converted synagogue is usually buzzing with activity long after the market traders have packed up. A lively place to share a bottle of wine or eat dinner; choose from the Middle Eastern- and South African-influenced menu. Mon–Fri 11am–1/2am, Sat & Sun 9am–midnight/2am.

Café Krull Sarphatipark 2. On the corner of 1e van der Helststraat, a few metres from the Albert Cuypstraat, this is an atmospheric and lively place. Drinks and snacks all day long from 11am.

Chocolate Bar 1e Van der Helststraat 62a. Cool, disco-inspired café-bar that's open for tasty food and cocktails at any time of the day. Perch at the bar on leather stools or lounge in the cosy room out back. It's a shame, though, that the service can be somewhat lackadaisical. Mon–Thurs 10am–1am, Fri & Sat 10am–3am, Sun 11am–1am.

East of Eden Linnaeusstraat 11. See map, p.136. A wonderfully relaxed café-bar across the road from the Tropenmuseum (see p.135), providing inexpensive food and good cocktails. There's an appealing combination of high-ceilinged splendour and gently waving palm trees – with James Dean pictures thrown in to boot. A good place to spend a sunny afternoon.

De Groene Vlinder Albert Cuypstraat 130. There are great views of the bustling market from this pleasant split-level café, with cheap daily specials and bulky salads. Daily 10am–1am (Fri & Sat till 3am).

Kingfisher Ferdinand Bolstraat 24. A nice neighbourhood café that's good for lunch or just a drink if you want to continue imbibing after the Heineken Experience (see p.127) – it's right around the corner. Mon–Thurs 11am–1am, Fri & Sat 11am–3am, Sun noon–1am.

Pilsvogel Gerard Douplein 14. A favourite drinking spot for style-conscious thirty-somethings enjoying the laid-back atmosphere and decent tapas, as well as the good selection of Spanish wines. Daily 10am–1am (Fri & Sat till 3am).

Cafés and tearooms

Amsterdam has plenty of **cafés and tearooms**, serving good coffee, sandwiches, light snacks and cakes at very affordable prices throughout the day. Some may serve alcohol but you wouldn't class them as bars. Usual opening hours are 9am or 10am to 5pm or 6pm; some are closed on Sundays.

Old Centre

De Bakkerswinkel Warmoesstraat 69. Part of an immensely popular chain where you can expect to queue up for a table at lunchtime. Mouth-watering scones with lemon curd and jam, muffins and home-made pies. Tues–Sat 8am–6pm, Sun 10am–4pm. Other branches at Roelof Hartstraat in the Old South and at the Westergasfabriek complex.

Café Beurs van Berlage Beursplein 1. The best chance to glimpse the interior of the Beurs (see p.45), and an elegantly furnished place for coffee or lunch. There are tables outside too. Mon–Sat 10am–6pm, Sun 11am–6pm.

Café Esprit Spui 10. Attached to the chain clothes shop, this is a swish, modern café, with wonderful sandwiches and rolls and superb salads. Mon–Fri & Sun 10am–6pm (Thurs till 8pm), Sat 10am–7pm.

Hofje van Wijs Zeedijk 43. A hidden treasure, this eighteenth-century courtyard sells Indonesian coffee and countless different tea blends. The home-made delicacies are mainly made with organic ingredients. Tues & Wed noon–6pm, Thurs 10am–10.30pm, Fri & Sat 9am–10.30pm, Sun 10am–7pm.

De Jaren Nieuwe Doelenstraat 20. One of the grandest of the grand cafés, overlooking the Amstel next to the university, with three

▲ De Jaren

floors, two terraces and a cool, light feel. A great place to read the Sunday paper – unusually, you'll find English ones here. Reasonably priced food too, and a great salad bar. There are sandwiches and snacks downstairs and a full restaurant upstairs. Daily 10am–1am (Fri & Sat till 2am).

Latei Zeedijk 143. Homely shop and café selling bric-a-brac as well as serving good coffee and decent lunches. Quite a find if you fancy something different from the Chinese restaurants that dominate this end of Zeedijk. Mon–Wed 8am–6pm, Thurs & Fri 8am–10pm, Sat 9am–10pm, Sun 11am–6pm.

Luxembourg Spui 22. The prime watering hole for Amsterdam's advertising and media brigade, this is a long, deep café-bar with a pleasant pavement terrace and an elegant, if faded, area at the back overlooking the Singel. Competent, reasonably priced bar food – and possibly the best hamburgers in town. Very popular. Daily 9am–1am (Fri & Sat till 2am).

't Nieuwe Kafé Eggerstraat 8. Adjoining the Nieuwe Kerk, this straightforward, modern café is popular with shoppers and tourists, serving good, reasonably priced breakfasts, lunches, light meals and great pancakes too, plus mountainous sundaes and ice creams. Daily 8am–6pm.

Puccini Staalstraat 21. This lovely café serves great salads, sandwiches, cakes and pastries, a few doors down from its sister chocolate shop (see p.224). Mon–Fri 8.30am–6pm, Sat & Sun 10am–6pm.

Restaurant 1e Klas Platform 2b, CS. Located in Centraal Station, this is more of a fully fledged restaurant than a café, with a sumptuous turn-of-the-twentieth-century interior and a solid menu of omelettes, sandwiches or more substantial meat and fish offerings at lunchtime. Certainly the best option in the station's immediate vicinity. Daily 8.30am–11pm.

Staalmeesters Kloveniersburgwal 127. Cosy, if slightly cramped, café, with wooden tables and a large replica of Rembrandt's *The Syndics of the Clothmaker's Guild* on the wall. Breakfast until 4.30pm for the genuine night crawler and a small selection of cocktails. The *frites* are served in paper cones. Daily 10am–10.30pm.

Tisfris St Antoniesbreestraat 142. Colourful, split-level café and bar metres from the Rembrandthuis – and minutes from

Waterlooplein. Youthful and popular, with hot rolls, sandwiches, salads and so forth. Daily 9am–7pm.

Villa Zeezicht Torensteeg 7. Small and central, this pastel-coloured café serves excellent rolls and sandwiches, plus some of the freshest apple cake in the city. Daily 8am–9pm.

Vlaamse Friethuis Voetboogstraat 33. This hole-in-the-wall takeaway has a long-established and pretty much undisputed reputation for serving the best *frites* in town. Mon & Sun noon–6pm, Tues–Sat 11am–6pm.

Grachtengordel west

Buffet van Odette & Yvette Herengracht 309. Neat little place decorated in attractive, modern style and serving tasty snacks and light meals, from home-made quiches, soups and pastas through to fruit tarts; cheese omelettes are the house speciality. Mon & Wed–Fri 8.30am–4.30pm, Sat 10am–5.30pm.

Greenwood's Singel 103. Pocket-sized café serving up a tasty line in salads, omelettes and cakes. Look out for the daily specials and order an English-style pot of tea. Mon–Thurs 9.30am–6pm, Fri–Sun till 7pm.

Lunchcafé Winkel Noordermarkt 43. Queue up along with the rest of Amsterdam (or so it seems) for mouth-watering, chunky apple-pie, home-made in the basement of this sober but agreeable lunchroom-cum-restaurant. Great coffee and fresh mint tea to go with it. Mon 7am–1am, Tues–Thurs 8am–1am, Fri 8am–3am, Sat 7am–3am, Sun 10am–1am.

Pompadour Patisserie Huidenstraat 12. This patisserie sells fifty different sorts of bonbon as well as a mouthwatering selection of cakes and candied fruits – take out or eat in. Mon–Fri 10am–6pm, Sat 9am–5pm.

Spanjer & van Twist Leliegracht 60. Hip café-bar with an airy air and brisk modern fittings. Tasty snacks and light meals plus an outdoor terrace right on the canal. Lunch served daily 10am–4pm, evening meals from 6pm.

Van Harte Hartenstraat 24. Crowded and cheerful spot for lunch, dinner and drinks with tasty sandwiches, a large tea selection, home-made pies and bonbons from *Pompadour* (see p.223). The Mediterranean-inspired mains go for around €18. Mon 10am–5.30pm, Tues–Sat 10am–midnight, Sun 11am–7pm.

Grachtengordel south

Bagels & Beans Keizersgracht 504. Bagel specialists, with all sorts of imaginative fillings, attracting a young clientele; their version of strawberries and cream cheese is a big favourite in the summer. The "Beans" part of the name refers to the coffee you can have with your bagel. There are also several other branches, including one in De Pijp (see p.185). This one is open Mon–Fri 9am–5.30pm, Sat & Sun 10am–6pm.

Café Americain American Hotel, Leidseplein 28. There was a time when this café was the trendiest spot in the city, attracting – at one time or another – artists, poets and TV folk. Nowadays, things are much more routine, even canteen-like, but the fanciful Art Nouveau decor, coordinated down to the doorknobs, has survived intact and makes a visit worthwhile(ish). Daily 7am–10pm.

🏃 **Metz Leidsestraat 34.** Pleasantly appointed café on the top floor of the Metz department store, offering panoramic views over the city centre. Asian food is the big deal here, but there are also salads and sandwiches; mains average €11. Mon 11am–6pm, Tues–Sat 9.30am–6pm & Sun noon–5pm.

Panini Vijzelgracht 3. Formica may be a thing of the past almost everywhere else, but not here, giving this split-level, Italian café-cum-restaurant a vaguely beatnik air. Great coffee, sandwiches, pastas and snacks during the day; reasonably priced meat, fish and pasta dishes at night. Mon–Sat 9.30am–11pm, Sun 11.30am–11pm.

Stacey's Pennywell Herengracht 558 ☎020/624 4111. Very stylish split-level café with a tile-covered bar, brassy chandeliers and comfortable lounge sofas. Inventive sandwiches make up the lunch menu; the small but well-balanced dinner menu offers main dishes like Ostrich steak or rack of lamb for around €18. Mon 9am–5pm, Tues–Sat 9.30am–10.30pm, Sun 9.30am–10.30pm.

The Jordaan and Western docklands

Arnold Cornelis Elandsgracht 78. Long-established confectioner and patisserie with a mouthwatering display of pastries and cakes. Take away or eat in the snug tearoom out back. Mon–Fri 8.30am–6pm, Sat 8.30am–5pm.

Festina Lente Looiersgracht 40b. Relaxed, neighbourhood café-bar with mismatched furniture and armchairs to laze in. The outside tables overlooking the canal are a suntrap in the summer when the locals come out to relax with friends for the afternoon; inside is cosy in the winter, and has a good selection of board games. As for the cons: service at the weekend can be slow. Mon noon–1am, Tues–Fri 10.30am–1/3am, Sat 11am–3am, Sun noon–1am.

Il Tramezzino Haarlemmerstraat 79. Richly filled sandwiches (€2.95) according to the old Venetian recipe, to be washed down with a superb espresso, ristretto or cappuccino in an up-to-the-minute setting. Mon & Tues–Sat 9am–6pm, Sun 9.30am–5pm.

The Old Jewish Quarter and Eastern docklands

Blijburg aan Zee Bert Haanstrakade 2004 ⊛ www.blijburg.nl. Last stop of tram #26 from CS. Amsterdam's city beach itself, situated on the IJsselmeer, might be something of a disappointment, but *Blijburg aan Zee* is very happening, with DJs in summer and live music in winter. Opening hours vary according to weather conditions.

De Hortus Plantage Middenlaan 2a. The pleasant café in the orangery of the Hortus Botanicus (see p.103) serves a good range of tasty sandwiches and rolls – plus the best blueberry cheesecake in the Western world. Unfortunately, you do have to pay entry for the gardens (€7) to get to the café. Mon–Fri 9am–5pm, Sat & Sun 10am–5pm; Dec & Jan till 4pm; July & Aug till 7pm.

Kadijk Kadijksplein 6. Tiny split-level place which – contrary to what the homely interior with Delft blue crockery might suggest – has an excellent Indonesian-inspired menu. Tasty *saté*, *soto ajam* and traditional Indonesian *spekkoek* (spiced cake) served with the coffee. Daily noon–10pm, Sat & Sun from 1pm.

The Museum Quarter and Vondelpark

't Blauwe Theehuis Vondelpark 5. These days this is a slightly shabby tearoom/café/bar in the middle of the Vondelpark, but its building dates from the De Stijl period. Downstairs it's a regular self-service park café; upstairs it's a pleasant, circular bar that hosts DJs on Friday and Saturday nights. April–Sept daily 9am–1am (Fri & Sat till 3am); Oct–March Mon–Wed 9am–7pm, Thurs 9am–11pm, Fri 9am–2am, Sat 9am–1am, Sun 9am–10pm.

Brasserie Patou PC Hooftstraat 63. The perfect spot to watch the shopping mania of the Dutch rich and famous, flashing their credit cards on the luxurious PC Hooftstraat. Service can be slow though. Daily 7.30am–6pm.

Cobra Hobbemastraat 18. This stand-alone asymmetric structure behind the Rijksmuseum mainly caters for tourists looking for a convenient place for a drink or a quick bite between exhibitions. It's also a popular late-night hangout, open from 10am until 3am at weekends, otherwise until 9pm.

Keyser Van Baerlestraat 96. In operation since 1905, and right next to the Concertgebouw, this café-restaurant exudes a *fin-de-siècle* charm, with ferns, gliding bow-tied waiters and a dark, carved-wood interior. It's open all day, and you can come here for dinner, but these days it's best as a venue for lunch or coffee. Daily 11am–11pm.

KinderKookKafé Vondelpark 6. A café entirely dedicated to making kids happy with a help-yourself bar where they can top their own sandwich, pizza or cake; the food is simple but tasty. Daily 10am–5pm. See "Kids' Amsterdam", p.241.

De Roos PC Hooftstraat 183. The downstairs café at this New Age centre on the edge of the Vondelpark is one of the most peaceful spots in the city, selling a range of drinks and organic snacks and meals. There's also an upstairs bookshop, and any number of courses in yoga and meditation. Mon–Fri 8.30am–9pm, Sat & Sun 8.30am–5.30pm.

Toussaint Café Bosboom Toussaintstraat 26. This cosy, very friendly café not far from the Vondelpark is a pleasant spot for lunch – excellent sandwiches, toasties and *uitsmijters*, as well as tapas-style options, although service can be slow. Daily 10am–midnight (Fri & Sat till 1am).

Vertigo Vondelpark 3. Attached to the Filmmuseum, this is a pleasant place to while away a summer afternoon at the tables outside overlooking the park; in winter, take refuge in the intimate basement interior. Good food, too, at all times of day. Mon–Fri 11am–1am, Sat & Sun 10am–1am.

The outer districts

Bagels & Beans Ferdinand Bolstraat 70. Large southern branch of this popular coffee and bagel joint, just opposite the Albert Cuypmarkt, with outside tables. Snacks include tuna melts, soups and club sandwiches. Mon–Fri 8.30am–5.30pm. Sat & Sun 9.30am–6pm.

Granny 1e van der Helststraat 45. Just off the Albert Cuypmarkt, with faded, old-fashioned Dutch appeal and terrific *appelgebak* and *pana montata*. Tues–Sat 9am–6pm.

Restaurants

Traditionally at least, **Dutch cuisine** lacks a certain finesse, with its origins firmly rooted in the meat, potato and cabbage school of cooking. That said, many restaurants offer tasty renditions of Dutch dishes, plus a healthy selection of vegetarian and seafood places. Nonetheless, it's the city's non-Dutch restaurants that usually steal the gastronomic limelight – especially the abundance of outstanding Indonesian restaurants.

Fish stalls

One of the pleasures of Amsterdam is to sample the various **fish and seafood specialities** sold from stalls dotted around the city centre – all delicious: raw herring (*haring*), smoked eel (*gerookte paling*), mackerel in a roll (*broodje makreel*), mussels (*mosselen*) and various kinds of deep-fried fish. Look out, too, for "green" or *maatje* haring, eaten raw with onions in early summer; hold the fish by the tail, tip your head back and dangle it into your mouth, Dutch-style. Among other places, there are stalls at the following city centre locations: Nieuwmarkt, Westermarkt, Stromarkt, Haarlemmerplein, Albert Cuypstraat.

Intense competition keeps **prices** down to manageable proportions, and in all but the ritziest of joints you can expect to pay no more than €20–25 for a main course, usually less. As for **opening hours**, the Dutch eat out early, with most restaurants opening at 5.30pm or 6pm and closing their doors around 10pm, though you'll still be served if you're already seated. At all but the least expensive places, it's a good idea to call ahead and **reserve** a table, especially on Thursday, Friday and Saturday nights. Almost all of the larger or smarter restaurants take **credit cards**, but don't assume this to be the case at smaller or cheaper places. A **tip** of about ten percent is pretty much expected; the custom is generally to hand some change directly to your server rather than adding it to the bill.

We've listed the restaurants below by **type of cuisine**, but there's an alphabetical list in the index at the back of the book; locations are marked on the colour **maps**, also at the back of this book.

The Old Centre

Chinese

Golden Chopsticks Oude Doelenstraat 1 ⓣ020/620 7040. Cheap and cheerful canteen-style Chinese food on the edge of the Red Light District. Very central, and,

▲ Hoi Tin

despite the Spartan interior, among the best Chinese food you'll find in Amsterdam. No credit cards. Daily 11.30am–1am.

Hoi Tin Zeedijk 122 ⓣ020/625 6451. You can always trust a restaurant where you have to walk through the kitchen to get to your table, and this one is no exception: a constantly busy Chinatown favourite with an enormous menu (in English too). Dim sum at lunchtime. Daily 11am–11.30pm.

🏃 **Nam Kee Zeedijk 111–113** ⓣ020/624 3470. Arguably the best of a number of Chinese diners along this stretch, and attracting a loyal clientele. Quick service, great food. There's another, slightly posher location at Gelderskade 117 (ⓣ020/639 2848). Both daily noon–midnight.

Wing Kee Zeedijk 76 ⓣ020/623 5683. Simple Chinese restaurant that's popular with the local Chinatown community. Good food, and very cheap too, although the service isn't great. Daily noon–10pm.

Dutch and Modern European

🏃 **Blauw Aan De Waal Oudezijds Achterburgwal 99** ⓣ020/330 2257. Quite a haven, situated down an alley in the heart of the Red Light District, with tremendous French-Dutch food and a wonderfully soothing environment after the mayhem outside. Mon–Sat 6–11.30pm.

Brasserie Harkema Nes 67 ☎020/428 2222.
Very sleek and stylish converted warehouse
restaurant, whose moderately priced food –
mains €14–19 – is sometimes good, and
sometimes more variable than you might
expect. The menu is appealing enough, but
service sometimes leaves something to be
desired, delivered by fresh-faced youths
who tend not to have a clue. Daily
11am–11pm.

Hemelse Modder Oude Waal 9 ☎020/624 3203.
Sleek, large restaurant serving a tasty menu
of Dutch and vaguely European food in an
informal atmosphere. Service is very
attentive and – despite the trendy environment – not at all precious, and the food is
excellent and reasonably priced. Deservedly
popular. Main courses for €19.50, and
three-course menus for €29.50. Daily
except Mon 6–11pm.

Keuken Van 1870 Spuistraat 4 ☎020/620 4018.
This large, light restaurant has been serving
hearty Dutch food to cheapskates for years
and continues – justifiably – to thrive. Its
three-course €7.50 menu is one of the city's
best bargains. Mon–Sat 5–10pm.

De Roode Leeuw Damrak 93 ☎020/555 0666.
Fusty old Dutch restaurant that's good for
both a quick bite at lunchtimes at the front –
pea soup, herrings, *uitsmijters* – or a full
evening meal in the more formal main
restaurant just behind. A good place if you
want to sample a traditional Dutch feed.
Main courses go for €15–20. Daily 7–10am
& noon–10pm.

De Silveren Spiegel Kattengat 4 ☎020/624 6589.
There's been a restaurant in this
location since 1614, and "The Silver Mirror"
is one of the best in the city, with a
delicately balanced menu of Dutch cuisine.
The proprietor lives on the coast and brings
in the fish himself. Spectacular food, with a
cellar of 350 wines. Four-course dinner for
two at a table set with silver is a cool €100,
though you can get a main course for €30.
Mon–Sat 5.30–10.30pm.

Skek Zeedijk 4 ☎020/427 0551, ⓦwww.skek
.nl. A no-nonsense cultural *eetcafé* run by
students. Cheap mains like Moroccan fish
stew or fried tortilla are accompanied by
seasonal vegetables. Check the website for
their frequent live music and exhibitions.
Free wi-fi access and student discounts.
Daily noon–10pm.

Supper Club Jonge Roelensteeg 21 ☎020/344 6400.
A five-course set menu is served at
8pm to customers lounging on mattresses
listening to a DJ on a raised stage. The
fusion food is of a very high standard,
though some may find the whole concept
pretentious or downright disconcerting – it's
not the most comfortable way to eat dinner.
Diners have free entry to the members-only
club downstairs. It's expensive, since there's
no à la carte and you have to have the set
dinner at €65 a pop (€70 at weekends);
booking essential. You can also try *Supper-
club Cruise*, which leaves from pier 4 behind
Centraal Station on Friday and Saturday
nights (☎020/344 6403). Daily
7.30pm–1am.

Van Beeren Koningsstraat 54 ☎020/622 2329.
This *eetcafé* serves a satisfying mixture of
Dutch staples and modern European dishes
in relaxed surroundings. The food is good,
and the setting cosy – and it remains a
moderately priced choice. Daily
5.30–10.15pm.

Van Kerkwijk Nes 41 ☎020/620 3316. It
looks like a bar but is more of a
restaurant these days, serving steaks, fish
and so on, from an ever-changing menu
that isn't written down, but heroically
memorized by the attentive waiting staff.
Good food, and cheap too – mains from
€12.50. Daily noon–10pm.

D' Vijff Vlieghen Spuistraat 294 ☎020/530 4060, ⓦwww.thefiveflies.com.
One of the city's best restaurants, "The Five Flies"
occupies immaculate ground-floor
premises kitted out in a smart version
of traditional Dutch style, from the tile-
and wood-panelled walls to the beamed
ceiling and antique embossed leather
hangings. Intimate and very cosy, its
enterprising menu features imaginative
renditions of traditional dishes, with herring
and suckling pig being two favourites.
Superb service. Main courses €28–32.
Daily 6–10pm.

In de Waag Nieuwmarkt ☎020/422 7772.
Comfortable café-restaurant housed in a
historic building bang in the centre of the
Nieuwmarkt. The building has been well
converted, there's outside seating, and the
food is reasonable, if not great.
Sandwiches, burgers and salads are
served at lunchtime, with more substantial
dishes in the evening – or there's a menu
of tapas, oysters and various other nibbles
if all you want is a snack with a drink. Daily
10am–midnight.

Fish

Kopke Adega Koggestraat 1 ☎020/€22 4587.
Mediterranean-style fish restaurant that
does a great *bouillabaisse*, as well as some
tasty, mainly Iberian fish and shellfish
dishes; you can sample them in the restaurant itself or in the more informal tapas bar.
Decent prices too – you'll spend no more
than about €30 for three courses à la carte.
Daily 6–10.30pm.

Lucius Spuistraat 247 ☎020/624 1831. This
long-established, bistro-style restaurant,
with its high-varnish wooden panelling, is
one of the best fish restaurants in town. The
lemon sole, when it's on the menu, is
excellent and so are the seafood platters.
Mains €25, a tad less for the daily special.
Daily 5pm–midnight.

French, Belgian and Swiss

De Brakke Grond Nes 43 ☎020/626 0044.
Modern, high-ceilinged *eetcafé* specializing
in Belgian beer and food, often full of people
discussing the performance they've just
seen at the adjacent Flemish Cultural
Centre. Daily 2–10pm.

🏃 **Café Bern** Nieuwmarkt 9 ☎020/622
0034. This place is really more of a
bar, but it's well known for its food, which is
excellent, for example the alcoholic cheese
fondue. It's very cosy and usually extremely
crowded, so it's best to book. If not, just get
plastered at the bar while you wait for a
table. Daily 6–11pm.

De Compagnon Guldenhandsteeg 17 ☎020/620
4225. This traditional restaurant serves
decent French food to a self-consciously
discerning clientele in an old-fashioned
atmosphere. There's a great, if not
especially cheap, wine list, too. It's
expensive – reckon on €25-plus for a main
course – and tends to be fully booked well
in advance, but you might get in for lunch.
Daily except Sun noon–2pm & 6–10pm;
evenings only on Sat.

Indonesian

Kantjil en de Tijger Spuistraat 291 ☎020/620
0994. This high-quality Indonesian restaurant
has been somewhat of an institution for over
twenty years. The traditional *rijsttafels* start
at €22 per person and are served in a
stylish wood-panelled setting. Mon–Fri
4.30–11pm, Sat & Sun noon–11pm.

Sie Joe Gravenstraat 24 ☎020/624 1830. Small
café-restaurant whose great value-for-money

menu is far from extensive but comprises
well-prepared, simple dishes such as *gado
gado*, *sateh* and *rendang*. Mon–Sat
11am–7pm, Thurs till 8pm.

Italian

🏃 **Mappa** Nes 59 ☎020/528 9170. Classic
Italian food with some inventive twists,
incorporating good home-made pasta
dishes and excellent service in an unpretentious and modern environment. Daily
6–9.45pm (Fri & Sat till 10.45pm).

Vasso Roozenboomsteeg 12 ☎020/626 0158.
Genuine, creative restaurant off a corner of
the Spui, housed in three curvy, sixteenth-
century buildings. Polite and attentive
service and moderate prices – around €20
for a main course. Daily 5–11pm.

Japanese

Kobe House Nieuwezijds Voorburgwal 77
☎020/622 6458. Not a lot of atmosphere,
partly because it's a big restaurant that
rarely seems to get full. But if you're craving
sushi or other Japanese treats, this is the
place. Daily noon–10.30pm.

Pancakes

Pannekoekhuis Upstairs Grimburgwal 2
☎020/626 5603. Minuscule place in a
tumbledown house opposite the university
buildings, with sweet and savoury pancakes
at low prices. Student discounts. Fri & Sat
noon–6pm, Sun noon–5pm.

Spanish and Portuguese

Centra Lange Niezel 29 ☎020/622 3050. This
authentic Spanish cantina is a long-standing
Red Light District favourite, with a wonderful
selection of Spanish food, masterfully
cooked and genially served. Daily
1.30–11pm. Cash only.

De Portugees Zeedijk 39 ☎020/427 2005. Truly
a little piece of Portugal on the Zeedijk, with
chaotic service and authentically hearty and
filling (rather than gourmet) food – tasty fish
stews, garlicky sausages, salt cod and
eggs. Tues–Sun 6–10.30pm.

Thai

🏃 **Bird** Zeedijk 77 ☎020/420 6289. This
Thai canteen is always packed, and
rightly so, drawing people from far and wide
for its cheap and authentic Thai fare. Its big
brother across the road (also called *Bird*)

serves much the same food in slightly more upscale surroundings. Daily 2–10pm.

Krua Thai Staalstraat 22 ☎020/622 9533. High-quality Thai restaurant with excellent fish and seafood dishes and moderate prices, with most main dishes going for around €15. Daily 5–10.30pm.

Grachtengordel west

Dutch and Modern European

Belhamel Brouwersgracht 60 ☎020/622 1095. Smashing restaurant where the Art Nouveau decor makes a delightful setting and the menu is short but extremely well chosen, mixing Dutch with French dishes. Main courses at around €20–25. The prime tables have charming canal views too. Daily 6–10pm.

De Luwte Leliegracht 26 ☎020/625 8548. This cordial restaurant is kitted out in attractive style, its yellow tables and pastel walls embellished with Art Nouveau flourishes. The small but well-chosen menu offers first-rate Dutch/Mediterranean cuisine – the seafood is especially delicious. Mains from €20. Daily 6–10pm.

Prego Herenstraat 25 ☎020/638 0148. Informal Mediterranean restaurant with sharp modern decor offering an inventive menu of rich dishes, including such delights as *coq au vin*, ravioli and red sea bass with couscous. Mains €25 and up. Daily 6–10.30pm.

Proeverij 274 Prinsengracht 274 ☎020/421 1848. Inviting split-level restaurant with sixteenth-century relics on the wall and a first-class menu offering classic dishes with a modern twist. Solely organic meat and in-season fish are served. Mains from €23 and up, but well worth splashing out on. Daily 5.30–10.30pm.

Saint Martin Prinsengracht 358 ☎020/620 2757. Cheerful little place offering Mediterranean cuisine, using only the freshest ingredients, in an informal setting. Attractively located on a canal. Wed–Sun 4–10pm.

Stout Haarlemmerstraat 73 ☎020/616 3664. Lively and fashionable café-restaurant, popular with locals. Great sandwiches and salads in the daytime, and everything from duck to fresh oysters in the evening. Comfortable velvet lounge seats outside. Daily 10am–11pm, Sun from 11am.

Werck Prinsengracht 277 ☎020/627 4079, ⓦwww.werck.nl. Located right next to the Anne Frank Huis this smart place offers flavoursome mains, such as pan-fried John Dory and venison stew for around €18. At night it's a livelier affair, with DJs. Tues–Sat 5–11pm.

't Zwaantje Berenstraat 12 ☎020/623 2373. Traditional Dutch restaurant, down to the mini-rugs on the tables, that serves up reasonably priced food with main courses around €15. Well known for its liver and onions. Daily 4.30–11pm.

French and Belgian

Chez Georges Herenstraat 3 ☎020/626 3332. Smart-to-formal, split-level, intimate restaurant offering highly rated, upmarket cuisine with an emphasis on meat dishes; mains €23 and up. Open from 6pm, but closed Wed & Sun.

D'Theeboom Singel 210 ☎020/623 8420. Traditional French restaurant in an old, attractive canal house a short walk from Dam Square. Relaxed atmosphere; attentive service. Mains from around €24. Mon–Sat 6–10pm.

Greek

De Twee Grieken Prinsenstraat 20 ☎020/625 5317. In a creatively renovated old shop, this appealing Greek restaurant, with its wood panelling and attractive outside terrace, offers all the favourites in an intimate, informal setting. Main courses average €15–20. Daily 5–11pm.

Indonesian

Cilubang Runstraat 10 ☎020/626 9755. Tiny but much-liked Indonesian restaurant, with a friendly atmosphere, serving well-presented, spicy dishes with mains hovering at around €20 and the traditional *rijsttafel* from €23 and up. Tues–Sun 6–11pm.

Italian

Bussia Reestraat 28 ☎020/627 8794. Recently opened top-notch Italian restaurant with fresh ingredients. Everything is home-made, from the original Italian *gelato* to the pasta. Many wines sold by the glass. Mains around €25, a bit less for pasta. Daily noon–3pm & 6–10.30pm.

Pancakes

Pancake Bakery Prinsengracht 191 ☎020/625 1333. Located in the basement of an old canal house, this long-established restaurant offers a mind-boggling range of fillings for its

▲ Bussia

pancakes. Very popular with tourists; pancakes for around €9. Daily noon–9.30pm.

Thai

Top Thai Herenstraat 28 ☎020/623 4633. Popular restaurant serving some of the best, spiciest and most authentic Thai food in the city – no mean feat given the quality of the opposition. Main courses average around €12. Daily 4.30–10.30pm.

Vegetarian

Bolhoed Prinsengracht 60 ☎020/626 1803. Something of an Amsterdam institution, this popular vegan and vegetarian restaurant features New Age decor and a daily changing menu, plus organic beer to wash it all down with. Main courses around €15. Daily noon–10pm.

Grachtengordel south

African

Axum Utrechtsedwarsstraat 85 ☎020/622 8389. Small and inexpensive Ethiopian café-restaurant offering a wide choice of authentic dishes. Daily except Mon from 5–11pm.

Dutch and Modern European

Kitsch Utrechtsestraat 42 ☎020/625 9251. Flower power goes over the top in this retro restaurant, with old movies projected on the wall and cushions in every thinkable design. The menu is less adventurous, ranging from a simple hamburger to lobster at reasonable prices. Tues–Sat 6–11pm.

Piet de Leeuw Noorderstraat 11 ☎020/623 7181. Arguably Amsterdam's best steakhouse, an old-fashioned, darkly lit, wood-panelled affair dating back to the 1940s. Doubles as a local bar, but the steaks, served in several different ways and costing around €16, are excellent. Mon–Fri noon–11pm, Sat & Sun 5–11pm.

Fish

Le Pêcheur Reguliersdwarsstraat 32 ☎020/624 3121. Smart, pastel-painted seafood restaurant with a lovely garden terrace in the summer. The fish arrives daily from the port of IJmuiden and defines both the menu and the daily specials. Prompt and efficient service. Main courses average around €25. Mon–Fri noon–3pm & Mon–Sat 5.30–11pm.

French and Belgian

Bonjour Keizersgracht 770 ☎020/626 6040. Bistro-style French restaurant in a cosy basement setting; particularly good charcoal-grilled dishes. Mains around €18. Wed–Sun 5–11pm.

Le Zinc... et les autres Prinsengracht 999 ☎020/622 9044. Wonderfully atmospheric little place decorated in rustic style and featuring imaginatively prepared French "peasant" food. Main courses in the region of €26, plus a particularly good wine list. Closed for renovation at the time of writing.

Quartier Latin Utrechtsestraat 49 ☎020/622 7419. Split-level, intimate, bistro-style restaurant serving up a (broadly) French menu – for example, *tournedos* with Roquefort sauce. Main courses €18–20. Tues–Sun 5.30–11pm.

Van de Kaart Prinsengracht 512 ☎020/625 9232. Excellent French/Mediterranean basement restaurant decorated in minimalist style and featuring an inventive menu, with stand-out dishes including poached lobster, home-cured bacon and mushroom risotto. Main courses for €28.50. There's a good cellar too. Mon–Sat 6.30–10.30pm.

Indian

Shiva Reguliersdwarsstraat 72 ☎020/624 8713. One of the city's best Indian restaurants in

terms of quality and price, with a good selection of dishes, all expertly prepared. Vegetarians are well catered for too. Main courses from as little as €12.50. Daily 5–11pm.

Indonesian

Bojo Lange Leidsedwarsstraat 51 ℡020/622 7434. One of the best-value Indonesian places in town. Recommended for its young, lively atmosphere and late opening hours, though the food itself is very much a hit-and-miss affair, and you may have to wait a long time both for a table and service. Main courses average €9–13. Mon–Thurs 4pm–2am, Fri 4pm–4am, Sat noon–4am, Sun noon–2am.

Puri Mas Lange Leidsedwarsstraat 37 ℡020/627 7627. Exceptionally good-value Indonesian restaurant near the Leidseplein. Friendly and informed service preludes spectacular *rijsttafels*, both meat and vegetarian. Main courses from €15. Daily from 6pm.

Tujuh Maret Utrechtsestraat 73 ℡020/427 9865. Impressive Indonesian food, notable for its rich combinations which don't compromise on authentic taste. Mains €15–25. Daily noon–10pm, Sun evening only.

Italian

D'Antica Reguliersdwarsstraat 80 ℡020/623 3862. Long-established restaurant serving authentic Italian cuisine in plain but pleasant premises; no pizza, and dreadful chips, but otherwise perfectly fine. Main courses average €25. Mon–Thurs 6–11pm, Fri & Sat 6pm–midnight.

Japanese

Japan-Inn Leidsekruisstraat 4 ℡020/620 4989. Warm and welcoming restaurant in the midst of the Leidseplein buzz. Sushi and sashimi popular with Japanese tourists and Dutch business folk alike. Main courses range from €15 to €35. Daily 5pm–midnight.

Tomo Sushi Reguliersdwarsstraat 131 ℡020/528 5208. Quality, hip Japanese grill and sushi place, popular with a young, professional crowd. Mains begin at €17. Daily 5.30–10.30pm.

Thai

Dynasty Reguliersdwarsstraat 30 ℡020/626 8400. Lavishly appointed restaurant – all orchids and murals – offering a first-rate choice of Indochinese food, with both Vietnamese and Thai options. Main courses from €20. Daily except Tues 5.30–10.30pm.

Vegetarian and organic

Golden Temple Utrechtsestraat 126 ℡020/626 8560. Laid-back place with a little more soul than the average Amsterdam veggie joint. Inexpensive, well-prepared, lacto-vegetarian food and pleasant, attentive service. No alcohol. Daily noon–3pm & 5–9.30pm.

The Jordaan and Western docklands

African

Semhar Marnixstraat 259 ℡020/638 1634. This small and popular restaurant's simple but authentic Ethiopian menu features meat, fish or vegetable dishes, such as lamb, catfish or chickpeas, soaked up with a large, flat, spongy bread. The vegetarian dish of lentils, spinach and pumpkin is delicious. Also try the African beer served in a *calabash*. Mains from €10.50. Daily except Mon 4–10pm.

Dutch and Modern European

Balthazar's Keuken Elandsgracht 108 ℡020/420 2114. As the name suggests (*keuken* being kitchen), this restaurant makes you feel like you've accidentally stumbled into someone's kitchen. The

▲ Bolhoed

weekly changing three-course menu is more sophisticated, made with only the freshest ingredients. Make sure to book ahead, as they have limited opening hours and tend to fill up quickly. Wed–Fri from 6pm.

Claes Claesz Egelantiersstraat 24 ⊕ 020/625 5306. Exceptionally friendly Jordaan restaurant that attracts a mixed crowd and serves excellent Dutch food. Fridays and Saturdays feature various Dutch theatrical and musical acts between courses. Their three-course menu will set you back about €27. Wed–Sun 6–11pm.

De Eettuin 2e Tuindwarsstraat 10 ⊕ 020/623 7706. Hefty, eminently affordable portions of Dutch food, with salad from a self-service bar. Non-meat-eaters can content themselves with a choice of tasty vegetarian dishes, and all mains (from €14) come with a choice of rice or potatoes. Daily 5.30–11.30pm.

Jur Egelantiersgracht 72 ⊕ 020/423 4287. Friendly restaurant and bar serving a varied menu, including fish, steaks and cheese fondue. Main courses €15–18. Tues–Fri from 4pm till late, Sat & Sun from noon.

Moeders Rozengracht 251 ⊕ 020/626 7957. Really cosy restaurant just across from the Singelgracht whose theme is obvious from the moment you step inside – mothers (*moeders*), photos of thousands of whom

plaster the walls. You're welcome to bring your own mother along, but if not then just savour the moderately priced Dutch staples and daily specials – traditional food, well presented and with the odd modern twist. Mains €13 and up, three-course menus €26–30. Daily 5–10.30pm.

Fish

Albatros Westerstraat 264 ⊕ 020/627 9932. Nautically themed, family-run restaurant, with a cosy conservatory out front, serving some mouthwateringly imaginative fish dishes. A great place to splash out and linger over a meal; mains from €25; three-course menu €35. Daily except Tues & Wed 6–11pm.

French and Belgian

Bordewijk Noordermarkt 7 ⊕ 020/624 3899. A chic, well-lit and roomy restaurant decorated in relaxed, minimalist style and serving delicious French cuisine with Italian gastronomic influences. Mains start at €26. Tues–Sun 6.30–10.30pm.

De Gouden Reael Zandhoek 14 ⊕ 020/623 3883. Fine French food in a unique setting up in the Westerdok. The bar, as described in the novel of the same name by Jan Mens, has a long association with dockworkers. Main courses hover around €15–20. Daily 6–10.30pm.

Italian

Burgers Patio 2e Tuindwarsstraat 12 ⊕ 020/623 6854. Despite the name (the site used to be occupied by a butcher's), there isn't a burger in sight in this long-established and convivial restaurant, which has managed to retain its informal atmosphere without compromising on service and taste. The food is wonderfully presented, with Italian-inspired dishes and a good choice of daily specials as well as vegetarian options. Mains from €15. Daily from 6pm till late.

Cinema Paradiso Westerstraat 186 ⊕ 020/623 7344. Fast-moving restaurant covering all the Italian classics with vim and gusto. It's in a former cinema, complete with chandeliers, and is very popular, so you may have to shout to be heard. Dress to kill/thrill. Pastas and pizzas kick off at around €12. Tues–Sun 6–11pm.

Yam Yam Frederik Hendrikstraat 90 ⊕ 020/681 5097. Top pizzeria and *trattoria* in a simple, traditonal dining room with an open kitchen. It attracts the couples

▲ Claes Claesz

and hip young parents of the neighbourhood with its excellent pizza toppings, including fresh *rucola* and truffle sauce. Pizzas €8–13. Booking strongly advised. Tues–Sun 6–10pm.

Middle Eastern

Nomads Rozengracht 133 ☎020/344 6401. The place to enjoy Arab meze while comfortably lying on kitschy sofas indulging the thousand and one nights atmosphere. A DJ takes over later in the evening. Meze for around €7. Daily 7pm–10.30pm (Fri & Sat till 11pm).

Spanish

Duende Lindengracht 62 ☎020 420 6692. Wonderful and busy tapas bar (€3–5), with a tiled interior, mismatched wood furniture, and a warm and inviting feel. Also includes a small venue out back for live dance and music performances, including regular flamenco every Saturday from 11pm. Mon–Fri 5–11pm, Sat & Sun 4–11pm.
La Oliva Egelantiersstraat 122 ☎020/320 4316. This sleek Jordaan eatery specializes in *pinxtos*, the delectable Basque snacks on sticks that make Spanish bar-hopping such a delight. With a nod to Dutch tastes perhaps, this is more of a restaurant than a bar, and the *pinxtos* anything but bite-sized; people come here to sit and feast on the grand works of art that cover the bar. But you're more than welcome to sit at the bar and sample one or two with a drink. Daily except Tues noon–10.30pm.

Thai

Rakang Thai Elandsgracht 29 ☎020/627 5012. Richly decorated restaurant with striking paintings and glassware. The Thai food is fresh and delicious and not too highly spiced. The adjacent takeaway is of the same good quality. Main courses average around €18. Daily 6–10.30pm.

Turkish

Divan Elandsgracht 14 ☎020 626 8239. A wonderful, uncomplicated restaurant, with attentive and knowledgeable staff, serving tasty Turkish food – good meze – along with a selection of fish dishes. Starters around €5, mains €16. Small terrace out front. Daily 5–11pm.

Vegetarian and organic

De Vliegende Schotel Nieuwe Leliestraat 162 ☎020/625 2041. Perhaps the pick of the city's cheap and wholesome vegetarian restaurants, "The Flying Saucer" serves delicious food in large portions. Lots of space and a peaceful ambience. Mains around €10. Daily 4–10.45pm.

The Old Jewish Quarter and Eastern docklands

African

Kilimanjaro Rapenburgerplein 6 ☎020/622 3485. Bright African restaurant in a largely forgotten part of town, serving such delicacies as West African antelope goulash, Moroccan tajine and crocodile steak. Vegetarian options available too. Small, moderately priced, simple and super-friendly. Tues–Sun 5–10pm.

Chinese

Nam Tin Jodenbreestraat 11 ☎020/428/8508. Vast cavernous restaurant almost opposite the Rembrandthuis that serves dim sum every day between noon and 5pm. Sister restaurant to *Nam Kee* on Zeedijk (p.186) and one of the best places for dim sum in the city. It serves a large regular menu too. Mon–Sat noon–11pm, Sun noon–10pm.

Dutch and Modern European

Fifteen Jollemanshof 9 ☎0900/343 8336. The Amsterdam branch of chef Jamie Oliver's successful formula, annually giving a bunch of youngsters the chance to prove themselves in a top-notch restaurant. Mediterranean, largely Italian-style menu, with a four-course meal for around €46. Also has a less formal *trattoria* and lounge. Daily noon–3pm & 6–11pm.
Greetje Peperstraat 23 ☎020/779 7450. A cosy, busy restaurant serving Dutch staples with a modern twist. A changing menu reflects the seasons and the favourite dishes of the owner's mother – a native of the southern Netherlands. Superb home cooking in a great atmosphere. Tues–Sun 5–10pm, Sat till 11pm.
Koffiehuis van de Volksbond Kadijksplein 4 ☎020/622 1209. Formerly a Communist Party café and the place where the local dockworkers used to receive their wages, this is now an Oosterdok neighbourhood restaurant with a varied and filling menu

ranging from grilled steak to Thai green curry with mussels. Homely decor and inexpensive food with mains from as little as €12.50. Mon–Sat 6–10pm, Sun 5–9pm. No credit cards.

Lloyd Hotel Oostelijke Handelskade 34 ☎020/561 3636, ⊛www.lloydhotel.com. Situated in the Eastern docklands, just 5min by tram #26 from Centraal Station, this is one of Amsterdam's most unusual hotels (see p.167). It comes complete with an airy, canteen-like, café-restaurant on the ground floor, where they serve a wide range of European dishes made with local ingredients. Mains cost €12–20, sandwiches €4–7. Daily 7am–10pm.

Fish

éénvistwéévis Schippersgracht 6 ☎020/623 2894. An uncomplicated fish restaurant serving an interesting selection of seafood, such as Thai-style mussels for starters and sea bass with rosemary and thyme for mains. No menu – the waiters will tell you what's cooking. Mains at around €20. Tues–Sun 6–10pm.

Italian

🏃 Rosario Peperstraat 10 ☎020/627 0280. Very attractive, canalside restaurant with smart modern decor serving top-quality Italian food in a slightly out-of-the-way corner of the city. There's an open kitchen, and the ravioli goes down a storm. Mains from €21. Tues–Sat 6–11pm.

The Museum Quarter and Vondelpark

African

Lalibela 1e Helmersstraat 249 ☎020/683 8332. Tram #1 or #6 along Overtoom to Jan Pieter Heijstraat. First-rate Ethiopian restaurant, with a well-balanced menu and attentive service. Mains from €8. Daily 5–11pm.

Dutch and Modern European

Bicken Overtoom 28 ☎020/689 3999. Trendy and minimalist restaurant offering fresh, seasonal products with an international twist. Creative mains will set you back around €23. Daily 5.30–10.30pm.

🏃 Loetje Johannes Vermeerstraat 52 ☎020/662 8173. Excellent steaks, fries and salads are the order of the day at this *eetcafé*. The service can be touch and go, but the food is great, and fairly inexpensive.

The pleasant outdoor terrace in the summer is a bonus. Mon–Fri 11am–10pm, Sat evening only.

French and Belgian

🏃 Gent aan de Schinkel Theophile de Bockstraat 1 ☎020/388 2851. Situated just outside the top end of the Vondelpark, a five-minute walk across the pedestrian bridge, this lovely corner restaurant overlooking the Sloterkade canal serves mainly Belgian food, and there's a huge range of bottled Belgian beers to enjoy on the summer terrace. Daily 5.30–10pm.

Le Garage Ruysdaelstraat 54 ☎020/679 7176. This elegant restaurant, with an eclectic French and Italian menu, is popular with a media crowd, since it's run by the well-known Dutch TV cook Joop Braakhekke. Call to reserve at least a week ahead and dress to impress. Prices are moderate, with mains around €30 and a three-course menu for €45. If you just want a snack, try the cocktail bar next door instead. Noon–2pm and 6–11pm; Sat & Sun dinner only.

Greek

Dionysos Overtoom 176 ☎020/689 4441. Inexpensive Greek restaurant just west of the Vondelpark, with a good selection of *meze* and occasional live music. Tues–Sun 5.30–11pm.

Indian

Dosa Overtoom 146 ☎020/616 4838. Halfway along the Vondelpark, this brightly lit corner restaurant concentrates on Southern Indian dishes at moderate prices – mains begin at around €15. Daily 5.30–11.30pm.

Indonesian

Orient Van Baerlestraat 21 ☎020/673 4958. This moderately priced Indonesian restaurant serves up a wide range of excellently prepared dishes, and vegetarians are very well taken care of. Expect to pay around €25 for a *rijsttafel*. Daily 5–10pm.

Sama Sebo P.C. Hooftstraat 27 ☎020/662 8146. Amsterdam's best-known Indonesian restaurant, especially for its *rijsttafel* (€27.50), although, if this seems a little pricey, it's easy to eat more economically by choosing à la carte dishes, and there's a reasonable set lunch for €15 a head too. The food is usually pretty good, though the waiters can be extravagantly rude. Mon–Sat noon–3pm & 5–10pm.

Thai

Khorat Top Thai 2e Const. Huygensstraat 64 ⊕020/683 1297. Small, simple restaurant serving generous helpings of inexpensive Thai food. Service is efficient, though not always with a smile. Mains from just €11. Daily 4–10pm.

The outer districts

Central American

Il Cantinero Marie Heinekenplein 4 ⊕020/618 1844. Right behind the Heineken Experience (see p.127), this fair-sized restaurant has a wide choice of good-value Mexican, Caribbean and Surinamese dishes. Average tapas dish €4.50 and main dishes €16. Worth a visit for its live salsa evenings from 6pm; at 10pm there's a DJ playing salsa and South American rumba tunes. Daily 4pm–1am (Fri & Sat till 3am).

Dutch and Modern European

Canvas op de 7e Wibautstraat 150 ⊕020/716 3817, ⊛www.canvasopde7e .nl. The city's newest hotspot, located in the canteen of a former national newspaper office. It's on the seventh floor, so panoramic views are guaranteed. Mains like tuna steak or vegetable quiche hover around €15 and are served in an urban setting at long picnic tables. It's hard to find the entrance, and you need to ring the doorbell to get in, but that adds to the exclusive feel. DJs on most evenings. Daily noon–4pm & 6–10pm.

De Duvel 1e van der Helststraat 59 ⊕020/675 7517. Immensely popular and always crowded so be sure to book ahead. Mains like duck breast, *saté* and huge salads for around €16. Also a fashionable spot for after-dinner drinks. Daily 11am–4pm & 6–11pm, no lunch on Mon.

De Ondeugd Ferdinand Bolstraat 13 ⊕020/672 0651. A long-standing local favourite, presenting a French-orientated menu with the occasional Eastern twist. Prices are reasonable, with a decent *boeuf bourguignon* or sea bass with chorizo sauce at around €18. Daily 6–11pm.

Hotel de Goudfazant Aambeeldstraat 10 ⊕020/636 5170. It's worth taking the ferry northbound from Centraal Station to try the

French-inspired dishes in the industrial setting of this former garage. A three-course menu with seasonal produce will set you back €30.50. Very trendy, so bookings are essential. Tues–Sun 6–10pm.

Trez Saenredamstraat 39 ⊕020/676 2495. Intimate little place, with good views of the chef cooking Mediterranean-inspired dishes in the open kitchen. Limited menu but very reasonably priced with nothing that exceeds €20. Three-course menu for €27.50. Tues–Thurs 6–10pm, Fri & Sat till 11pm.

Italian

L'Angoletto Hemonystraat 18 ⊕020/676 4182. This small, traditional *trattoria* in the De Pijp neighbourhood has a reputation for simple, hearty food. It's inexpensive and always packed, with long wooden tables and benches creating a sociable atmosphere. Service can be slow and plain rude, so just go for the good food and ignore the rest. Not everything they serve is on the menu so keep an eye on the glass showcase in front of the kitchen for any specials. No bookings, so just turn up and hope for the best. Daily except Sat 6–11.30pm; closed Aug.

Palma Johannes Verhulststraat 104 ⊕020/379 5900. See map, pp.132–133. Within comfortable walking distance of the Concertgebouw, this excellent southern European and Mediterranean mezzanine restaurant, with tables out front for warm summer evenings, offers a good choice of steak, fish and pasta. Portions are large and the atmosphere is relaxed. Three-course menu €37.50, mains €17–25. Daily 6–11pm.

Japanese

Yamazato and Teppanyaki Sazanka Ferdinand Bolstraat 333 ⊕020/678 7111. **Tram #25 from CS to Cornelis Troostplein.** Situated in the swanky *Okura Hotel* (see p.169), and dating back over thirty years, this was the first place to serve Japanese *haute cuisine* food in the Netherlands. Today two of the hotel's four restaurants (including the French *Ciel Bleu*, on the 23rd floor) have Michelin stars, and this is one of the best places to eat Japanese food in the city; *Yamazato* is a very traditional sushi restaurant with over fifty specialities, and an à la carte menu featuring expertly prepared tempura, sashimi and sukiyaki. Reckon on paying €65–75 per person. *Teppanyaki Sazanka* is

▲ Yamazato

mosaic tiles everywhere, serving inexpensive tapas (€4.75) and an interesting variety of main dishes (€9.50–11.50). There's outside seating, too, on a leafy intersection. Thurs–Sun 4.30–10.30pm (also Wednesday in summer).

Surinamese

Warung Swietie 1e Sweelinckstraat 1 ℡020/671 5833. Cheap and cheerful Surinamese–Javanese *eetcafé*, with only a few seats. Budget prices: nothing over €10. Daily 11am–9pm, Sun from 2pm.

Turkish

Saray Gerard Doustraat 33 ℡020/671 9216. Excellent Turkish eatery in the De Pijp neighbourhood. It's cheap too, with an intimate living-room ambience and main courses for €11.50–14.50; mixed meze from €7 per person. Tues–Sun 5–11pm.

Vegetarian and organic

De Waaghals Frans Halsstraat 29 ℡020/679 9609. Well-prepared organic dishes in this cooperative-run restaurant near the Albert Cuypmarkt. This place gets busy early so book ahead to be sure of a table. The menu changes twice a month, and though food takes a while to prepare, the results are generous and delicious. Mains around €13. Tues–Sun 5–9.30pm.

De Witte Uyl Frans Halsstraat 26 ℡020/670 0458. Good restaurant serving free-range poultry and meat and organic vegetables; dishes include grilled barramundi and home-made goat sausages. Two-course menu €39.50. Tues–Sat 6–11pm.

the renowned grill restaurant, where the chef prepares fish, steaks and vegetables at the table; seasonal menu for €92.50. Advance bookings essential. Daily 6.30–10pm.

Middle Eastern

Artist 2e Jan Steenstraat 1 ℡020/671 4264. A small Lebanese restaurant just off Albert Cuypstraat. Inexpensive, though not a place for a drawn-out meal. Set menus €13, smaller dishes around €6. Daily except Mon 5–10pm.

Spanish

Más Tapas Saenredamstraat 37 ℡020/664 0066. Small, Moorish-style restaurant with

Coffeeshops

This is the one Western country where the purchase of **cannabis** has been de-criminalized (see Basics p.31), the most conspicuous result of which has been the rise of the licensed **coffeeshop**, selling bags of dope in much the same way as bars sell glasses of beer. When you first walk into a coffeeshop, however, it isn't immediately apparent how to buy the stuff – it's illegal to advertise cannabis in any way, which includes calling attention to the fact that it's available at all. What you have to do is ask to see the **menu**, which is normally kept behind the counter. This will list all the different hashes and grasses on offer, along with (if it's a reputable place) exactly how many grams you get for your money. The in-house dealer will be able to help you out with queries. The seedier coffeeshops are concentrated in and around the Red Light District; the more congenial in the Grachtengordel. Current **prices** per gram of hash and marijuana range from €10 for low-grade stuff up to €25 for top-quality hash,

Smoking ban

A serious hurdle for coffeeshops was the **new law** introduced in July 2008, banning the smoking of tobacco in public areas, including restaurants and bars. Many of them feared closure, but the coffeeshops bounced back with creative solutions, such as selling **pure weed joints** (not for the faint-hearted!) or joints mixed with **tobacco substitutes**. Like many bars, the larger coffeeshops have also built designated smoking areas.

Another major setback was mayor Cohen's proposal to close down coffeeshops located within 250 metres of a high school, following cities like Rotterdam and The Hague. If this law goes ahead, 43 coffeeshops, including the famous *Bulldog* on the Leidseplein, will have to close by December 2011.

and as high as €60 for really strong grass; most coffeeshops open around 10am or 11am and close around midnight.

The **hash** on sale originates in various countries and is pretty self-explanatory, apart from Pollem, which is compressed resin and stronger than normal. **Marijuana** is a different story, and the old days of imported Colombian, Thai and sensimilia are fading away; taking their place are limitless varieties of *Nederwiet* – Dutch-grown under UV lights and more potent than anything you're likely to have come across. Skunk, Haze and Northern Lights are all popular types of Dutch weed, and should be treated with caution – a smoker of low-grade British draw will be laid low (or high) for hours by a single spliff of skunk. You would be equally well advised to take care with **space-cakes** (cakes or biscuits baked with hash), which are widely available: you can never be sure exactly what's in them and they tend to have a delayed reaction (up to two hours before you notice anything strange – don't get impatient and gobble down another one!). Once they kick in, they can bring on an extremely intense, bewildering high – ten to twelve hours is common. You may also come across cannabis seeds for growing your own; while locals are permitted to grow a small amount of marijuana for personal use, the import of cannabis seeds is illegal in any country, so don't even think about trying to take some home.

Although it might be tempting, don't buy drugs of any sort on the street; if you do, you're simply asking for trouble. The ⓦ www.coffeeshop.freeuk.com website gives potted descriptions of all the city's main coffeeshops. The locations of those listed below are marked on the colour **maps** at the back of this book.

Old Centre

Abraxas Jonge Roelensteeg 12. Quirky mezzanine coffeeshop with spiral staircases that can prove challenging after a spliff. The hot chocolate with added hash is not for the susceptible. Daily 10am–1am.

The Bulldog Oudezijds Voorburgwal 132. The biggest and most famous of the coffeeshop chains with three Oudezijds Voorburgwal outlets at nos. 90, 132 and 218. This one is open daily 10am–1am, till 2am at weekends.

Dampkring Handboogstraat 29. Colourful coffeeshop with loud music and laid-back atmosphere, known for its good-quality hash. Daily 10am–1am.

Extase Oude Hoogstraat 2. Part of a chain run by the founder of the Hash Museum (see p.59). Considerably less chichi than the better-known coffeeshops, but a handy Red Light District standby. Daily 10am–1am.

Grasshopper Oudebrugsteeg 16. This multi-level coffeeshop, with bar, sports screen and restaurant, has tried to steal some thunder from *The Bulldog* over recent years, and is one of the city's more welcoming places for visitors, although its proximity to Centraal Station means that at times it can be overwhelmed by tourists. There's another branch – the original – at Nieuwezijds Voorburgwal 59. Daily 8am–1am.

Homegrown Fantasy Nieuwezijds Voorburgwal 87a. Attached to the Dutch Passion Seed Company, this sells the widest selection of marijuana in Amsterdam, most of it local, hence the name. Daily noon–11pm, till midnight at weekends.

Kadinsky Rosmarijnsteeg 9. Fairly small, but still the largest of the three branches of this small chain. Strictly accurate deals weighed out to a background of jazz dance. The chocolate chip cookies are to die for. Daily 10am–1am, till 2am at weekends.

Rusland Rusland 16. One of the first Amsterdam coffeeshops, a cramped but vibrant place that's a favourite with both dope fans and tea addicts (it has forty different kinds). A cut above the rest. Daily 10am–midnight, till 1am at weekends.

Grachtengordel west

Amnesia Herengracht 133. Stylish and dimly lit coffeeshop with a canalside terrace. Daily 10am–1am.

La Tertulia Prinsengracht 312. Tiny corner coffeeshop, complete with indoor rockery and tinkling fountain. Much better outside, though, as it's on a particularly fine stretch of canal. Tues–Sat 11am–7pm.

Siberië Brouwersgracht 11. Bright, modern coffeeshop set up by the former staff of *Rusland* (see above) and notable for having avoided the over-commercialization of the

larger chains. Very relaxed, very friendly, and worth a visit whether you want to smoke or not; has a good selection of magazines as well as a chessboard. Daily 11am–11pm (Fri & Sat till midnight).

Grachtengordel south

The Bulldog Leidseplein 15 Ⓦ www.bulldog.nl. The biggest and most famous of the coffee-shop chains, and a long way from its pokey Red Light District origins, the main branch of *The Bulldog* is here on the Leidseplein, housed in a former police station. It has a large cocktail bar, coffeeshop, juice bar and souvenir shop, all with separate entrances. It's big and brash, not at all the place for a quiet smoke, though the dope they sell (packaged up in neat little brand-labelled bags) is reliably good. Daily 9am–1am, till 3am at weekends.

Happy Feelings Kerkstraat 51. Formerly a hippie hangout, this is now a fresh and trendy coffeeshop with flatscreen TVs on the walls, attracting a selective crowd. Daily 1pm–1am.

Mellow Yellow Vijzelgracht 33. Spartan but bright coffeeshop with a small, good-quality dope list. It's a little out of the way, but makes up for it in friendliness. Mon–Thurs 9am–midnight, Fri–Sun 8am–1am.

The Otherside Reguliersdwarsstraat 6. Popular with (but not exclusively occupied by) gay smokers, this is a crowded and fun coffeeshop near the Muntplein. In Dutch, "the other side" is a euphemism for homosexuality. Daily 11am–1am.

Stix Utrechtsestraat 21. The quietest branch of an Amsterdam institution for dope-smoking. You can get it all here: coffee, newspaper and a smoke. Daily 11am–1am.

The Jordaan and Western docklands

Barney's Breakfast Bar Haarlemmerstraat 102. This extremely popular café-cum-coffeeshop is simply the most civilized place in town to enjoy a big hit with a fine breakfast – at any time of day. A few doors down, at no. 98, *Barney's Farm* affords a nice sunny spot in the morning and serves alcohol, and across the street *Barney's Uptown* has good cocktails in a trendier environment. Daily 7am–10pm.

Bronx Marnixstraat 92. Smart-looking, multi-level place equipped with a large coma-inducing fish tank and internet

▲ Kadinsky

access up on the mezzanine floor. Daily 10am–midnight.

Paradox 1e Bloemdwarsstraat 2. If you're fed up with the usual coffeeshop food offerings, *Paradox* satisfies the munchies with outstanding natural food, including spectacular fresh fruit smoothies and veggie burgers. Daily 10am–8pm.

Old Jewish Quarter and Eastern docklands

Pollinator Company Nieuwe Herengracht 25 ⓦ **www.pollinator.nl.** Not strictly a coffeeshop, this place is for those serious about growing their own marijuana. The owner can tell you everything you need to know, and stocks the products you need to do it, from seeds to compost, as well as various peripherals such as pipes, cannabis lollies and hemp rock. The small chill-out area offers free tea

and coffee and has a large collection of back issues of *High Times.* Mon noon–7pm, Tues–Fri 11am–7pm, Sat 1.30–7pm.

The outer districts

Greenhouse Tolstraat 91. Tram #4 or #25 from CS. Consistently sweeps the board at the annual Cannabis Cup (see p.251), with medals for its dope as well as for "Best Coffeeshop". Staff are extremely knowledgeable in their "grassy" field; if you're only buying once, buy here. There are also branches at Waterlooplein 345 and OZ Voorburgwal 191. Daily 9am–1am.

Yo-Yo 2e Jan van der Heijdenstraat 79. About as local as you can get, down in De Pijp, to the east of the Sarphatipark, this is a small, airy little place in which to seek out smoking solitude. A little gallery at the back exhibits works by local artists. Daily noon–8pm.

EATING AND DRINKING | Coffeeshops

Entertainment and nightlife

Amsterdam offers a broad range of **music, dance and film**, partly due to its youthful population, and partly thanks to its government subsidies. Indeed, the city is often at the cutting edge of the arts and its frequent **festivals** and fringe events (see Chapter 15) provide plenty of offbeat entertainment. Furthermore, the city is crammed with places offering a wide range of affordable entertainment. Something of a Mecca for **clubbers**, the city comes into its own after dark, with numerous venues clustered around Leidseplein and its environs buzzing into the small hours. Lovers of the **performing arts** are particularly well catered for, with venues such as the state-of-the-art Muziekgebouw (see p.208) and the prestigious Concertgebouw (see p.208) top of the list, not to mention a host of concert halls, theatres and churches hosting all manner of cultural happenings, from modern dance to stand-up comedy.

Information

For information about **what's on**, a good place to start is the **Amsterdam Uitburo**, or **AUB** (Mon–Sat 10am–7.30pm, Sun noon–7.30pm), the city council's cultural office, housed in a corner of the Stadsschouwburg theatre on Leidseplein. You can get advice on anything remotely cultural here, as well as tickets and copies of listings magazines. Of the **listings magazines**, the AUB's own monthly *Uitkrant* is comprehensive and free, but in Dutch; or you could settle for the VVV's bland, English-language *Day By Day* (also free). Alternatively, the free *NL20* magazine (in Dutch) is the most up-to-date and complete reference source and can be found in many supermarkets, cafés and shops. In addition, the Wednesday entertainment supplement of the newspaper *Het Parool* also gives a good overview of most cultural activities and *Amsterdam Weekly* is a free cultural newspaper in English, which comes out every Wednesday and has information on film, music and the arts. Any cinema can provide the fold-out *Film Agenda*, which gives details of all films showing in the city that week (Thurs–Wed). Bars and restaurants often stock similar fortnightly or monthly listings leaflets.

Tickets

Tickets for most concerts and events can be bought from the Uitburo and VVV offices, or reserved by phone through the **AUB Uitlijn** (☎020/795 9950, 9am–8pm); in all cases a booking fee applies, usually 1–2 percent. You can also buy tickets for any live music event in the country at the GWK bureau de change offices at the Leidseplein and at Centraal Station, for a fee of around €3–4. If you're under 30 and plan to take in a few events, you might want to buy a **Cultureel Jongeren Passport** (**CJP**), which costs €15 and gets you reductions on entry to theatres, concerts and *filmhuizen*, and is available from the AUB. Aside from CJP cardholders, the only people generally eligible for **discounts** at cultural events and venues are students and over-65s (though most places will only accept Dutch ID).

Clubbing

After a long lull, **clubbing** in Amsterdam has been re-invigorated by a good range of decent venues that bear comparison with clubs in any other European city, plus plenty of bars hosting regular DJs – most playing variations on house, trance, garage and techno. The best place to find out what's on is the free weekly **listings** magazine *NL20* or pick up the printed "flyer-newspaper" *guestlist.nu* (Ⓦwww.guestlist.nu), which has information on upcoming events. Also check for flyers at Midtown Records, Nieuwendijk 104 (Old Centre), which runs a ticket service for most dance events.

Most clubs charge for entry, with **ticket prices** hovering between €10 and €15 at weekends and dropping to around €7 during the week. A singular feature of Amsterdam clubbing, however, is that you're expected to tip the bouncer if you want to get back into the same place next week; €1 or €2 in the palm of his hand will do very nicely. **Drinks** prices are just slightly more expensive than in cafés at around €3–4, though you'll usually pay more for spirits, but not excessively so. **Dress** up if you want to get into some of the smaller, hipper clubs where space is limited and door staff have carte blanche about who they let in. **Smoking** is not allowed inside, but most clubs have purpose-built smoking lounges. As far as **drugs** go, smoking joints in the designated area is generally fine. Should you need reminding, ecstasy, acid, speed and cocaine are all illegal, and you can expect less than favourable treatment from the bouncers (and the law) if you're caught consuming.

Although all the places listed below **open** at either 10pm or 11pm, there's not much point turning up anywhere before midnight; unless stated otherwise, everywhere stays open until 5am on Friday and Saturday nights, 4am on other nights.

For gay and lesbian clubs see Chapter 12.

Clubs

Arena 's Gravensandestraat 51 (The Old Jewish Quarter and Eastern Docklands) ☎020/850 2410, Ⓦwww.hotelarena.nl.
Part of a large, trendy hotel (see p.167), this club, situated in a former chapel, opens Friday and Saturday only. Occasionally hosts popular international acts, such as Hed Kandi.

Bitterzoet Spuistraat 2 (Old Centre) ☎020/521 3001, Ⓦwww.bitterzoet.com. Spacious but cosy two-floored bar and theatre hosting a mixed bag of events: DJs playing acid jazz, R&B, funk and disco, film screenings and occasional urban poetry nights.

't Blauwe Theehuis Vondelpark 5 (Museum Quarter and Vondelpark) ☏020/662 0254, ⓦwww.blauwetheehuis.nl. Free open-air dancing with DJs playing throughout the summer in the Vondelpark; usually weekends but check website for programme.

Club Home Wagenstraat 3 (Grachtengordel south) ☏020/620 1375, ⓦwww.clubhome.nl. Relaxed dance club, spread over three floors and offering all styles of house and club music. Mixed audience with mainly students on Thursdays and the hip(per) on weekends. Thurs 11pm–4am, Fri & Sat 10pm–5am.

Club NL Nieuwezijds Voorburgwal 169 (Old Centre) ☏020/622 7510, ⓦwww.clubnl.nl. What used to be the city's first lounge bar is now a posh, stylish house club, frequented by the rich and famous. Daily 10pm–3am, Fri & Sat till 4am.

Dansen bij Jansen Handboogstraat 11 (Old Centre) ☏020/620 1779, ⓦwww .dansenbijjansen.nl. Founded by – and for – students, the popular dance nights here have an emphasis on disco, club classics and R&B – and, as you would expect, cheap beer. Open nightly from 11pm; officially you need student ID to get in.

Escape Rembrandtplein 11 (Grachtengordel south) ☏020/622 1111, ⓦwww.escape.nl. This vast club has space enough to house two thousand people, but its glory days – when it was home to Amsterdam's cutting edge Chemistry nights – are long gone, and it now focuses on weekly club nights that pull in crowds of mainstream punters. Recent renovations and the opening of the *Escape* café, lounge and studio should pull in more trendsetting crowds. Impressive sound system and visuals. Thurs–Sun from 11pm.

Heineken Music Hall ArenA Boulevard (Amsterdam Oost) ☏0900/68742 4255, ⓦwww .heineken-music-hall.nl. Metro or train to Bijlmer station. Hosts dance events featuring well-known Dutch DJs, including the renowned Tiesto.

Jimmy Woo Korte Leidsedwarsstraat 18 (Grachtengordel south) ☏020/626 3150, ⓦwww.jimmywoo.nl. Intimate and stylish club spread over two floors. Upstairs, the black lacquered walls, Japanese lamps and cosy booths with leather couches ooze sexy chic, while downstairs a packed dancefloor throbs under the oscillating light from hundreds of light bulbs studded into the ceiling. Popular with young, well-dressed locals, so look smart if you want to join in. Thurs–Sun from 11pm.

Melkweg Lijnbaansgracht 234a (Grachtengordel south) ☏020/531 8181, ⓦwww.melkweg.nl. After the bands have finished, excellent offbeat disco sessions go on well into the small hours, sometimes featuring the best DJs in town. Also plays host to some of the most enjoyable theme nights around, ranging from African dance to experimental jazz-trance.

Nachttheater Sugar Factory Lijnbaansgracht 238 (Grachtengordel south) ☏020/627 0008, ⓦwww.sugarfactory.nl. Busy Leidseplein's "theatrical nightclub" hosts a stimulating programme of cabaret, live music, poetry and theatre – up to two events a night, plus a late-night club that kicks off after the last show. Pulls in a young, trendy crowd. Closed Tues & Wed.

Odeon Singel 460 (Grachtengordel west) ☏020/521 8555, ⓦwww.odeontheater.nl. Originally a brewery, this beautifully restored seventeenth-century canal house has since been a theatre, a cinema and a concert hall, until it was gutted in a fire in 1990. Rescued by the owners of the *Hotel Arena* (see p.167), it's now a stylish nightclub hosting Eighties parties and regular club nights (Fri & Sat) with a splendid bar overlooking the canal. There's also a restaurant (Tues–Sat) and a café (daily).

▲ Odeon

Panama Oostelijke Handelskade 4 (Old Jewish Quarter and Eastern docklands) ☎020/311 8686, ⓦwww.panama.nl. One of Amsterdam's coolest clubs, *Panama* overlooks the IJ and plays host to top-name international DJs Thurs–Sun. Dress to impress. There's also a restaurant, which is open daily from noon.

Paradiso Weteringschans 6–8 (Grachtengordel south) ☎020/626 4521, ⓦwww.paradiso.nl. One of the principal venues in the city, this converted church just around the corner from the Leidseplein is popular with an alternative crowd. On Wednesdays and Thursdays alternative dance night "Noodlanding" continues to draw in the crowds, and look out for DJ sets featuring live performances on Saturdays.

The Powerzone Spaklerweg (Outer districts) ☎020/681 8866, ⓦwww.thepowerzone.nl. Metro Spaklerweg. Situated near Amstel station, southeast of the centre, this is a Saturday-night party zone, with good trance and techno DJs – both Dutch and international – and a capacity of five thousand.

Studio 80 Rembrandtplein 17 (Grachtengordel south) ☎020/521 8333, ⓦwww.studio-80.nl. Right on the Rembrandtplein, this new club attracts the more fashionable underground scene with techno, soul, funk, minimal and electro. A creative breeding ground for young and upcoming DJs, bands and acts. Wed–Mon 11pm–4/5am.

▲ Panama

Winston Kingdom Warmoesstraat 131 (Old Centre) ☎020/623 1380, ⓦwww.winston.nl. This small venue adjacent to the *Winston Hotel* (see p.163) offers eclectic club nights and performances.

Zebra Lounge Korte Leidsedwarsstraat 14 (Grachtengordel south) ☎020/612 6153, ⓦwww.the-zebra.nl. This small, stylish bar set over two floors attracts a lively, younger crowd than the neighbouring *Jimmy Woo* – possibly owing to its less picky door staff. Fri & Sat only.

Rock and pop

As far as **live music** goes, Amsterdam is a regular tour stop for many major artists – so keep an eye on the listings magazines. **Dutch rock and pop** bands are often worth seeking out too. Look out for the celebrated Zuco 103, with a distinctive Brazilian sound, Junky XL and other members of the dance/hip-hop scene, or try to catch rock bands such as Bløf, Kane or Spinvis. Anouk is also a popular draw.

In the southeastern suburbs, the superb 50,000-seater Amsterdam ArenA doubles as the city's music **stadium** for big-name rock bands and artists. The Heineken Music Hall, a simple but acoustically impressive black box close to the ArenA, hosts medium-sized acts, while the two dedicated **music venues** in Amsterdam city centre – the Paradiso and the Melkweg – are on a much smaller scale, and supply a daily programme of music to suit all tastes (and budgets). At the time of writing, plans were ahead to build a new music venue near the Amsterdam ArenA with a capacity of 15,000 visitors to fill the musical gap between stadium acts and smaller venues; **Ziggo Dome** is scheduled to open early 2011. Alongside the main venues, the city's clubs, bars and multimedia centres host occasional performances by live bands.

As far as **prices** go, for big names you'll pay anything between €30 and €60 a ticket; ordinary gigs cost €8–15, although some places charge a membership fee (*lidmaatschap*) on top.

Folk and world

The Dutch **folk music** tradition is virtually extinct in Amsterdam, except for occasional performances by the duo Acda and de Munnik. There are still one or two touring folk singers who perform traditional *smartlappen* ("torchsongs") at the Carré Theater and a few other sympathetic venues, but the best place to catch these traditional songs – a brash and sentimental adaptation of French chanson – is the café *Nol* (see p.180), in the heart of the Jordaan, where they made their name. More accessible is **world music**, for which there are several good venues, including the Akhnaton, the Tropentheater and the Melkweg, the latter two being venues for the **Amsterdam Roots Festival** held in June (see p.250).

Rock, pop and folk festivals

Amsterdam doesn't have many **outdoor music festivals**, but the few events that do take place are usually well attended. Aside from the summer concerts held in the Vondelpark (see p.123), the Oosterpark hosts the free Roots Open Air Festival, a huge one-day event that attracts over 60,000 people and kicks off the aforementioned Roots Festival, though at the time of writing the future of the Roots Festival was uncertain. A new initiative is **Live at Westerpark** (ⓦ www.liveatwesterpark.nl), a chain of concerts held in July on consecutive days around the Westergasterrein area (see p.91), with artists such as Radiohead, R.E.M. and Lenny Kravitz.

Of the **music festivals outside the city**, the most famous is the Pinkpop Festival (ⓦ www.pinkpop.nl) in May/June, down in the south in Landgraaf, near Maastricht. Others include A Campingflight to Lowlands (ⓦ www .lowlands.nl), held over a weekend in August in Flevoland, and Parkpop (ⓦ www.parkpop.nl), Europe's largest free festival, taking place in June at The Hague's Zuiderpark. Major **dance festivals** include Dancevalley (ⓦ www .dancevalley.nl) in Spaarnwoude between Haarlem and Amsterdam, Mystery-land (ⓦ www.mysteryland.nl) in Hoofddorp near Haarlem and Extrema Outdoor (ⓦ www.extrema.nl) near Eindhoven in the south, all held in July/ August. Dates vary, so check the websites before making plans.

Major venues

Amsterdam ArenA ArenA Boulevard (Amsterdam Oost) ☏ 020/311 1333, ⓦ www.amsterdamarena .nl. Metro or train to Bijlmer station. The Ajax soccer stadium also plays host to world-class music acts such as the Rolling Stones and Madonna.

Heineken Music Hall See p.202. A hi-tech music venue attracting international bands ranging from Pink to Franz Ferdinand.

🏃 **Melkweg** See p.202. The Melkweg ("Milky Way") is probably Amsterdam's most famous entertainment venue and also ranks as one of the city's prime multimedia arts centres, with a young, hip clientele. A former dairy (hence the name) just round the corner from Leidseplein, it has two separate halls for live music, hosting a broad range of genres, from reggae to rock. Excellent DJ sessions go on till late at the weekend, with anything from dancehall to indie pop on Saturdays. There's also a monthly film programme, as well as a theatre, gallery and café-restaurant (Marnixstraat entrance; Wed–Sun noon–9pm).

Paradiso Weteringschans 6–8 (Grachtengordel south) ☎020/626 4521, ⒲www
.paradiso.nl. This converted church near the Leidseplein, revered by many for its atmosphere and excellent programme, features local and international bands, ranging from the newly signed to the more established. The venue has also been known to host classical concerts, as well as debates and multimedia events.

Smaller venues

Akhnaton Nieuwezijds Kolk 25 (Old Centre) ☎020/624 3396, ⒲www.akhnaton.nl. A "Centre for World Culture" hosting a wide-ranging programme of events, from salsa nights to Turkish dance parties. On a good night, the place heaves.

Badcuyp Eerste Sweelinckstraat 10 (De Pijp, Outer districts) ☎020/675 9669, ⒲www.badcuyp.nl. Unpretentious music venue located just off the bustling Albert Cuypmarkt, hosting mainly jazz and world music performances with an adjacent convivial *eetcafé*. Dinner concerts on Thursday and Sunday.

De Buurvrouw St Pieterspoortsteeg 29 (Old Centre) ☎020/625 9654. Eclectic, alternative bar, occasionally featuring loud local bands. From 9pm.

Cruise Inn Zuiderzeeweg 29 (Old Jewish Quarter and Eastern docklands) ⒲www.cruise-inn.com. Tram #26 from CS. This volunteer-run clubhouse was set up over twenty years ago by a group of rockabillys. Open Saturdays only from 9pm and located somewhat off the beaten track in Zeeburg, to the northeast of the Oosterdok, but worth the trek, with jam sessions and great live band nights with music from the 1950s and 1960s.

De Heeren van Aemstel Thorbeckeplein 5 (Grachtengordel south) ☎020/620 2173, ⒲www .deheerenvanaemstel.nl. Warm, atmospheric café with swinging soul, jazz and funk gigs. Wed–Sun.

Maloe Melo Lijnbaansgracht 163 (Jordaan and Western docklands) ☎020/420 4592, ⒲www .maloemelo.nl. Dark, low-ceilinged bar, with a small back room featuring lively local blues

acts every day of the week. Jam sessions Sun–Tues & Thurs. Free before 11pm, €5 thereafter.

Mulligan's Amstel 100 (Grachtengordel south) ☎020/622 1330, ⒲www.mulligans.nl. Irish bar that's head and shoulders above the rest for atmosphere and authenticity, with Gaelic musicians and storytellers most nights for free.

OCCII Amstelveenseweg 134 (Museum Quarter and Vondelpark) ☎020/671 7778, ⒲www.occii.org. Former squat bar opposite the western entrance of the Vondelpark, with live alternative music, from indie pop to electro-punk.

Pakhuis Wilhelmina Veemkade 576 (Old Jewish Quarter and Eastern docklands) ☎020/419 3368, ⒲www.cafepakhuiswilhelmina.nl. Tucked away in an old warehouse, this underground venue hosts everything from jazz to pop, funk, punk and folk with live gigs and DJs from Thursday to Sunday.

Skek Zeedijk 4 (Old Centre) ☎020/427 0551, ⒲www.skek.nl. Frequent performances from Thursday to Sunday by singer-songwriters, hip-hop, rock and jazz acts in this pleasant *eetcafé* run by students.

Tropentheater Linnaeusstraat 2 (Amsterdam Oost) ☎020/568 8500, ⒲www.tropentheater.nl. Tram #9 from CS, or #10 from Leidseplein. Part of the Royal Tropeninstituut, east of Artis Zoo, this formal theatre specializes in non-Western drama, dance, film and music. A great place to take in live acts that you wouldn't normally get to see.

The Waterhole Korte Leidsedwarsstraat 49 (Grachtengordel south) ☎020/620 8904, ⒲www .thewaterhole.nl. Late-night bar with live music every night, ranging from punk and rock to jazz and blues. Popular for its regular Monday jam sessions, which attract a raucous but friendly crowd, and for its pool table and cheap beer. Sunday night is ladies' night, with half-price drinks.

Winston International Warmoesstraat 123 (Old Centre) ☎020/623 1380, ⒲www.winston.nl. Part of the arty *Winston Hotel* (see p.163), this adventurous small venue attracts an eclectic crowd and offers a mix of live bands, electro, drum 'n' bass and cheesy pop nights.

Jazz and Latin

For **jazz** fans, Amsterdam can be a treat. Ever since the 1940s and 1950s, when American jazz musicians began moving to Europe, the city has had a soft spot for jazz. Paris stole much of the limelight, but Chet Baker lived and died in

Amsterdam, and he and any number of legendary jazzbos could once be found jamming into the small hours at Casablanca on Zeedijk. Venues have changed a lot since then, varying from tiny bars staging everything from Dixieland to avant-garde, to the large, modern Bimhuis – the city's major jazz venue – which plays host to both international names and home-grown talent. Pianist Michiel Borstlap, cellist Ernst Reijseger and sought-after percussionist Han Bennink – member of the acclaimed contemporary jazz collective, ICP – are among the **Dutch musicians** you might come across, and they're well worth catching if you get the chance.

The **jazz season** runs from September to July, with concerts and festivals held all over the country. The Netherlands boasts one of the best jazz festivals in the world, the **North Sea Jazz Festival**, held in July at the Ahoy in Rotterdam. Comprising three days and nights of continuous jazz on fourteen stages, the event involves around 1200 musicians, among them world-class performers, from Oscar Peterson to Guru's Jazzmatazz. **Tickets** cost from about €75 a day, with supplements for the big names. Information on the event is available from ☎015/214 8393, ⓦ www.northseajazz.com.

The Dutch connection with **Surinam** – a former colony tucked in between Venezuela and Brazil – means that there's a sizeable **Latin American** community in the city, and plenty of authentic salsa and other Latin sounds to be discovered; the best venue for this type of music is Akhnaton, while the Melkweg and Paradiso put on occasional salsa nights.

Venues

Akhnaton See p.205. This crowded, lively venue is your best bet for Latin music.

Bimhuis Piet Heinkade 3 (Old Jewish Quarter and Eastern docklands) ☎020/788 2150, ⓦ www.bimhuis.nl. The city's premier jazz and improvised music venue is located right next to the Muziekgebouw, beside the River IJ to the east of Centraal Station. The Bimhuis showcases gigs from Dutch and international artists throughout the week, as well as jam sessions and workshops. There's also a bar and restaurant for concertgoers with pleasant views over the river.

Bourbon Street Leidsekruisstraat 6 (Grachtengordel south) ☎020/623 3440, ⓦ www .bourbonstreet.nl. Friendly bar with a relaxed atmosphere and quality blues and jazz nightly, Mon–Thurs & Sun until 4am, Fri & Sat until 5am. Free entry before 11pm.

Café Alto Korte Leidsedwarsstraat 115 (Grachtengordel south) ☎020/626 3249, ⓦ www.jazz-cafe-alto.nl. It's worth hunting out this legendary little jazz bar just off Leidseplein for the quality modern jazz every night from 9pm until 3am (and often much later). Though slightly cramped, it's big on atmosphere. Entry is free, and you don't have to buy a beer to hang out and watch the band.

Casablanca Zeedijk 26 (Old Centre) ☎020/625 5685, ⓦ www.casablanca-amsterdam.nl. Though a shadow of its former self, Casablanca still hosts live jazz most nights of the week, when it's not putting on variety and cabaret shows. Check website for programme details.

De Engelbewaarder Kloveniersburgwal 59 (Old Centre) ☎020/625 3772. Comfy old bar with excellent live jazz sessions Sunday afternoons 4–7pm.

Classical and opera

There's no shortage of **classical music** concerts in Amsterdam, with two major orchestras based in the city, plus regular visits by other Dutch ensembles. The **Royal Concertgebouw Orchestra** remains one of the most dynamic in the world, and occupies one of the finest concert halls to boot. The other resident orchestra is the **Netherlands Philharmonic**, also based in the Concertgebouw, which has a wide symphonic repertoire and also performs with the Netherlands Opera at the Muziektheater. Among visiting orchestras, the Rotterdam Philharmonic has a world-class reputation, as does the Radio Philharmonic Orchestra, based in Hilversum outside Amsterdam.

As well as the main concert halls, a number of Amsterdam's churches (and former churches) host regular performances of classical and chamber music – both types of venue are listed here. Others, including the Nieuwe Kerk on Dam Square, the Westerkerk, the Noorderkerk, the Mozes en Aaronkerk on Waterlooplein, and the tiny Amstelkerk on Kerkstraat, occasionally put on one-off concerts, often at very reasonable prices (check with venues for programme details).

The most prestigious venue for **opera** is the Muziektheater (otherwise known as the "Stopera") on Waterlooplein, which is home to the Netherlands Opera company as well as the Dutch National Ballet. Visiting companies sometimes perform here, but more often at the Stadsschouwburg or the Carré Theater.

Tickets are excellent value and aren't as exclusively priced as some European cities, starting from as little as €7.50 for matinee concerts, and rising to €70 for big-name performers.

As far as **contemporary classical music** goes, the Muziekgebouw, overlooking the River IJ, is the city's leading showcase for musicians from all over the world. Local talent is headed by the Asko and Schoenberg ensembles, as well as the Nieuw Ensemble and the Volharding Orchestra. Look out also for Willem Breuker and Maarten Altena, two popular musicians who successfully combine improvised jazz with composed, contemporary classical music.

Classical music festivals

By far the most prestigious multi-venue Dutch festival for contemporary classical music is the annual **Holland Festival** (ⓦ www.hollandfestival.nl) in June, which attracts the best of the country's mainstream and fringe performers in all areas of the arts, as well as an exciting international line-up. Otherwise, one of the more interesting, music-oriented events is the popular **Grachtenfestival**, held at the end of August, a week-long classical music festival (ⓦ www.grachtenfestival.nl), which concludes with a piano recital on a floating stage outside the *Pulitzer Hotel* on the Prinsengracht – with the whole area floodlit and filled with small boats; this can be a wonderfully atmospheric evening. Also around this time – and from two ends of the musical spectrum – Utrecht plays host to the internationally renowned **Early Music Festival** (ⓦ www.oudemuziek.nl), while in early September, Amsterdam holds the **International Gaudeamus Music Week** (ⓦ www.gaudeamus.nl), a forum for debate and premiere performances of cutting-edge contemporary music.

Venues

Beurs van Berlage Damrak 277 (Old Centre) ☎ 020/521 7575, ⓦ www.berlage.com. The splendid interior of the former stock exchange s the setting for regular exhibitions and concerts, though nowadays it's used more for conferences. The resident Netherlands Philharmonic rehearse in the huge Amvest Zaal, the former Corn Exchange Hall, a glassed-in pavilion. The glass-roofed Yakult Zaal (Main Hall) was the location for the royal wedding of Prince Willem-Alexander and Princess Máxima in 2002.

Carré Theater Amstel 115–125 (Grachtengordel south) ☎ 020/524 9452, ⓦ www.theatercarre.nl. This splendid late nineteenth-century

▲ Carré Theater

structure (originally built for a circus) represents the ultimate venue for Dutch folk artists, and hosts all kinds of international performances: anything from Antony and the Johnsons to *Carmen*, with reputable touring orchestras and opera companies squeezed in between.

Concertgebouw Concertgebouwplein 2–6 (Museum Quarter and Vondelpark) ☎020/671 8345, Ⓦwww.concertgebouw.nl. Hearing a concert at the Concertgebouw, one of the most impressive looking – and sounding – venues in the city, is a great experience, especially when the Netherlands Philharmonic Orchestra put on one of their regular performances. The acoustics of the Grote Zaal (Great Hall) are unparalleled, while the smaller Kleine Zaal regularly hosts chamber concerts. Though both halls boast a star-studded international programme, prices are very reasonable, ranging from €15 to €50 (€15 for the sponsored Sunday-morning events, June–Sept). Free Wednesday lunchtime concerts are held from Sept to May (doors open 12.15pm; arrive early), and in July and Aug there's a heavily subsidized series of summer concerts. Look out also for occasional world music and swing/jazz nights.

Engelse Kerk Begijnhof 48 (Old Centre) ☎020/624 9665. The church with the biggest programme: three to four performances a week, usually Fri, Sat & Sun (performances

at 3.15pm or 8.15pm). Tickets are available from the church 30min before the start of performance or in advance from the Uitburo (see p.200).

Marionetten Theater Nieuwe Jonkerstraat 8 (Old Centre) ☎020/620 8027, Ⓦwww .marionettentheater.nl. Maintains an old European tradition with its performances of operas by Mozart and Offenbach. Although they tour the Netherlands and the rest of Europe for most of the year, the wooden marionettes return to Amsterdam in spring, October and Christmas. Call for details of performances, and to find out about their opera dinners.

Muziekgebouw Piet Heinkade 1 (Old Jewish Quarter and Eastern docklands) ☎020/788 2000, Ⓦwww.muziekgebouw.nl. East of Centraal Station, Amsterdam's newest concert hall for over a hundred years, with two new medium-sized concert halls, a café, bar and state-of-the-art acoustics, has given new impetus to the redevelopment going on along the IJ. Its top-quality programme of opera and orchestral music draws a highbrow crowd to this part of town. Worth a visit for the building alone; the café offers great views over the water. The same development also includes the relocated Bimhuis.

Muziektheater Waterlooplein 22 (Old Jewish Quarter and Eastern docklands) ☎020/625 5455, Ⓦwww.hetmuziektheater.nl. Part of the €150 million complex that includes the city hall. The theatre's resident company, Netherlands Opera, offers the fullest, and most reasonably priced, programme of opera in Amsterdam; not surprisingly, tickets go very quickly.

Oude Kerk Oudekerksplein 23 (Old Centre) ☎020/625 8284, Ⓦwww.oudekerk.nl. Hosts organ and carillon recitals, as well as occasional choral events.

Stadsschouwburg Leidseplein 26 (Grachtengordel south) ☎020/624 2311, Ⓦwww.ssba.nl. Somewhat overshadowed by the Muziektheater these days, but still staging significant opera, theatre and dance, as well as occasionally hosting visiting English-language theatre companies. At the time of writing, the construction of their newest concert hall, which will be built over the roof of the Melkweg, was in progress.

Waalse Kerk Oudezijds Achterburgwal 159 (Old Centre) ☎020/623 2074, Ⓦwww .waalsekerk-amsterdam.nl. Weekend afternoon and evening concerts of early classical and chamber music.

Theatre, cabaret and comedy

Surprisingly for a city that functions so much in English, there is next to no **English-language drama** to be seen in Amsterdam, though a handful of amateur companies put on two or three English productions during the summer, and there are also occasional performances by touring groups at the theatres listed below and at other venues dotted around town.

English-language **comedy** and **cabaret**, on the other hand, has gained some ground in Amsterdam, spearheaded by the resident and extremely successful "Boom Chicago" comedy company. During the summer in particular, a number of small venues host mini-seasons of English-language stand-up comedy and cabaret, featuring touring British performers and material that's generally targeted at visitors to the city.

Most of Amsterdam's **larger theatre companies** concentrate either on foreign works in translation or Dutch-language theatre, neither of which is likely to be terribly interesting for the non–Dutch speaker. However, there are plenty of **avant-garde** theatre groups in the city, much of whose work relies on visual rather than verbal impact, as well as one or two companies devoted to **mime**. Look out also for performances at the Amsterdam Marionetten Theater (see opposite). The Amsterdamse Bos Theatre (Ⓦ www.bostheater.nl) puts on summertime open-air performances of Shakespeare's plays (in Dutch). It's an atmospheric evening, with audiences picnicking before the show.

The main event to watch out for, apart from the mainstream Holland Festival (see p.207), is the summer-long **Over Het IJ Festival** (info ☎020/624 6380, Ⓦ www.overhetij.nl), a showcase for all kinds of performance arts at large, often outdoor locations in Amsterdam Noord (thus "over the IJ"). The participation of many interesting small companies pushes the standard of the average production well above that of the usual fringe festival acts. In June, the **International Theatre School Festival** (Ⓦ www.itsfestival.nl) sees the four theatres on Nes, a tiny alley running from Dam square parallel to Rokin, host productions by local and international theatre schools.

Major venues

De Balie Kleine-Gartmanplantsoen 10 (Grachtengordel south) ☎020/553 5151, Ⓦ www.debalie .nl. A multimedia centre for arts and culture located off the Leidseplein, which often plays host to drama, debates, international symposia and the like, sometimes in conjunction with the Paradiso next door. Also has a lovely, roomy, mezzanine bar.

Boom Chicago Leidseplein 12 (Grachtengordel south) ☎020/423 0101, Ⓦ www.boomchicago.nl. Something of a phenomenon in Amsterdam, this rapid-fire improv comedy troupe hailing from America performs at the Leidseplein Theater nightly to crowds of both tourists and locals, and receives rave reviews. Inexpensive food, cocktails and beer served in pitchers.

Carré Theater See p.207. A chunky old building on the eastern bank of the Amstel which, aside from its folk associations, hosts all kinds of top international acts, with an emphasis on hit musicals.

Comedy Café Max Euweplein 43 (Grachtengordel south) ☎020/638 3971, Ⓦ www .comedycafe.nl. Small stand-up theatre with a bar and restaurant that sometimes hosts English-language acts; look out for Sunday night's "In Your Face", an improv show in English.

De Kleine Komedie Amstel 56 (Grachtengordel south) ☎020/624 0534, Ⓦ www .dekleinekomedie.nl. One of Amsterdam's oldest theatres, established in 1786, which occasionally hosts English-language shows.

Melkweg See p.202. At the centre of the city's cultural scene, this is often the first-choice venue for foreign touring companies.

Stadsschouwburg See opposite. Occasionally hosts productions on tour from London or New York.

Avant-garde and mime

De Brakke Grond Nes 45 (Old Centre) ☎020/622 9014, ⓦwww.brakkegrond.nl. See also ⓦwww .nestheaters.nl. Mainly Flemish productions.
DasArts Mauritskade 56 (Old Jewish Quarter and Eastern docklands) ☎020/586 9636, ⓦwww.dasarts.nl. Situated east of the centre, beyond Artis Zoo, this is less of a venue than a global clubhouse for theatre-makers, a think-tank and postgraduate institute, with international workshops and performances.

Felix Meritis Keizersgracht 324 (Grachtengordel south) ☎020/626 2321, ⓦwww.felix.meritis.nl. Unique, restored eighteenth-century centre for arts and sciences. Hosts theatre, debate, music and visual arts events, and features a foyer bar and café that's open 9am–7pm during the week and at weekends if there's an event.
De Nieuw Amsterdam Grote Bickersstraat 2 (Jordaan and Western docklands) ☎020/627 8672, ⓦwww.denieuwamsterdam.nl. Theatre company with a multicultural background and a focus on non-Western productions.

Dance

Of the major **dance companies** based in Amsterdam, the largest and most prestigious is the Muziektheater's **Dutch National Ballet**, under Ted Brandsen. For fans of **folk dancing**, the excellent Internationaal Danstheater is based in the city.

Among the most innovative of the other leading **Dutch dance companies** that tour Amsterdam – or visit nearby Rotterdam and The Hague – is The Hague's Netherlands Dance Theatre, with a repertoire of ballet and modern dance featuring inspired choreography by Jirí Kylian and artistic director Jim Vincent. The oldest company in the country, the Scapino Ballet (based in Rotterdam), has spruced up its image under artistic director Ed Wubbe and is gathering a new generation of admirers.

Amsterdam is particularly receptive to the latest trends in **modern dance**, and has many experimental dance groups; small productions staged by dance students also abound. Look out for performances by the Dans Werkplaats Amsterdam, as well as mime specialists Griftheater and Shusaku Takeuchi's vast, open-air, water-based extravaganzas. Modern dance and movement theatre companies from outside Amsterdam who often perform in the city include the Dance Works Rotterdamse and Introdans, similar in style to the Netherlands Dance Theatre.

Dance festivals

Dance **festivals** are a little thin on the ground: **Julidans** (ⓦwww.julidans.nl), held in theatres around the Leidseplein area every July, is the leading event in the city; beyond, there's **Dansweek** (ⓦwww.dansweek.nl), an event held throughout the Netherlands in October. The Hague – just a 45-minute train ride from Centraal Station – hosts two dance festivals: the **Holland Dance Festival** (ⓦwww.hollanddancefestival.com), which takes place every two years (Oct 2009 & 2011) and attracts many leading international companies; and the biennial **CaDance** (ⓦwww.cadance.nl; next festival in Oct/Nov 2010), which premieres contemporary dance works.

Venues

Dans Werkplaats Amsterdam Arie Biemond-straat 107b (Jordaan and Western docklands)

☎020/689 1789, ⓦwww.danswerkplaats .nl. A dance company staging productions by young, up-and-coming choreographers.

Internationaal Danstheater Kloveniersburgwal 87 (Old Centre) ⊕020/623 9112, ⓦwww .intdanstheater.nl. Original folk dancing from around the world, featuring international choreographers.

🎿 Melkweg See p.202. Upstairs in this pop and world music venue, there's a little theatre which puts on modern productions.

Muziektheater See p.208. Home of the National Ballet, but with a third of its dance schedule given over to international companies.
Stadsschouwburg See p.208. This theatre is the principal host to the Julidans dance festival in July, and also stages regular productions.

Film

Most of Amsterdam's commercial **cinemas** are huge multiplex affairs showing a selection of general releases. There's also a scattering of film houses (*filmhuizen*) showing **revival and art-house films** and occasional retrospectives. Two Amsterdam cinemas worth a visit no matter what's showing are the extravagant Art Deco Tuschinski (see p.212) and the atmospheric The Movies (see p.212).

Pick up a copy of the weekly *Film Agenda* from any cinema for details of all films showing in the city, or check ⓦwww.filmladder.nl. Weekly programmes change on Thursdays. All foreign movies playing in Amsterdam (Dutch movies are something of a rarity) are shown in their **original language** and subtitled in Dutch – which is fine for British or American films, but a little difficult if you fancy Tarkovsky or Pasolini. If you're interested in seeing a non-English-language movie, check with the venue whether it's been **subtitled** in English (*Engels Ondertiteld*) before you go. Films are almost never dubbed into Dutch; if they are, *Nederlands Gesproken* will be printed in the listings. **Tickets** cost between €4.50 and €8.50, depending on the day and time you go.

Film festivals

Amsterdam's only regular event is the excellent **International Documentary Film Festival** in November/December (ⓦwww.idfa.nl), when up to three hundred documentaries from all over the world are shown over ten days, making it the largest documentary festival in the world. Simultaneously, there's the **Shadowfestival** (ⓦwww.shadowfestival.nl), which showcases alternative documentaries, while the **Netherlands Film Festival** (ⓦwww.filmfestival.nl), held each September in Utrecht, features home-grown productions only.

Cinemas

ArenA ArenA Boulevard 600 (Amsterdam Oost) ⊕0900/1458, ⓦwww.pathe.nl/arena. Metro or train to Bijlmer station. With 14 screens, this is the largest cinema in Amsterdam located right next to the ArenA stadium.
De Balie See p.209. Cultural centre for theatre, politics, film and new media, showing movies on selected evenings during the week, often with English subtitles.
Cavia Van Hallstraat (Jordaan and Western Docklands) 52 ⊕020/681 1419, ⓦwww .filmhuiscavia.nl. This is one of the best of

the small *filmhuizen*, with an eclectic and non-commercial programme of international and art-house movies.
Cinecenter Lijnbaansgracht 236 (Grachtengordel south) ⊕020/623 6615, ⓦwww.cinecenter.nl. Opposite the Melkweg, this cinema shows independent and quality commercial films, the majority originating from non-English-speaking countries, shown with an interval.
Filmmuseum Vondelpark 3 (Museum Quarter and Vondelpark) ⊕020/589 1400, ⓦwww .filmmuseum.nl. Subsidized by the government since the 1940s, the Filmmuseum has a library of tens of thousands of films. Dutch

▲ Tuschinski Theater

films show regularly, along with all kinds of movies from all corners of the globe, sometimes with a themed run, such as retrospectives of directors' work. Silent movies often have live piano accompaniment, and on summer weekend evenings there are free open-air screenings on the terrace. Matinees are often cheap Most films have English subtitles.

Kriterion Roeterstraat 170 (Old Jewish Quarter and Eastern docklands) ☎020/623 1708, ⓦwww.kriterion.nl. Weesperplein metro. Stylish duplex cinema showing art-house and quality commercial films, with late-night cult favourites. Friendly bar attached.

🏃 **Melkweg** See p.202. As well as music, art and dance, the Melkweg manages to maintain a consistently good monthly film programme, ranging from mainstream fodder through to more obscure imports.

The Movies Haarlemmerdijk 161 (Jordaan and Western docklands) ☎020/638 6016, ⓦwww .themovies.nl. A beautiful Art Deco cinema, and a charming setting for independent films. Worth visiting for the bar and restaurant alone, fully restored to their original appearance. "Filmdinner" nights (Mon–Thurs) include a three-course meal and film from €35. There are late showings (11.45pm) of classic or cult films at weekends.

De Munt Vijzelstraat 15 (Grachtengordel south) ☎0900/1458, ⓦwww.pathe.nl/demunt. Huge multi-screen cinema with up to six showings a day of mainstream films, as well as a few home-grown productions.

Rialto Ceintuurbaan 338 (De Pijp) ☎020/676 8700, ⓦwww.rialtofilm.nl. The only fully authentic art-house cinema in Amsterdam, showing an enormously varied programme of European and World movies supplemented by themed series and classics. The cinema boasts a large café open to the public, and the place has a friendly, welcoming atmosphere.

Smart Cinema 1e Const. Huygensstraat 10 (Museum Quarter and Vondelpark) ☎020/427 5951, ⓦwww.smartprojectspace.net. Tram #3 or #12 to Overtoom. Small cinema near the Filmmuseum showing the best non-mainstream offerings, with short experimental films, sometimes video art, before the film begins.

Studio K Timorplein 62 (Old Jewish Quarter and Eastern docklands) ☎020/692 0422, ⓦwww .studio-k.nu. Cultural hotspot containing a small cinema, theatre, music venue and restaurant in the eastern part of the city; run solely by students. Small selection of art-house movies for €7. Conveniently located in the same building as the *Stay Okay Zeeburg* hostel (see p.171).

Tropentheater See p.205. Attached to the Tropenmuseum, this theatre concentrates mostly on music and dance, but puts on ad hoc themed film events focusing on cultures from around the world. No screenings in June & July.

Tuschinski Theater Reguliersbreestraat 26 (Grachtengordel south), ⓦwww.pathe.nl /tuschinski. Fabulous Art Deco theatre, famous for its hand-woven carpet and hand-painted wallpaper, this film house shows the artier offerings from the mainstream list.

De Uitkijk Prinsengracht 452 (Grachtengordel south) ☎020/623 7460, ⓦwww.uitkijk.nl. Pronounced "out-kike", the oldest cinema in the Netherlands is a converted canal house with no bar, no ice cream and no popcorn – but low prices. Shows popular movies for months on end.

⑪

Shopping

V ariety is the essence of Amsterdam **shopping**. Whereas in other or cities you can spend days trudging around in search of something interesting, here you'll find every kind of store packed into a relatively small area, plus a handful of great **street markets**. There are, of course, the obligatory generic malls and pedestrianized shopping streets, where you can find exactly the same stuff you'd see at home, but where Amsterdam scores is in its excellent, unusual **speciality shops** – dedicated to rubber stamps, Indonesian arts or condoms, to name but three, almost always owned by a family or individual.

Shopping in Amsterdam can be divided roughly by **area**, with similar shops often huddled together in neighbouring streets. Broadly speaking, the **Nieuwendijk/Kalverstraat** strip running just west of Dam Square in the Old Centre is home to high-street fashion and mainstream department stores – crowded Saturday afternoons here can be a grim experience – while nearby **Koningsplein** and **Leidsestraat** offer a good selection of affordable designer clothes and shoe stores. In the **Grachtengordel** and the **Jordaan**, further to the south and west, many local artists ply their wares; you can find individual items of genuine interest here, as well as more specialized and offbeat clothes shops and some affordable antiques. Bear in mind, that the major canals of the Grachtengordel (Herengracht, Keizersgracht and Prinsengracht) are mostly given over to homes and offices, and it's along the small radial streets that connect them that you'll find the more interesting and quirky shops, many of which are listed on the website ⓦwww.theninestreets.com; the **nine streets** concerned extend south from Reestraat/Hartenstraat to Runstraat/Huidenstraat in Grachtengordel west.

Elsewhere, pricier antiques – the cream of Amsterdam's renowned trade – can be found in the Spiegelkwartier, centred on **Nieuwe Spiegelstraat**, while to the south of the centre, **P.C. Hooftstraat**, **Van Baerlestraat** and, further south still, **Beethovenstraat** play host to designer clothes shops, upmarket ceramics stores, confectioners and delicatessens.

As regards **opening hours**, many shops take Monday morning off, not opening until noon or 1pm and closing again at 6pm. On Tuesday, Wednesday and Friday, hours are mostly a standard 9am to 6pm, although the larger shops in the centre have shifted towards a 7pm closing time. Thursday is late-opening night (*koopavond*), with most places staying open from 9am until 9pm and Saturday hours are normally 8.30 or 9am to 5 or 5.30pm. On Sundays, many of the larger shops in the city centre now open from noon to 5pm, but their smaller rivals are mostly closed. A few "night shops" are open between roughly 4pm and 1am – see the box on p.222.

▲ Shopping on the nine streets

Finally, note that some small and medium-sized shops won't accept **credit cards** – ask if in doubt; traveller's cheques are accepted hardly anywhere.

Shops

Antiques

By necessity, this is only a sample of what's on offer – you'll find **antiques** shops in every corner of Amsterdam – but there is a top-end-of-the-market concentration in the **Spiegelkwartier**

along Nieuwe Spiegelstraat and Spiegelgracht.

Affaire D'Eau Haarlemmerdijk 150 (Jordaan and Western docklands) ☎020/422 0411. Antique bathtubs, taps, sinks and toilets, as well as lamps, mirrors and soaps. Mon–Fri 10.30am–6pm, Sat 10.30am–5pm.

Jan Beekhuizen Nieuwe Spiegelstraat 49 (Grachtengordel south) ☏020/626 3912, ⒲www.janbeekhuizen.nl. European pewter from the fifteenth century onwards. Daily 10am–6pm.

Jan Best Keizersgracht 357 (Grachtengordel west) ☏020/623 2736. Famed antique lamp shop, with some wonderfully kitsch examples. Offbeat new lamps and lights too. Corner Huidenstraat. Mon–Fri 10.30am–6pm & Sat 10.30am–5pm, Sun 1.30-5pm.

Gallery de Munt Munttoren, Muntplein 12 (Old Centre) ☏020/623 2271. One of the best

outlets for gifts of antique delftware, pottery, hand-painted tiles and the like. Mon–Sat 9.30am–6pm, Sun 11am–6pm.

Harrie van Gennip Govert Flinckstraat 402 (De Pijp, Outer districts) ☏020/679 3025, ⒲www .harrievangennip.nl. A huge collection of old and antique stoves from all parts of Europe, lovingly restored and all in working order. Thurs 1–6pm & Sat 11am–4pm.

Eduard Kramer Nieuwe Spiegelstraat 64 (Grachtengordel south) ☏020/623 0832, ⒲www.antique-tileshop.nl. Holds a wonderful selection of Dutch tiles from the fifteenth century onwards, and operates an online

Amsterdam's commercial art galleries

Amsterdam has a small but thriving **commercial art scene** and some great private galleries, and these are well worth visiting either to view specific exhibitions or to buy some art.

Arti et Amicitae Rokin 112 (Old Centre) ☏020/623 3508, ⒲www.arti.nl. This centrally situated gallery, part of a private art academy, is one of the city's most prestigious exhibition spaces, with a gallery at the top of a Berlage-designed staircase, usually given over to exhibitions of modern art in a variety of media. Tues–Sun noon–6pm.

Binnen Galerie Keizersgracht 82 (Grachtengordel west) ☏020/625 9603. A gallery of interior design, with regular exhibitions of furniture and a small permanent collection too. At Prinsenstraat. Wed–Sat noon–6pm.

Chiellerie Raamgracht 58 (Old Centre) ☏020/320 9448, ⒲www.chiellerie.nl. Cutting-edge gallery off Kloveniersburgwal that focuses on photography and has regular temporary exhibitions. Daily 2–6pm.

FOAM Keizersgracht 609 (Grachtengordel south) ☏020/551 6500, ⒲www.foam.nl. One of the city's major exhibition spaces for photography, with regular large exhibits and a small collection of material that's always on view. Entrance €7.50. Daily 10am–6pm, Thurs & Fri till 9pm.

Huis Marseille Keizersgracht 401 (Grachtengordel west) ☏020/539 8181, ⒲www .huismarseille.nl. The city's prime photo exhibition space, housed in a fabulous location in a restored, mid-seventeenth-century canal house that was once the home of a French merchant – hence the name. It hosts quarterly exhibitions, to which admission is usually around €5. At Runstraat. Tues–Sun 11am–6pm.

Mokum OZ Voorburgwal 334 (Old Centre), ☏020/624 3958, ⒲www.galeriemokum .nl. This historic Amsterdam gallery, named after the Jewish word for the city and a famous magical realist novel, still exhibits both fantastical and realist modern works. Wed–Sat noon–5pm, Sun 1–5pm.

Reflex Modern Art Gallery Weteringschans 79a (Grachtengordel south) ☏020/627 2832, ⒲www.reflex-art.nl. You'll always find something interesting in this gallery, which represents some big international names, most notably some of the artists of the CoBrA school – Appel, Corneille and others. At Spiegelgracht. Tues–Sat 11am–6pm.

Torch Lauriergracht 94 (Jordaan and Western docklands) ☏020/626 0284, ⒲www .torchgallery.com. One of the city's most challenging contemporary galleries. Thurs–Sat 2–6pm.

W139 Warmoesstraat 139 (Old Centre) ☏020/622 9434, ⒲www.w139.nl. Long-established gallery in the heart of the city that can always be relied upon to take a chance on new, up-and-coming artists. Daily 11am–7pm.

ordering service. Mon–Sat 10am–6pm, Sun 1–6pm.

Thom & Lenny Nelis Keizersgracht 541 (Grachtengordel south) ⓣ020/623 1546. Medical antiques and spectacles. Just off Spiegelstraat. Thurs–Sat 11am–5pm.

Tóth Ikonen Nieuwe Spiegelstraat 68 (Grachtengordel south) ⓣ020/420 7359, ⓦwww .tothikonen.com. Antique Russian icons from the sixteenth to the nineteenth century. Tues–Sat 11am–5.30pm.

Van Dreven Nieuwe Spiegelstraat 38 (Grachtengordel south) ⓣ020/428 8442, ⓦwww.antique-horology.org/vandreven. Antique clocks, barometers and music boxes. Tues–Sun 10.30am–6pm.

Van Hier tot Tokio Prinsengracht 262 (Grachtengordel west) ⓣ020/428 2682, ⓦwww .vanhiertottokio.com. This split-level store just south of Reestraat has a good selection of modern and antique Japanese furniture, crafts, kimonos and the like. Tues–Fri noon–6pm, Sat 11am–6pm & Sun noon–5pm.

Art supplies, postcards and posters

Art Unlimited Keizersgracht 510 (Grachtengordel south) ⓣ020/624 8419, ⓦwww.artunlimited .com. Sprawling postcard, card and poster shop, with excellent stock. All kinds of images: good for communiqués home that avoid windmills and clogs. Near the corner of Leidsestraat. Mon 1–6pm, Tues, Wed & Sat 10am–6pm, Thurs 10am–8pm, Fri 10am–noon, Sun noon–5pm.

Van Beek Stadhouderskade 62–65 (De Pijp, Outer districts) ⓣ020/662 1670. Long-established outlet for art materials of all kinds. Mon 1–6pm, Tues–Fri 9am–8pm, Sat 10am–5pm.

Van Ginkel Bilderdijkstraat 99 (Oud West, Outer districts) ⓣ020/618 9827. Supplier of art materials, with an emphasis on print-making. Mon–Fri 9.30am–6pm, Sat 9.30am–5pm.

Bikes

While in Amsterdam you may want to buy a **bike**, but don't be tempted by anything you're offered on the street or in a bar – more often than not you'll end up with a stolen edition. Try instead the shops listed here, which sell, rent and repair bikes of all qualities; buying a well-worn model

will cost around €100, maybe less, while €150 and up should get you a fairly decent secondhand machine. To rent one you'll need to show ID and pay a €50 or €100 deposit, or leave a credit card; see Basics for further details. If you find that no one in the shop speaks English, check out the glossary of basic bike terms on p.291.

Damstraat Rent-a-Bike Damstraat 20–22 (Old Centre) ⓣ020/625 5029, ⓦwww.bikes.nl. Traditional Dutch bikes for sale, both used and new. Bike repair and rental from €6.50 for three hours, €9.50 a day, €35 a week, insurance excluded. Daily 9am–6pm.

Freewheel Akoleienstraat 7 (Jordaan and Western docklands) ⓣ020/627 7252. Women-run bike sales and repairs. Tues–Fri 9am–6pm, Sat 10am–5pm.

MacBike Centraal Station (Eastpoint), Stations-plein; Mr Visserplein 2; and Weteringschans 2, on the edge of Leidseplein ⓣ020/620 0985, ⓦwww.macbike.nl. Three locations (but one central phone number) for this well-established and very popular bike sales, rental and repair firm, though the circular MacBike disks sported by every one of their bikes do look distinctly un-cool. They also organize city tours. Rental from €7 for three hours, €9.50 a day and €30.80 a week. Daily 9am–5.45pm.

Books and comics

Virtually all of Amsterdam's many **bookshops** stock at least a small selection of English-language books, though prices are always inflated (sometimes dramatically). A particular speciality is the city's range of **second-hand and antiquarian** bookshops, several of which are listed here, but for a comprehensive list pick up the free *Antiquarian & Secondhand Bookshops of Amsterdam* leaflet at any of them. For gay and lesbian bookstores see Chapter 12.

General bookstores

American Book Center Spui 12 (Old Centre) ⓣ020/625 5537. This store has a vast stock of books in English, as well as lots of imported US magazines and books. Mon 11am–7pm, Tues–Sat 10am–8pm (Thurs till 9pm), Sun 11am–6.30pm.

Athenaeum Spui 14–16 (Old Centre) ☎020/514
1460. Perhaps the city's most appealing
bookshop, and although it's relatively short
on stuff in English, its array of books about
Amsterdam is always current, and its
selection of international newspapers and
magazines is one of the best in the city.
Mon 11am–6pm, Tues–Sat 9.30am–6pm
(Thurs till 9pm), Sun noon–5.30pm.

The English Bookshop Lauriergracht 71
(Jordaan and Western docklands) ☎020/626
4230, ⊛www.englishbookshop.nl. A small,
quirky collection of titles on a wide range of
subjects, in particular literature, but also
cookery, travel and children's books. Tues–
Sat 11am–6pm.

Martyrium Van Baerlestraat 170–172
(Museum Quarter and Vondelpark) ☎020/673
2092. Good general bookshop with lots of
material in English. Mon–Fri 9am–6pm, Sat
9am–5pm, Sun noon–5pm.

🏃 **Selexyz Scheltema** Koningsplein 20
(Grachtengordel south) ☎020/523 1411,
⊛www.scheltema.nl. Amsterdam's biggest
and arguably best bookshop. Six floors of
absolutely everything (mostly in Dutch).
Mon–Sat 10am–6pm (Thurs till 9pm), Sun
noon–5pm.

De Slegte Kalverstraat 48–52 (Old Centre)
☎020/622 5933. The Amsterdam branch of a
nationwide chain specializing in new and
used books at a discount. Mon 11am–6pm,
Tues–Sat 9.30am–6pm (Thurs till 9pm), Sun
noon–5pm.

Waterstone's Kalverstraat 152 (Old Centre)
☎020/638 3821. Amsterdam branch of
the UK high-street chain, with four
floors of books and magazines. A
predictable selection, but prices are
sometimes cheaper here than elsewhere.
Sun & Mon 11am–6pm, Tues & Wed
9am–6pm, Thurs 9am–9pm, Fri
9am–7pm, Sat 10am–7pm.

Secondhand and antiquarian

Boekenmarkt Spui (Old Centre). Open-air book
market every Friday 10am–6pm.

The Book Exchange Kloveniersburgwal 58 (Old
Centre) ☎020/626 6266. Large and rambling
old shop with a friendly American proprietor,
and a great selection of secondhand books
in English. Mon–Sat 10am–6pm, Sun
11.30am–4pm.

Book Traffic Leliegracht 50 (Grachtengordel
west) ☎020/620 4690. An excellent and well-
organized selection of mostly secondhand

books. Mon–Fri 11am–6pm, Sat 11am–6pm
& Sun noon–5pm.

Brinkman Singel 319 (Grachtengordel west)
☎020/623 8353, ⊛www.antiquariaatbrinkman
.nl. A stalwart of the Amsterdam antiquarian
book trade, *Brinkman* has occupied the
same premises for forty years. Lots of good
local stuff. Corner Ramsteeg. Mon–Fri
10am–5pm & Sat 11am–5pm.

Egidius Haarlemmerstraat 87 (Jordaan and
Western docklands) ☎020/624 3255. A good
selection of literature, art and poetry, plus a
gallery selling lithographs. Tues–Fri
11am–6pm, Sat 11am–5pm.

Fenix Frans Halsstraat 88 (De Pijp, Outer
districts) ☎020/673 9459. General secondhand bookstore, with piles of stuff stacked
up on the floor. A good range of books in
English, with the emphasis on Celtic literature, history and culture. Tues–Sat
noon–6pm.

De Kloof Kloveniersburgwal 44 (Old Centre)
☎020/622 3828, ⊛www.kloof.nl. Enormous,
higgledy-piggledy used bookshop on four
floors – great for a rummage. Lots of titles in
English, especially on law, history, science
and philosophy. Thurs–Sat 1.30–5.30pm.

A. Kok Oude Hoogstraat 14 (Old Centre)
☎020/623 1191. Vintage and secondhand
bookstore, especially strong on prints and
maps. Mon–Fri 9.30am–6pm, Sat
9.30am–5pm.

Magic Galaxies Oude Schans 140 (Old Centre)
☎020/627 6261. Run from home by a
couple whose spare time is spent
collecting science fiction, fantasy and other
esoteric books, many of which are in
English. Call first.

Oudemanhuispoort Book Market Mon–Fri
11am–4pm. See p.62.

Art and architecture

Architectura & Natura Leliegracht 22 (Grachtengordel west) ☎020/623 6186, ⊛www
.architectura.nl. Books on architecture and
interior design. An eclectic collection with
many English titles. Mon noon–6pm, Tues
9am–6pm, Wed–Fri 9am–6.30pm, Sat
10am–6pm.

🏃 **Boekie Woekie** Berenstraat 16 (Grachtengordel west) ☎020/639 0507. Books on
– and by – leading Dutch artists and graphic
designers. Entertaining postcards too. Daily
noon–6pm.

Mendo Berenstraat 11 (Grachtengordel west)
☎020/612 1216. Stylish, à la mode

bookshop specializing in architecture, art, interior design, photography and graphic design. Mon–Sat noon–5.30pm, Sun 1–5pm.

Nijhoff en Lee Staalstraat 13a (Old Centre) ☏020/620 39 80. This small corner store specializes in art, architecture and design titles, and is especially good on the art of printing, typography and lithography. Mon noon–6pm, Tues–Sat 10am–6pm, Sun noon–6pm.

Robert Premsela Van Baerlestraat 78 (Museum Quarter and Vondelpark) ☏020/662 4266. Great art and architecture book specialist, with lots of stuff in English. Mon noon–6pm, Tues–Fri 10am–6pm, Sat 10am–5.30pm, Sun 11am–5pm.

Comics

Gojoker Zeedijk 31a (Old Centre) ☏020/620 5078. Classic and contemporary comic store. Mon & Sat 11am–6pm, Tues–Fri 10am–7pm (Thurs till 9pm), closed for lunch.

Lambiek Kerkstraat 132 (Grachtengordel south) ☏020/626 7543, ⓦwww.lambiek.nl. The city's largest, oldest and best comic bookshop and gallery, with an international stock. Their website features the biggest comiclopedia in the world. Mon–Fri 11am–6pm, Sat 11am–5pm & Sun 1–5pm.

Vandal Com-x Rozengracht 31 (Jordaan and Western docklands) ☏020/420 2144, ⓦwww.vandalcomx.com. US comic imports, as well as related toy figures, games and masks.

▲ Pied-à-Terre

Mon 1–5.30pm, Tues–Thurs 11am–5.30pm, Fri 11am–6pm, Sat 11am–5pm.

Language

Intertaal Van Baerlestraat 76 (Museum Quarter and Vondelpark) ☏020/575 6756. Teach-yourself books and dictionaries in every language you can think of, and then some. Tues–Fri 10am–6pm, Sat 10am–5pm.

Selexyz Scheltema See p.217. Amsterdam's biggest and best bookshop has an excellent range of language books and all sorts of stuff on the Dutch and their habits.

Politics and society

Fort van Sjakoo Jodenbreestraat 24 (Jewish Quarter and Eastern docklands) ☏020/625 8979, ⓦwww.sjakoo.nl. Anarchist bookshop stocking a wide selection of radical political publications. Mon–Fri 11am–6pm, Sat 11am–5pm.

Religion and occult

Au Bout du Monde Singel 313 (Grachtengordel west) ☏020/625 1397, ⓦwww.auboutdumonde.nl. Astrology, philosophy, psychology and mysticism, with classical music playing while you browse. Near Raamsteeg. Mon 1–6pm, Tues–Sat 10am–6pm, Sun 1–5pm.

Theatre and film

Cine-Qua-Non Staalstraat 14 (Old Centre) ☏020/625 5588. Film and cinema history books, posters and other film paraphernalia. Tues–Fri 1–6pm.

Travel

A la Carte Utrechtsestraat 110 (Grachtengordel south) ☏020/625 0679. Large and friendly travel bookshop. Prinsengracht cross-street. Mon 1–6pm, Tues–Fri 10am–6pm (Thurs till 9pm), Sat 10am–5.30pm, Sun noon–5pm.

Evenaar Singel 348 (Grachtengordel west) ☏020/624 6289. Concentrates less on guidebooks and more on travel literature, of which it has an exemplary selection in both English and Dutch. Near Raamsteeg. Mon–Sat 12.15–6pm.

🏃 **Pied-à-Terre Overtoom 135 (Museum Quarter and Vondelpark)** ☏020/627 4455, ⓦwww.piedaterre.nl. The city's best travel bookshop, with knowledgeable staff and a huge selection of books and maps. Also sells inflatable and illuminated globes and hiking maps for Holland and beyond, mostly in English, as well as adventure holiday guides. Mon 1–6pm, Tues–Fri 10am–6pm (Thurs till 9pm), Sat 10am–5pm.

Women's

Xantippe Unlimited Prinsengracht 290 (Grachtengordel west) ☏020/623 5854, ⓦwww .xantippe.nl. Amsterdam's foremost women's bookshop, with a wide selection of new feminist titles in English, plus guidebooks and postcards too. At Berenstraat. Mon 1–7pm, Tues–Fri 10am–7pm, Sat 10am–6pm, Sun noon–5pm.

Clothes and accessories

In many ways, Amsterdam is an ideal place for **clothes shopping**; prices aren't too high and the city is sufficiently compact to save lots of shoe leather. On the other hand, don't expect the huge choice of, say, London or New York. There are good-value, if somewhat predictable, mainstream styles along **Kalverstraat** and **Nieuwendijk**, with better-quality wares along **Rokin** and **Leidsestraat**; the really fancy goods are to be found down in the south of the city on **P.C. Hooftstraat**, **Van Baerlestraat** and, further south still, on **Beethovenstraat**.

There's a fair range of one-off **secondhand clothing shops** dotted around the Jordaan, on **Oude and Nieuwe Hoogstraat**, and along the narrow streets that connect the major canals in **Grachtengordel west**. The **Waterlooplein** flea market (see p.229) is also a great hunting ground for vintage bargains. For children's clothes, see "Kids' Amsterdam", p.241.

High-street and designer clothes

Agnès B Rokin 126 (Old Centre) ☏020/627 1465. Amsterdam city-centre shop of the chic French designer, Agnès Troublé.
Antonia Gasthuismolensteeg 18–20 (Grachten-gordel west) ☏020/320 9443, ⓦwww .antoniabyyvette.nl. High-fashion shoes, slippers and handbags spread over two smallish shops. Mon noon–6pm, Tues–Sat 10am–6pm (Thurs till 8pm), Sun 1–5pm.
Hemp Works Nieuwendijk 13 (Old Centre) ☏020/421 1762. Not all hemp is like

sackcloth – check out the silky hemp shirts, fleeces and jeans in this clothing store that sells nothing but clothes made from the stuff. Mon–Wed 11am–7pm, Thurs–Sat 11am–9pm, Sun 11am–7pm.
Cora Kemperman Leidsestraat 72 (Grachten-gordel south) ☏020/625 1284, ⓦwww .corakemperman.nl. Well-made, elegant, relaxed designer womenswear that won't break the bank. Mon noon–6pm, Tues–Sat 10am–6pm (Thurs till 9pm), Sun noon–6pm.
Laundry Industry Spui 1 (Old Centre) ☏020/420 2554. On the corner of the Rokin, this Dutch clothing brand does chic, youthful clothes for women and men. There's another branch in Magna Plaza (Old Centre) and a third at Van Baerlestraat 76 (Museum Quarter and Vondelpark). Mon 11am–6.30pm, Tues–Fri 10am–6.30pm (Thurs till 9pm), Sat 10am–6pm, Sun noon–6pm.
Linhard Van Baerlestraat 50 (Museum Quarter and Vondelpark) ☏020/679 0755. Cheerful, fairly priced clothes. Mon 1–6pm, Tues–Fri 10am–6pm, Sat 10am–5.30pm.
Local Service Keizersgracht 400 (Grachten-gordel west) ☏020/626 6840. Men's and women's fashions. Ultra-trendy in an alter-native kind of way – but expensive. At Runstraat. Mon–Fri 10am–6pm (Thurs till 7.30pm), Sat 10am–5pm, Sun 1–5.30pm.
Margriet Nannings Prinsenstraat 8 (Grachten-gordel west) ☏020/620 7672. Pricey designer clothes for women, mostly casual chic. Classy handbags and jewellery too. There's also a menswear shop next door at Prinsenstraat 6. Mon 1–6pm, Tues–Sat 10.30am–6pm (Thurs till 8pm).
Marlies Dekkers Berenstraat 18 (Grachtengordel west) ☏020/421 1900, ⓦwww.marliesdekkers.com. Holland's most successful lingerie designer, known for her daring collection and stylish shop displays. Mon 1–6pm, Tues–Wed 11am–6pm, Thurs 11am–7pm, Sat 10am–8pm, Sun noon–5pm.
Robin's Bodywear Nieuwe Hoogstraat 20 (Old Centre) ☏020/620 1552. Great lingerie and swimwear shop, with all the designer names and good, personal service. Mon 1–6pm, Tues–Sat 11am–6pm.
Rodolfo's Sarphatistraat 59 (Outer districts) ☏020/623 1214. Huge collection of skates and skateboards, plus the latest matching fashions. Mon noon–6pm, Tues–Sat 10am–6pm (Thurs till 9pm).

Sissy Boy Leidsestraat 15 (Grachtengordel south) ☎020/623 8949, ⓦ www.sissyboy.nl. Simply designed but classy and affordably priced clothes for men and women. A number of designer labels are featured here. Also at six other locations in Amsterdam. Mon 11am–6pm, Tues–Sat 9.30am–6pm (Thurs till 9pm), Sun noon–5pm.

Solid Haarlemmerdijk 20 (Jordaan and Western docklands) ☎020/627 4114. Interesting and hip womenswear from well-known designers. Mon 1–6pm, Tues–Sat 10am–6pm.

Secondhand/vintage clothes

Daffodil Jacob Obrechtstraat 41 (Museum Quarter and Vondelpark) ☎020/679 5634. Right behind the Concertgebouw, this store sells secondhand designer labels only. Tues–Fri noon–6pm, Sat noon–5pm.

Episode Berenstraat 1 (Grachtengordel west) ☎020/626 4679. One of the larger second-hand stores, with everything from army jackets to hats, fur coats, shoes and belts, specializing in stock from the 1970s and 1980s. Mon & Sun 1–6pm, Tues–Wed 11am–6pm, Thurs 11am–8pm, Fri 11am–7pm, Sat 10am–7pm.

Jojo Huidenstraat 23 (Grachtengordel west) ☎020/623 3476. If you're hankering after a natty suit with a certain vintage cut, this charmingly antiquated gentlemen's outfitters has plenty. There are also shirts and ties in

▲ Zipper

a myriad of colours plus some rather nifty accessories. Mon noon–6pm, Tues–Sat 11am–6pm (Thurs till 7pm), Sun 2–6pm.

🏃 **Lady Day** Hartenstraat 9 (Grachtengordel west) ☎020/623 5820, ⓦ www .ladydayvintage.com. A wide-ranging selection of secondhand and vintage fashion in this spacious store. Lady Day also has a good military section, with old sailors' wide-leg pants and military dress jackets, plus the usual 1950s-to-1980s array of men's and women's fashion. Mon–Sat 11am–6pm (Thurs till 9pm), Sun 1–6pm.

🏃 **Laura Dols** Wolvenstraat 6 & 7 (Grachtengordel west) ☎020/624 9066, ⓦ www .lauradols.nl. Top dog on the vintage fashion scene, Laura Dols is split into two shops opposite each other on Wolvenstraat. One has rails groaning under the weight of countless dresses, all sorted according to colour to make things easier for the seasoned buyer. There is also a multitude of vintage pieces for both women and men, including some excellent swimwear, stunningly printed fabrics from the 1950s and 1960s, piles of vintage pillowcases, tablecloths, tea towels, and even a superb selection of children's and baby clothes. But the quality vintage pieces are across the road in the stylish sister store; prices are high, but not unaffordable, for 1920s flapper dresses, 1930s hats and 1950s skirts. Mon–Sat 11am–6pm (Thurs till 9pm), Sun 1–6pm.

Second Best Wolvenstraat 18 (Grachtengordel west) ☎020/422 0274. Most things here are from the last fifteen years, so don't expect to dig out a1950s prom dress from the racks of classy cast-offs. There is, however, some great modern(ish) stuff to be found if you're prepared to rummage – and pay a little over the odds. Mon 1–6pm, Tues–Sat 11am–6pm.

Zipper Huidenstraat 7 (Grachtengordel west) ☎020/623 7302. Zipper has mainly cheap and cheerful stuff from the 1960s, 1970s and 1980s, and is great for jeans. Pay attention though, as they stock new clothes alongside the vintage ones and that 1960s-style shift dress may not be all that it seems. They also have a good selection of accessories, both vintage and modern. Mon noon–6pm, Tues–Sat 11am–6pm (Thurs till 9pm), Sun 1–5pm. Also in the Old Centre at Nieuwe Hoogstraat 8 (same hours; ☎020/627 0353).

Shoes, bags and other accessories

Body Sox Leidsestraat 35 (Grachtengordel south) ☎020/422 3544. Socks, tights and stockings in every conceivable colour and design. Mon–Sat 9.30am–6pm (Thurs till 9pm), Sun noon–6pm.

Dr Adam's P.C. Hooftstraat 90 (Museum Quarter and Vondelpark) ☎020/662 3835. One of the city's widest selections of fashionable shoes. Also at Leidsestraat 25 (☎020/626 4460; Grachtengordel south). Mon–Fri 10am–6pm (Thurs till 9pm), Sat 10am–7pm, Sun noon–7pm.

The English Hatter Heiligeweg 40 (Old Centre) ☎020/623 4781, ⊛www.english-hatter.nl. Ties, hats and various other accessories, alongside classic menswear, from shirts to cricket sweaters. Mon noon–5.30pm, Tues–Fri 9am–5.30pm (Thurs till 9pm), Sat 9am–5pm, Sun noon–5pm.

Fred de la Bretonière St Luciensteeg 20 ☎020/623 4152; Utrechtsestraat 77 ☎020/626 9627 (both Grachtengordel south). Designer famous for his high-quality handbags and shoes, all sold at reasonable – or at least affordable – prices. Both shops Mon 1–6pm, Tues–Fri 10am–6pm (Thurs till 9pm), Sat 10am–5pm; St Luciensteeg store also Sun noon–5pm and Thurs till 7pm.

De Grote Tas Oude Hoogstraat 6 (Old Centre) ☎020/623 0110. Family-run store now in the third generation, selling a wide selection of serious bags, briefcases and suitcases. Mon 11am–6pm, Tues–Sat 10am–6pm, Sun noon–6pm.

Hoeden M/V Herengracht 422 (Grachtengordel west) ☎020/626 3038, ⊛www.hoeden-mv.com. Pricey designer hats galore, from felt Borsalinos to straw Panamas. Gloves and umbrellas too. At Leidsestraat. Tues–Fri 11am–6pm (Thurs till 9pm), Sat 11am–5pm, Sun 1–6pm.

Jan Jansen Rokin 42 (Old Centre) ☎020/625 1350, ⊛www.janjansenshoes.com. This famous Dutch designer sells handmade shoes with bizarre designs. Tues–Sat 11am–6pm.

Mono Haarlemmerstraat 16 (Grachtengordel west) ☎020/421 5378. Everything in this tiny store is retro, from the bags to the funky T-shirts and belts. Mon–Wed 10.30am–5.30pm, Thurs–Sat 10.30am–6pm, Sun noon–5pm.

Patta Nieuwezijds Voorburgwal 142 (Old Centre) ☎020/528 5994. The trendiest sneaker store in town selling Adidas, Vans and Asics

among others. Also clothes by Alife, Rockwell and Reigning Champ. Mon–Sat noon–7pm (Thurs till 9pm), Sun 1–8pm.

Shoebaloo PC Hoofstraat 80 (Museum Quarter and Vondelpark) ☎020/671 2210. Perhaps the city's coolest shoe shop for both men and women, with other branches at Koningsplein 7 (men's; Grachtengordel south) and Leidsestraat 10 (women's & children's; Grachtengordel south). All stores Mon noon–6pm, Tues–Sat 10am–6pm (Thurs till 9pm), Sun 1–6pm.

Department stores and shopping malls

On the whole, Amsterdam's **department stores** are really rather insipid, and the same applies to most of the city's **shopping malls**, the bulk of which are consigned to the suburbs. An exception is **Magna Plaza**, a shopping mall imaginatively sited in the old neo-Gothic post office building behind Dam Square at Nieuwezijds Voorburgwal 182, though even here the shops themselves – comprising the usual big-brand stuff – don't match the setting.

De Bijenkorf Dam 1 (Old Centre) ☎020/552 1700. Dominating the northern corner of Dam Square, this is the city's top department store with an interesting history (see p.46), a huge bustling place whose name means "beehive". It's good for clothes, accessories and kids' stuff. Mon 11am–7pm, Tues & Wed 9.30am–7pm, Thurs & Fri 9.30am–9pm, Sat 9.30am–6pm, Sun noon–6pm.

HEMA Nieuwendijk 174 (Old Centre) ☎020/623 4176. A cross between Woolworths and Marks & Spencer, great for stocking up on all the important things you need – underwear, toiletries and other essentials, plus occasional designer delights. Surprises include wine and salami at the back of the shop, and a good bakery and cheese counter; great sweets too. Plus, their Fotoservice is convenient and promises same-day delivery. There's another branch at Kalverstraat 212 (Old Centre; ☎020/422 8988). Mon 10.30am–6pm, Tues–Sat 9.30am–6pm (Thurs till 9pm), Sun noon–6pm.

Maison de Bonneterie Rokin 140 (Old Centre) ☎020/626 2162. A venerable old department store that has somewhat reinvented itself as a hub of mainstream designer fashion. The building is attractive too, rising through balustraded balconies to a high central dome. There's also a small lunch café. Mon 11am–6pm, Tues & Wed 10am–6pm, Thurs 10am–9pm, Fri & Sat 10am–6.30pm, Sun noon–5pm.

Metz & Co Leidsestraat 34 (Grachtengordel south) ☏020/520 7020. Large department store with floor upon floor of clothing, furniture and household appliances. The rooftop café offers a particularly enjoyable view over the city centre. Mon 11am–6pm, Tues–Sat 9.30am–6pm (Thurs till 9pm), Sun noon–5pm.

Peek & Cloppenburg Dam 20 (Old Centre) ☏020/623 2837. Less a department store than a multistorey clothes shop with some painfully middle-of-the-road styles. Nonetheless, this remains an Amsterdam institution. Mon noon–6pm, Tues–Sat 10am–6pm (Thurs till 9pm), Sun noon–6pm.

Vroom & Dreesmann Kalverstraat 203 (entrance also from Rokin; Old Centre) ☏020/622 0171. The main Amsterdam branch of a middle-range nationwide chain, near Muntplein. It's pretty unadventurous, but take comfort from the fact that the restaurant is quite outstanding for a department store, and they bake fresh bread on the premises as well. Check out also the listening stands in the CD section on the top floor – the best place for a free Mozart recital with a canal view. Mon 11am–8pm, Tues–Sat 10am–8pm (Thurs till 9pm), Sun noon–8pm.

Food and drink

While the city centre's supermarkets may not impress, there's also a whole host of **speciality food stores** where you can buy anything from local fish to imported Heinz baked beans. The **wine and spirits shops** listed here have been chosen for their location, their specialities – or simply because they're good value.

Supermarkets

Supermarkets are thin on the ground in central Amsterdam and most – apart from Albert Heijn's flagship store (see below) – are crowded and cramped. If you're buying **fruit and vegetables**, note you'll usually need to weigh and price them yourself (unless a price is given per item, *per stuk*); put them on the scale, press the little picture, then press BON to get a sticky barcode. If you're buying beer, juice or water in **bottles** (glass or plastic), a deposit of €0.10–0.50 will be added on at the checkout; you get it back when you return the empties – to a different store if you like.

Albert Heijn NZ Voorburgwal 226 (Old Centre) ☏020/421 8344. Located just behind Dam Square, this is the biggest of the city's forty-odd Albert Heijn supermarkets. None of them take credit cards. There are other

Night shops

Most **night shops** (*avondwinkels*) open when other stores are starting to think about closing up, and they stay open until well into the night – which sounds great, but you have to pay for the privilege: essentials can cost three times the regular price. There are one or two exceptions, but most are located a fair walk from the city centre and may take time to seek out. For a complete list, see the Gouden Gids (Yellow Pages) under "*avondverkoop*". Bear in mind also that Albert Heijn supermarkets (see above) are mostly open until 10pm Monday to Saturday.

De Avondmarkt De Wittenkade 94–96 (Jordaan and Western docklands) ☏020/686 4919. One of the largest and cheapest night shops in town with a good selection of fresh products, spirits and home-made takeaway meals. Mon–Fri 4pm–midnight, Sat 3pm–midnight, Sun 2pm–midnight.

Sterk De Clercqstraat 1–9 (Jordaan and Western docklands) ☏020/618 1727. Less a night shop than a city-centre institution, with all kinds of breads and pastries baked on the premises, a large fresh produce section, a deli and friendly staff. Beats the pants off most regular supermarkets. On the far side of the Jordaan from the Old Centre via Rozengracht. Daily 9am–1am.

central branches at Koningsplein 4 (Grachtengordel south); Vijzelstraat 113 (Grachtengordel south); Westerstraat 79 (Jordaan and Western docklands); Haarlemmerdijk 1 (Jordaan and Western docklands); and Overtoom 454 (Museum Quarter and Vondelpark). Daily 8am–10pm.

Dirk van den Broek Marie Heinekenplein 25 (De Pijp, Outer districts) T020/611 0812. **Tram #16, #24 or #25.** Beats Albert Heijn hands down in everything except image. Cheaper across the board and bigger too. More branches dotted around the suburbs. Daily 8am–9pm.

De Natuurwinkel 1e Van Swindenstraat 30 (Jewish Quarter and Eastern docklands) T020/693 5909, W www.denatuurwinkel.com. Main branch of a chain selling only organic food. Much better-tasting fruit and vegetables than anywhere else; also grains, pulses, Bonbon Jeanette chocolates and superb bread. Also at Haarlemmerdijk 174 (Jordaan and Western docklands) and smaller branches around town. Daily 8am–7pm.

Beer, wine, spirits and water

The **legal age** at which you can be sold beer is 16; for wines and spirits you need to be 18. The Dutch word for an off-licence (liquor store) is *slijterij*.

De Bierkoning Paleisstraat 125 (Old Centre) T020/625 2336. The "Beer King" is aptly named: 950 different beers, with the appropriate glasses to drink them from. Mon 1–7pm, Tues–Fri 11am–7pm, Sat 11am–6pm, Sun 1–6pm.

Chabrol Haarlemmerstraat 7 (Jordaan and Western docklands) T020/622 2781, W www .chabrolwines.com. Excellent selection of wines (over 1500) and champagne, plus extremely knowledgeable staff. Mon–Wed & Sat 9.30am–7.30pm, Thurs & Fri 9.30am–8pm, Sun noon–6pm.

Gall & Gall Nieuwezijds Voorburgwal 226 (Old Centre) T020/421 8370. The most central branch of the largest chain of wine merchants in Amsterdam, with a good choice of wines and regular tastings. Good range of *jenevers* (Dutch gins) too. Among others, there are also outlets at Jodenbreestraat 23 (T020/428 7060; Jewish Quarter and Eastern docklands) and Rozengracht 72 (T020/624 4666; Jordaan & Western docklands). Mon–Sat 10am–10pm, Sun 11am–8pm.

Le Cellier Spuistraat 116 (Old Centre) T020/638 6573. The largest wine, beer and spirits

shop in the city centre, with a huge selection. Mon 11am–6pm, Tues–Fri 9.30am–6pm, Sat 9.30am–5.30pm.

Vintner Otterman Keizersgracht 300 (Grachtengordel west) T020/625 5088. Medium-sized, notably unpretentious store selling a first-rate selection of French wines. At Berenstraat. Mon 1–6pm, Tues–Fri 10.30am–6pm, Sat 10.30am–5pm.

Waterwinkel Roelof Hartstraat 10 (Oud Zuid, Outer districts) T020/675 5923, W www.springwater.nl. Every type of mineral water imaginable. Mon–Fri 10am–6pm, Sat 10am–5pm.

Bread, pastries, chocolates, sweets and ice cream

Amsterdam has a bevy of **bread and pastry shops**: a *warme bakkerij* sells bread and rolls baked on the premises, a *banketbakkerij* pastries and cream cakes. Specialist **chocolatiers** are much less common, but several of them are quite simply outstanding.

Bakkerij Paul Année Runstraat 25 (Grachtengordel west) T020/623 5322. The best wholegrain and sourdough breads in town, bar none – all made from organic grains. Mon–Fri 8am–6pm, Sat 8.30am–5pm.

J.G. Beune Haarlemmerdijk 156 (Jordaan and Western docklands) T020/624 8356. Long-established chocolatier with enticing window displays. Mon–Fri 8.30am–6pm, Sat 8am–5pm.

Jordino Haarlemmerdijk 25a T020/420 3225. You can sample some of Amsterdam's best ice cream and chocolates at this Haarlemmerdijk institution. Mon 1–7pm, Tues–Sat 10–7pm, Sun 1–7pm.

Lanskroon Singel 385 (Grachtengordel west) T020/623 7743. Famously good pastry shop, with a small area for on-the-spot consumption. Near the south end of Spuistraat. Mon–Fri 8am–5.30pm, Sat 9am–5.30pm, Sun 10am–5.30pm.

Oud-Hollandsch Snoepwinkeltje Tweede Egelantierdwarsstraat 2 (Jordaan and Western docklands) T020/420 7390. All kinds of mouth-watering Dutch sweets, piled up in glass jars and attracting hordes of neighbourhood kids. The ideal place to try the typical Dutch salted liquorice. Tues–Sat 11am–6.30pm, Sun noon–5pm.

Pompadour Chocolaterie Huidenstraat 12 (Grachtengordel west) T020/623 9554. Delicious chocolates and lots of home-made pastries (usually smothered in or filled with chocolate). Mon–Sat 9am–6pm, Sun noon–6pm.

Puccini Singel 184 (Grachtengordel west) ☎020/427 8341, ⊛www.puccinibomboni.com. Arguably the best chocolatier in town, selling a wonderfully creative range of chocolates in all shapes and sizes. This mini-chain has also abandoned the tweeness of the traditional chocolatier for brisk, modern decor. At the junction of Oude Leliestraat. Mon noon–6pm, Tues–Sat 11am–6pm. Also at Staalstraat 17 (Old Centre), ☎020/626 5474; Mon & Sun noon–6pm, Tues–Sat 9am–6pm.

Cheese

Arxhoek Damstraat 19 (Old Centre) ☎020/622 9118. Centrally situated general cheese shop. Mon–Fri 9am–6pm, Sat 9am–5pm, Sun noon–4pm.
De Kaaskamer Runstraat 7 (Grachtengordel west) ☎020/623 3483. Friendly shop with a comprehensive selection of Dutch cheeses, plus international wines, cheeses and olives. Mon noon–6pm, Tues–Fri 9am–6pm, Sat 9am–5pm, Sun noon–5pm.
Kaasland Haarlemmerdijk 1 (Jordaan and Western docklands) ☎020/625 7945. As the name suggests, this shop offers a huge selection of cheeses, plus breads and sandwiches. Mon–Fri 8am–8pm, Sat 8am–7pm, Sun 10am–7pm.

▲ Puccini

Coffee and tea

Geels & Co Warmoesstraat 67 (Old Centre) ☎020/624 0683. Oddly situated among Warmoesstraat's loud bars and porn shops, this is one of the city's oldest and best-equipped coffee and tea specialists, with low prices on beans and utensils, and a fantastic stock of coffees and teas. It also has a small museum of coffee upstairs. Mon–Sat 9.30am–6pm.
Levelt Prinsengracht 180 (Grachtengordel west) ☎020/624 0823. This specialist tea and coffee company has occupied the same premises for over 150 years and, although there are now Levelts dotted across the city, this is the best. Friendly service too. At Westermarkt. Mon–Fri 10am–6pm, Sat 10am–5pm, Sun 1–5pm.

Delis and imported foods

Eichholtz Leidsestraat 48 (Grachtengordel south) ☎020/622 0305. Old-fashioned store specializing in imported foods from Britain and the US – the place to find Oreo cookies, Pop Tarts and Heinz beans. Mon 10am–6pm, Tues–Sat 9am–6.30pm (Thurs till 9pm), Sun noon–6pm.
Meeuwig & Zn. Haarlemmerstraat 70 (Grachtengordel west) ☎020/626 5286. Oil from every thinkable country sold from large silver barrels. Also a wide selection of vinegar, over thirty kinds of mustard and tasty fresh olives. Mon–Fri 10.30am–6pm, Sat 10am–5.30pm.
Olivaria Hazenstraat 2a (Jordaan and Western docklands) ☎020/638 3552. Olive oil – and nothing but. Incredible range of oils, all self-imported from small- and medium-sized concerns around the world. Expert advice and a well-stocked tasting table. Mon 2–6pm, Tues–Sat 11am–6pm.
Oriental Commodities Nieuwmarkt 27 (Old Centre) ☎020/626 2797. Large and warren-like Chinese supermarket. All sorts of stuff is squirrelled away in corners – seaweed, water chestnuts, spicy prawn crackers. Get there early for the handmade tofu. Mon–Sat 9am–6pm.

Fish and seafood

Although there are lots of fresh herring and **seafood stalls** dotted around the city at strategic locations, including one or two excellent ones in the Albert Cuypmarkt (see p.228), perhaps the best is the award-winning **Bloemberg** on Van Baerlestraat, just along from the Van Gogh Museum. Others worth trying are on the corner of Singel and Haarlemmerstraat, Singel and Raadhuisstraat, and Utrechtsestraat and Keizersgracht.

Organic and natural food

De Aanzet Frans Halsstraat 27 (De Pijp, Outer districts) ☎020/673 3415. Small, organic co-operative supermarket in De Pijp. Mon–Fri 9am–6pm, Sat 9am–5pm.
Boerenmarkt See p.229. Weekly organic farmers' market.
De Natuurwinkel See p.223. The city's widest selection of organic and natural food.
Natuurwinkel Waterlooplein Waterlooplein 131 (Old Jewish Quarter and Eastern docklands) ☎020/624 1765. Friendly natural food shop right on the Waterlooplein flea market. Mon–Fri 8am–7pm, Sat 9am–6pm, Sun 11am–6pm.

Music

The price of **CDs** in Amsterdam is higher than in Britain – and outrageous compared to the US. Where the city scores points, however, is in its variety: there are lots of small, low-key independent shops specializing in one type of music or another and it's here you can uncover vintage items unavailable elsewhere. If it's **vinyl** you're after, on the other hand, you've come to the wrong city. Some places still sell records, but it's very much taken for granted that music comes on CD. The main exception is the **Waterlooplein flea market** (see p.229), which has stacks of old records – and CDs – on offer.

Back Beat Records Egelantiersstraat 19 (Jordaan and Western docklands) ☎020/627 1657, Ⓦwww.backbeat.nl. Small specialist in soul, blues, jazz, funk, etc, with a helpful and enthusiastic owner. Mon–Sat 11am–6pm.
Blue Note Gravenstraat 12 (Old Centre) ☎020/428 1029. A great selection of jazz records and CDs. Tues–Sat 11am–7pm, Sun noon–5pm.
Broekmans & Van Poppel Van Baerlestraat 92–94 (Museum Quarter and Vondelpark) ☎020/675 6979, Ⓦwww.broekmans.com. Specialists in classical and opera CDs and sheet music, of which they have perhaps

Smart shops

Riding on the coat-tails of Amsterdam's liberal policy towards cannabis are a number of what have become known as "**smart shops**". Ostensibly established as outlets for "smart" drugs (memory enhancers, concentration aids, and so on), they do most of their business selling natural alternatives to hard drugs such as LSD, speed or ecstasy – as well as a variety of natural aphrodisiacs. These substitutes often have many or all of the effects of the real thing, but with greatly reduced health risks – and the added bonus of legality. Smart shops were once allowed to sell the popular alternative to LSD, **magic mushrooms**, which grow wild all over northern Europe. However, new legislation introduced in December 2008 has put a halt to this, partly prompted by the death of a French teenager who committed suicide after using the psychotropic drug. Smart shops now sell mushroom seeds for home growing, and truffles, which supposedly have a similar effect to mushrooms.

Conscious Dreams Kokopelli Warmoesstraat 12 (Old Centre) ☎020/421 7000, Ⓦwww.consciousdreams.nl. Magic mushrooms, aphrodisiacs, herbal remedies and psychedelic experiences at this city-centre smart shop. Daily 11am–10pm.
The Magic Mushroom Gallery Spuistraat 249 (Old Centre) ☎020/427 5765, Ⓦwww.magicmushroom.com. One of the city's oldest smart shops, with the usual array of sexual stimulants, hallucinogens, pipes and basic drug accessories – and of course the truffles. Daily 10am–10pm.
When Nature Calls Keizersgracht 508 (Grachtengordel south) ☎020/330 0700, Ⓦwww.whennaturecalls.nl. Another shop selling cannabis products such as hemp chocolate and beer, plus seeds. At the corner of Leidsestraat. Daily 10am–10pm.

the best selection in the city. Mon 10am–6pm, Tues–Fri 9am–6pm, Sat 9am–5pm.

Concerto Utrechtsestraat 54 (Grachtengordel south) ☎020/623 5228, ⊛www.concertomania .nl. New and used records and CDs in all categories; equally good on baroque as on grunge. One of the best all-round selections in the city, with the option to listen before you buy. Mon–Sat 10am–6pm (Thurs till 9pm), Sun noon–6pm.

Discostars Haarlemmerdijk 86 ☎020/626 1777. Brilliantly chaotic CD and vinyl store, with a vast collection of stuff you won't find anywhere else. Mon 1–6pm, Tues–Sat 10–6pm, Sun 1–6pm.

Distortion Records Westerstraat 244 (Jordaan and Western docklands) ☎020/627 0904, ⊛www.distortion.nl. Secondhand independent shop with vinyl everywhere. Tues–Fri 11am–6pm (Thurs till 9pm), Sat 10am–6pm.

Fame Kalverstraat 2 (Old Centre) ☎020/638 2525. The only large music warehouse in town; predictable selection of CDs and tapes. Books and computer games too. Mon & Sun noon–7pm, Tues–Sat 10am–7pm (Thurs till 9pm).

Free Record Shop Kalverstraat 32 & 230 (Old Centre) ☎020/626 5808. One of the better pop/rock chains. No vinyl. Also at Leidsestraat 24 (Grachtengordel south), Centraal Station and Nieuwendijk 229 (both Old Centre).

Killa Cutz Nieuwe Nieuwstraat 19 (Old Centre) ☎020/428 4040. Specializes in all the latest techno and electronic music. Daily 10am–6pm, closed on Wed in winter.

Phantasio 2e Tuindwarssatraat 53 (Jordaan and Western docklands) ☎020/421 7110. Large shop with a good collection of mainstream alternative music – CDs only – and a "listening table" equipped with headphones. Good for flyers. Mon & Sun noon–6pm, Tues–Fri 11am–7pm (Fri till 8pm), Sat 10am–7pm.

South Miami Plaza Albert Cuypstraat 116 (De Pijp, Outer districts) ☎020/662 2817. Large store specializing in Portuguese and Surinamese music, but plenty of other styles too, along with posters and DVDs. Mon–Sat 9am–6pm.

Speciality shops

Perhaps more than any other city in Europe, Amsterdam is a great source of idiosyncratic little shops devoted to one particular product or special interest. What follows is a selection of the city's more distinctive offerings.

3-D Holograms Grimburgwal 2 (Old Centre) ☎020/624 7225. All kinds of holographic art, big and small – and erotic too. Mon & Sun 1–5.30pm, Tues–Fri noon–6pm, Sat noon–6pm.

Absolute Danny OZ Achterburgwal 78 (Old Centre) ☎020/421 0915. A so-called "erotic lifestyle store", specializing in rubberwear, bondage gear, basques, etc. Mon–Sat 11am–9pm, Sun noon–9pm.

Ajax Fan Shop Arena Boulevard 1–3 (Outer districts) ☎020/311 1688. Official club shop selling the current strips and sportsgear, as well as the usual hats and duvet covers. There's also an unofficial outlet at Kalverstraat 86 (Grachtengordel west) if you can't be bothered to schlep all the way out to the stadium. Mon–Sat 9.30am–5pm, last Sun of the month 10am–5pm, match days 10am until 5min before kick-off.

Akkerman Kalverstraat 149 (Old Centre) ☎020/623 1649. The city's poshest pen shop, with an excellent selection of writing accessories. Mon–Fri 10am–5.45pm (Thurs till 8.45pm), Sat 10am–5pm, Sun 1–5pm.

Appenzeller Grimburgwal 1 (Old Centre) ☎020/616 6865. State-of-the-art designer jewellery, watches and spectacles. Tues–Sat 11am–5.30pm.

Baobab Elandsgracht 105 (Jordaan and Western docklands) ☎020/626 8398, ⊛www .baobab-aziatica.nl. Textiles and ceramics from Indonesia and the Far East, plus a huge selection of well-priced silver jewellery. Mon & Sun 1–6pm, Tues–Sat 11am–6pm.

Beadazzled Sarphatipark 6 (De Pijp, Outer districts) ☎020/673 4587. Beads in all shapes and colours as well as bags, cheerfully decorated lamps and other accessories. Mon 1–6pm, Tues–Fri 10.30am–6pm, Sat 10am–5pm.

Bloembollenwinkel Prinsengracht 112 (Grachtengordel west) ☎020/421 0095, ⊛www.amsterdamtulipmuseum.com. Charming little shop selling packets of tulip bulbs in season, as well as cards and gifts such as tulip-patterned pillows and pottery. Downstairs is a small museum that charts the tulip's history from the gardens of the Ottoman Empire to its role as Amsterdam's most iconic flower. Daily 10am–6pm.

Blond Gerard Doustraat 69 (De Pijp, Outer districts) ☎020/428 4929. Popular gift shop with hand-painted and personalized pottery, bed linen, towels and note blocs, mainly in the colour pink. Tues–Fri 10am–6pm, Sat 10am–5pm.

 Condomerie Het Gulden Vlies Warmoesstraat 141 (Old Centre) ☎020/627 4174. This shop sells condoms of every shape, size and flavour imaginable (and unimaginable) – all in the best possible taste. Mon–Sat 11am–6pm.

Coppenhagen Rozengracht 54 (Jordaan and Western docklands) ☎020/624 3681. The only thing you'll find here is beads and beady accessories – including everything you need to make your own jewellery. Tues–Fri 10am–6pm, Sat 10am–5pm.

Delftshop Muntplein 12 (Old Centre) ☎020/623 2271, ⓦwww.delftshop.com. If you're after that elusive present and don't want to settle for tourist tat, this is the place – a great selection of delftware, from small ashtrays and trinkets for €2 to more elaborate designs such as the €7500 replica of a tulip vase held in the Rijksmuseum. Other branches at Spiegelgracht 13 (Grachtengordel south) and Prinsengracht 440 (Grachtengordel west). Mon–Sat 9.30–6pm, Sun 11am–6pm.

Demmenie Sports Marnixstraat 2 (Jordaan and Western docklands) ☎020/624 3652, ⓦwww .demmeniesport.nl. Large sports shop spread over two floors, selling everything you could need for hiking, camping and wilderness survival. Mon 1–6pm, Tues–Fri 10am–6pm (Thurs till 7pm), Sat 10am–5pm.

Peter Doeswijk Vijzelgracht 11 (Grachtengordel south) ☎020/420 3133, ⓦwww.peterdoeswijk .nl. Idiosyncratic, brightly coloured, street-art style miscellany, from phones and toilet seats to painted wooden canal houses in wobbly mirror shapes – much, much better than the usual tourist stuff. Opening times vary – ring ahead to check.

Droog Design Staalstraat 7 (Old Centre) ☎020/523 5050, ⓦwww.droogdesign.nl. Founded in 1993, Droog Design has made a serious contribution to the international reinvention of design. Some of their products, such as their milk bottle chandelier, have ended up in museum collections; this is their gallery and shop. Tues–Sat noon–6pm.

Fair Trade Shop Heiligeweg 45 (Old Centre) ☎020/625 2245, ⓦwww.fairtrade.nl. Fair trade goods of all kinds – food, household items, books and cards. Mon 1–6pm, Tues–Fri 10am–6pm (Thurs till 9pm), Sat 10am–5.30pm, Sun noon–5pm.

Frozen Fountain Prinsengracht 629 (Grachtengordel south) ☎020/622 9375, ⓦwww.frozenfountain.nl. Contemporary furniture and interior design with the emphasis on all things Dutch. At Leidsegracht. Mon 1–6pm, Tues–Fri 10am–6pm, Sat 10am–5pm.

Gamekeeper Hartenstraat 14 (Grachtengordel west) ☎020/638 1579, ⓦwww.gamekeeper.nl. The place to go if you're into games. All kinds of "fantasy" games, mainly for adults, from Games Workshop to role-play games, collectible cards, backgammon, magic accessories, etc. Mon noon–6pm, Tues–Fri 10.30am–6.30pm, Sat 10am–6pm, Sun 11am–6pm.

Gerda's Runstraat 16 (Grachtengordel west) ☎020/624 2912, ⓦwww.gerdasflowers.com. Amsterdam is full of flower shops, but this one is the most imaginative and sensual. Bouquets to melt the hardest of hearts. Mon–Fri 9am–6pm, Sat 9am–5pm.

P.G.C. Hajenius Rokin 92 (Old Centre) ☎020/623 7494. Long-established tobacconist selling its own and other brands of cigars, tobacco, smoking accessories, and every make of cigarette you can think of. There's also a room at the back where you can sit and smoke and have a coffee as you view the amazing range of cigars, pipes and smoking accessories, and even leaf through a magazine or book from its library. Mon noon–6pm, Tues–Sat 9.30am–6pm, Sun noon–5pm.

The Head Shop Kloveniersburgwal 39 (Old Centre) ☎020/624 9061. Every dope-smoking accessory you could possibly need, along with assorted marijuana memorabilia. Mon–Fri 11am–6pm, Sat 11am–7pm, Sun noon–7pm.

Hera Candles Overtoom 402 (Museum Quarter and Vondelpark) ☎020/616 2886. A wonderful little all-wood shop selling nothing but handmade candles of all shapes, sizes and scents. Wed 2–6pm, Thurs & Fri 11am–6pm, Sat 11am–5pm.

Himalaya Warmoesstraat 56 (Old Centre) ☎020/626 0899. Something of an oasis of calm in the Red Light District, this cosy shop has a wide selection of books and magazines from around the world, with New Age music, tarot cards and bric-a-brac, as well as readings, a changing photo/art exhibition, and a café with a terrace and canal view out back. Mon noon–6.30pm, Tues–Sat 10.30am–6.30pm (Sat from 10am), Sun 11.30am–5.30pm.

Jacob Hooij Kloveniersburgwal 10–12 (Old Centre) ☎020/624 3041. Homeopathic chemist with any amount of herbs and natural cosmetics, as well as a huge stock of *drop* (Dutch liquorice). In business at this address since 1778 – and the shop and its stock seem as if they are the same now as then. Mon 1–6pm, Tues–Fri 10am–6pm, Sat 10am–5pm.

Joe's Vliegerwinkel Nieuwe Hoogstraat 19 (Old Centre) ☎020/625 0139. Kites, frisbees, boomerangs, diabolos, yo-yos, juggling balls and clubs. Tues–Fri noon–6pm, Sat noon–5pm.

Kitsch Kitchen Rozengracht 8 (Jordaan and Western docklands) ☎020/622 8261, ⓦwww .kitschkitchen.nl. Crammed full of chunky furniture, bowls and kitsch home stuff, plus bags, aprons, umbrellas and diaries, all in bright primary colours. Mon–Sat 10am–6pm, Sun noon–5pm.

't Klompenhuisje Nieuwe Hoogstraat 9a (Old Centre) ☎020/622 8100. Amsterdam's best and brightest array of clogs and kids' shoes. Mon–Sat 10am–6pm.

Kramer and Pontifex Reestraat 20 (Grachtengordel west) ☎020/626 5274. On one side of the shop, Mr Kramer repairs old broken dolls and teddies; on the other, Pontifex sells all kinds of candles, oils and incense. Mon–Sat 10am–6pm.

Kruiderij De Munt Vijzelstraat 1 (Grachtengordel south) ☎020/624 4533. A very wide range of herbal remedies, essential oils, teas and dietary supplements. Mon–Sat 10am–6.30pm (Thurs till 9pm), Sun noon–6pm.

Posthumus Sint Luciensteeg 23 (Old Centre) ☎020/625 5812. Upmarket stationery, cards and, best of all, hundreds of rubber stamps. Mon noon–5pm, Tues–Fri 9am–5pm, Sat 11am–4pm.

De Roos PC Hooftstraat 183 (Museum Quarter and Vondelpark) ☎020/689 0436, ⓦwww.roos .nl. New Age bookshop with a wide selection of esoteric books, crystals and remedies. Part of a larger centre with a café (see p.185) and lots of training/learning courses. Mon–Fri 10am–8pm, Sat & Sun 11am–5.30pm.

Santa Jet Prinsenstraat 7 (Grachtengordel west) ☎020/427 2070. Handmade Latin American

items, from collectables to humorous knick-knacks to religious icons – and a selection of hand-painted skulls. Mon–Fri 11am–6pm, Sat 10am–5pm, Sun noon–5pm.

Saskya & Co Stromarkt 5 ☎020/420 0840. A better class of Dutch souvenir, with ceramics, textiles and other bits and pieces that are a cut above the stuff you find elsewhere around the centre. Not exactly cheap though. Daily 11am–8pm, except Thurs until 7pm.

Tibet Winkel Spuistraat 185a (Old Centre) ☎020/420 4538, ⓦwww.tibetwinkel.nl. Books, music, jewellery and more, all made by Tibetan refugees in Nepal and India. The Tibet Support Group (☎020/623 7699) can give travel advice and information on Tibetan restaurants in Holland and anything else concerned with Tibet. Mon 1–6pm, Tues–Sat 10am–6pm, Sun 1–5pm.

Tikal Hartenstraat 2a (Grachtengordel west) ☎020/623 2147. Colourful textiles and jewellery from Mexico and Guatemala. Mon 1–6pm, Tues–Fri 11am–6pm, Sat 11am–5.30pm.

Witte Tandenwinkel Runstraat 5 (Grachtengordel west) ☎020/623 3443. The "White Teeth Shop" sells wacky toothbrushes and just about every dental hygiene accoutrement you could ever need – and then some. Mon 1–5.30pm, Tues–Fri 10am–5.30pm, Sat 10am–5pm.

Wonderwood Rusland 3 (Old Centre) ☎020/625 3738, ⓦwww.wonderwood.nl. Claims to be a cross between a shop and a gallery, and it certainly is a good place to browse, packed as it is with vintage furniture designs in wood from the 1940s to the 1960s – as well as its own creations based on the classics. Wed–Sat noon–6pm.

Markets

Albert Cuypmarkt Albert Cuypstraat (De Pijp, Outer districts). The city's principal general goods and food market, with some great bargains to be had – including fashionwear and shoes. Mon–Sat 9am–5pm.

Amstelveld Prinsengracht, near Utrechtsestraat (Grachtengordel south). This market sells flowers and plants, but with much less of a scrum than the Bloemenmarkt. Mon 10am–3pm.

Artplein Spui (Old Centre). Low-key but high-quality art market, with much lower prices than you'll find in the galleries; prints and occasional books as well. March–Dec Sun 10am–6pm.

Bloemenmarkt Singel, between Koningsplein and Muntplein (Grachtengordel south). Flowers and plants, ostensibly for tourists, but regularly frequented by locals. Bulbs for export (with health certificate). Some stalls open on Sunday as well. Mon–Sat 9am–5.30pm.

Boerenmarkt Noordermarkt, next to the Noorderkerk (Jordaan and Western docklands). Organic farmers' market selling all kinds of produce, including amazing fresh breads, exotic fungi, fresh herbs and home-made mustards. Sat 9am–4pm.

Kunstmarkt Thorbeckeplein, south of Rembrandtplein (Grachtengordel south). Quality art market with more reasonable prices than you'll find in the galleries; vintage books too. March–Oct Sun 9am–5pm.

Lindengracht Lindengracht, south of Brouwers-gracht (Jordaan and Western docklands). Rowdy and raucous general household supplies market, a complete switch from the gentility of the neighbouring Boerenmarkt (see above). Sat 9am–5pm.

Noordermarkt Noordermarkt, next to the Noorderkerk (Jordaan and Western docklands). Junk-lover's gold mine, full of all kinds of bargains tucked away beneath piles of useless rubbish. Get there early. Mon 9am–2pm.

Waterlooplein Waterlooplein, behind the Stadhuis (Old Jewish Quarter and Eastern docklands). A real Amsterdam institution, and the city's best flea market by far. Sprawling and chaotic, it's the final resting

▲ Albert Cuypmarkt

place for many a pair of yellow corduroy flares; but there are more wearable clothes to be found too, and some wonderful antique/junk stalls to root through. Some secondhand vinyl available. Mon–Sat 9am–5pm.

Westermarkt Westerstraat, from the Noorderkerk onwards (Jordaan and Western docklands). Another general goods market, though the emphasis here is on fabrics and textiles, roll after roll of the stuff. Very popular with the Jordaan locals. Mon 8am–1pm.

12

Gay and lesbian Amsterdam

In keeping with the Dutch reputation for tolerance, no other city in Europe accepts **gay people** quite as readily as Amsterdam, a liberalism that is displayed publicly at all gay events and festivals organized throughout the year: Amsterdam Pride is a huge occasion on the gay calendar, as is Queen's Day and the many memorial events that take place around the **Homomonument** (see p.70). Furthermore, with the Dutch willingness to speak English, French and just about any other language, and with a good network of advice centres, bars, clubs and cinemas, Amsterdam has become a magnet for the **international gay scene**. That said, a worrying recent development is an increase in the number of reports of homophobic activity. One specific example was at a 2008 Queen's Day fashion show to promote gay tolerance, during which a gay model was dragged off the catwalk by a group of young protesters. Local politicians have taken the incident very seriously and gay tolerance has become a key issue on the political agenda.

Homosexuality was decriminalized in the Netherlands way back in 1811; a century later – still sixty years ahead of the UK – the gay **age of consent** was reduced to 21, and in 1971 it was brought into line with that of heterosexuals, at 16. In 2001 the Netherlands was again at the vanguard of gay and lesbian rights, when the country legalized **same-sex marriages** and introduced non-discriminatory adoption rights, with gay couples enjoying equal legal rights with heterosexuals. Same-sex couples holding hands and kissing in the streets are no more worthy of comment than straight couples; however, it's fair to say that gay men in Amsterdam are much better catered for than **lesbians**. Although there is a sizeable lesbian community, the city lacks strictly women-only establishments, and the lesbian scene is largely limited to a few nights held in men-only or mixed clubs.

The city has four recognized gay areas: **Reguliersdwarsstraat**, with its trendy bars and clubs, is the best known, attracting a young, lively and international crowd, while quieter **Kerkstraat** is populated as much by locals as visitors, and includes a smattering of straight venues. The streets just north of **Rembrandtplein** and along the Amstel are a camp focus, as well as being home to a number of traditional Dutch pubs and rent-boy bars, while **Warmoesstraat**, in the heart of the Red Light District, is cruisey and mainly leather-oriented. **Cruising** is generally tolerated in places where it's not likely to cause offence, such as in known gay areas, and most bars and clubs have **darkrooms**, which are legally obliged to provide safe sex information and condoms.

If you want more information, get a copy of the free **Amsterdam Gay Map** for visitors, published by the producers of the monthly magazine **Gay News** (€3.75), both of which can be picked up from the COC (see below) or from most of the bars and shops listed in this chapter. The Gay Amsterdam website, Ⓦ www.gayamsterdam.com, is also a good resource for bar and club listings, and another free map, **Friends Gaymap Amsterdam**, is available online at Ⓦ www .gaymap.info. You could also purchase a copy of *The Bent Guide To Gay & Lesbian Amsterdam* (€9.95), a practical and witty **guidebook** written in English by the volunteers at Pink Point (see below) and available from the booth at Westermarkt or from bookshops listed on p.235. Among the many local gay **newspapers and magazines**, *Gay & Night* (Ⓦ www.gay-night.nl), which is published monthly and costs €3.60 in newsagents (or free in a number of bars and shops), features interviews, news and film reviews. The fortnightly *Gay Krant* (€2.95; Ⓦ www .gk.nl) has all the details you could conceivably need, including up-to-the-minute listings, though it is available in Dutch only. Flyers and brochures for parties and gay-oriented shops can be found in most gay bars and businesses.

   Gay-friendly hotels and bars are reviewed in this chapter and marked on the colour maps at the back of the book.

Resources and contacts

In addition to the organizations and centres listed in this section, there are two important sources of information on the gay and lesbian scene: the **Gay and Lesbian Switchboard** (℡ 020/623 6565, Ⓦ www.switchboard.nl; Mon–Fri noon–6pm, Sat & Sun 4–6pm), an English-speaking service providing help and advice on all manner of things, including where to go out in Amsterdam; and **MVS Radio** (Ⓦ www.mvs.nl), Amsterdam's gay and lesbian radio station, which broadcasts Monday to Saturday from 7pm to 8pm on 106.8FM (or 103.3 via cable).

COC Rozenstraat 14 (Jordaan and Western docklands) ℡ 020/626 3087, Ⓦ www .cocamsterdam.nl. Amsterdam branch of the national gay and lesbian organization, offering advice and contacts. Mon–Fri 10am–4pm.
Gala ℡ 020/412 4463, Ⓦ www.gala-amsterdam .nl. Organization co-responsible for Pink Point and the various Homomonument festivals, including those on Queen's Day, Roze Wester and Amsterdam Pride, and themed parties at *Club Church* (see p.233).
Pink Point Near the Homomonument, Westermarkt (Jordaan and Western docklands) ℡ 020/428 1070, Ⓦ www.pinkpoint.org. This free advice and information point run by a team of knowledgeable volunteers offers

practical information about where to go and what to do in the city, and is stocked with flyers and brochures, as well as a range of souvenirs and T-shirts. Also publishes the excellent *Bent Guide*. Daily 11am–6pm.
Schorer Sarphatistraat 35 (Grachtengordel south) ℡ 020/573 9444, Ⓦ www.schorer.nl. Gay and lesbian counselling centre offering professional and politically conscious advice on identity, sexuality and lifestyle (Mon–Fri 9am–5pm; July & Aug noon–4pm). Its clinic, held at the Municipal Health Department, provides STD examinations and treatment.
Stichting Tijgertje Ⓦ www.tijgertje.nl. Website providing information on gay and lesbian sports clubs throughout Amsterdam.

Accommodation

The city's **gay-friendly hotels** are reviewed here, and prices are for the cheapest double in high season (see also p.161). There are no women-only hotels as such, but all the places listed below are lesbian-friendly. Note that it's illegal for any hotel to refuse entry to anyone on the grounds of sexual orientation.

Old Centre

Anco Oudezijds Voorburgwal 55 ☎020/624 1126, ⓦwww.ancohotel.nl. Ten-minute walk from CS. Small and friendly hotel in the Red Light District, with a private bar catering exclusively to leather-wearing gay men. There are three- and four-person dorms (€43 per person) with shared facilities and a studio with private bathroom and kitchenette (€135). Booking advised. Doubles with shared facilities €90.

Grachtengordel south

Amistad Kerkstraat 42 ☎020/624 8074, ⓦwww.amistad.nl. Tram #1, #2 or #5 to Koningsplein. Stylish and cosy gay hotel, conveniently located for the Kerkstraat area. Each room is equipped with soft lighting, snug duvets, TV, fridge, minibar and safe. Standard rooms come without shower; deluxe room (€150) has a bathtub and stereo. Breakfast is served in a convivial communal room 9am–1pm, which later becomes a public internet lounge. From €94.

Golden Bear Kerkstraat 37 ☎020/624 4785, ⓦwww.goldenbear.nl. Tram #1, #2 or #5 to Prinsengracht. Amsterdam's first gay hotel has recently been refurbished, its bright red walls adding some colour to this solid, well-managed option. The clean, comfortable rooms – some en suite – all come with sinks, fridges and DVD players. Booking essential. From €118.

The Museum Quarter and the Vondelpark

Sander Jacob Obrechtstraat 69 ☎020/662 7574, ⓦwww.hotel-sander.nl. Tram #16 to Jacob Obrechtstraat. Right behind the Concertgebouw, this spacious, pleasant hotel has twenty en-suite rooms; it is welcoming to gay men and women, and everyone else too. Triples and quads also available. Small bar open to guests only. From €100.

Nightlife and entertainment

The main nightlife areas in the Old Centre and the Grachtengordel are dotted with **gay bars and clubs**. Some venues have both gay-only and mixed gay/straight nights, as indicated. Pink Point (see p.231), near the Homomonument, has flyers and can provide good, reliable advice on where to go in the city, as can Nighttours, ⓦwww.nighttours.nl (in English), which features a guide to events, clubs and bars, as well as more general information on Amsterdam's gay scene. Although there are currently no clubs exclusively for lesbians, lesbian-only nights are on the increase, and the gay bars and clubs which welcome women are indicated below. Further information for women on where to go in Amsterdam can be obtained from the Gay and Lesbian Switchboard (see p.231) or from the Nighttours website (see above).

The only **cinema** showing **gay films** on a regularly is the Filmhuis Cavia (see p.211) which, in conjunction with De Balie (see p.209), hosts an annual event in December called **De Roze Filmdagen** ("Pink Film Days"; ⓦwww .rozefilmdagen.nl), a mini-season of gay and lesbian movies. Call the Gay and Lesbian Switchboard (see p.231) for details of gay film showings around town, or take a look at the AUB's *Uitlijst* (see p.200).

Bars

Old Centre

Anco Oudezijds Voorburgwal 55. Hotel leather bar with a large darkroom. Daily 9am–10pm.

Argos Warmoesstraat 95. Europe's oldest leather bar, with two bars and a cellar darkroom. Not for the faint-hearted. Daily 10pm–3am (Fri & Sat till 4am).
Cuckoo's Nest Nieuwezijds Kolk 6. An ever-popular cruisey leather bar, this is described

as "the best place in town for chance encounters". Vast and infamous darkroom. Daily 1pm–1am (Fri & Sat till 2am).

Prik Spuistraat 109. Voted best gay bar of 2008 with tasty cocktails, smoothies and snacks, plus DJs on weekends. Daily 4pm–1am (Fri & Sat till 3am).

The Web St Jacobsstraat 6. Strict but friendly leather and bear bar-club that attracts an older crowd. Dance floor, darkrooms and a pool table. Daily 1pm–2am (Fri & Sat till 3am).

Grachtengordel south

Arc Reguliersdwarsstraat 44. Trendy, mixed, neon-lit club, with comfy couches, friendly bar staff and late-night dancing. Small fusion menu. Happy hour 5–7pm. Daily 4pm–1am (Fri & Sat till 3am).

Downtown Reguliersdwarsstraat 31. Popular café that's a favourite with visitors and locals. Relaxed and friendly, with inexpensive meals. Mon–Wed noon–8pm, Thurs–Sun 10am–8pm.

Entre Nous Halvemaansteeg 14. Camp and often outrageous small bar. Can be packed at peak times, when everyone joins in the sing-alongs to cheesy Eighties music. Women welcome. Daily 8pm–3am (Fri & Sat till 4am).

Lellebel Utrechtsestraat 4. Small and popular drag-show bar, with a lively and cheerful atmosphere. Mon–Thurs 9pm–3am, Fri & Sat 8pm–4am, Sun 3pm–3am.

Mankind Weteringstraat 60. Quiet, non-scene, traditional Dutch bar away from the usual gay hangouts, with its own terrace beside the canal attracting locals and visitors alike. Inexpensive meals. Lovely in summer. Daily noon–midnight.

Mix Café Amstel 50. *Gezellig* Dutch bar, playing the Top 40 and Europop. Daily 8pm–3am (Fri & Sat till 4am).

Montmartre de Paris Halvemaansteeg 17. A convivial brown café that's usually packed, with the emphasis on music and entertainment (courtesy of Whitney and Madonna). Happy hour 6–8pm. Daily 5pm–1am (Fri & Sat till 3am).

Rouge Amstel 60. Welcoming bar, popular with both tourists and locals. Mon, Thurs & Sun 4pm–1am, Fri & Sat 4pm–3am.

Sappho Vijzelstraat 103. Friendly café with a small stage and a range of weekly and monthly nights. Tuesday is open-mic night for singer-songwriters, Friday is women-only

night, and every first Saturday of the month there's a mixed gay and lesbian club night. Small and cosy, the place fills up very quickly. Simple menu available till 10pm. Tues–Thurs & Sun 6pm–1am, Fri & Sat 8pm–3am.

De Spijker Kerkstraat 4. Friendly leather and denim bar showing porn movies, with an upstairs darkroom. Happy hour 5–7pm. Women welcome. Bingo every Sat from 6pm plus monthly leather parties (Sun from 7pm). Open Mon–Thurs 3pm–1am, Fri & Sat 1pm–3am, Sun 1pm–1am.

Vivelavie Amstelstraat 7. Small, campy bar patronized mostly, but not exclusively, by women, but gay men are very welcome. Quiet during the week, but packed at the weekend. Daily 4pm–1am (Fri & Sat till 3am).

The Jordaan and Western docklands

Saarein Elandsstraat 119. Amsterdam's first women-only bar, *Saarein* finally opened its doors to men in 1999, though its clientele remains mostly female. Some of the former glory of this split-level café may be gone, but it's still a warm, relaxing place, with a cheerful atmosphere. Also a useful source of contacts and information. Open 4pm–1am (Fri & Sat till 2am). Closed Mon.

Clubs

Old Centre

Cockring Warmoesstraat 96 ☎020/623 9604, ⒲www.clubcockring.com. One of Amsterdam's most popular – and cruisey – gay men's clubs with a small dancefloor and bars on three levels. Expect lots of shirtless men dancing to techno. Strip shows on Thurs, Sat & Sun from 1am. Get there early at the weekend to avoid queuing. Daily 11pm–4am (Fri & Sat till 5am); entry €3.50–5.

Getto Warmoestraat 51 ☎020/421 5151, ⒲www.getto.nl. Relaxed, local bar-club situated in the heart of the Red Light District, serving food and cocktails. Happy hour 5–7pm. Tarot readings every Sun from 8pm. Tues–Thurs 4pm–1am, Fri & Sat 4pm–2am, Sun 4pm–midnight.

Grachtengordel south

Club Church Kerkstraat 52 ⒲www.clubchurch .nl. The most recent addition to the

Amsterdam cruising scene, featuring fetish and themed nights hosted by the Gala foundation. Wed & Thurs 8pm–midnight, Fri & Sat 10pm–4am, Sun 4–8pm.

Club Roque Amstel 178 ⓦ www.clubroque.nl. Incredibly stylish gay-minded discotheque with dance tunes and a cocktail bar. Thursday is hosted by the Netherlands's most famous transvestite, Nicky Nicole. Happy hour from Thurs–Sat from 9–11pm. Wed & Thurs 9pm–4am, Fri & Sat 9pm–5am, Sun 6pm–midnight.

Exit Reguliersdwarsstraat 42 ⓣ 020/625 8788, ⓦ www.clubexit.eu. A classic gay club ideally situated for the fallout from the surrounding area's bars and cafés, with four bars each

playing different music, from R&B to house, to an upbeat, cruisey crowd. Predominantly male, though women are admitted. Fri & Sat 11pm–5am.

The Jordaan and Western docklands

De Trut Bilderdijkstraat 165. Housed in a former factory building, this popular squat venue holds a gay/lesbian-only dance party on Sunday nights, with a large dancefloor, cheap drinks and a varied mix of music. Very popular with both men and women – the doors close at midnight and if you arrive after 11pm you may not get in. Its basement location means it can get very hot. 11pm–4am; €1.50.

Events

The two leading events in Amsterdam's gay calendar are **Remembrance Day** (May 4) and **Liberation Day** (May 5), both of which prompt ceremonies and events around the Homomonument, the symbolic focus of the city's gay community (see p.70). A few days before, there's **Queen's Day** (April 30), when the whole city has a big knees-up, with gay parties and drag acts hosted throughout the city, and also the **Roze Wester festival**, commencing the evening of April 29 with the Drag Queen Olympics at the Homomonument, and ending on Liberation Day. Other events include **Leather Pride** (ⓦ www.leatherpride.nl), held in October and November, and the infamous organized fetish parties, Trash (ⓦ www.clubtrash.com) and Wasteland (ⓦ www.wasteland.nl), although the latter is not strictly aimed at the gay community. Both events are held regularly throughout the year; look out for flyers in bars and shops.

The first **Amsterdam Pride** (ⓦ www.amsterdamgaypride.nl) took place in 1996 with street parties and performances, and is now one of the busiest annual events, with a "Canal Pride" flotilla of boats cruising down the Prinsengracht to musical accompaniment. If you're in the city for the first weekend in August, keep an eye out for bars and clubs holding parties over the weekend.

Finally, there's the old Amsterdam tradition of **Hartjesdag** ("Day of Hearts"; ⓦ www.hartjesdagen.nl), which ceased to be observed just before World War II, then was rediscovered and popularized by a researcher in Gay and Lesbian Studies at the University of Amsterdam. During the third weekend in August, it was once common for Amsterdammers to dress up in the clothes of the opposite sex, and, although the majority of the population have hardly flocked to the cross-dressing banner, nightclubs and bars around the Zeedijk and Nieuwmarkt often host a themed drag event during this weekend, including a drag parade on the Sunday from 4pm.

For more information on the above events or other special parties held throughout the year, see ⓦ www.nighttours.nl.

▲ Amsterdam Pride

Shops and services

Bookshops

American Book Center Spui 12 (Old Centre)
☎020/625 5537, Ⓦ www.abc.nl. Large general
bookstore, with a fine gay and lesbian
section. Mon 11am–7pm, Tues–Sat
10am–8pm (Thurs till 9pm), Sun
11am–6.30pm.
Intermale Spuistraat 251 (Old Centre) ☎020/625
0009, Ⓦ www.intermale.nl. Well-stocked gay

bookshop, with a wide selection of English,
French, Spanish, German and Dutch literature, as well as cards, newspapers,
magazines and DVDs. They have a
worldwide mail order service. Mon
11am–6pm, Tues–Sat 10am–6pm (Thurs till
9pm), Sun noon–5pm.
Vrolijk Paleisstraat 135 (Old Centre) ☎020/623
5142, Ⓦ www.vrolijk.nu. "The largest gay and
lesbian bookstore on the continent", with a

vast stock of new and secondhand books and magazines, as well as music and DVDs. Mon 11am–6pm, Tues–Fri 10am–6pm, Sat 10am–5pm, Sun 1–5pm.

Xantippe Unlimited Prinsengracht 290 (Grachtengordel west) T 020/623 5854, W www .xantippe.nl. Small, general bookstore with an impressive range of books and resources by, for and about women, including a large lesbian section. Mon 1–7pm, Tues–Fri 10am–7pm, Sat 10am–6pm, Sun noon–5pm.

Sex shops and cinemas

Adonis Warmoesstraat 92 (Old Centre) T 020/627 2959, W www.adonis-4men.info. This long-standing gay cinema (entry €8) also stocks toys, books and videos. Mon–Thurs & Sun 10am–1am, Fri & Sat 10am–3am.

Black Body Lijnbaansgracht 292 (Grachtengordel south) T 020/626 2553, W www .blackbody.nl. Huge selection of rubber and leather, plus toys and much more. Online ordering service available. Mon–Fri 10am–6.30pm, Sat 11am–6pm.

Bronx Kerkstraat 53–55 (Grachtengordel south) T 020/623 1548, W www.bronx.nl. Strictly porn books, magazines and videos for men. Daily noon–9pm.

Christine le Duc Spui 6 (Old Centre) T 020/624 8265, W www.christineleduc.com. One of the least sleazy sex shops in Amsterdam, selling quality underwear and sex toys, with a good selection of DVDs for men and women. Mon–Sat 10am–9pm (Thurs till 10pm), Sun noon–6.30pm.

Demask Zeedijk 64 (Old Centre) T 020/620 5603, W www.demask.com. Expensive rubber and leather fetish store for men and women. Mon–Sat 11am–7pm.

Drake's Damrak 61 (Old Centre) T 020/627 9544, W www.drakes.nl. Gay porn cinema above a souvenir and sex shop. Entry €10, under-25s half price, free to under-20s. Daily 9am–midnight.

Female and Partners Spuistraat 100 (Old Centre) T 020/620 9152, W www.femaleandpartners.nl. Staffed by women and with an emphasis on products for women, this shop has a good

selection of lingerie, plus an array of sex toys, with one of the best selections of vibrators in the city. Mon & Sun 1–6pm, Tues–Sat 11am–6pm (Thurs till 9pm).

Mantalk Reguliersdwarsstraat 39 (Grachtengordel south) T 020/627 2525. Small shop with an enormous choice of quality underwear and T-shirts which, owing to its location, is very popular with gay men. Mon 1–6pm, Tues–Sat 10am–6pm (Thurs till 9pm).

Mister B Warmoesstraat 89 (Old Centre) T 020/422 0003, W www.misterb.com. Multi-level store selling rubber and leather clothing and sex toys. Piercing and tattoos by appointment. Mon–Fri 10.30am–7pm (Thurs till 9pm), Sat 11am–6pm, Sun 1–6pm.

RoB Amsterdam Warmoesstraat 71 (Old Centre) T 020/627 3000, W www.rob.nl. Top-quality made-to-measure leather wear, with a worldwide mail order service. Mon–Sat 11am–7pm, Sun 1–6pm.

Robin and Rik Runstraat 30 (Grachtengordel west) T 020/627 8924. Handmade, quality leather clothes and accessories. Mon 2–6pm, Tues–Sat 11am–6pm.

Stout Berenstraat 9 (Grachtengordel west) T 020/620 1676, W www.stoutinternational .com. A wide range of designer underwear and erotica for women in a smart environment and with helpful (female) staff. Mon–Fri noon–7pm, Sat 11am–6pm, Sun 1–5pm.

Saunas

Sauna Damrak Damrak 54 (Old Centre) T 020/622 6012. Centrally located gay men's sauna; €14.50, including towels. You can also get a private sauna for two for €33 per hour; towels extra. Mon–Fri 10am–11pm, Sat & Sun noon–8pm.

Thermos Sauna Raamstraat 33 (Jordaan and Western docklands) T 020/623 9158, W www .thermos.nl. Modern gay men's sauna, with steam room, swimming pool, sun beds, cinema, café and bar spread over five floors. Daily noon–8am; day pass €19, under-25s €14. There's also a beauty salon, offering facials, waxing, body treatments and massage (daily noon–8pm).

Kids' Amsterdam

W ith its canals, narrow cobbled alleys and trams, the novelty value of Amsterdam can prove entertaining enough for many kids aged six and above. There's also a whole host of **attractions** specifically aimed at young children, ranging from circuses and puppet theatres to urban farms and one of the best zoos in Europe, with a Planetarium attached. There are also plenty of opportunities for play – practically all of the city's **parks** and most patches of greenery have some form of playground, and the recreation area in the Vondelpark is heaven for kids and parents alike.

You'll find most places pretty child-friendly; the majority of restaurants have highchairs and special children's menus, and bars don't seem to mind accompanied kids, as long as they're well behaved. Indeed, having a small child in your care is unlikely to close many doors to you in Amsterdam.

Though not all hotels welcome young children, this will be made clear to you when you book. If you require a **babysitting** service, contact Oppascentrale Kriterion (daily 4.30–8pm, Mon also 9–11am; ☎020/624 5848, ⓦwww .oppascentralekriterion.nl), a long-established agency with a good reputation.

Activities

For older children, a good introduction to Amsterdam might be one of the **canal trips** that start from Centraal Station or Damrak. Much more fun, though, is a ride on a **canal bike**. This can get tiring, but jetties where these pedalo-style bikes can be picked up and dropped off are numerous, and it's quite safe; see p.25 for details. If your kids enjoy being on the water, you could also take them on a free **ferry ride** to Amsterdam Noord (only 5min away). The *Buiksloterwegveer* is a small, tug-like ferry, which leaves day and night every six to twelve minutes or so from behind Centraal Station and travels back and forth to the north side of the River IJ. Cars aren't allowed, but you can take bikes and motorbikes. For more details on the city's **canal cruises and bike tours**, see p.37.

For panoramic **views** of the city, try climbing the **tower** of the Westerkerk (summer only; see p.70). Alternatively, see Amsterdam on two wheels: it's possible to take the kids along when you're **cycling** around the city, by renting either a bike with a child seat attached, or a tandem, depending on the size of the child. Bike City at Bloemgracht 70 (☎020/626 3721, ⓦwww.bikecity.nl) rents out both types and gives friendly advice too.

In the winter, there's **ice skating** at the Jaap Eden IJsbanen (see p.245), which has indoor and outdoor rinks. If the canals are frozen over and you don't have any skates, just teeter along on the ice with everybody else; see p.245 for safety points before venturing out. Another option is **bowling**; the centre near the RAI complex has eighteen lanes and a café (see p.244).

The best **swimming pool** for kids is the indoor, tropical-style Mirandabad, De Mirandalaan 9 (☏020/546 4444; tram #25), which has all sorts of gimmicks such as wave machines, slides and whirlpools; there's also a separate toddlers' pool. In summer, the most popular outdoor pool is in the Flevopark; for details of this and other outdoor pools, see p.247.

The **Huis van Aristoteles** at the Westergasfabriek (Wed, Sat & Sun 10am–11.30am & 2–5pm; €5 per person; ☏020/486 2499) is a giant play area for kids, with lots of little houses and levels to explore and regular film and theatre showings.

Finally, **TunFun** (Mr Visserplein 7 ☏020/689 4300, ⓦwww.tunfun.nl; tram #9 from CS or #14 to Mr Visserplein), near the Esnoga (Portuguese synagogue), is a large underground playground with slides, trampolines and climbing apparatus, for children aged 1 to 12. Activities include gymnastics, bowling and indoor football, as well as organized events such as discos and birthday parties, and there's plenty of equipment to clamber into, under and over. It's open daily from 10am to 6pm, and costs €7.50 for 1- to 12-year-olds (free for adults and under-1s). Children must be accompanied by an adult, but there is a café to escape to.

Parks and farms

The city's most central park, the leafy and lawned **Vondelpark** (ⓦwww .vondelpark.nl; see p.123) has an excellent playground, as well as sandpits, paddling pools and a couple of cafés where you can take a break. *De Vondeltuin*, a café on the Amstelveen side of the park, rents out skates in the summer and is perfectly situated opposite the playground. Also in summertime, the open-air theatre, Openluchttheater, usually puts on some free entertainment for kids – mime, puppets, acrobats and the like.

Most other city parks offer something to keep children entertained, the best being the **Gaasperpark**, located about 8km southeast of the centre (metro stop Gaasperplas), which has a play area and paddling pools. In the **Amsterdamse Bos** (ⓦwww.amsterdamsebos.nl; see p.133) you'll find playgrounds, lakes, cycle paths and a nature reserve with bison and sheep, and you can also rent canoes and pedaloes to explore the waterways, or visit the **Geitenhouderij Ridammerhoeve** (March–Oct daily 10am–5pm, except Tues; Nov–Feb also closed Mon; ☏020/645 5034, ⓦwww.geitenhouderij.nl), an enjoyable mini-farm with a herd of goats and their kids. The visitors' information centre near the Bosbaan entrance has a kids' area and exhibitions about the park.

There are also plenty of **urban farms** dotted around the city – look in the phone book under *Kinderboerderij* for a full list. One of the best is the **Artis Zoo Children's Farm**, which can be visited alongside a trip to the zoo itself; see p.240 for details.

Theatres, circuses and funfairs

A number of **theatres** put on inexpensive (around €3–4) entertainment for children most afternoons. Furthermore, a fair proportion offer **mime**- or **puppet**-based shows, suitable for English-speakers: check the children's section ("Jeugdagenda") of the monthly *Uitkrant* (see p.200), and look for the words *mimegroep* and *poppentheater*. Public holidays and the summer season bring touring **circuses** and the occasional travelling **funfair** (*kermis*) to the city, usually setting up on Dam Square or in one of the city's many parks. Lastly, check out the **festivals** listings in Chapter 15; many of them, such as the Queen's Day celebrations, are enjoyable for kids too.

Circustheater Elleboog Passeerdersgracht 32 (Jordaan and Western docklands) ☏020/623 5326, ⓦwww.elleboog.nl. This club runs regular courses for children aged 6–12 on how to juggle, walk the tightrope, unicycle and do conjuring tricks. Workshops also available for around €10 during school holidays. Students put on occasional shows at various venues around the city. Phone or email for full details of times and prices.

De Krakeling Nieuwe Passeerdersstraat 1 (Jordaan and Western docklands) ☏020/624 5123, ⓦwww.krakeling.nl. Permanent children's theatre, with shows for youngsters up to the age of 18, often with an emphasis on full-scale audience participation. Performances are mostly in Dutch, though the theatre also puts on a number of dance events which non-Dutch speakers will appreciate.

The zoo and museums

A trip to **Artis Zoo** is one of the best days out for kids in the city. The ticket price includes entry to the zoo and its botanical gardens, the Zoological Museum, the Geological Museum, the Aquarium and the Planetarium. You can

▲ Artis Zoo

also go on a canal cruise; the Artis Express runs daily 10am–2pm every thirty minutes from Centraal Station to the zoo, including a detour through the city on the return journey (departs zoo hourly 2.15–5.15pm). A return ticket costs €21.50, or €17 for 3- to 9-year-olds, and includes entry to the zoo. Further information on ℡020/530 1090 or Ⓦwww.lovers.nl.

Artis Zoo Plantage Kerklaan 3E–40 (Old Jewish Quarter and Eastern docklands) ℡020/523 3400, Ⓦwww.artis.nl; metro Waterlooplein, tram #9, #10 or #14. Opened in 1838, this is the oldest zoo in the country, and it's now one of the city's top tourist attractions, though thankfully its layout and refreshing lack of bars and cages mean that it never feels overcrowded. Highlights include an African savanna environment, huge aquariums and an aviary. In addition to the usual lions, monkeys and creepy-crawlies, there's also a children's farm where kids come nose-to-nose with sheep, calves, goats, etc. Feeding times always draw a crowd and take place as follows: 10.45am birds of prey; 11.30am and 3.45pm seals and sea lions; 12.30pm crocodiles (Sun only); 2pm pelicans; 3pm lions and tigers (not Thurs); 3.30pm penguins. The on-site Planetarium has five or six shows daily, all in Dutch, though you can pick up a leaflet with an English translation from the desk. An English guidebook for the whole complex costs €2.50. No dogs allowed. Daily: April–Oct 9am–6pm; Nov–March 9am–5pm; June–Aug till sundown on Sat with special activities. Adults €18.50, 3- to 9-year-olds €15.

Madame Tussaud's Dam 20 (Old Centre) ℡020/523 0623, Ⓦwww.madametussauds.nl. Large waxworks collection with the usual smattering of famous people and rock stars, as well as Dutch celebrities and the royal family, plus a few Amsterdam peasants and merchants thrown in for local colour. Hardly the high point of anyone's trip to the city, but some parts might be of interest to teenagers, such as Karaoke Corner, the "Models" zone, and the odd actor jumping out at you at unexpected moments. Daily 10am–5.30pm, school summer holidays till 8.30pm. Adults €21; 5- to 15-year-olds €16; family tickets available.

NEMO Oosterdok 2 (Old Jewish Quarter and Eastern docklands) ℡020/531 3233, Ⓦwww.e-nemo.nl; bus #22 to Kadijksplein,

ten-minute walk from CS. The whopping great green building that marks the entrance to the IJ tunnel is home to NEMO, a large, six-floor science and technology centre, whose interactive exhibits are geared towards children. Interaction is encouraged and the whole experience is very hands-on. Labelling is in Dutch and English. Tues–Sun 10am–5pm, plus Mon during school holidays in July & Aug. €12.50, under-4s free.

The Amsterdam Dungeon Rokin 78 (Old Centre) ℡020/530 8500, Ⓦwww.thedungeons.com. Tram #4, #9, #16, #24 or #25 from CS. Popular but rather pricey sight housed in a former church. Tours last for around an hour, during which you're handed from one ham actor to another, making believe you have been sentenced by the Inquisition, press-ganged onto the high seas, chased by witches and surrounded by plague victims – until you're finally swept around the interior of the church on a short roller coaster ride. Discount coupons are available in many hotels. Daily 11am–5pm; €21, children €16, half-price if booked online.

Tropenmuseum Junior Tropenmuseum, Linnaeusstraat 2 (Amsterdam Oost) ℡020/568 8233, Ⓦwww.tropenmuseumjunior.nl; tram #9 from CS. Designed especially for children between the ages of 4 and 12, the museum's aim is to promote international understanding through exhibitions, tours and performances on other cultures. It's nowhere near as dry as it sounds, and although the show is in Dutch only, this is more than compensated for by the lively exhibits, which are expertly presented and supported by music and dance performances, all designed to fascinate children, with lots of things for kids to get their hands on. Workshops on Sat, Sun & school holidays 1pm & 3pm, plus Wed 3pm; call to reserve. Adults €8, 6- to 17-year-olds €4, under-5s free.

Cafés and pancake houses

**KinderKookKafé Vondelpark 6b/Overtoom
325 (Museum Quarter and Vondelpark)**
☎020/625 3257, ⓦwww.kinderkookkafe.nl. A
café especially for kids, with a self-service
bar where kids can prepare their own food,
like pizzas, sandwiches and cakes. The
café is open to all, unless booked for a
party. Booking essential at weekends
(times vary so check the website). Adults
€10, 6- to 12-year-olds €5 (€10 if cooking),
under-6s €2.50.
**The Pancake Bakery Prinsengracht 191
(Grachtengordel west)** ☎020/625 1333, ⓦwww
.pancake.nl. Busy, well-known pancake and
omelette house that caters especially well
for children. The pancakes are delicious,
and kids are kept entertained at the table
with pens, paper and novelty toys.
Children's pancakes start at around €5.50
with toy; adults' pancakes also start from
€5.50 – but no toy. Daily noon–9.30pm.

▲ KinderKookKafé

Shops

**Azzurro Kids P.C. Hooftstraat 122 (Museum
Quarter and Vondelpark)** ☎020/673 0457,
ⓦwww.azzurrokids.nl. Perhaps the city's
chicest kids' clothes store, stocking labels
such as Diesel, Replay, Armani and Baby
Dior. Mon 1–6pm, Tues–Sat 10am–6pm
(Thurs till 9pm), Sun noon–5pm.
De Beestenwinkel Staalstraat 11 (Old Centre)
☎020/623 1805, ⓦwww.beestenwinkel.nl.
Well-made stuffed toy animals, in all shapes
and sizes. Mon noon–6pm, Tues–Fri
10am–6pm, Sat 10am–5.30pm, Sun
noon–5.30pm.
De Bijenkorf Dam 1 (Old Centre) ☎020/552
1700. This department store has one of the
best (and most reasonably priced) toy
sections in town. Mon 11am–7pm, Tues &
Wed 9.30am–7pm, Thurs & Fri 9.30am–
9pm, Sat 9.30am–7pm, Sun noon–6pm.
**Broer & Zus Rozengracht 104 (Jordaan and
Western docklands)** ☎020/422 9002, ⓦwww
.broerenzus.nl. Cool, urban streetwear and
gifts with a funky twist for babies and
children up to age 8, from T-shirts with
logos to wooden toys and cute bags. The
range includes the store's own clothing label
plus a few mid-range Dutch children's

designers. Tues–Fri 10.30am–6pm, Sat
10am–6pm.
**De Geboortewinkel Bosboom Toussaintstraat 22
(Museum Quarter and Vondelpark)** ☎020/683
1806, ⓦwww.degeboortewinkel.nl. Specialists
in all kinds of stuff for new or expectant
parents, from quality clothes and bedding to
prams and furniture. Mon 1–6pm, Tues–Sat
10am–6pm.
Intertoys Heiligeweg 26 (Old Centre) ☎020/638
3356, ⓦwww.intertoys.nl. Amsterdam's
largest toy shop, with branches throughout
the city. Mon 11am–6pm, Tues–Fri 9.30am–
6pm (Thurs till 9pm) Sat 9.30am–5.30pm,
Sun noon–5pm.
**De Kinderbrillenwinkel Nieuwezijds Voorburgwal
129–131 (Old Centre)** ☎020/626 4091, ⓦwww
.kinderbrillenwinkel.com. Shop specializing in
spectacles for children of all ages, with a
selection of very stylish frames for adults
available next door at Marcel Barlag Visuals.
Wed–Sat 11am–6pm (till 5pm Sat).
**Oilily P.C. Hooftstraat 131–133 (Museum Quarter
and Vondelpark)** ☎020/672 3361. This marvellous children's clothing chain has been
dressing the luckiest Dutch kids in colourful
– and, let's face it, pretty expensive – outfits

since the 1960s, and is still going strong here in its flagship Amsterdam location. Mon 1–6pm, Tues–Sat 10am–6pm (Thurs till 9pm).

Teuntje Haarlemmerdijk 132 (Jordaan and Western docklands) ℡020/625 3432, ⓦwww .teuntje.nu. Large shop stocking a wide range of prams and strollers, including models by Bugaboo and Easywalker, as well as carriers and highchairs. The store

also sells toys, a good range of clothing (0–8yrs) and shoes. Mon 1–6pm, Tues–Fri 10am–6pm, Sat 10am–5pm.

Tinkerbell Spiegelgracht 10 (Grachtengordel south) ℡020/625 8830, ⓦwww.tinkerbelltoys .nl. A wonderful shop full of old-fashioned toys, mobiles, models and kids' books, with all purchases beautifully gift-wrapped. Mon 1–6pm, Tues–Sat 10am–6pm, Sun noon–5pm.

Sports and activities

M ost visitors to Amsterdam tend to confine their exercise to walking around the major sights, but if you do get the urge to stretch your muscles, there's a wide range of sports to enjoy. In winter – if it's cold enough – **skating** on the frozen waterways is the most popular and enjoyable activity; other winter sports are mostly played in private health or sports clubs, to which you can usually get a day pass, though many are well outside the city centre.

The chief spectator sport is **football**. Amsterdam is home to the legendary Ajax (pronounced "eye-axe") who play in the impressive ArenA stadium situated in the eastern suburbs. Less mainstream offerings include Holland's own *korfbal* and *carambole*. For up-to-the-minute details on all sporting activities in the city, call the city's sport and recreation information service on ☏020/552 2490 (Mon–Fri 9am–5pm), or go to ⓦwww.sport.amsterdam.nl, though this website is in Dutch only.

Baseball (Honkbal)

Local team the **Amsterdam Pirates** are in the top baseball division, and based at Sportpark Ookmeer in Osdorp (☏020/616 2151; tram #17 then bus #19 or #192), 4km west of the centre. Matches take place on either Saturday or Sunday afternoons (2pm) in the summer, and most games are free.

Beaches

The Netherlands has some great sandy **beaches**, although it has to be said that the weather is notoriously unreliable. Temperatures can be bracing and the North Sea is pretty murky and often teeming with jellyfish. For swimming and sunbathing, the nearest resort is **Zandvoort**, a couple of short train rides from Amsterdam (via Haarlem), but there are nicer, quieter stretches of coast nearby, most notably amid the wild expanse of dune and beach that makes up the **National Park Zuid-Kennemerland**; the park is easily reached by bus from Haarlem bus station. Amsterdam's own city beach is **Blijburg**, a small stretch of sand on the IJsselmeer, a popular spot on warm summer days. The improvised beach bar *Blijburg aan Zee* (see p.184) has frequent live music and cheap food. To reach Blijburg, take tram #26 from Centraal Station and get off at the last stop.

Bowling

The closest **bowling alley** to the city centre is **Knijn Bowling Centre**, Scheldeplein 3, opposite the RAI complex (☎020/664 2211; Mon–Thurs 10am–midnight, Fri 10am–1am, Sat noon–1am, Sun noon–11pm; tram #4 or #25 from CS), with eighteen lanes and a café. Lanes cost between €20 and €26.50 per hour, with a maximum of six people per lane. Reservations recommended. Friday and Saturday evenings have "twilight bowling" (€11.50 per person), accompanied by a DJ.

Football

It's a mark of the dominance of Amsterdam's **Ajax**, Eindhoven's **PSV** and Rotterdam's **Feyenoord** that most foreigners would be hard pushed to name any other Dutch football team. More generally familiar, perhaps, is the Dutch style of play – based on secure passing with sudden, decisive breaks – which has made Dutch players highly sought-after all over Europe. Not surprisingly, therefore, getting hold of tickets to watch Ajax play at their extravagant all-seater ArenA stadium in the Amsterdam suburbs takes a little time and effort. You can't buy a ticket without a Clubcard, and although these only cost €6 for two years, you must apply in advance (☎020/311 6666) and wait up to five weeks for your application to be processed. Having done all that, you can then buy your ticket (€15–50). Much easier for visitors from abroad is to book a package through **Ajax Travel & Events** (☎020/311 1940), which costs €80–100 and includes a guided tour of the grounds, lunch or dinner and entry to a match, though you'll still need to book your trip well in advance.

Buying tickets for Feyenoord and PSV, whose grounds are both within easy striking distance of Amsterdam by public transport, is similarly awkward; most games require a club card, and limited numbers of tickets are available for visitors from abroad, purchased only by prior application. The football season runs from September to May, and matches are generally on Sundays at 2.30pm, with occasional games at 8pm on Wednesdays. Your best bet is to catch a game on screen in a bar. Try the *Globe* at Oudezijds Voorburgwal 3.

Ajax Amsterdam Amsterdam ArenA, Bijlmer ☎020/311 4444, ⓦwww.ajax.nl. Metro Bijlmer.
Feyenoord Rotterdam Olympiaweg 50, Rotterdam ☎010/292 3888, ⓦwww.feyenoord.nl. Trains from Amsterdam stop near the ground.

PSV Eindhoven Frederiklaan 10a, Eindhoven ☎040/250 5505, ⓦwww.psv.nl. Matches are played at the Philips Stadium, a 10min walk from Eindhoven train station.

Dance and gyms

Dancestreet 1e Rozendwarsstraat 10 (Jordaan and Western docklands) ☎020/489 7676, ⓦwww.dancestreet.net. Dance and yoga centre offering a wide range of classes, from belly-dancing to flamenco, and various forms of yoga, as well as Pilates. Dance classes €10–12, yoga €14.50. Massage available. A café (10am–9pm) overlooks the main studio.

Fitness & Health Garden Jodenbreestrat 158 (Old Jewish Quarter and Eastern docklands) ☎020/320 3666, ⓦwww.healthgarden.nl. This health club mainly offers classes (yoga, t'ai chi, Pilates and aerobics among others), as well as saunas, solarium and massage. Classes €9.50; sauna €11; class & sauna €13. Mon, Wed & Fri 9am–10.30pm, Tues & Thurs noon–10.30pm, Sat & Sun 9am–5.30pm.

Splash **Looiersgracht 26 (Jordaan and Western docklands)** ☎020/624 8404, ⓦwww .splashhealthclubs.nl. Very popular hi-tech fitness centre with sauna, tanning salon, Turkish bath and a range of daily aerobic classes from €10 for non-members. Day pass €20; week pass also available. Mon–Fri 7am–midnight, Sat & Sun 7am–9pm.

Horseriding

Amsterdamse Manege Nieuwe Kalfjeslaan, Amstelveen (Nieuw Zuid) ☎020/643 1342, ⓦwww.deamsterdamsemanege.nl. Superbly located in the Amsterdamse Bos, although unfortunately it's not possible to go for a ride unless you are a regular customer. You can however book a lesson; an hour costs €20 for adults and €16 for under-16s. Mon–Thurs 8.30am–11pm, Fri 8.30am–10pm, Sat 8.30am–6pm, Sun 8.30am–5pm.

Hollandsche Manege Vondelstraat 140 (Museum Quarter and Vondelpark) ☎020/618 0942, ⓦwww.dehollanschemanege.nl. Stables built in 1882 in neo-Renaissance style on the edge of the Vondelpark. You'll need your own boots, though hats can be rented. A one-hour lesson costs €22.50 for adults, €19.50 for 11- to 17-year-olds, and €17.50 for under-11s. Group lessons also available.

Ice skating

One of the great events in Holland's sporting calendar, when it happens, is the **Elfstedentocht**, a race across eleven towns and 200km of frozen waterways in Friesland, in the north of the Netherlands. If you're around in January and the ice is good, you'll hear talk of little else, but it's been over ten years since the last big freeze allowed it to go ahead, so you'll have to be very lucky to catch the race.

However, whenever the city's canals and waterways freeze over (which does not happen every winter by any means), local **skaters** are spoiled for choice, with almost every stretch of water utilized, providing an exhilarating way to whizz round the city – much more fun than a rink. Surprisingly, canal cruises continue even when the waterways are frozen over, with the boats crunching their way up and down the Prinsengracht, but they leave the Keizersgracht well alone, to be occupied by bundled-up Amsterdammers who take to the ice in droves. Most locals have their own skates, and buying a pair from a department store will set you back over €100. Your best option is to visit one of Amsterdam's ice rinks (see below), which rent out their own skates.

However, if you're not a pro skater, the easiest and safest option is probably the **Jaap Eden IJsbanen**, Radioweg 64 (outdoor rink Oct to mid-March: Mon, Thurs, Fri: 8am–4pm & 9–11pm, Tues 9.20am–4pm & 9–11pm, Wed 8am–4pm, Sat noon–4.30pm, Sun 10.30am–5.30pm; indoor rink Mon–Fri 1–3.45pm, Sat & Sun noon–4pm; disco skating Sat 8.40–11.30pm; €5.80; ☎020/694 9652, ⓦwww .jaapeden.nl; tram #9 from CS), a large ice-skating complex to the east of the city centre, with an indoor and an outdoor rink. You can rent skates for €5.50 from Waterman Sport next door (☎020/694 9884), but only if you use them at Jaap Eden, and you're required to leave your passport or driving licence as a deposit.

If you do decide to try skating on the canals, take note of a few **safety points** before you venture out onto the ice:

• If no one's on the ice, don't try skating – locals have a better idea of its thickness.
• To gain confidence, start off on the smaller ponds in the Vondelpark.
• Be careful under bridges, where the ice takes longest to freeze.
• If the ice gives way and you find yourself underneath, head for the darkest spot you can see in the ice above – that's the hole.

In-line skating

If you're equipped with **skates or a skateboard**, head for the free public **ramp** at the northeastern edge of the Museumplein (see p.113). For the more experienced skater there's also the free Friday Night Skate (Ⓦwww.fridaynightskate .nl), a twenty-kilometre tour around Amsterdam, which takes place – weather permitting – every week at 8.30pm, departing from the Filmmuseum in the Vondelpark. You can **rent** skates, gear and boards at De Vondeltuin at the Amstelveen entrance of the Vondelpark (summer only; Ⓣ020/664 5091; €5 per hour); alternatively, buy your own pair at Rodolfo's skate shop (Sarphatistraat 59 Ⓣ020/622 5488). If you're renting to skate around town, take care not to get stuck in the tram tracks.

▲ Skating in the Vondelpark

Korfbal

Korfbal is a home-grown sport, cobbled together from netball, basketball and volleyball, and played with mixed teams and a high basket. **Blauw Wit** (ⓦ www .akcblauw-wit.nl) play at the Joos Banckersweg (☎ 020/616 0894; tram #12 from train station Amsterdam Sloterdijk), with matches usually held on Sundays from September to June.

Pool and carambole

A number of bars and cafés across the city have **pool** tables, although you may have to go to a hall to play snooker. A popular local variation on billiards (*biljart*) is **carambole**, played on a table without pockets. You score by *caroming* (rebounding) off the cue ball and the opponent's ball; the skill of some of the locals, often spinning the ball through impossible angles, is often unbelievable. You'll find tables dotted around the city in cafés, and you'll get plenty of advice on how to play if you so much as look at a ball.

Snooker and Pool Centre Van Ostadestraat 97 (Oud Zuid) ☎ 020/676 4059. Tram #25 from CS. The first, third and fourth floors comprise the pool centre, with 26 tables costing a flat rate of €8.50 per hour. The second floor is the snooker centre, which has seven tables and there's also one *carambole* table, all charged at €8.50 per hour as well. Daily 2pm–1am, Fri & Sat till 2am.

Saunas and flotation

Hammam Zaanstraat 88 (Jordaan and Western docklands) ☎ 020/681 4818, ⓦ www .hammamamsterdam.nl. Situated north of the Westerpark (walk through the underpass near the northeast entrance, and turn left), this Turkish bath is a wonderful social institution for women only. Comprises hot and cold rooms and top-to-toe cleansing; treatments such as full-body scrub and massage also available. Entry costs €17. Tues–Fri noon–10pm, Sat & Sun noon–8pm.

Koan Float Herengracht 321 (Grachtengordel west) ☎ 020/555 0333, ⓦ www.koan-float.com. The place to come in Amsterdam to float in a large bath of warm water. Magnesium and sodium salt are added to aid muscular relaxation and provide buoyancy, and because the water is the same temperature as your body, the sensation is of floating freely. There are three individual soundproof floating cabins, each with its own shower; once you're inside, lights, music and clothing are optional. Advance reservations are essential. Prices start from €32.50 for 45min or €38.50 for an hour. The centre also offers massage. Towels and bathrobes are provided. Daily 9.30am–11pm.

Sauna Damrak Damrak 54 (Old Centre) ☎ 020/622 6012. Centrally located gay sauna, though women are also welcome at weekends. See p.236.

Sauna Deco Herengracht 115 (Grachtengordel west) ☎ 020/623 8215, ⓦ www.saunadeco.nl. Built in 1920, this is possibly Amsterdam's most stylish sauna and steam bath, with a magnificent Art Deco interior. Massage available. Entry costs €19.50 (€17 Mon, Wed–Fri noon–3pm); towels and bathrobes extra. No credit cards. Mon, Wed–Sat noon–11pm, Tues 3–11pm, Sun 1–7pm.

Swimming pools

It's a good idea to call before setting out for any of the pools (*zwembaden*) listed below, since certain times are set aside for small children, family groups or classes.

Flevoparkbad **Insulindeweg 1002 (Amsterdam Oost)** ☎020/692 5030. **Tram #7 from Leidseplein or #14 from Dam Square.** The best outdoor pool in the city; gets very busy on sunny days. May to early Sept daily 10am–5.30pm, until 7pm on warm days. Admission €2.65.

Mirandabad **De Mirandalaan 9 (Nieuw Zuid)** ☎020/546 4444. Superbly equipped swimming centre (outdoor and indoor

pools), with wave machine, whirlpools and slides. Admission €3.55.

Zuiderbad **Hobbemastraat 26 (Museum Quarter and Vondelpark)** ☎020/678 1390. Lovely old pool dating from the nineteenth century and refreshingly gimmick-free, though they do have a naturist hour on Sunday from 4.30 to 5.30pm. Pool opens weekdays 7am, Sat 8am, Sun 10am; phone for details, as hours vary according to age. Admission €3.

Tennis and squash

Most outdoor **tennis** courts are for members only, and those that aren't need to be reserved well in advance. Your best chance of getting a game at short notice is either at the open-air tennis courts in the Vondelpark, or at one of the following.

Frans Otten Stadion **IJsbaanpad 43 (Nieuw Zuid)** ☎020/662 8767, ⓦwww.fransottenstadion.nl. **Tram #6 from Leidseplein, #16 or #24 from CS.** This complex has eight indoor and fifteen outdoor tennis courts, as well as 21 squash courts. Tennis courts €17.50–27 per hour; squash courts €16–22 per hour. Racket rental €3. Call ahead to reserve a court in the evening. Mon–Fri 9am–midnight, Sat & Sun 9am–8pm.

Squash City **Ketelmakerstraat 6 (Jordaan and Western docklands)** ☎020/626 7883, ⓦwww.squashcity.nl. Situated west of Centraal Station, with thirteen squash courts at €9.90–11.90 per member for 45min; membership costs €25 and also includes use of the sauna. Racket rental €2.50. Call ahead to reserve courts. Mon–Thurs 7am–midnight, Fri 7am–11.30pm, Sat & Sun 8.45am–8pm.

Festivals and events

M ost of Amsterdam's festivals are music and arts events, supplemented by a sprinkling of religious celebrations, and, as you might expect, the majority take place in the summer. The Queen's Birthday (also referred to as **Queen's Day**) at the end of April is the city's most touted and exciting annual event, with a large portion of the city given over to an impromptu flea market and lots of street parties. On a more cultural level, the **Holland Festival** art extravaganza, held throughout June, attracts a handful of big names. Check with the VVV (see p.36) for the latest details, and remember that many other interesting events, such as the Easter performance of Bach's *St Matthew Passion* in the Grote Kerk at Naarden and the North Sea Jazz Festival in Rotterdam (ⓦ www.northseajazz.nl), are only a short train ride away. See p.35 for a list of **public holidays**.

January

Chinese New Year Late Jan/early Feb depending on lunar calendar. Dragon dance and fireworks, held at Nieuwmarkt and along the Zeedijk.

February

Februaristaking (Commemoration of the February Strike) Feb 25 ⓦ www .februaristaking.nl. Speeches and wreath-laying at the Dokwerker (Dockworker) statue on J.D. Meijerplein (see p.101).

March

Stille Omgang (Silent Procession) Sunday closest to March 15 ⓦ www.stille-omgang.nl. Procession by local Catholics commemo-rating the Miracle of Amsterdam (see p.56), starting and finishing at Spui and passing through the Red Light District.

April

Nationaal Museumweekend First or second weekend ⓦ www.museumweekend.nl. Free or discounted entrance to most of the museums in the Netherlands. Contact the VVV for more information.

Koninginnedag (Queen's Day/the Queen's Birthday) April 30. This is one of the most popular dates in the Dutch diary, a street event *par excellence,* which seems to grow annually and is almost worth planning a visit

▲ Queen's Day

around, despite claims that it has become too commercialized in recent years. Celebrations in honour of Queen Beatrix take place throughout the Netherlands, though festivities in Amsterdam tend to be somewhat wilder and larger in scale. Special club nights and parties are held both the night before and the night after; however, to gain entry you'll need to book in advance either at the club itself or at record stores. The next day sees the city's streets and canals lined with people, most of whom are dressed in ridiculous costumes (not surprisingly, Queen's Day is one of the most flamboyant events on the gay calendar as well). Anything goes, especially if it's orange – the Dutch national colour. A fair is held in Dam Square, and music blasts continuously from huge sound systems set up across most of the major squares. This is also the one day of the year when goods can be bought and sold tax-free to anyone on the streets, and numerous stalls are set up in front of people's houses.

May

Herdenkingsdag (Remembrance Day) May 4 Ⓦ www.4en5mei.nl. There's a wreath-laying ceremony and a two-minute silence at the National Monument in Dam Square, commemorating the Dutch dead of World War II, as well as a smaller event at the Homomonument in Westermarkt in honour of the country's gay soldiers who died in the conflict.

Bevrijdingsdag (Liberation Day) May 5 Ⓦ www.4en5mei.nl. The country celebrates the 1945 liberation from Nazi occupation with bands, speeches and impromptu markets around the city.

National Windmill Day Second Saturday. On this day over half the country's remaining windmills and watermills, indicated by blue flags, are opened to the public free of charge. Contact Vereniging De Hollandsche Molen (Ⓣ020/623 8703, Ⓦ www.molens.nl) or the VVV (see p.36) for further details.

Art Amsterdam (former KunstRai) Second week Ⓦ www.artamsterdam.nl. Metro Rai or tram #4. The city's annual mainstream contemporary arts fair, held in the RAI conference space south of the centre, featuring works from over 120 galleries. Entry costs €20. A less commercial alternative is the Kunstvlaai (Ⓦ www.kunstvlaai.nl)

at the Westergasfabriek (see p.91), usually held the week before or after Art Amsterdam.

June

Open Garden Days Third weekend Ⓦ www .opentuinendagen.nl. Three-day event which sees some thirty private gardens – usually arranged around a particular theme – open their gates to the public. Gardens are open 10am–5pm and there's a canal boat to take you around. Tickets €15.

Amsterdam Roots Festival Third Sunday Ⓦ www.amsterdamroots.nl. Tram #3, #7 or #9 from CS. Free open-air concert in Oosterpark with stalls, workshops and a parade that opens a week-long world music and film festival, with over sixty acts performing in the Concertgebouw, Melkweg, Paradiso and Tropentheater.

Holland Festival Throughout June Ⓦ www .hollandfestival.nl. The largest music, dance and drama event in the Netherlands, aimed at making the dramatic arts more accessible. Showcasing around forty productions, from theatre and dance to music and opera, at various venues around the city, it features a mix of established and new talent.

International Theatre School Festival Third or last week Ⓦ www.itsfestival.nl. Ten-day programme of events showcasing aspiring actors, dancers, musicians and opera singers in theatres on Nes, off Dam Square, culminating in an award night with a prize presented to the most promising director.

Vondelpark Open-Air Theatre (Openluchttheater) June–Aug Ⓦ www.openluchttheater.nl. Free theatre, dance and music performances throughout the summer, Wed–Sun only, with anything from jazz and classical concerts through to stand-up comedy.

July

Julidans First half of July Ⓦ www.julidans.nl. Twelve-day festival dedicated to contemporary dance, hosting both renowned and up-and-coming choreographers. Held at numerous locations around the Leidseplein, with the Stadsschouwburg as its main focus.

Kwakoe Zomer Festival Weekends only throughout July and August Ⓦ www.kwakoe.nl. Metro Bijlmer. A Surinamese and Antillian festival held in Bijlmerpark, close to the

Amsterdam ArenA in the southeastern suburbs, featuring music, workshops, dance acts and stand-up comedy. In the middle of the festival there's a football competition between several teams. Caribbean delicacies such as *roti* and Surinamese *bakabana,* baked banana with peanut sauce, are widely available from stalls around the festival site.

August

De Parade First two weeks ⓦ www.deparade .nl. Tram #25 from CS. An excellent sixteen-day travelling theatrical fair, which puts on a host of short, independent performances, ranging from cabaret to theatre, given in or in front of artists' tents. Held in the Martin Luther King park, next to the River Amstel, with special kid-friendly performances in the afternoon.
Amsterdam Pride First or second weekend ⓦ www.amsterdampride.nl. The city's gay community celebrates, with street parties and performances held along the Amstel, Warmoesstraat and Reguliersdwarsstraat. The Canal Parade takes place on the 2pm and Saturday between 2–6pm, a flotilla of up to 75 boats cruising along the Prinsengracht, watched by over 350,000 people.
Grachtenfestival Starts second or third weekend ⓦ www.grachtenfestival.nl. For nine days international musicians perform at over ninety classical music events at historical locations around the three main canals, as well as the River IJ. Includes the Prinsengracht Concert, one of the world's most prestigious free open-air concerts, held opposite the *Pulitzer* hotel.
Uitmarkt Last weekend ⓦ www.uitmarkt.nl. Every cultural organization in the city, from opera to dance, advertises its forthcoming programme of events during this weekend, with free preview performances held over three days around Dam Square, Waterlooplein and Nieuwmarkt.

September

Open Monument Day Second weekend ⓦ www .openmonumentendag.nl. For two days monuments throughout the Netherlands that are normally closed or have restricted opening times throw open their doors to the public for free.
Jordaan Festival Second or third weekend ⓦ www.jordaanfestival.nl. A three-day street festival in the Jordaan. There's a commercial fair on Palmgracht, talent contests on Elandsgracht, a few street parties and a culinary fair on the Sunday afternoon at the Noordermarkt.

October

Amsterdam City Marathon Usually third Sunday ⓦ www.amsterdammarathon.nl. A 42-kilometre course around Amsterdam starting at and finishing inside the Olympic Stadium, passing through the old city centre along the way.
Amsterdam Dance Event Late Oct ⓦ www .amsterdam-dance-event.nl. A four-day club festival, hosting hundreds of national and international DJs taking over every dance venue in the city. Also a conference for turntable professionals. Tickets for all events have to be purchased separately and tend to sell out quickly.

November

Museum Night First Saturday ⓦ www.n8.nl. Around forty museums open their doors to the public from 7pm to 2am, with various events put on, accompanied by DJs and music. Tickets €20.
Parade of Sint Nicolaas Second or third Sunday. The traditional parade of *Sinterklaas* (Santa Claus) through the city on his white horse. Starting from behind Centraal Station where he arrives by steam boat, he proceeds down the Damrak towards Rembrandtplein, accompanied by his helpers the *Zwarte Pieten* ("Black Peters") – so called because of their blackened faces – who hand out sweets and little presents. It all finishes in Leidseplein on the balcony of the Stadsschouwburg.
International Documentary Film Festival Mid- to late Nov ⓦ www.idfa.nl. The world's largest documentary festival held over ten days in the Tuschinski (see p.212) and De Munt (see p.212) showing around 250 domestic and international documentaries.
Cannabis Cup Late Nov ⓦ www .hightimes.com. Five-day "harvest festival" organized by *High Times* magazine with seminars, tours and music events held at the *Powerzone* (see p.203), which also hosts a competition to find the best cultivated seed. Judging is open to the general public, but a judge pass is pricey (€250).

December

Pakjesavond (Present Evening) Dec 5. Though it tends to be a private affair, Pakjesavond, rather than Christmas Day, is when Dutch kids receive their Christmas presents. If you're in the city on that day and have Dutch friends, it's worth knowing that it's traditional to give a present together with an amusing poem you have written caricaturing the recipient.

New Year's Eve Dec 31. New Year's Eve is big in Amsterdam, with fireworks and celebrations everywhere. Most bars and clubs stay open until morning – make sure you get tickets in advance. This might just qualify as the wildest and most reckless street partying in Europe, but a word of warning: Amsterdammers seem to love the idea of throwing lit fireworks around and won't hesitate to send one careering into the crowd.

Contexts

Contexts

History

To a large extent, a **history of Amsterdam** is a history of the whole of the Netherlands, which includes the province of Holland. In turn, the Netherlands of today was an integral part of the **Low Countries** – modern Belgium, Luxembourg and the Netherlands – until the late sixteenth century. It was then that the Dutch broke with their Spanish Habsburg masters and, ever since, Amsterdam has been at the centre of Dutch events. The city was the country's most glorious cultural and trading centre throughout its seventeenth-century heyday, the so-called **Golden Age**, and, after a long downturn in the eighteenth century, picked itself up to emerge as a major metropolis in the nineteenth. In the 1960s Amsterdam was galvanized by its youth, who took to **hippy culture** with gusto; their legacy is a social progressiveness – most conspicuously over drugs and prostitution – that still underpins the city's international reputation, good and bad, today.

Medieval foundations

Amsterdam's earliest history is as murky as the marshes from which it arose. Legend asserts that two Frisian fishermen were the first inhabitants and, it is indeed likely that the city began as a fishing village at the mouth of the **River Amstel**. Previously, this area had been a stretch of peat bog and marsh, but a modest fall in the sea level permitted settlement on the high ground along the riverside. The village was first given some significance when the local lord built a castle here around 1204, and then, some sixty years later, the Amstel was dammed – hence Amstelredam – and it received its municipal **charter** from a new feudal overlord, Count Floris V, in 1275. Designating the village a toll port for beer imported from Hamburg, the charter led to Amsterdam flourishing as a trading centre from around 1300, when it also became an important transit port for Baltic grain, destined for the burgeoning cities of the Low Countries (broadly Belgium and the Netherlands).

As Amsterdam grew, its **trade** diversified. In particular, it made a handsome profit from English **wool**, which was imported into the city, barged onto Leiden and Haarlem – where it was turned into cloth – and then much of it returned to Amsterdam to be exported. The cloth trade drew workers into the town to work along Warmoesstraat and the Amstel, and ships were able to sail right up to Dam Square to pick up the finished work and drop off imported wood, fish, salt and spices.

Though the city's **population** rose steadily in the early sixteenth century, to around 12,000, Amsterdam was still small compared with Antwerp or London; building on the waterlogged soil was difficult and slow, requiring timber piles to be driven into the firmer sand below. And with the extensive use of timber and thatch, **fires** were a frequent occurrence. A particularly disastrous blaze in 1452 resulted in such destruction that the city council made building with slate, brick and stone obligatory; one of the few wooden houses that survived the fire still stands today in the Begijnhof (see p.52). In the mid-sixteenth century the city underwent its first major **expansion**, as burgeoning trade with the Hanseatic towns of the Baltic made the city second only to Antwerp as a marketplace and warehouse for northern and western Europe. The trade in cloth, grain and wine brought craftsmen to the city, and its merchant fleet grew; by the 1550s three-quarters of all grain cargo out of the Baltic was carried in Amsterdam vessels. The foundations were being laid for the wealth of the Golden Age.

The rise of Protestantism

At the beginning of the sixteenth century, the corruption and elaborate ritual of the established (Catholic) **Church** found itself under attack throughout northern Europe. First, Erasmus of Rotterdam promoted ideas of reforma-tion, and then, in 1517, **Martin Luther** (1483–1546) went one step – or rather, leap – further, producing his 95 theses against the Church practice of indulgences, a prelude to his more comprehensive assault on the entire institution. Furthermore, when Luther's works were disseminated his ideas gained a European following among a range of reforming groups branded as **Lutheran** by the Church, while other reformers were drawn to the doctrines of **John Calvin** (1509–64). Luther asserted that the Church's political power should be subservient to that of the state; Calvin emphasized the importance of individual conscience and the need for redemption through the grace of Christ rather than the confessional. Luther's writings and Bible translations were printed in the Netherlands, but the doctrines of Calvin proved more popular in Amsterdam, setting the seal on the city's religious transformation. Calvin was insistent on the separation of Church and State, but the lines were easily fudged in Amsterdam by the Church's ruling council of ministers and annually elected elders, who soon came to exercise considerable political clout. The council also had little time for other (more egalitarian) Protestant sects, and matters came to a head when, in 1535, one of the radical splinter groups, the **Anabaptists**, occupied Amsterdam's town hall, calling on passers-by to repent. Previously the town council had tolerated the Anabaptists, but, prompted by the Calvinists, it acted swiftly when civic rule was challenged; the town hall was besieged and, after its capture, the leaders of the Anabaptists were executed on the Dam.

The revolt of the Netherlands

In 1555, the fanatically Catholic **Philip II** succeeded to the Spanish throne. Through a series of marriages the Spanish monarchy – and **Habsburg** family – had come to rule over the Low Countries, and Philip was determined to rid his empire of its heretics, regardless of whether they were Calvinists or Anabap-tists. Philip promptly garrisoned the towns of the Low Countries with Spanish mercenaries, imported the **Inquisition** and passed a series of anti-Protestant edicts. However, other pressures on the Habsburg Empire forced him into a tactical withdrawal and he transferred control of the Low Countries to his sister, **Margaret of Parma**, in 1559. Based in Brussels, the equally resolute Margaret implemented the policies of her brother with gusto. In 1561 she reorganized the Church and created fourteen new bishoprics, a move that was construed as a wresting of power from civil authority, and an attempt to destroy the local aristocracy's powers of religious patronage. Right across the Low Countries, **Protestantism** – and Protestant sympathies – spread to the nobility, who now formed the "League of the Nobility" to counter Habsburg policy. The League petitioned Margaret for moderation but were dismissed out of hand by one of her (French-speaking) advisers, who called them "*ces geux*" (those beggars), an epithet that was to be enthusiastically adopted by the rebels. In 1565 a harvest failure caused a winter famine among the urban workers of the region and, after years of repression, they struck back. In 1566 a Protestant sermon in the tiny Flemish textile town of Steenvoorde incited the congregation to purge the local church of its "papist" idolatry. The crowd smashed up the church's reliquaries and shrines, broke the stained-glass windows and terrorized the priests, thereby igniting what is commonly called the **Iconoclastic Fury**. The rioting spread like wildfire and within ten days churches had been ransacked from one end of the Low Countries to the other, nowhere more so than in Amsterdam – hence the plain, whitewashed interiors of many of the city's churches today.

The Council of Blood and the Waterguezen

The ferocity of this outbreak shocked the upper classes into renewed support for Spain, and Margaret regained the allegiance of most nobles – with the principal exception of the country's greatest landowner, Prince William of Orange-Nassau, known as **William the Silent**, who prudently slipped away to his estates in Germany. Meanwhile, Philip II was keen to capitalize on the increase in support for Margaret and, in 1567, he dispatched the **Duke of Albe**, with an army of ten thousand men, to the Low Countries to suppress his religious opponents absolutely. One of Albe's first acts was to set up the Commission of Civil Unrest, which was soon nicknamed the "Council of Blood", after its habit of executing those it examined. No fewer than twelve thousand citizens were polished off, mostly for taking part in the Fury. Initially the repression worked; in 1568, when William attempted an invasion from Germany, the towns, including Amsterdam, offered no support. William withdrew and conceived other means of defeating Albe, sponsoring the Protestant privateers, the so-called **Waterguezen** or sea-beggars, who took their name from the epithet provided by Margaret's advisor. In April 1572, the Waterguezen entered Brielle on the Maas and captured it from the Spanish in the first of several commando-style attacks. At first, the Waterguezen were obliged to operate from England, but it was soon possible for them to secure bases in the Netherlands, whose citizens had grown to loathe the autocratic Albe and his Spanish army.

After the success at Brielle, the revolt spread rapidly. By June the rebels controlled all of the province of Holland except for Amsterdam, which steadfastly refused to come off the fence. Albe and his son Frederick fought back, but William's superior naval power frustrated him and a mightily irritated Philip replaced Albe with **Luis de Resquesens**. Initially, Resquesens had some success in the south, where the Catholic majority were more willing to compromise with Spanish rule than their northern neighbours, but the tide of war was against him – most pointedly in William's triumphant relief of Leiden in 1574. Two years later, Resquesens died and the (unpaid) Habsburg garrison in Antwerp mutinied and assaulted the town, slaughtering some eight thousand of its people in what was known as the **Spanish Fury**. The massacre alienated the south and pushed its peoples – including the doubting Thomases of Amsterdam – into the arms of William, whose troops now swept into Brussels, the heart of imperial power. Momentarily, it seemed possible for the whole region to unite behind William and all signed the **Union of Brussels**, which demanded the departure of foreign troops as a condition for accepting a diluted Habsburg sovereignty.

The formation of the United Provinces

Philip was, however, not inclined to compromise, especially when he realized that William's Calvinist sympathies were giving his newly found Walloon and Flemish allies (of modern-day Belgium) the jitters. The king bided his time until 1578, when, with his enemies arguing among themselves, he sent another army from Spain to the Low Countries under the command of Alessandro Farnese, the **Duke of Parma**. Events played into Parma's hands. In 1579, tiring of all the wrangling, seven northern provinces agreed to sign the **Union of Utrecht**, an alliance against Spain that was to be the first unification of the Netherlands as an identifiable country – the **United Provinces**. It was then that Amsterdam formally declared for the rebels and switched from Catholicism to Calvinism in what became known as the "**Alteratie**" of 1578. The rebels had conceded freedom of religious belief, but in Amsterdam, as elsewhere, this did not extend to freedom of worship. Nonetheless, a pragmatic compromise was reached in which a blind eye was turned to the celebration of the Mass if it was done privately and inconspicuously. It was this ad hoc arrangement that gave rise to "clandestine" Catholic churches (*schuilkerken*) like that of the Amstelkring on Oudezijds Voorburgwal (see p.58).

The assembly of these United Provinces was known as the **States General**, and it met at Den Haag (The Hague); it had no domestic legislative authority, and could only carry out foreign policy by unanimous decision, a formula designed to reassure the independent-minded merchants of every Dutch city. The role of **Stadholder** was the most important in each province, roughly equivalent to that of governor, though the same person could occupy this position in any number of provinces. Meanwhile, in the south – and also in 1579 – representatives of the southern provinces signed the **Union of Arras**, a Catholic-led agreement that declared loyalty to Philip II and counterbalanced the Union of Utrecht in the north. Thus, the Low Countries were, de facto, divided into two – the **Spanish Netherlands** and the United Provinces – beginning a separation that would lead, after many changes, to the creation of Belgium, Luxembourg and the Netherlands. With the return of more settled times, Amsterdam was now free to carry on with what it did best – trading and making money.

The Golden Age

The brilliance of Amsterdam's explosion onto the European scene is as difficult to underestimate as it is to detail. The size of its **merchant fleet** carrying Baltic grain into Europe had long been considerable and even the Spaniards had been unable to undermine Dutch maritime strength. Furthermore, with the decline of Antwerp, whose skilled workers had fled north after their city had been incorporated into the Spanish Netherlands, Amsterdam now became the unrivalled emporium for the products of northern and southern Europe as well as the East and West Indies. The city didn't prosper from its market alone, though, as Amsterdam ships also carried produce, a cargo trade that greatly increased the city's wealth. Dutch **banking and investment** brought further prosperity, and by the middle of the seventeenth century Amsterdam's wealth was spectacular. The Calvinist bourgeoisie indulged themselves in fine canal houses, and commissioned images of themselves in

Tulipomania

Nothing exemplifies the economic bubble of seventeenth-century Amsterdam more than the arrival of the **tulip**. As a relatively exotic flower, a native of Turkey, it had already captured the imagination of other parts of Europe, and its arrival in the United Provinces – coinciding as it did with an abrupt rise in personal domestic wealth – led to it becoming the bloom of choice for the discerning collector and horticulturalist. New varieties were developed voraciously and the trade in **tulip bulbs** boomed in the 1630s, with prices spiralling out of control and culminating in three rare bulbs changing hands for the price of a house. By this time it was less about flowers, and more about speculation, with tulips being seen as a way of getting rich quick. However, such speculation couldn't be sustained, and the bottom fell out of the tulip market in 1637, when, in the space of three months, prices collapsed to around ten percent of their previous value, and thousands lost everything they possessed. Today tulips and other blooms still define some of the Dutch landscape, but seeing them up close is easiest at the Keukenhof Gardens (see p.146), if you're here in springtime, or at Amsterdam's Bloemenmarkt (p.82).

group portraits. Civic pride knew no bounds as great monuments to self-aggrandizement, such as the new **town hall** (now the Koninklijk Paleis, see p.48), were hastily erected, and, if some went hungry, few starved, as the poor were cared for in municipal almshouses.

The arts flourished and **religious tolerance** was extended even to the traditional scapegoats, the Jews, and in particular the Sephardic Jews, who had been hounded from Spain by the Inquisition, but were guaranteed freedom from religious persecution under the terms of the Union of Utrecht. By the end of the eighteenth century, Jews accounted for ten percent of the city's population. Guilds and craft associations thrived, and in the first half of the seventeenth century Amsterdam's population quadrupled; the relatively high wages paid by the city's industries attracted agricultural workers from every part of the country and Protestant refugees arrived from every corner of Catholic Europe.

Expansion – and the East and West India companies

To accommodate its growing populace, Amsterdam **expanded** several times during the seventeenth century. The grandest and most elaborate plan to enlarge the city was begun in 1613, with the digging of the western stretches of the Herengracht, Keizersgracht and Prinsengracht, the three great canals of the **Grachtengordel** (literally "girdle of canals") that epitomized the wealth and self-confidence of the Golden Age. In 1663 this sweeping crescent was extended beyond the River Amstel, but by this time the population had begun to stabilize, and the stretch that would have completed the ring of canals around the city was left only partially developed – an area that would in time become the Jewish Quarter (see Chapter 4).

One organization that kept the city's coffers brimming throughout the Golden Age was the **East India Company** (Verenigde OostIndische Compagnie, VOC). Formed in 1602, this Amsterdam-controlled enterprise sent ships to Asia, Indonesia and China to bring back spices, wood and other assorted plunder. Given a trading monopoly in all lands east of the Cape of Good Hope, it also exercised unlimited military powers over the lands it controlled, and was effectively the occupying government in Malaya, Ceylon (Sri Lanka) and Malacca. The speed of the VOC's vessels amazed the company's competitors and may well have given rise to the legend of the **Flying Dutchman**. One story has it that the fastest VOC captain of them all, a certain Bernard Fokke, only achieved the sailing times he did with the help of the devil – and his reward is to sail the seven seas forever; another has the VOC's Captain Hendrik van der Decken sailing round the Cape of Good Hope for eternity after blaspheming against the wind and the waves.

Twenty years after the founding of the VOC, the **West India Company** (Westindische Compagnie, WIC) was inaugurated to protect new Dutch interests in the Americas and Africa. It never achieved the success of the East India Company, expending its energies in waging war on Spanish and Portuguese colonies from a base in Surinam, but it did make handsome profits until the 1660s. The company was dismantled in 1674, ten years after its small colony of New Amsterdam had been ceded to the British – and renamed **New York**. Elsewhere, the Dutch held on to their colonies for as long as possible – Indonesia, its principal possession, only secured its independence in 1949.

Decline – 1660 to 1795

Although the economics of the Golden Age were dazzling, the **politics** were dismal. The United Provinces was dogged by interminable wrangling between those who hankered for a central, unified government under the pre-eminent **House of Orange**-Nassau and those who championed provincial autonomy. Frederick Henry, the powerful head of the House of Orange-Nassau who had kept a firm centralizing grip, died in 1647 and his successor, William II, lasted just three years before his death from smallpox. A week after William's death, his wife bore the son who would become William III of England, but in the meantime the leaders of the province of Holland, with the full support of Amsterdam, seized their opportunity. They forced measures through the States General abolishing the position of Stadholder, thereby reducing the powers of the Orangists and increasing those of the provinces, chiefly Holland itself. Holland's foremost figure in these years was **Johan de Witt**, Council Pensionary (chief minister) to the States General. He guided the country through wars with England and Sweden, concluding a triple alliance between the two countries and the United Provinces in 1668. This was a striking reversal of policy; the economic rivalry between the United Provinces and England had already precipitated two **Anglo-Dutch wars** (in 1652–54 and 1665–67) and there was much bitterness in Anglo-Dutch relations – a popular English pamphlet of the time was titled *A Relation Shewing How They [the Dutch] Were First Bred and Descended from a Horse-Turd Which Was Enclosed in a Butter-Box*. Much of the ill feeling came from an embarrassing defeat in the second Anglo–Dutch war, when **Admiral Michiel de Ruyter** had sailed up the Thames and caught the English fleet napping. This infuriated England's Charles II, who was quite willing to break with his new-found allies and join a French attack on the Provinces in 1672. The republic was now in deep trouble – previous victories had been at sea, and the army, weak and disorganized, could not withstand the onslaught. In panic, the country turned to **William III** of Orange for leadership and Johan de Witt was brutally murdered by a mob of Orangist sympathizers in Den Haag. By 1678 William had defeated the French and made peace with the English – and was rewarded (along with his wife Mary, the daughter of Charles I of England) with the English crown ten years later.

The French covet the Low Countries

Though King William III had defeated the French, **Louis XIV** retained designs on the United Provinces and the military pot was kept boiling in a long series of dynastic wars that ranged across northern Europe. In 1700, Charles II of Spain, the last of the Spanish Habsburgs, died childless, bequeathing the Spanish throne and control of the Spanish Netherlands (now Belgium) to Philip of Anjou, Louis' grandson. Louis promptly forced Philip to cede the latter to France, which was, with every justification, construed as a threat to the balance of power by France's neighbours. The **War of the Spanish Succession** ensued, with the United Provinces, England and Austria forming the **Triple Alliance** to thwart the French king. The war itself was a haphazard, long-winded affair distinguished by the spectacular victories of the Duke of Marlborough at Blenheim, Ramillies and Malplaquet. It dragged on until the **Treaty of Utrecht** of 1713 in which France finally abandoned its claim to the Spanish Netherlands, which reverted to the Austrian Habsburgs (as the Austrian Netherlands).

However, the fighting had drained the United Provinces' reserves and a slow economic decline began, accelerated by a reactive trend towards conservatism. This in turn reflected the development of an increasingly socially static society, with power and wealth concentrated within a small, self-regarding elite. Furthermore, with the threat of foreign conquest effectively removed, the Dutch ruling class divided into two main camps – the **Orangists** and the pro-French "**Patriots**" – whose interminable squabbling soon brought political life to a virtual standstill. The situation deteriorated even further in the latter half of the century, and the last few years of the United Provinces present a sorry state of affairs.

French occupation and the United Kingdom of the Netherlands

In 1795 the **French**, aided by the Patriots, invaded, setting up the **Batavian Republic** and dissolving the United Provinces – along with many of the privileges of the richer Dutch merchants. Now part of the Napoleonic empire, the Netherlands were obliged to wage unenthusiastic war with England, and in 1806 Napoleon appointed his brother **Louis** as their king in an attempt to unite the rival Dutch groups under one (notionally independent) ruler. **Louis** was installed in Amsterdam's town hall, giving it its title of Koninklijk Paleis (Royal Palace; see p.48). Louis, however, wasn't willing to allow the Netherlands to become a simple satellite of France; he ignored Napoleon's directives and after just four years of rule was forced to abdicate. The country was then formally incorporated into the French Empire, and for three gloomy years suffered occupation and heavy taxation to finance French military adventures.

Following Napoleon's disastrous retreat from Moscow, the **Orangist faction** surfaced to exploit weakening French control. In 1813, Frederick William, son of the exiled William V, returned to the country and eight months later, under the terms of the **Congress of Vienna**, was crowned King William I of the **United Kingdom of the Netherlands**, incorporating both the old United

Provinces and the Austrian Netherlands. A strong-willed man, he spent much of the later part of his life trying to control his disparate kingdom but failed, primarily because of the Protestant north's attempt – or perceived attempt – to dominate the Catholic south. The southern provinces revolted against his rule and in 1830 the separate Kingdom of **Belgium** was proclaimed. During the years of the United Kingdom, Amsterdam's status was dramatically reduced. Previously, the self-governing city, made bold by its wealth, could (and frequently did) act in its own self-interest, at the expense of the nation. From 1815, however, it was integrated within the country, with no more rights than any other city. The seat of government (and the centre for all decision-making) was Den Haag (The Hague), and so it remained after the southern provinces broke away.

The nineteenth century

In the first decades of the nineteenth century, the erosion of Amsterdam's pre-eminent position among Dutch cities was largely camouflaged by its profitable colonial trade with the East Indies (Indonesia). This trade was however hampered by the character of the **Zuider Zee**, whose shallows and sandbanks presented all sorts of navigational problems given the increasing size of merchant ships. The **Noordhollandskanaal** (North Holland Canal), completed in 1824 and running north from Amsterdam to bypass the Zuider Zee, made little difference, and it was Rotterdam, strategically placed on the Rhine inlets between the industries of the Ruhr and Britain, that prospered at Amsterdam's expense. Even the 1876 opening of the **Nordzeekanaal** (North Sea Canal), which provided a direct link west from Amsterdam to the North Sea, failed to push Amsterdam's trade ahead of rival Rotterdam's, though the city did hold on to much of the country's **shipbuilding industry**, remnants of which can still be seen at the 't Kromhout shipyard (see p.110). The city council was also slow to catch on to the possibilities of rail, but finally, in 1889, the opening of **Centraal Station** put the city back on the main transport routes. Nonetheless, Amsterdam was far from being a backwater; in the second half of the nineteenth century its industries boomed, attracting a new wave of migrants, who were settled outside of the centre in the vast tenements of De Pijp and the Oud Zuid (Old South). These same workers were soon to radicalize the city, supporting a veritable raft of Socialist and Communist politicians. One marker was a reforming **Housing Act** of 1901 that pushed the city council into a concerted effort to clear the city's slums. Even better, the new municipal housing was frequently designed to the highest specifications, no more so than under the guidance of the two leading architects of the (broadly Expressionist) **Amsterdam School**, Michael de Klerk (1884–1923) and Piet Kramer (1881–1961). The duo were responsible for the layout of much of the Nieuw Zuid (New South; see pp.131–133) in general and the De Dageraad housing project in particular (see p.139).

The Netherlands reconfigures

Nationally, **Jan Rudolph Thorbecke** (1798–1872), the outstanding political figure of the times, formed three ruling cabinets (in 1849–53, 1862–66 and 1872) and steered the Netherlands through a profound attitudinal change. The political parties of the late eighteenth century had wanted to resurrect the power and prestige of the seventeenth-century Netherlands; Thorbecke and his liberal allies resigned themselves to the country's reduced status as a small power and eulogized its advantages. For the first time, from about 1850, liberty was seen as a luxury made possible by the country's very lack of power, and the malaise that had long disturbed public life gave way to a positive appreciation of the very narrowness of its national existence. One of the results of Thorbecke's liberalism was a gradual extension of the franchise, culminating in the **Act of Universal Suffrage** in 1917.

The war years

The Netherlands remained neutral during **World War I** and although it suffered privations as a by-product of the Allied blockade of German war materials, this was offset by the profits many Dutch merchants made by trading with both sides. Similar attempts to remain neutral in **World War II**, however, failed. The **Germans invaded** on May 10, 1940, and the Netherlands was quickly overrun. Queen Wilhelmina fled to London to set up a government-in-exile, and members of the **NSB**, the Dutch fascist party which had welcomed the invaders, was rewarded with positions of authority. Nevertheless, in the early months of the occupation, life for ordinary Amsterdammers went on pretty much as usual. Even when the first roundups of the **Jews** began in late 1940, many managed to turn a blind eye, though in February 1941 Amsterdam's newly outlawed Communist Party did organize a widely supported strike, spearheaded by the city's transport and refuse workers, shipbuilders and dockers in support of the Jews. It was a gesture rather than a move to undermine German control, but an important one all the same. Interviewed after the war, one of the leaders summarized it thus: "If just one of Amsterdam's Jews did not feel forgotten and abandoned as he was packed off in a train, then the strike was well worth it."

As the war progressed, so the German grip got tighter and the Dutch **Resistance** stronger, its activities trumpeted by underground newspapers such as *Het Parool* (The Password), which survives in good form today. For the most part, the Resistance focused on industrial and transportation sabotage as well as the forgery of identity papers, a real Dutch speciality, but it paid a heavy price with some 23,000 of its fighters and sympathizers losing their lives. The city's Jews (see box, p.98), however, took the worst punishment. In 1940, Amsterdam's Jewish population, swollen by refugees from Hitler's Germany, was around 140,000, but when the Allies liberated the city in May 1945 only a few thousand were left. The Old Jewish Quarter (see Chapter 4) lay deserted, a rare crumb of comfort being the survival of the diary of a young Jewish girl – **Anne Frank**.

Reconstruction – 1945 to 1960

The **postwar years** were spent patching up the damage of occupation, though at first progress was hindered by a desperate shortage of food, fuel and building materials. Indeed, things were in such short supply – and the winter of 1945–46 so cold – that hundreds of Amsterdammers died of hunger and/ or hypothermia, their black cardboard coffins being trundled to mass graves.

Neither did it help that the retreating Germans had blown up all the dykes and sluices on the North Sea coast at IJmuiden, at the mouth of the Nordzeekanaal. Nevertheless, Amsterdam had not received an aerial pounding like the ones dished out to Rotterdam and Arnhem, and the reconstruction soon built up a head of steam. One feature was the creation of giant suburbs like **Bijlmermeer**, to the southeast of the city, the last word in early 1960s large-scale residential planning, with low-cost modern housing, play areas and foot and cycle paths.

Two events marred Dutch reconstruction in the late 1940s and early 1950s. The former **Dutch colonies** of Java and Sumatra, taken by the Japanese at the outbreak of the war, were now ruled by a nationalist republican government that refused to recognize Dutch sovereignty. Following the failure of talks between Den Haag and the nationalists in 1947, the Dutch sent the troops in – a colonial enterprise that soon became a bloody debacle. International opposition was intense and, after much condemnation and pressure, the Dutch reluctantly surrendered their most important Asian colonies, which were ultimately incorporated as **Indonesia** in 1950. Back at home, tragedy struck on February 1, 1953 when an unusually high tide was pushed over Zeeland's sea defences by a westerly gale, flooding 160 square kilometres of land and drowning over 1800 people. The response was the **Delta Project**, which closed off the western part of the Scheldt and Maas estuaries with massive sea dykes, thereby ensuring the safety of cities to the south of Amsterdam, though Amsterdam itself had already been secured by the completion of the **Afsluitdijk** in 1932. This dyke closed off the **Zuider Zee**, turning it into the freshwater IJsselmeer with the Markermeer hived off later.

The Provos and the 1960s

The radical, youthful mass movements that swept through the West in the 1960s transformed Amsterdam from a middling, rather conservative city into a turbo-charged hotbed of **hippy action**. In 1963, one-time window cleaner and magician extraordinaire **Jasper Grootveld** won celebrity status by painting "K" – for *kanker* ("cancer") – on cigarette billboards throughout the city. Two years later, he proclaimed the statue of the *Lieverdje* ("Loveable Rascal") on the Spui (see p.47) the symbol of "tomorrow's addicted consumer" – since it had been donated to the city by a cigarette manufacturer – and organized large-scale gatherings there once a week. His actions enthused others, most notably **Roel van Duyn**, a philosophy student at Amsterdam University, who assembled a left-wing-cum-anarchist movement known as the **Provos** – short for *provocatie* ("provocation"). The Provos participated in Grootveld's meetings and then proceeded to organize their own street "**happenings**", which proved to be fantastically popular among young Amsterdammers. The number of Provos never exceeded about thirty and the group had no coherent structure, but they did have one clear aim – to bring points of political or social conflict to public attention by spectacular means. More than anything, they were masters of publicity, and pursued their "games" with a spirit of fun rather than grim political fanaticism. The reaction of the police, however, was aggressive; the first two issues of the Provos' magazine were confiscated and, in July 1965, they intervened at a Saturday-night "happening", setting a pattern for future confrontations. The magazine itself contained the Provos' manifesto, a set of policies that later appeared under the title "**The White Plans**". These included the famously popular **white bicycle plan**, which proposed that the council ban all cars in the city centre and supply 20,000 bicycles (painted white) for general public use.

Princess Beatrix gets married

There were regular police-Provos confrontations throughout 1965, but it was the **wedding of Princess Beatrix** to Claus von Amsberg on March 10, 1966, that provoked the most serious unrest. Amsberg had served in the German army during World War II and many Netherlanders were deeply offended by the marriage. Consequently, when hundreds took to the streets to protest, pelting the wedding procession with smoke bombs, a huge swathe of Dutch opinion supported them – to some degree or another. Amsberg himself got no more than he deserved when he was jeered with the refrain "Give us back the bikes", a reference to the commandeering of hundreds of bikes by the retreating German army in 1945. The wedding over, the next crisis came in June when, much to the horror of the authorities, it appeared that students, workers and Provos were about to combine. In panic, the Hague government ordered the dismissal of Amsterdam's police chief, who was deemed to be losing control, but in the event the Provos had peaked and the workers proved far from revolutionary, settling for arbitration on their various complaints.

The 1970s and 1980s – and the squatters

In 1967, the Provos formally dissolved their movement at a happening in the Vondelpark, but many of their supporters promptly moved on to **neighbourhood committees**, set up to oppose the more outlandish development plans of the city council. The most hated scheme by a long chalk was the plan to build a **metro line** through the Nieuwmarkt to the new suburb of Bijlmermeer, as this involved both wholesale demolitions and compulsory relocations. For six months there were regular confrontations between the police and the protestors and, although the council eventually had its way, the scene was set for more trouble. In particular, the council seemed to many to be unwilling to tackle Amsterdam's acute **housing shortage**, neglecting the needs of its poorer citizens in favour of business interests. It was this perception that fuelled the **squatter movement**, which coalesced around a handful of symbolic squats. The first major incident came in March 1980 when several hundred police evicted squatters from premises on **Vondelstraat**. Afterwards, there was widespread rioting, but this was minor in comparison with the protests of April 30, 1980 – the **coronation day of Queen Beatrix** – when a mixed bag of squatters and leftists vigorously protested both the lavishness of the proceedings and the expense of refurbishing Beatrix's palace in Den Haag. Once again there was widespread rioting and this time it spread to other Dutch cities, though the unrest proved to be short-lived.

Now at its peak, Amsterdam's squatting movement boasted around ten thousand activists, many of whom were involved in two more major confrontations with the police – the first at the **Lucky Luyk** squat, on Jan Luykenstraat, the second at the **Wyers** building, when, in February 1984, the squatters were forcibly cleared to make way for a Holiday Inn, now the *Crowne Plaza Hotel*.

The final showdown – the **Stopera** campaign – arrived with the construction of the **Muziektheater/Stadhuis** complex on Waterlooplein (see p.99). Thereafter, the movement faded away, at least partly because of its repeated failure to stop the developers, who now claim, with some justification, to be more sensitive to community needs.

The 1990s and the rise of Pim Fortuyn

In the 1990s, Amsterdam's street protests and massive squats became an increasingly distant memory, but some of the old ideas – and ideals – were carried forward by the **Greens**, who attracted – and continue to attract – a small but significant following in every municipal and national election. One of the recurring political problems was that the city's finely balanced system of **proportional representation** brought little rapid change, often getting mired in interminable compromise and debate. The same is true **nationally**, where politics has long seemed a bland if necessary business conducted between the three main parties, the **Protestant-Catholic CDA** coalition, the **Liberal VVD** and the **Socialist PVDA**. However, the entire political class received a jolt in the national elections of May 2002 when a brand-new rightist grouping – **Leefbaar Neederlands** (Liveable Netherlands) – led by Rotterdam's **Pim Fortuyn**, swept to second place behind the CDA, securing seventeen percent of the national vote. Stylish and witty, openly gay and a former Marxist, Fortuyn managed to cover several popular bases at the same time, from the need for law and order through to tighter immigration controls. Most crucially, he also attacked the liberal establishment's espousal of multiculturalism even when the representatives of minority groups were deeply reactionary, anti-gay and sexist. Politically, it worked a treat, but a year later Fortuyn was assassinated and his party rapidly unravelled, losing most of its seats in the general election of January 2003 (see below).

One of the reasons for Fortuyn's electoral success reflected the other shock to the Dutch system, which came with the publication of a damning report on the failure of the Dutch army to protect the Bosnian Muslims ensconced in the UN safe-haven of **Srebrenica** in 1995. Published in April 2002, the report told a tale of extraordinary incompetence; the UN's Dutch soldiers were inadequately armed, but still refused American assistance, and watched as Serb troops separated Muslim men and women in preparation for the mass executions, which the Dutch soldiers then did nothing to stop (though they were never involved). In a country that prides itself on its internationalism, the report was an especially hard blow and the whole of the PVDA-led government, under **Wim Kok**, resigned in April 2002.

The early 2000s – Theo van Gogh and Ayaan Hirsi Ali

The general election of 2003 was a close-run thing, and there was certainly a revival in PVDA fortunes, but a **rightist alliance** – consisting of the VVD, the CDA and the Lijst Pim Fortuyn (formerly Leefbaar Neederlands) – still managed to cobble together an administration under the leadership of **Jan Peter**

Balkenende. In the event, this coalition proved most unstable, but Balkenende soldiered on (with different partners) until the national election of November 2006. This saw modest gains for the far right and left, but not enough to unseat Balkenende, who is now at the head of a majority CDA, PVDA and Christian Union (CU) administration. Superficially, therefore, and with Leefbaar Neederlands dead and gone (the party dissolved itself), it seemed that normal political service had been resumed, but although the CDA and the PVDA were once again the largest parties, there was an uneasy undertow. In truth, Fortuyn's popularity pushed certain sorts of social debate, particularly on **immigration**, to the right. The situation got much worse – and race relations much more tense – when, in late 2004, filmmaker **Theo van Gogh** was shot dead on an Amsterdam street by a Moroccan who objected to a film he had made – *Submission* – about Islamic violence against women. Shown on Dutch TV, the film was scripted by a politician, **Ayaan Hirsi Ali**, a Somali refugee and Dutch citizen, whose pronouncements on this same subject have been hard-hitting and headline-grabbing in equal measure. In an interview with the UK's *Daily Telegraph* in December 2004, she is reported to have said: "But tell me why any Muslim man would want Islamic women to be educated and emancipated? Would a Roman voluntarily have given up his slaves?" Unfortunately for Ali, she was engulfed by controversy of a different kind in 2006, when it turned out that her application for asylum had not been entirely truthful – and the ensuing furore created parliamentary panic.

To its credit, the Amsterdam city council, and especially the mayor, Job Cohen, handled the racial tension with aplomb and, largely as a result, he was mandated for a second term as mayor in 2006. Also in 2006, **municipal elections** saw the PVDA runaway winners in terms of the popular vote, but still needing the support of another party – in this case, the leftist **GroenLinks** ("GreenLeft") – to form a majority administration. This coalition remains in power at the time of writing.

The present

In the 1970s, many Amsterdammers may have had their misgivings, but the vast majority came to accept that their country's liberal attitude to soft drugs and prostitution was sane and pragmatic. They couldn't have foreseen that almost nobody else in Europe would follow in their slipstream and that, as a result, Amsterdam would become a target for thousands of tourists after the city's indulgences. By the 1990s, a solid bloc of Amsterdammers was appalled by this state of affairs and this played into the hands of a new breed of city politician, who wanted to cast Amsterdam as a dynamic metropolis. To this new breed, the Red Light District was unpleasant, if not downright offensive, and in recent years there have been political rumblings about closing the "window brothels" down. The mayor himself railed against people trafficking, gangsterism and money laundering, and others proposed to have the whole lot moved to the polders east of the city, though the only result so far has been a reduction in the number of window brothel licences. But really it was **redevelopment** that became the name of the game with the first major target being the old docklands bordering the River IJ. The initial phases of this colossal project went down well and Amsterdammers did indeed begin to think that their city could become an ultra-modern metropolis – but then came the **Noord–Zuidlijn**. Begun in 2003, the plan was to construct a

10km-long metro running north–south underneath Amsterdam. It has been little short of a disaster: costs have ballooned, there have been endless problems keeping the tunnels dry, several houses have actually collapsed as a result of the diggings and finally, to add insult to injury, the work won't be completed until at least 2015 – much later than was intended.

Perhaps more than anything else, the Noord-Zuidlijn fiasco has contributed to a sense of malaise amongst Amsterdammers – a feeling they share with many other Netherlanders. Most hope for better times, but others are voting with their feet: in 2006, 132,000 mostly middle-class Dutch citizens emigrated, the largest number ever.

Dutch art

Designed to serve only as a quick reference, the following **outline** is the very briefest of introductions to a subject that has rightly filled volumes. Inevitably, it covers artists that lived and worked in both the Netherlands and Belgium, as these two countries have – along with Luxembourg – been bound together as the "**Low Countries**" for most of their history. For in-depth and academic studies, see the recommendations in "Books" on p.282.

Beginnings – the Flemish Primitives

Throughout the medieval period, **Flanders**, in modern-day Belgium, was one of the most artistically productive parts of Europe, and it was here that the solid realist base of later Dutch painting developed. Today, the works of these early Flemish painters, the **Flemish Primitives**, are highly prized, and although examples are fairly rare in the Netherlands, Amsterdam's Rijksmuseum has a healthy sample, though unfortunately many of them are not on display during the museum's long-winded refurbishment (see p.115).

Jan van Eyck (1385–1441) is generally regarded as the first of the Flemish Primitives, and has even been credited with the invention of oil painting – though it seems more likely that he simply perfected a new technique by thinning his paint with turpentine (at the time a new discovery), thus making it more flexible. The most famous of his works still in the Low Countries is the altarpiece in Belgium's Ghent Cathedral, which was revolutionary in its realism, for the first time using elements of native landscape in depicting biblical themes. Van Eyck's style and technique were to influence several generations of the region's artists.

Firmly in the Eyckian tradition were the **Master of Flemalle** (1387–1444) and **Rogier van der Weyden** (1400–64), one-time official painter to the city of Brussels. The Flemalle master is a shadowy figure; some believe he was the teacher of Van der Weyden, others that the two artists were in fact the same person. There are differences between the two, however; the Flemalle master's paintings are close to Van Eyck's, whereas van der Weyden shows a greater degree of emotional intensity in his religious works. Van der Weyden also produced serene portraits of the bigwigs of his day and these were much admired across a large swathe of western Europe. His style, never mind his success, influenced many painters, one of the most talented of these being **Dieric Bouts** (1415–75). Born in Haarlem but active in (Belgium's) Leuven, Bouts is recognizable by his stiff, rather elongated figures and penchant for horrific subject matter – the tortures of damnation for example – all set against carefully drawn landscapes.

Few doubt that **Hans Memling** (1440–94) was a pupil of van der Weyden. Active in Bruges throughout his life, he is best remembered for the pastoral charm of his landscapes and the quality of his portraiture, much of which survives on the rescued side panels of triptychs. **Gerard David** (1460–1523) was a native of Oudewater, near Gouda, but he moved to Bruges in 1484, becoming the last of the great painters to work in that city, producing formal religious works of traditional bent. Strikingly different, but broadly contemporaneous, was **Hieronymus Bosch** (1450–1516), who lived for most of his life in the Netherlands, though his style is linked to that of his Flemish contemporaries. His frequently reprinted religious allegories are filled with macabre visions of tortured people and grotesque beasts, and appear at first faintly unhinged, though it's now thought that these are visual representations of contemporary sayings, idioms and parables. While their interpretation is far from resolved, Bosch's paintings draw strongly on subconscious fears and archetypes, giving them a lasting, haunting fascination.

The sixteenth century

At the end of the fifteenth century, Flanders was in economic and political decline and the leading artists of the day were drawn instead to the booming port of **Antwerp**, also in present-day Belgium. The artists who worked here soon began to integrate the finely observed detail that characterized the Flemish tradition with the style of the Italian painters of the Renaissance. **Quentin Matsys** (1464–1530) introduced florid classical architectural details and intricate landscapes to his works, influenced perhaps by the work of Leonardo da Vinci. As well as religious works, he painted portraits and genre scenes, all of which have recognizably Italian facets – and in the process he paved the way for the Dutch genre painters of later years. **Jan Gossaert** (1478–1532) made the pilgrimage to Italy too, and his dynamic works are packed with detail, especially finely drawn classical architectural backdrops. He was the first Low Countries artist to introduce the subjects of classical mythology into his paintings, part of a steady trend towards secular subject matter, which can also be seen in the work of **Joachim Patenier** (d.1524), who painted small landscapes of fantastical scenery.

The middle of the sixteenth century was dominated by the work of **Pieter Bruegel the Elder** (c.1525–69), whose gruesome allegories and innovative interpretations of religious subjects are firmly placed in Low Countries settings. Pieter also painted finely observed peasant scenes, though he himself was well connected in court circles in Antwerp and, later, Brussels. **Pieter Aertsen** (1508–75) also worked in the peasant genre, adding aspects of still life; his paintings often show a detailed kitchen scene in the foreground, with a religious episode going on behind. Bruegel's two sons, **Pieter Bruegel the Younger** (1564–1638) and **Jan Bruegel** (1568–1625), were lesser painters; the former produced fairly insipid copies of his father's work, while Jan developed a style of his own – delicately rendered flower paintings and genre pieces that earned him the nickname "Velvet". Towards the latter half of the sixteenth century highly stylized Italianate portraits became the dominant fashion, with **Frans Pourbus the Younger** (1569–1622) the leading practitioner. Frans hobnobbed across Europe, working for the likes of the Habsburgs and the Médicis.

The Dutch get going

Meanwhile, there were artistic rumblings in the province of Holland. Leading the charge was **Geertgen tot Sint Jans** (Little Gerard of the Brotherhood of St John; d.1490), who worked in Haarlem, initiating – in a strangely naive style – an artistic vision that would come to dominate the

Dutch in the seventeenth century. There was a tender melancholy in his work very different from the stylized paintings produced in Flanders, and, most importantly, a new sensitivity to light. **Jan Mostaert** (1475–1555) took over after Geertgen's death, developing similar themes, but the first painter to effect real changes in northern painting was **Lucas van Leyden** (1489–1533). Born in Leiden, his bright colours and narrative technique were refreshingly novel, and he introduced a new dynamism into what had become a rigidly formal treatment of devotional subjects. There was rivalry, of course. Eager to publicize Haarlem as the artistic capital of the northern Netherlands, **Karel van Mander** (see below) claimed **Jan van Scorel** (1495–1562) as the better painter, complaining, too, of van Leyden's dandyish ways. Certainly van Scorel's influence should not be underestimated. Like many of his contemporaries, van Scorel hotfooted it to Italy to view the works of the Renaissance, but in Rome his career went into overdrive when he found favour with Pope Hadrian VI, one-time bishop of Utrecht, who installed him as court painter in 1520. Van Scorel stayed in Rome for four years and when he returned to Utrecht, armed with all that papal prestige, he combined the ideas he had picked up in Italy with those underpinning Haarlem realism, thereby modifying what had previously been an independent artistic tradition once and for all. Amongst his several students, probably the most talented was **Maerten van Heemskerck** (1498–1574), who duly went off to Italy himself in 1532, staying there five years before doubling back to Haarlem.

The Golden Age

The seventeenth century begins with **Karel van Mander** (1548–1606), Haarlem painter, art impresario and one of the few contemporary chroniclers of the art of the Low Countries. His *Schilderboek* of 1604 put Flemish and Dutch traditions into context for the first time, and in addition specified the rules of fine painting. Examples of his own work are rare – though Haarlem's Frans Hals Museum (see p.143) weighs in with a couple – but his followers were many. Among them was **Cornelius Cornelisz van Haarlem** (1562–1638), who produced elegant renditions of biblical and mythical themes; and **Hendrik Goltzius** (1558–1616), who was a skilled engraver and an integral member of van Mander's Haarlem academy. The enthusiasm these painters had for Italian art, combined with the influence of a late revival of Gothicism, resulted in works that combined **Mannerist and Classical** elements. An interest in realism was also felt, but, for them, the subject became less important than the way in which it was depicted; biblical stories became merely a vehicle whereby artists could apply their skills in painting the human body, landscapes, or copious displays of food. All of this served to break the religious stranglehold on art, and make legitimate a whole range of everyday subjects for the painter.

In what is now the Netherlands (and this was where the north and the south finally diverged) this break with tradition was compounded by the **Reformation**: the austere Calvinism that had replaced the Catholic faith in the United (ie northern) Provinces had no use for images or symbols of devotion in its churches. Instead, painters catered to the burgeoning middle class, and no longer visited (Catholic) Italy to learn their craft. Indeed, the real giants of the seventeenth century – Hals, Rembrandt, Vermeer – stayed in the Netherlands all their lives. Another innovation was that painting split into more distinct categories – genre, portrait, landscape – and artists tended (with notable exceptions) to confine themselves to one field throughout their careers. So began the **Golden Age** of Dutch art.

Historical and religious painting

The artistic influence of Renaissance Italy may have been in decline, but Italian painters still had clout with the Dutch, most notably **Caravaggio** (1571–1610), who was much admired for his new realism. Taking Caravaggio's cue, many artists – Rembrandt for one – continued to portray classical subjects, but in a way that was totally at odds with the Mannerists' stylish flights of imagination. The Utrecht artist **Abraham Bloemaert** (1564–1651), though a solid Mannerist throughout his career, encouraged these new ideas, and his students – **Gerard van Honthorst** (1590–1656), **Hendrik Terbrugghen** (1588–1629) and **Dirck van Baburen** (1590–1624) – formed the nucleus of the influential **Utrecht School**, which followed Caravaggio almost to the point of slavishness. Honthorst was perhaps the leading figure, learning his craft from Bloemaert and travelling to Rome, where he was nicknamed "Gerardo delle Notti" for his ingenious handling of light and shade. In his later paintings, however, this was to become more routine technique than inspired invention, and though a supremely competent artist, Honthorst is somewhat discredited among critics today. Terbrugghen's reputation seems to have aged rather better; he soon forgot Caravaggio and developed a more individual style, his later, lighter work having a great influence on the young Vermeer. After a jaunt to Rome, Baburen shared a studio with Terbrugghen and produced some fairly original work – work which also had some influence on Vermeer – but today he is the least studied member of the group and few of his paintings survive.

Rembrandt

The gilded reputation of **Rembrandt van Rijn** (1606–69) is still relatively recent – nineteenth-century connoisseurs preferred Gerard Dou – but he is now justly regarded as one of the greatest and most versatile painters of all time. Born in Leiden, the son of a miller, he was a boy apprentice to Jacob van Swanenburgh, a then quite important, though singularly uninventive, local artist. Rembrandt shared a studio with Jan Lievens, a promising painter and something of a rival, though now all but forgotten, before venturing forth to Amsterdam to study under the fashionable Pieter Lastman. Soon he was painting commissions for the city's elite and became an accepted member of their circle.

Above all others, Rembrandt was the most original historical artist of the seventeenth century, also chipping in with religious paintings throughout his career. In the 1630s, the poet and statesman Constantijn Huygens procured for him his greatest commission – a series of five paintings of the Passion, beautifully composed and uncompromisingly realistic. Later, however, Rembrandt drifted away from the mainstream, ignoring the smooth brushwork of his contemporaries and choosing instead a rougher, darker and more disjointed style for his biblical and historical subjects. This may well have contributed to a decline in his artistic fortunes and it is significant that while the more conventional Jordaens, Honthorst and van Everdingen were busy decorating the Huis ten Bosch near Den Haag for the Stadholder Frederick Henry, Rembrandt was having his monumental *Conspiracy of Julius Civilis* – painted for the new Amsterdam Town Hall – thrown out. The reasons for this rejection have been hotly debated, but it seems likely that Rembrandt's rendition was thought too suggestive of cabalistic conspiracy – the commissioners wanted to see a romantic hero and certainly not a plot in the making: Julius had organized a revolt against the Romans, an important event in early Dutch history, which had obvious resonance in a country just freed from the Habsburgs. Even worse, perhaps, Rembrandt had shown Julius to be blind in one eye, which was historically accurate but not at all what the city's burghers had in mind.

Genre painting

Often misunderstood, the term **genre painting** was initially applied to everything from animal paintings and still lifes through to historical works and landscapes, but later – from around the middle of the seventeenth century – came to be applied only to **scenes of everyday life**. Its target market was the region's burgeoning middle class, who had a penchant for non-idealized portrayals of common scenes, both with and without symbols – or subtly disguised details – making one moral point or another. One of its early practitioners was Antwerp's **Frans Snijders** (1579–1657), who took up still-life painting where Aertsen (see p.270) left off, amplifying his subject – food and drink – to even larger, more sumptuous canvases. Snijders also doubled up as a member of the Rubens art machine (see p.277), painting animals and still-life sections for the master's works. In Utrecht, Hendrik Terbrugghen and Gerard van Honthorst adapted the realism and strong chiaroscuro learned from Caravaggio to a number of tableaux of everyday life, though they were more concerned with religious works (see p.272), while Haarlem's Frans Hals dabbled in genre too, but is better known as a portraitist. The opposite is true of one of Hal's pupils, **Adriaen Brouwer** (1605–38), whose riotous tavern scenes were well received in their day and collected by, among others, Rubens and Rembrandt. Brouwer spent only a couple of years in Haarlem under Hals before returning to his native Flanders, where he influenced the inventive **David Teniers the Younger** (1610–90), who worked in Antwerp, and later in Brussels. Teniers' early paintings are Brouwer-like peasant scenes, although his later work is more delicate and diverse, including *kortegaardje* – guardroom scenes that show soldiers carousing. **Adriaen van Ostade** (1610–85), on the other hand, stayed in Haarlem most of his life, skilfully painting groups of peasants and tavern brawls – though his later acceptance by the establishment led him to water down the realism he had learnt from Brouwer. He was teacher to his brother **Isaak** (1621–49), who produced a large number of open-air peasant scenes, subtle combinations of genre and landscape work.

Jan Steen

The English critic E.V. Lucas dubbed Teniers, Brouwer and Ostade "coarse and boorish" compared with **Jan Steen** (1625–79) who, along with Vermeer, is probably the most admired Dutch genre painter. Steen's paintings offer the same Rabelaisian peasantry in full fling, but they go their debauched ways in broad daylight, and nowhere do you see the filthy rogues in shadowy hovels favoured by Brouwer and Ostade. Steen offers more humour, too, as well as more moralizing, identifying with the hedonistic mob and reproaching them at the same time. Indeed, many of his pictures are illustrations of well-known proverbs of the time – popular epithets on the evils of drink or the transience of human existence that were supposed to teach as well as entertain.

Gerrit Dou, Nicholas Maes and their contemporaries

Leiden's **Gerrit Dou** (1613–75) was one of Rembrandt's first pupils. It's difficult to detect any trace of the master's influence in his work, however, as Dou initiated a style of his own: tiny, minutely realized and beautifully finished views of a kind of ordinary life that was decidedly more genteel than Brouwer's – or even Steen's for that matter. He was admired, above all, for his painstaking attention to detail; and he would, it's said, sit in his studio for hours waiting for the dust to settle before starting work. Among his students, **Frans van Mieris** (1635–81) continued the highly finished portrayals of the Dutch bourgeoisie, as did **Gabriel Metsu** (1629–67) – perhaps Dou's most talented pupil – whose pictures often convey an overtly moral message. Another pupil of Rembrandt's, though a much later one, was **Nicholas Maes** (1629–93), whose early works were almost entirely genre paintings, sensitively executed and with an obvious didacticism. His later paintings show the influence of a more refined style of portraiture, which he had picked up in France.

Gerard ter Borch and Pieter de Hooch

As a native of Zwolle, well to the east of Amsterdam, **Gerard ter Borch** (1619–81) found himself far from all these Leiden/Rembrandt connections; despite trips abroad to most of the artistic capitals of Europe, he remained very much a provincial painter. He depicted the country's merchant class at play and became renowned for his curious doll-like figures and his ability to capture the textures of different cloths. His domestic scenes were not unlike those of **Pieter de Hooch** (1629–84), whose simple depictions of everyday life are deliberately unsentimental, and have little or no moral commentary. De Hooch's favourite trick was to paint darkened rooms with an open door leading through to a sunlit courtyard, a practice that, along with his trademark rusty red colour, makes his work easy to identify and, at its best, exquisite. That said, his later pictures lose their spartan quality, reflecting the increasing opulence of the Dutch Republic; the rooms are more richly decorated, the arrangements more contrived and the subjects far less homely.

Jan Vermeer

It was **Jan Vermeer** (1632–75) who brought the most sophisticated methods to painting interiors, depicting the play of natural light on indoor surfaces with superlative skill – and the tranquil intimacy for which he is now famous the world over. Another observer of the better-heeled Dutch household and, like de Hooch, without a moral tone, he is regarded (with Hals and Rembrandt) as one of the big three Dutch painters – though he was, it seems, a slow worker. As a result, only about forty paintings can be attributed to him with any certainty. Living all his life in Delft, to the south of Amsterdam, Vermeer is perhaps the epitome of the seventeenth-century Dutch painter – rejecting the pomp and ostentation of the High Renaissance to record quietly his contemporaries at home, painting for a public that demanded no more than that: bourgeois art at its most complete.

Portraits

Predictably enough, the ruling bourgeoisie of the United Provinces was keen to record and celebrate its success, and consequently portraiture was a reliable way for a young painter to make a living. **Michiel Jansz Miereveld** (1567–1641), court painter to Frederick Henry of Orange-Nassau in Den Haag, was the first real portraitist of the Dutch Republic, but it wasn't long before his stiff and rather conservative figures were superseded by the more spontaneous renderings of **Frans Hals** (1585–1666). Hals is perhaps best known for his "corporation pictures" – group portraits of the Dutch civil guard regiments that had been formed in most of the larger towns during the war with Spain, but subsequently became social clubs. These large group pieces demanded superlative technique, since the painter had to create a collection of individual portraits while retaining a sense of the group, and accord prominence based on the relative importance of the sitters and the size of the payment each had made. Hals was particularly good at this, using innovative lighting effects, arranging his sitters subtly, and putting all the elements together in a fluid and dynamic composition. He also painted many individual portraits, making the ability to capture fleeting and telling expressions his trademark; his pictures of children are particularly sensitive. Later in life, however, his work became darker and more akin to Rembrandt's, spurred − it is conjectured − by his penury.

Jan Cornelisz Verspronck (1597−1662) and **Bartholomeus van der Helst** (1613−70) were the other great Haarlem portraitists after Frans Hals − Verspronck recognizable by the smooth, shiny glow he always gave to his sitters' faces, van der Helst by a competent but unadventurous style. Of the two, van der Helst was the more popular, influencing a number of later painters and leaving Haarlem as a young man to begin a solidly successful career as portrait painter to Amsterdam's upper crust.

Rembrandt the portraitist

With poet and statesman Constantijn Huygens acting as his agent, **Rembrandt** was given more lucrative jobs, and in 1634 the artist married Saskia van Ulenborch, daughter of the burgomaster of Leeuwarden and quite a catch for a relatively humble artist. His self-portraits from this period show the confident face of security − on top of things and quite sure of where he's going.

Rembrandt would not always be the darling of the Amsterdam burghers, but his fall from grace was still some way off when he painted *The Night Watch* (see p.118), a group portrait often − but inaccurately − associated with the artist's decline in popularity. Indeed, although Rembrandt's fluent arrangement of his subjects was totally original, there's no evidence that the military company who commissioned the painting was anything but pleased with the result. More likely culprits are the artist's later pieces, whose obscure lighting and psychological insights took the conservative Amsterdam merchants by surprise − and his personal irascibility. Whatever the reason, his patrons were certainly not sufficiently enthusiastic about his later work to support both his taste for art collecting and his expensive house on Jodenbreestraat (see p.96), the result being that Rembrandt was declared bankrupt in 1656. Rembrandt died thirteen years later, a broken and embittered old man − as his last self-portraits show. Throughout his career he maintained a large studio, and his influence pervaded the next generation of Dutch painters. Some − Dou and Maes − more famous for their genre work, have already been mentioned. Others turned to portraiture.

Govert Flinck, Ferdinand Bol and Carel Fabritius

Govert Flinck (1615−60) was perhaps Rembrandt's most faithful follower, and he was, ironically enough, given the job of decorating Amsterdam's new Town Hall after his teacher had been passed over. Unluckily for him, Flinck died before he could execute his designs and Rembrandt took over, but although the latter's *Conspiracy of Julius Civilis* was installed in 1662, it was discarded a year later (see p.272). The early work of **Ferdinand Bol** (1616−80) was also heavily influenced by Rembrandt, so much so that for centuries art historians couldn't tell the two apart, though Bol's later paintings are readily distinguishable, blandly elegant portraits which proved very popular with the wealthy. At the age of 53, Bol married a wealthy widow and promptly hung up his brush – perhaps he knew just how emotionally tacky his work had become. Most of the pitifully slim extant work of **Carel Fabritius** (1622–54) was portraiture, but he too died young, before he could properly realize his promise as perhaps the most gifted of all Rembrandt's students. Generally regarded as the teacher of Vermeer, he forms a link between the two masters, combining Rembrandt's technique with his own practice of painting figures against a dark background, prefiguring the lighting and colouring of Vermeer.

Landscapes

Aside from Pieter Bruegel the Elder (see p.270), whose depictions of his native surroundings make him the first true Low Countries landscape painter, **Gillis van Coninxloo** (1544–1607) stands out as the earliest Dutch landscapist. He imbued his native scenery with elements of fantasy, painting the richly wooded views he had seen on his travels around Europe as backdrops to biblical scenes. In the early seventeenth century, **Hercules Seghers** (1590–1638), apprenticed to Coninxloo, carried on his mentor's style of depicting forested and mountainous landscapes, some real, others not; his work is scarce but is believed to have had considerable influence on the landscape work of Rembrandt himself. **Esaias van der Velde**'s (1591–1632) quaint and unpretentious scenes show the first real affinity with the Dutch countryside, but while his influence was likewise considerable, he was soon overshadowed by his pupil **Jan van Goyen** (1596–1656). A remarkable painter, who belongs to the so-called "tonal phase" of Dutch landscape painting, van Goyen's early pictures were highly coloured and close to those of his teacher, but it didn't take him long to develop a marked touch of his own, using tones of green, brown and grey to lend everything a characteristic translucent haze. His paintings are, above all, of nature, and if he included figures it was just for the sake of scale. A long-neglected artist, van Goyen only received recognition with the arrival of the Impressionists, when his fluid and rapid brushwork was at last fully appreciated.

Another "tonal" painter, Haarlem's **Salomon van Ruysdael** (1600–70) was also directly affected by Esaias van der Velde, and his simple and atmospheric, though not terribly adventurous, landscapes were for a long time consistently confused with those of van Goyen. More esteemed is his nephew, **Jacob van Ruysdael** (1628–82), generally considered the greatest of all Dutch landscapists, whose fastidiously observed views of quiet flatlands dominated by stormy skies were to influence European landscapists right up to the nineteenth century. John Constable, certainly, acknowledged a debt to him. Ruysdael's foremost pupil was **Meindert Hobbema** (1638–1709), who followed the master faithfully, sometimes even painting the same views as in his *Avenue at Middelharnis*.

The Italianizers

Nicholas Berchem (1620–83) and **Jan Both** (1618–52) were the "Italianizers" of Dutch landscapes. They studied in Rome, taking back to the Netherlands rich, golden views of the world, full of steep gorges and hills, picturesque ruins and wandering shepherds. **Allart van Everdingen** (1621–75) had a similar approach, but his subject matter stemmed from his travels in Norway, which, after his return to the Netherlands, he reproduced in all its mountainous glory. **Aelbert Cuyp** (1620–91), on the other hand, stayed in Dordrecht all his life, painting what was probably the favourite city skyline of Dutch landscapists. He inherited the warm tones of the Italianizers, and his pictures are always suffused with a deep, golden glow.

The specialists

Of a number of specialist seventeenth-century painters who can be included here, **Paulus Potter** (1625–54) is rated as the best painter of domestic animals. He produced a surprisingly large number of paintings in his short life, the most reputed being his lovingly executed pictures of cows and horses. The accurate rendering of architectural features also became a specialized field in which **Pieter Saenredam** (1597–1665), with his finely realized paintings of Dutch church interiors, is the most widely known exponent. **Emanuel de Witte** (1616–92) continued in the same vein, though his churches lack the austere crispness of Saenredam's. **Gerrit Berckheyde** (1638–98) worked in Haarlem soon after, but he limited his views to the outside of buildings, producing variations on the same townscapes. Nautical scenes in praise of the Dutch navy were, on the other hand, the speciality of **Willem van der Velde II** (1633–1707), whose melodramatic canvases, complete with churning seas and chasing skies, are displayed to greatest advantage in the Nederlands Scheepvaartmuseum in Amsterdam (see p.108) – or at least will be again when it reopens.

A further thriving category of seventeenth-century painting was the still life, in which objects were gathered together to remind the viewer of the transience of human life and the meaninglessness of worldly pursuits. Thus, a skull would often be shown alongside a book, pipe or goblet, and some half-eaten food. Two Haarlem painters dominated this field: **Pieter Claesz** (1598–1660) and **Willem Heda** (1594–1680), who confined themselves almost entirely to this type of painting.

Rubens and his followers

Down in the south, in Antwerp, **Pieter Paul Rubens** (1577–1640) was easily the most important exponent of the Baroque in northern Europe. Born in Siegen, Westphalia, he was raised in Antwerp, where he entered the painters' Guild in 1598. Two years later, he became court painter to the Duke of Mantua and thereafter he travelled extensively in Italy, absorbing the art of the High Renaissance and classical architecture. By the time of his return to Antwerp in 1608 he had acquired an enormous artistic vocabulary and, like his Dutch contemporaries, the paintings of Caravaggio were to greatly influence his work. His first major success was *The Raising of the Cross*, painted in 1610 and displayed today in Antwerp cathedral. A large, dynamic work, it caused a sensation at the time, establishing Rubens' reputation and leading to a string of commissions that enabled him to set up his own studio.

The division of labour in Rubens' studio, and the talent of the artists working there (who included Anthony van Dyck and Jacob Jordaens – see p.278) ensured an extraordinary output of excellent work. The degree to which Rubens personally worked on a canvas would vary – and would determine its price. From the early 1620s onwards he turned his hand to a plethora of themes and subjects – religious works, portraits, tapestry designs, landscapes, mythological scenes, ceiling paintings – each of which was handled with supreme vitality and virtuosity. From his Flemish antecedents he inherited an acute sense of light, and used it not to dramatize his subjects (a technique favoured by Caravaggio and other Italian artists), but in association with colour and form. The drama in his works comes from the vigorous animation of his characters. His large-scale allegorical works, especially, are packed with heaving, writhing figures that appear to tumble out from the canvas.

The energy of Rubens' paintings was reflected in his private life. In addition to his career as an artist, he also undertook diplomatic missions to Spain and

England, and used these opportunities to study the works of other artists and – as in the case of Velázquez – to meet them personally. In the 1630s, **gout** began to hamper his activities, and from this time his painting became more domestic and meditative. Hélène Fourment, his second wife, was the subject of many portraits and served as a model for characters in his allegorical paintings, her figure epitomizing the buxom, well-rounded women found throughout his work.

Rubens' pupils

Rubens' influence on the artists of the period was enormous. The huge output of his studio meant that his works were universally seen and also widely disseminated by the engravers he employed to copy him. Chief among his followers was the portraitist **Anthony van Dyck** (1599–1641), who worked in Rubens' studio from 1618, often taking on the depiction of religious figures in his master's works, or at least those that required particular sensitivity and pathos. Like Rubens, van Dyck was born in Antwerp and travelled widely in Italy, though his initial work was influenced less by the Italian artists than by Rubens himself. Eventually, van Dyck developed his own distinct style and technique, establishing himself as court painter to Charles I in England, and creating portraits of a nervous elegance that would influence the genre there for the next 150 years. **Jacob Jordaens** (1593–1678) was also an Antwerp native who studied under Rubens. Although he was commissioned to complete several works left unfinished by Rubens at the time of his death, his robustly naturalistic works have an earthy – and sensuous – realism that is quite different and distinct in style and technique.

The eighteenth century

Accompanying the Netherlands's economic decline was a gradual deterioration in the quality and originality of Dutch painting. The subtle delicacies of the great seventeenth-century painters was replaced by finicky still lifes and minute studies of flowers, or overly finessed portraiture and religious scenes; the work of **Adrian van der Werff** (1659–1722) is typical. Of the era's other big names, **Gerard de Lairesse** (1640–1711) spent most of his time decorating a rash of brand-new civic halls and mansions, but, like the buildings he worked on, his style and influences were French. **Jacob de Wit** (1695–1754) continued where Lairesse left off, painting burgher ceiling after ceiling in flashy style. He also benefited from a relaxation in the laws against Catholics, decorating several of their (newly legal) churches. The eighteenth century's only painter of any real talent was **Cornelis Troost** (1697–1750) who, although he didn't produce anything stunningly original, painted competent portraits and some neat, faintly satirical pieces that have since earned him the title of "The Dutch Hogarth". Cosy interiors also continued to prove popular, and the Haarlem painter **Wybrand Hendriks** (1744–1831) satisfied demand with numerous proficient examples.

The nineteenth century

Johann Barthold Jongkind (1819–91) was the first important artist to emerge in the nineteenth century, painting landscapes and seascapes that were to influence Monet and the early Impressionists. He spent most of his life in France and his work was exhibited in Paris with the Barbizon painters, though he owed less to them than to van Goyen and the seventeenth-century "tonal" artists of the United Provinces. Jongkind's work was a logical precursor to the art of the **Hague School**. Based in and around Den Haag between 1870 and 1900, this prolific group of painters tried to re-establish a characteristically Dutch national school of painting. They produced atmospheric studies of the dunes and polders around Den Haag, nature pictures that are characterized by grey, rain-filled skies, windswept seas and silvery, flat beaches – pictures that, for some, verge on the sentimental. **J.H. Weissenbruch** (1824–1903) was a founding member, a specialist in low, flat beach scenes dotted with stranded boats. The banker-turned-artist **H.W. Mesdag** (1831–1915) did the same but with more skill than imagination, while **Jacob Maris** (1837–99), one of three artist brothers, was perhaps the most typical with his rural and sea scenes heavily covered by grey, chasing skies. His brother **Matthijs** (1839–1917) was less predictable, ultimately tiring of his colleagues' interest in straight observation and going to London to design windows, while the youngest brother **Willem** (1844–1910) is best known for his small, unpretentious studies of nature.

Anton Mauve (1838–88) is better known, an exponent of soft, pastel landscapes and an early teacher of van Gogh. Profoundly influenced by the French Barbizon painters – Corot, Millet et al – he went to Hilversum near Amsterdam in 1885 to set up his own group, which became known as the "Dutch Barbizon". **Jozef Israëls** (1826–1911) has often been likened to Millet, though it's generally agreed that he had more in common with the Impressionists, and his best pictures are his melancholy portraits and interiors. Lastly, **Johan Bosboom**'s (1817–91) church interiors may be said to sum up the romanticized nostalgia of the Hague School; shadowy and populated by figures in seventeenth-century dress, they seem to yearn for the country's Golden Age.

Very different, and slightly later, **Jan Toorop** (1858–1928) went through multiple artistic changes, radically adapting his technique from a fairly conventional pointillism through a tired Expressionism to Symbolism with an Art Nouveau feel. Roughly contemporary, **George Hendrik Breitner** (1857–1923) was a better painter, and one who refined his style rather than changed it. His snapshot-like impressions of his beloved Amsterdam figure among his best work.

Van Gogh

Vincent van Gogh (1853–90) was one of the least "Dutch" of Dutch artists, and he spent most of his relatively short painting career in France. After countless studies of Dutch peasant life – studies which culminated in his sombre *Potato Eaters* (see p.120) – he went to live in Paris with his art-dealer brother Theo. There, under the influence of the Impressionists, he lightened his palette, following the pointillist work of Seurat and "trying to render intense colour and not a grey harmony". Two years later he went south to Arles, the "land of blue tones and gay colours", and, struck by the brilliance of Mediterranean light, his characteristic style began to develop. A disastrous attempt to live with Gauguin, and the much-publicized episode in which he cut off part of his ear and presented it to a local prostitute (see p.121), led to his committal in an asylum at St-Rémy. Here he produced some of his most famous, and most Expressionistic, canvases – strongly coloured and with the paint thickly, almost frantically, applied. Now one of the world's most popular – and popularized –

painters, Amsterdam's Van Gogh Museum has the world's finest collection of his work (see pp.119–121).

The twentieth century – De Stijl

Each of the major modern art movements has had – or has – its followers in the Netherlands and each has been diluted or altered according to local taste. Of many lesser names, **Jan Sluyters** (1881–1957) stands out as the Dutch pioneer of Cubism, but this is small beer when compared with the one specifically Dutch movement – **De Stijl** (The Style). **Piet Mondriaan** (1872–1944) was De Stijl's leading figure, developing the realism he had learned from the Hague School painters – via Cubism, which he criticized for being too cowardly to depart totally from representation – into a complete abstraction of form which he called Neo-Plasticism. Mondriaan was something of a mystic, and this was to some extent responsible for the direction that De Stijl – and his paintings – took: canvases painted with grids of lines and blocks made up of the three primary colours plus white, black and grey. Mondriaan believed this freed his art from the vagaries of personal perception, making it possible to obtain what he called "a true vision of reality".

De Stijl took other forms too; there was a magazine of the same name, and the movement introduced new concepts into every aspect of design, from painting to interior design and architecture. But in all these media, lines were kept simple, colours bold and clear. **Theo van Doesburg** (1883–1931) was a De Stijl cofounder and major theorist. His work is similar to Mondriaan's except for the noticeable absence of thick, black borders and the diagonals that he introduced into his work, calling his paintings "contra-compositions" – which, he said, were both more dynamic and more in touch with the twentieth century. **Bart van der Leck** (1876–1958) was the third member of the circle, identifiable by white canvases covered by seemingly randomly placed inter-locking coloured triangles. Mondriaan split with De Stijl in 1925, going on to attain new artistic extremes of clarity and soberness before moving to New York in the 1940s and producing atypically exuberant works such as *Victory Boogie Woogie* – named for the artist's love of jazz.

From De Stijl to the present day

During and after De Stijl, a number of other movements flourished in the Netherlands, though their impact was not so great and their influence was largely local. The Expressionist **Bergen School** was probably the most local-ized, its best-known exponent **Charley Toorop** (1891–1955), daughter of Jan, developing a distinctively glaring but strangely sensitive realism. **De Ploeg** (The Plough), centred in Groningen, was headed by **Jan Wiegers** (1893–1959) and influenced by Ernst Ludwig Kirchner and the German Expressionists; the group's artists set out to capture the uninviting landscapes around their native town, and produced violently coloured canvases that hark back to van Gogh. Another group, known as the **Magic Realists**, surfaced in the 1930s, painting quasi-surrealistic scenes that, according to their leading light, **Carel Willink** (1900–83), revealed "a world stranger and more dreadful in its haughty impen-etrability than the most terrifying nightmare".

Postwar Dutch art began with **CoBrA**: a loose grouping of like-minded painters from Denmark, Belgium and the Netherlands, whose name derives

Amsterdam galleries: a hit list

Of the galleries in Amsterdam, the **Rijksmuseum** (see pp.113–119) owns a fabulous and wonderfully comprehensive collection of Dutch/Low Countries art, but much of it is out of sight during a major refurbishment, which is scheduled to last until 2013. In the meantime, one wing of the museum remains open and features the major artists of the Golden Age, most memorably Rembrandt. The **Van Gogh Museum** (see pp.119–121) is best for the Impressionists and, of course, van Gogh, while for contemporary Dutch art there's both the inventive **De Appel** (see p.77) and the **Stedelijk Museum** (see p.121), which will reopen after an extensive refit in 2010. Contemporary photographers, on the other hand, are featured at the **Huis Marseille** (see p.74) and **FOAM** (see p.215). In the city's southern suburbs, the **CoBrA Museum** (see p.134) is dedicated to the CoBrA art movement of the 1950s and 1960s, and the neighbouring town of **Haarlem** possesses the excellent **Frans Hals Museum** (see p.143), which holds some of the best work of Hals, his predecessors and successors. For commercial art galleries, see box, p.215.

from the initial letters of their respective capital cities. Their first exhibition at Amsterdam's Stedelijk Museum in 1949 provoked a furore, at the centre of which was **Karel Appel** (1921–2006), whose brutal Abstract Expressionist pieces, plastered with paint inches thick, were, he maintained, necessary for the era – indeed, inevitable reflections of it. "I paint like a barbarian in a barbarous age," he claimed. In the graphic arts, the most famous twentieth-century Dutch figure was **Maurits Cornelis Escher** (1898–1972), whose Surrealistic illusions and allusions were underpinned by his fascination with mathematics.

As for today, a vibrant contemporary art scene sustains an ambitious programme of temporary exhibitions, most notably at De Appel (see p.77), and nourishes about a dozen premier private/commercial art galleries (see box, p.77). Among modern Dutch artists, look out for the abstract work of **Edgar Fernhout** (1912–74) and **Ad Dekkers** (1938–74); the reliefs of **Jan Schoonhoven** (1914–94); the multimedia productions of **Jan Dibbets** (b.1941); the imprecisely coloured geometric designs of **Rob van Koningsbruggen** (b.1948); the smeary Expressionism of **Toon Verhoef** (b.1946); the exuberant figures of **Rene Daniels** (b.1950); the exquisite realism of **Karel Buskes** (b.1962) and **Joke Frima** (b.1952); and the witty, hip furniture designs of **Piet Hein Eek** (b.1967) – to name just ten of the more important figures.

Books

M ost of the books listed below are in print and in paperback, and those that are out of print (o/p) should be easy to track down either in second-hand bookshops or online. Note also that while we recommend all the books we've listed below, we do have favourites – and these have been marked with ⚓.

History, politics and general

Leo Akveld *et al The Colourful World of the VOC*. Beautifully illustrated, coffee-table sized book on the VOC – the East India Company. The subject is dealt with in a series of intriguing essays on the likes of the uses of Eastern spices, Indonesian fashion and furniture, rituals and beliefs. The only problem is that it is hard to get hold of outside Amsterdam.

Ayaan Hirsi Ali *Infidel: My Life*. This powerful and moving autobiography, written by one of the Netherlands's most controversial figures, begins with Ali's harsh and sometimes brutal childhood in Somalia and then Saudi Arabia, where – among other tribulations – her grandmother insisted she have her clitoris cut off when she was 5. Later, in 1992, Ali wound up in the Netherlands at least partly to evade an arranged marriage. Thereafter, she made a remarkable transition from factory cleaner to MP, becoming a leading light of the rightist VVD political party and remaining outspoken in her denunciations of militant Islam (see p.267). Due to death threats, Ali was forced to go into hiding in 2004, only returning to parliament in 2005. She now lives in the US.

J.C.H. Blom (ed.) *History of the Low Countries*. Books on the totality of Dutch history are thin on the ground, so this heavyweight volume fills a few gaps, though it's hardly sun-lounge reading. A series of historians weigh in with their specialities, from Roman times onwards.

Taken as a whole, its forte is in picking out those cultural, political and economic themes that give the region its distinctive character.

Mike Dash *Tulipomania*. An examination of the introduction of the tulip into the Low Countries at the height of the Golden Age – and the extraordinarily inflated and speculative market that ensued. There's a lot of padding and scene-setting, but it's an engaging though read, and has nice detail on seventeenth-century Amsterdam, Leiden and Haarlem.

Pieter Geyl *The Revolt of The Netherlands 1555–1609 and The Netherlands in the Seventeenth Century 1609–1648*. Geyl presents a detailed account of the Netherlands during its formative years, chronicling the uprising against the Spanish and the formation of the United Provinces. First published in 1932, it has long been regarded as the classic text on the subject, though it is a hard and ponderous read.

A.C. Grayling *Descartes: The Life and Times of a Genius*. One of the greatest philosophers of all time, René Descartes (1596–1650) was a key figure in the transition from medieval to early modern Europe. He also made key contributions to optics and geometry and, among his miscellaneous travels, spent time living in Amsterdam (see p.71). This crisply written, erudite biography deals skilfully with the philosophy – Grayling is himself a philosophy professor – and argues that Descartes was almost certainly a Jesuit spy acting on behalf of the Habsburg interest during his time here in Amsterdam.

Christopher Hibbert *Cities and Civilisation*. Includes a diverting chapter on Amsterdam in the age of Rembrandt. Hibbert, one of the UK's best historians, is always a pleasure to read.

Lisa Jardine *The Awful End of Prince William the Silent*. Great title for an intriguing book on the premature demise of one of the country's most acclaimed heroes, who was assassinated in Delft in 1584. At just 160 pages, the tale is told succinctly, but – unless you have a particular interest in early firearms – there is a bit too much information on guns.

Carol Ann Lee *Roses from the Earth: the Biography of Anne Frank*. Among a spate of publications trawling through and over the life of the young Jewish diarist, this is probably the best, written in a straightforward and insightful manner without sentimentality. Working the same mine is the same author's *The Hidden Life of Otto Frank* – clear, lucid and equally as interesting.

🏃 **Geert Mak** *Amsterdam: A Brief Life of the City*. First published in 1995, this infinitely readable trawl through the city's past is a simply wonderful book – amusing and perceptive, alternately tart and indulgent. It's more a social history than anything else, so – for example – it's here you'll find out quite why Rembrandt lived in the Jewish Quarter and why the city's merchant elite ossified in the eighteenth century. It's light and accessible enough to read from cover to cover, but its index of places makes it easy to dip into. Highly recommended.

🏃 **Geoffrey Parker** *The Dutch Revolt*. Compelling account of the struggle between the Netherlands and Spain. Quite the best

thing you can read on the period. Also *The Army of Flanders and the Spanish Road 1567–1659*. The title may sound academic, but this book gives a fascinating insight into the Habsburg army that occupied the Low Countries for well over a hundred years – how it functioned, was fed and moved from Spain to the Low Countries along the so-called Spanish Road.

Simon Schama *The Embarrassment of Riches: An Interpretation of Dutch Culture in the Golden Age*. Long before his reinvention on British TV, Schama had a reputation as a specialist in Dutch history, and this chunky volume draws on a huge variety of archive sources. Also by Schama, *Patriots and Liberators: Revolution in the Netherlands 1780–1813* focuses on one of the less familiar periods of Dutch history and is particularly good on the Batavian Republic set up in the Netherlands under French auspices. Both are heavyweight tomes, and leftists might well find Schama too reactionary. See also Schama's *Rembrandt's Eyes* (p.284).

Andrew Wheatcroft *The Habsburgs*. Excellent and well-researched trawl through the family's history, from eleventh-century beginnings to its eclipse at the end of World War I. Enjoyable background reading.

🏃 **Manfred Wolf** (ed.) *Amsterdam: A Traveler's Literary Companion*. Published by an independent American press, Whereabout Press, these anthologies aim to get to the heart of the modern cities they cover, and this well-chosen mixture of travel pieces, short fiction and reportage does exactly that, uncovering a low-life aspect to the city of Amsterdam that exists beyond the tourist brochures. A high-quality and evocative selection, and often the only chance you'll get to read some of this material in translation. Published in 2001.

Art and architecture

Svetlana Alpers *Rembrandt's Enterprise*. Intriguing 1988 study of Rembrandt, positing the theory – in line with findings of the Leiden-based Rembrandt Research Project – that many previously accepted Rembrandt paintings are not his at all, but merely the products of his studio. Bad news if you own one.

Anthony Bailey *A View of Delft*. Concise, startlingly well-researched book on Vermeer, complete with an accurate and well-considered exploration of his milieu.

R.H. Fuchs *Dutch Painting*. As complete an introduction to the subject – from Flemish origins to the present day – as you could wish for, in just a couple of hundred pages. First published in the 1970s, but still the classic text. o/p

Walter S. Gibson *Hieronymus Bosch* and *Bruegel*. Two wonderfully illustrated Thames & Hudson titles on these two exquisite allegorical painters. The former contains everything you wanted to know about Hieronymus Bosch, his paintings and his late fifteenth-century milieu, while the latter takes a detailed look at Pieter Bruegel the Elder's art, with nine well-argued chapters investigating its various components. Both published in the 1970s, but there has been nothing better yet. o/p

Melissa McQuillan *Van Gogh*. Extensive, in-depth look at Vincent's paintings, as well as his life and times. Superbly researched and illustrated.

Simon Schama *Rembrandt's Eyes*. Published in 1999, this erudite work received good reviews, but it's very, very long – and often very long-winded.

🏃 **Mariet Westerman** An all-you-could-ever-want-to-know book about Rembrandt and a fascinating *Art and Home: Dutch Interiors in the Age of Rembrandt*, but this will cost £60 from Amazon.

Christopher White *Rembrandt*. White is something of a Rembrandt specialist, writing a series of books on the man and his times. Most of these books are expensive and aimed at the specialist art market, but this particular title is perfect for the general reader. Well illustrated plus a wonderfully incisive and extremely detailed commentary. Published in 1984, but still very much to the point.

Frank Wynne *I was Vermeer: The Legend of the Forger who Swindled the Nazis*. Amsterdam's Han van Meegeren (see p.74) fooled everyone, including Hermann Goering, with his "lost" Vermeers, when in fact he painted them himself. This story of bluff, bluster and fine art is an intriguing tale no doubt, but Wynne's newly published book, though extremely well informed, is overly long.

Literature

A.C. Baantjer *De Kok and the Mask of Death*. An ex-Amsterdam policeman, who racked up nearly forty years service, Baantjer is currently the most widely read author in the Netherlands. This rattling good yarn, the latest in the Inspector De Kok series, has all the typical ingredients – crisp plotting, some gruesomeness and a batch of nice characterizations on the way. More? Try *De Kok and the Somber Nude*.

Tracey Chevalier *Girl with a Pearl Earring*. Chevalier's novel is a fanciful piece of fiction, building a story around the subject of one of Vermeer's most enigmatic paintings. It's an absorbing read, if a tad too detailed and slow-moving for some tastes, and it paints a convincing picture of seventeenth-century Delft, exploring its social structures and values.

Anne Frank *The Diary of a Young Girl*. Lucid and moving, the most revealing book you can read on the plight of Amsterdam's Jews during the German occupation. An international bestseller since its original publication in 1947.

Nicolas Freeling *Love in Amsterdam* (o/p); *Dwarf Kingdom* (o/p); *A Long Silence* (o/p); *A City Solitary* (o/p). Freeling wrote detective novels, and his most famous creation was the rebel cop van der Valk. These are light, carefully crafted tales, with just the right amount of twists to make them classic cops 'n' robbers reading – and with good Amsterdam (and Dutch) locations. London-born, Freeling (1927–2003) evoked Amsterdam (and Amsterdammers) as well as any writer has, subtly and unsentimentally using the city and its people as a vivid backdrop to the fast-moving action.

Willem Frederik Hermans *The Dark Room of Damocles*. Along with Jan Wolkers, Harry, Mulisch (see p.286) and Gerard Reve, Hermans is considered one of the four major literary figures of the Dutch post-war generation. This particular title, published in 1958, but only recently translated, is all about the German occupation and its concomitants – betrayal, paranoia and treason. Indeed, the reader is rarely certain what is truth and what is false-hood. If this whets your appetite for Hermans, try the same author's *Beyond Sleep*, which has also been translated recently. Hermans died in 1995.

Etty Hillesum *An Interrupted Life: the Diaries and Letters of Etty Hillesum,*

1941–43. The Germans transported Hillesum, a young Jewish woman, from her home in Amsterdam to Auschwitz, where she died. As with Anne Frank's more famous journal, penetratingly written – though on the whole a tad less readable.

Arthur Japin *The Two Hearts of Kwasi Boachi*. Inventive re-creation of a true story in which the epony-mous Ashanti prince was dispatched to the court of King William of the Netherlands in 1837. Kwasi and his companion Kwame were ostensibly sent to Den Haag to further their education, but there was a strong colonial subtext. Superb descriptions of Ashanti-land in its pre-colonial pomp. Also Japin's *Lucia's Eyes*, an imaginative extrapolation of a casual anecdote found in Casanova's memoirs and set for the most part in eighteenth-century Amsterdam.

Sylvie Matton *Rembrandt's Whore*. Taking its cue from Chevalier's *Girl with a Pearl Earring* (see p.284), this slim novel tries hard to conjure Rembrandt's life and times, with some success. Matton certainly knows her Rembrandt – she worked for two years on a film of his life.

Sarah Emily Miano *Van Rijn*. Carefully composed re-creation of Rembrandt's milieu, based on the (documented) visit of Cosimo de Medici to the artist's house. As an attempt to venture into Rembrandt's soul it does well – but not brilliantly.

Deborah Moggach *Tulip Fever*. At first Deborah Moggach's novel seems no more than an attempt to build a story out of her favourite domestic Dutch interiors, genre scenes and still-life paintings. But ultimately the story is a basic one – of lust, greed, mistaken identity and tragedy. The Golden Age Amsterdam backdrop is well realized, but almost incidental.

Marcel Moring *In Babylon*. Popular Dutch author with an intense style spliced with thought-provoking, philosophical content. *In Babylon* has an older Jewish man and his niece trapped in a cabin in the eastern Netherlands and here they ruminate on their family's history. Moring's *Dream Room* is also gracefully nostalgic in its concentration on the family of Boris and his son, David, while Moring's latest novel, *In a Dark Wood*, is set in the town of Assen, again in the east of the country, during the annual Dutch TT motor-bike races.

Harry Mulisch *The Assault.* Set part in Haarlem, part in Amsterdam, this novel traces the story of a young boy who loses his family in a reprisal-raid by the Nazis. A powerful tale, made into an excellent and effective film. Also, *The Discovery of Heaven*, a gripping yarn of adventure and happenstance; *The Procedure*, featuring a modern-day Dutch scientist investigating strange goings-on in sixteenth-century Prague; and *Siegfried: a Black Idyll*, whose central question is whether a work of imagination can help to understand the nature of evil in general and Hitler in particular.

Multatuli *Max Havelaar: Or, The Coffee Auctions of the Dutch Trading Company.* Classic, nineteenth-century Dutch satire of colonial life in the East Indies. Eloquent and intermittently amusing. If you have Dutch friends, they should be impressed (dumbstruck) if you have actually read it, not least since it's 352 pages long. For more on Multatuli, see p.67.

Cees Nooteboom *Rituals.* Nooteboom published his first novel in 1955, but only hit the literary headlines with this, his third novel, in 1980. The central theme of all his work is the phenomenon of time; *Rituals* in particular is about the passing of time and the different ways of controlling the process. Inni Wintrop, the main character, is an outsider, a well-heeled, antique-dabbling "dilettante" as he describes himself. The book is almost entirely set in Amsterdam, and although it describes the inner life of Inni himself, it also paints a strong picture of the city.

David Veronese *Jana.* A hip thriller set in the druggy underworld of Amsterdam and London.

Janwillem van de Wetering *Tumbleweed*; *Hard Rain*; *Corpse on the Dyke; Outsider in Amsterdam.* Offbeat detective tales set in Amsterdam and the provinces. Humane, quirky and humorous, Wetering's novels have inventive plots and feature unusual characters in interesting locations, though the prose itself can be a tad indigestible.

Language

Language

Dutch

I t's unlikely that you'll need to speak anything other than English while you're in Amsterdam; the Dutch have a seemingly natural talent for languages, and your attempts at speaking theirs may be met with some bewilderment – though this can have as much to do with your pronunciation (Dutch is very difficult to get right) as their surprise that you're making an effort. Outside Amsterdam, people aren't quite as cosmopolitan, but even so, the Dutch **words and phrases** below should be the most you'll need to get by; also included is a basic **food and drink glossary**, though menus are nearly always multilingual; where they aren't, ask and one will almost invariably appear.

Dutch is a Germanic language – the word "Dutch" itself is a corruption of Deutsche, a label inaccurately given by English sailors in the seventeenth century, and indeed, although the Dutch are at pains to stress the differences between the two languages, if you know any German you'll spot many similarities. As for phrasebooks, the *Rough Guide to Dutch* is pocket-sized, and has a good dictionary section (English–Dutch and Dutch–English), as well as a menu reader; it also provides a useful introduction to grammar and pronunciation.

Pronunciation

Dutch is **pronounced** in much the same way as English. However, there are a few Dutch sounds that don't exist in English, which can be difficult to get right without practice.

Consonants

Double-consonant combinations generally keep their separate sounds in Dutch: *kn*, for example, is never like the English "knight". Note also the following consonants and consonant combinations:

j is an English **y**

ch and g indicate a throaty sound, as at the end of the Scottish word lo**ch**. The Dutch word for canal – *gracht* – is especially tricky, since it has two of these sounds – it comes out along the lines of *khrakht*. A

common word for hello is Dag! – pronounced like *daakh*

ng as in bri**ng**

nj as in o**ni**on

y is not a consonant, but another way of writing **ij**

Vowels and diphthongs

A good rule of thumb is that doubling the letter lengthens the vowel sound.

a is like the English **a**pple

aa like c**a**rt

e like l**e**t

ee like l**a**te

o as in p**o**p

oo in p**o**pe

u is like the French **tu** if preceded by a consonant; it's like w**oo**d if followed by a consonant uu is the French t**u**

au and ou like h**ow**

ei and ij as in f**i**ne, though this varies strongly from region to region; sometimes it can sound more like l**a**ne

oe as in s**oo**n

eu is like the diphthong in the French l**eur**

ui is the hardest Dutch diphthong of all, pronounced like h**ow** but much further forward in the mouth, with lips pursed (as if to say "oo")

Words and phrases

Basics

yes	ja	**Do you speak English?**	Spreekt u Engels?
no	nee	**I don't understand**	Ik begrijp het niet
please	alstublieft	**women/men**	vrouwen/mannen
(no) thank you	(nee) dank u or bedankt	**children**	kinderen
hello	hallo, dag or hoi	**men's/women's toilets**	heren/dames
good morning	goedemorgen		
good afternoon	goedemiddag	**I want...**	Ik wil...
good evening	goedenavond	**I don't want to...**	Ik wil niet...(+verb)
goodbye	tot ziens	**I don't want any...**	Ik wil geen...(+noun)
see you later	tot straks	**How much is...?**	Wat kost...?

Travel, directions and shopping

How do I get to...?	Hoe kom ik in...?	**here/there**	hier/daar
Where is...?	Waar is...?	**good/bad**	goed/slecht
How far is it to...?	Hoe ver is het naar...?	**big/small**	groot/klein
far/near	ver/dichtbij	**open/closed**	open/gesloten
left/right	links/rechts	**push/pull**	duwen/trekken
straight ahead	rechtdoor	**new/old**	nieuw/oud
airport	luchthaven	**cheap/expensive**	goedkoop/duur
post office	postkantoor	**hot/cold**	heet or warm/koud
postbox	postbus	**with/without**	met/zonder
stamp(s)	postzegel(s)	**North**	noord
money exchange	geldwisselkantoor	**South**	zuid
cash desk	kassa	**East**	oost
railway platform	spoor or perron	**West**	west
ticket office	loket		

Signs and abbreviations

A.U.B.	alstublieft: please (also shown as S.V.P., from French)	**BTW**	Belasting Toegevoegde Waarde: VAT
BG	begane grond: ground floor	**Geen toegang**	no entry
		gesloten	closed

ingang	entrance	toegang	entrance
K	kelder: basement	**uitgang**	exit
let op!	attention!	**V.A.**	vanaf: from
heren/dames	men's/women's toilets	**Z.O.Z.**	please turn over
open	open		(page, leaflet, etc)
T/M	tot en met: up to and including		

Useful cycling terms

tyre	band	pedal	trapper
puncture	lek	**pump**	pomp
brake	rem	**handlebars**	stuur
chain	ketting	**broken**	kapot
wheel	wiel	**cycle path**	fietspad

Days of the week

Sunday	zondag	today	vandaag
Monday	maandag	**tomorrow**	morgen
Tuesday	dinsdag	**tomorrow morning**	morgenochtend
Wednesday	woensdag	**year**	jaar
Thursday	donderdag	**month**	maand
Friday	vrijdag	**week**	week
Saturday	zaterdag	**day**	dag
yesterday	gisteren		

Months of the year

January	januari	July	juli
February	februari	**August**	augustus
March	maart	**September**	september
April	april	**October**	oktober
May	mei	**November**	november
June	juni	**December**	december

Time

hour	uur	3.30	half vier
minute	minuut	3.35	vijf over half vier
What time is it?	Hoe laat is het?	3.40	tien over half vier
It's...	Het is...	3.45	kwart voor vier
3.00	drie uur	3.50	tien voor vier
3.05	vijf over drie	3.55	vijf voor vier
3.10	tien over drie	8am	acht uur 's ochtends
3.15	kwart over drie	1pm	een uur 's middags
3.20	tien voor half vier	8pm	acht uur 's avonds
3.25	vijf voor half vier	1am	een uur 's nachts

Numbers

When saying a number, the Dutch generally transpose the last two digits: for example, €3.25 is *drie euro vijf en twintig*.

0	nul	19	negentien
1	een	20	twintig
2	twee	21	een en twintig
3	drie	22	twee en twintig
4	vier	30	dertig
5	vijf	40	veertig
6	zes	50	vijftig
7	zeven	60	zestig
8	acht	70	zeventig
9	negen	80	tachtig
10	tien	90	negentig
11	elf	100	honderd
12	twaalf	101	honderd en een
13	dertien	200	twee honderd
14	veertien	201	twee honderd en een
15	vijftien	500	vijf honderd
16	zestien	525	vijf honderd vijf en twintig
17	zeventien	1000	duizend
18	achttien		

Food and drink

Basics

boter	butter	pindakaas	peanut butter
boterham/broodje	sandwich/roll	sla/salade	salad
brood	bread	slagroom	whipped cream
dranken	drinks	smeerkaas	cheese spread
eieren	eggs	stokbrood	French bread
gerst	barley	suiker	sugar
groenten	vegetables	vegetarisch	vegetarian
honing	honey	vis	fish
hoofdgerechten	main courses	vlees	meat
kaas	cheese	voorgerechten	starters/hors d'oeuvres
koud	cold	vruchten	fruit
nagerechten	desserts	warm	hot
peper	pepper	zout	salt

Starters and snacks

erwtensoep/snert	thick pea soup with bacon or sausage	huzarensalade	potato salad with pickles

koffietafel	light midday meal of cold meats, cheese, bread and perhaps soup	patat/friet	chips/French fries
		soep	soup
		uitsmijter	ham or cheese with eggs on bread

Meat

biefstuk (hollandse)	steak	kip	chicken
biefstuk (duitse)	hamburger	kroket	spiced veal or beef in hash, coated in breadcrumbs
eend	duck		
fricandeau	roast pork		
fricandel	frankfurter-like sausage	lamsvlees	lamb
		lever	liver
gehakt	mince	ossenhaas	beef tenderloin
ham	ham	rookvlees	smoked beef
kalfsvlees	veal	spek	bacon
kalkoen	turkey	worst	sausages
karbonade	a chop		

Fish

forel	trout	oesters	oysters
garnalen	prawns	paling	eel
haring	herring	schelvis	haddock
haringsalade	herring salad	schol	plaice
kabeljauw	cod	tong	sole
makreel	mackerel	zalm	salmon
mosselen	mussels		

Vegetables

aardappelen	potatoes	rijst	rice
bloemkool	cauliflower	sla	salad, lettuce
bonen	beans	stampot andijvie	mashed potato and endive
champignons	mushrooms		
erwten	peas	stampot boerenkool	mashed potato and cabbage
hutspot	mashed potatoes and carrots	uien	onions
knoflook	garlic	wortelen	carrots
komkommer	cucumber	zuurkool	sauerkraut
prei	leek		

Cooking terms

belegd	filled or topped, as in belegde broodjes (bread rolls topped with cheese, etc)	doorbakken	well-done
		gebakken	fried/baked
		gebraden	roasted
		gegrild	grilled

gekookt	boiled	half doorbakken	medium-done
geraspt	grated	Hollandse saus	hollandaise (a milk and egg sauce)
gerookt	smoked		
gestoofd	stewed	rood	rare

Indonesian dishes and terms

ajam	chicken	nasi rames	a rijsttafel on a single plate
bami	noodles with meat and vegetables		
		pedis	hot and spicy
daging	beef	pisang	banana
gado gado	vegetables in peanut sauce	rijsttafel	assortment of spicy dishes served with plain rice
goreng	fried		
ikan	fish	sambal	hot chilli-based sauce
katjang	peanut	sate	meat on a skewer
kroepoek	prawn crackers	satesaus	peanut sauce to accompany meat grilled on skewers
loempia	spring rolls		
nasi	rice		
nasi goreng	fried rice with meat/chicken and vegetables	seroendeng	spicy, shredded and fried coconut
		tauge	bean sprouts

Sweets and desserts

appeltaart/appelgebak	apple tart or cake	pannenkoeken	pancakes
drop	Dutch liquorice, available in zoet (sweet) or zout (salted) varieties; the latter an acquired taste	pepernoten	Dutch ginger nuts
		poffertjes	small pancakes/fritters
		(slag)room	(whipped) cream
		speculaas	spice- and cinnamon-flavoured biscuit
gebak	pastry		
ijs	ice cream	stroopwafels	waffles
koekjes	biscuits	taai-taai	spicy Dutch cake
oliebollen	traditional sweet sold at New Year – similar to a doughnut	vla	custard

Fruits and nuts

aardbei	strawberry	hazelnoot	hazelnut
amandel	almond	kers	cherry
appel	apple	kokosnoot	coconut
appelmoes	apple purée	peer	pear
citroen	lemon	perzik	peach
druiven	grape	pinda	peanut
framboos	raspberry	pruim	plum/prune

Drinks

anijsmelk	aniseed-flavoured warm milk	**kopstoot**	beer with a jenever chaser
appelsap	apple juice	**melk**	milk
bessenjenever	blackcurrant gin	**met ijs**	with ice
chocomel	chocolate milk	**met slagroom**	with whipped cream
warme chocolade melk	hot chocolate	**pils**	Dutch beer
		proost!	cheers!
citroenjenever	lemon gin	**sinaasappelsap**	orange juice
droog	dry	**thee**	tea
frisdranken	soft drinks	**tomatensap**	tomato juice
jenever	Dutch gin	**vruchtensap**	fruit juice
karnemelk	buttermilk	**wijn**	wine
koffie	coffee	**(wit/rood/rosé)**	(white/red/rosé)
koffie verkeerd	coffee with warm milk	**Vieux**	Dutch brandy

Glossary

Abdij Abbey

Amsterdammertje Phallic-shaped bollard placed in rows alongside many Amsterdam streets to keep drivers off pavements – and out of the canals.

Begijnhof Similar to a *hofje* (see below), but occupied by Catholic women (*begijns*) who led semi-religious lives without taking full vows.

Beiaard Carillon chimes

Belfort Belfry

Beurs Stock exchange

Botermarkt Butter market

Brug Bridge

BTW (Belasting Toegevoegde Waarde) – VAT (sales tax)

Burgher Member of the upper or mercantile classes of a town, usually with certain civic powers

Gasthuis Hospice for the sick or infirm

Geen toegang No entry

Gemeente Municipal, as in *gemeentehuis* (town hall)

Gerechtshof Law courts

Gesloten Closed

Gezellig A hard term to translate – something like "cosy", "comfortable" and "inviting", all in one – but a term which is often said to lie at the heart of the Dutch psyche. A long, relaxed meal in a favourite restaurant with friends is *gezellig*; grabbing a quick snack is not. The best brown cafés ooze *gezelligheid*; Kalverstraat on a Saturday afternoon definitely doesn't.

Gilde Guild

Gracht Canal

Groentenmarkt Vegetable market

Grote Kerk Literally "big church" – the main church of a town or village.

Hal Hall

Hijsbalk Pulley beam, often decorated, fixed to the top of a gable to lift goods, furniture etc. Essential in canal houses whose staircases were – and mostly still are – narrow and steep; *hijsbalken* are still very much in use today.

Hof Courtyard

Hofje Almshouse, usually for elderly women who could look after themselves but needed small charities such as food and fuel; usually comprising a number of buildings centred around a small, enclosed courtyard.

Huis House

Ingang Entrance

Jeugdherberg Youth hostel

Kasteel Castle

Kerk Church

Koning King

Koningin Queen

Koninklijk Royal

Kunst Art

Lakenhal Cloth hall: the building in medieval weaving towns where cloth would be weighed, graded and sold.

Markt Central town square and the heart of most Dutch communities, normally still the site of weekly markets.

Mokum A Yiddish word meaning "city", originally used by the Jewish community to indicate Amsterdam; now in general usage as a nickname for the city.

Molen Windmill

Nederland The Netherlands

Nederlands Dutch

Omgang Procession

Paleis Palace

Plein A square or open space

Polder An area of land that has been reclaimed from the sea.

Poort Gate

Raadhuis Town hall

Randstad Literally "rim-town", this refers to the urban conurbation that makes up much of Noord- and Zuid-Holland, stretching from Amsterdam in the north to Rotterdam and Dordrecht in the south.

Rijk State

Schepenzaal Alderman's hall

Schone kunsten Fine arts

Schouwburg Theatre

Sierkunst Decorative arts

Spionnetje Small mirror on a canal house enabling the occupant to see who is at the door without descending the stairs.

Spoor Train station platform

Stadhuis The most common word for a town hall.

Stedelijk Civic, municipal

Steeg Alley

Steen Stone

Stichting Institute or foundation

Straat Street

Toegang Entrance

Toren Tower

Tuin Garden

Uitgang Exit

V.S. (Verenigde Staten) United States

Vleeshuis Meat market

Volkskunde Folklore

VVV Tourist information office

Waag Old public weighing house, a common feature of Dutch towns.

Weg Way

Wijk District

Art and architecture glossary

Ambulatory Covered passage around the outer edge of the choir of a church.

Apse Semicircular protrusion, usually at the east end of a church.

Art Deco Geometrical style of art and architecture popular in the 1930s.

Art Nouveau Style of art, architecture and design based on highly stylized vegetal forms, especially popular in the early part of the twentieth century.

Balustrade An ornamental rail, running, almost invariably, along the top of a building.

Baroque The art and architecture of the Counter-Reformation, dating from around 1600 onwards. Distinguished by extreme ornateness and by the complex but harmonious spatial arrangement of interiors.

Carillon A set of tuned church bells, either operated by an automatic mechanism or played on a keyboard.

Caryatid A sculptured female figure used as a column.

Chancel The eastern part of a church, often separated from the nave by a screen (see "rood screen"). Contains the choir and ambulatory.

Classical Architectural style incorporating Greek and Roman elements – pillars, domes, colonnades, etc – at its height in the seventeenth century and revived, as Neoclassical, in the nineteenth.

Diptych Carved or painted work on two panels. Often used as an altarpiece – both static and, more occasionally, portable.

Expressionism Artistic style popular at the beginning of the twentieth century, characterized by the exaggeration of shape or colour; often accompanied by the extensive use of symbolism.

Flamboyant Florid form of Gothic.

Fresco Wall painting – durable through application to wet plaster.

Gable The triangular upper portion of a wall – decorative or supporting a roof – which is a feature of many Amsterdam canal houses. Initially fairly simple, they became more ostentatious in the late seventeenth century, before turning to a more restrained if imposing classicism in the eighteenth and nineteenth centuries.

Genre painting In the seventeenth century the term "genre painting" applied to everything from animal paintings and still lifes through to historical works and landscapes. In the eighteenth century, the term came to be applied only to scenes of everyday life.

Gothic Architectural style of the thirteenth to sixteenth centuries, characterized by pointed arches, rib vaulting, flying buttresses and a general emphasis on verticality.

Grisaille A technique of monochrome painting in shades of grey.

Misericord Ledge on a choir stall on which the occupant can be supported while standing; often carved with secular subjects (bottoms were not thought worthy of religious subject matter).

Nave Main body of a church.

Neoclassical A style of classical architecture evived in the nineteenth century, popular in the Low Countries during and after the Napoleonic occupation.

Neo-Gothic Revived Gothic style of architecture popular between the late eighteenth and nineteenth centuries.

Pediment Feature of a gable, usually triangular and often sporting a relief.

Pilaster A shallow rectangular column projecting, but only slightly, from a wall.

Renaissance The period of European history marking the end of the medieval period and the rise of the modern world. Defined, among many criteria, by an increase in classical scholarship, geographical discovery, the rise of secular values and the growth of individualism. Began in Italy in the fourteenth century. Also refers to the art and architecture of the period.

Rococo Highly florid, light and intricate eighteenth-century style of architecture, painting and interior design, forming the last phase of Baroque.

Romanesque Early medieval architecture distinguished by squat, heavy forms, rounded arches and naive sculpture.

Rood screen Decorative screen separating the nave from the chancel. A rood loft is the gallery (or space) on top of it.

Stucco Marble-based plaster used to embellish ceilings, etc.

Transept Arms of a cross-shaped church, placed at ninety degrees to nave and chancel.

Triptych Carved or painted work on three panels. Often used as an altarpiece.

Tympanum Sculpted, usually recessed, panel above a door.

Vault Arched ceiling or roof.

Small print and

Index

A Rough Guide to Rough Guides

Rough Guide credits

Text editor: Lara Kavanagh
Layout: Ajay Verma
Cartography: Rajesh Mishra
Picture editor: Mark Thomas
Production: Rebecca Short
Proofreader: Susannah Wight
Cover design: Chloë Roberts
Photographer: Mark Thomas, Natasha Sturny
Editorial: Ruth Blackmore, Andy Turner, Keith Drew, Edward Aves, Alice Park, Lucy White, Jo Kirby, James Smart, Natasha Foges, Róisín Cameron, Emma Traynor, Emma Gibbs, Kathryn Lane, Monica Woods, Mani Ramaswamy, Harry Wilson, Lucy Cowie, Amanda Howard, Alison Roberts, Joe Staines, Peter Buckley, Matthew Milton, Tracy Hopkins, Ruth Tidball; **Delhi** Madhavi Singh, Karen D'Souza, Lubna Shaheen
Design & Pictures: **London** Scott Stickland, Dan May, Diana Jarvis, Nicole Newman, Sarah Cummins, Emily Taylor; **Delhi** Umesh Aggarwal, Jessica Subramanian, Ankur Guha, Pradeep Thapliyal, Sachin Tanwar, Anita Singh, Nikhil Agarwal, Sachin Gupta
Production: Vicky Baldwin

Cartography: **London** Maxine Repath, Ed Wright, Katie Lloyd-Jones; **Delhi** Rajesh Chhibber, Ashutosh Bharti, Animesh Pathak, Jasbir Sandhu, Karobi Gogoi, Alakananda Bhattacharya, Swati Handoo, Deshpal Dabas
Online: **London** George Atwell, Faye Hellon, Jeanette Angell, Fergus Day, Justine Bright, Clare Bryson, Aine Fearon, Adrian Low, Ezgi Celebi, Amber Bloomfield; **Delhi** Amit Verma, Rahul Kumar, Narender Kumar, Ravi Yadav, Debojit Borah, Rakesh Kumar, Ganesh Sharma, Shisir Basumatari
Marketing & Publicity: **London** Liz Statham, Niki Hanmer, Louise Maher, Jess Carter, Vanessa Godden, Vivienne Watton, Anna Paynton, Rachel Sprackett, Libby Jellie, Laura Vipond, Vanessa McDonald; **New York** Katy Ball, Judi Powers, Nancy Lambert; **Delhi** Ragini Govind
Manager India: Punita Singh
Reference Director: Andrew Lockett
Operations Manager: Helen Phillips
PA to Publishing Director: Nicola Henderson
Publishing Director: Martin Dunford
Commercial Manager: Gino Magnotta
Managing Director: John Duhigg

Publishing information

This tenth edition published January 2010 by
Rough Guides Ltd,
80 Strand, London WC2R 0RL
14 Local Shopping Centre, Panchsheel Park, New Delhi 110017, India

Distributed by the Penguin Group
Penguin Books Ltd,
80 Strand, London WC2R 0RL
Penguin Group (USA)
375 Hudson Street, NY 10014, USA
Penguin Group (Australia)
250 Camberwell Road, Camberwell,
Victoria 3124, Australia
Penguin Group (Canada)
195 Harry Walker Parkway N, Newmarket, ON,
L3Y 7B3 Canada
Penguin Group (NZ)
67 Apollo Drive, Mairangi Bay, Auckland 1310,
New Zealand
Cover concept by Peter Dyer.

Typeset in Bembo and Helvetica to an original design by Henry Iles.

Printed in Singapore

© Martin Dunford/Phil Lee/Karoline Thomas, 2010

Maps © Rough Guides

No part of this book may be reproduced in any form without permission from the publisher except for the quotation of brief passages in reviews.

312pp includes index

A catalogue record for this book is available from the British Library

ISBN: 978-1-84836-515-5

The publishers and authors have done their best to ensure the accuracy and currency of all the information in **The Rough Guide to Amsterdam**, however, they can accept no responsibility for any loss, injury, or inconvenience sustained by any traveller as a result of information or advice contained in the guide.

1 3 5 7 9 8 6 4 2

Help us update

We've gone to a lot of effort to ensure that the tenth edition of **The Rough Guide to Amsterdam** is accurate and up-to-date. However, things change – places get "discovered", opening hours are notoriously fickle, restaurants and rooms raise prices or lower standards. If you feel we've got it wrong or left something out, we'd like to know, and if you can remember the address, the price, the hours, the phone number, so much the better.

Please send your comments with the subject line "**Rough Guide Amsterdam Update**" to ℗mail@roughguides.com. We'll credit all contributions and send a copy of the next edition (or any other Rough Guide if you prefer) for the very best emails.

Have your questions answered and tell others about your trip at ℗www.roughguides.com

Acknowledgements

Martin Dunford would like to thank Eric Toren, Lara Kavanagh and as always Caroline, Daisy and Lucy.

Phil Lee would like to thank his editor, Lara Kavanagh, for her good-humoured efficiency during the preparation of this new edition of Amsterdam. Special thanks also to Malijn Maat for her help with all sorts of queries, and to my co-authors, Martin Dunford and Suzanne Morton-Taylor.

SMALL PRINT

Readers' letters

Thanks to all the readers who have taken the time to write in with comments and suggestions (and apologies if we've inadvertently omitted or misspelt anyone's name):

Julie Beckford; Johanneke Braam; David Buckley; Mark Burns; A M Castro; Martin Christlieb; Lyndsey Daley; Annette Gahlings; Claes De Groot; Maarten van der Gulik; David Jenkins; Michael Kirby; Leo Lacey; Richard Lamey; Stav Louizou; Tom Marrinan; Leann Nelson; Judith Orford; Jill Pearson; Bill Paton; Nick Reeves; Fiona Rempt; Mandy Revel; Lesa Rollo; Bobby Russell; Nigel Sandford; Toby Screech; Carolien Selderijk; Johanna Sleeswijk; Hilary Smith; K Tan; Dunya Verwey; Anna Vidou; Ronald Walgreen; Clare Webster; Susan Webster; Christel van Weezep; Paul Weston; B. White; J Wood; Karen Woods; Alison Young; Liz Young.

Photo credits

All photography by Natascha Sturny & Mark Thomas © Rough Guides except the following:

Things not to miss
01 The Jordaan © Ingolf Pompe 2/Alamy
05 The Grachtengordel © Iain Masterton/Alamy
09 Secret door in Anne Frank Huis © Image courtesy of Anne Frank Huis
15 Amstelkring © Sergio Pitamitz/Alamy
19 Heineken Experience © Image courtesy of the Heineken Experience

Black and whites
p.97 The Rembrandthuis © Yadid Levy/Alamy
p.109 ARCAM building © Richard Wareham/Alamy
p.122 Interior of the Concertgebouw © Lebrecht/Alamy

p.154 Alkmaar cheese market © Koen Suyk/Corbis
p.166 Marcel van Woerkom © Mark Thomas
p.208 Carré Theatre © Caro/Alamy
p.229 Albert Cuypmarkt © Andy Marshall/Alamy
p.235 Gay pride parade © Michel Porro/Getty
p.249 Queen's Day © Martin Dunford/Rough Guides

Amsterdam on the water colour section
Zeeburg © Hugo Nienhuis/Alamy
Marken © Peter Adams/Alamy
Amsterdam NAP © Richard Wareham/Alamy

Index

Map entries are in colour.

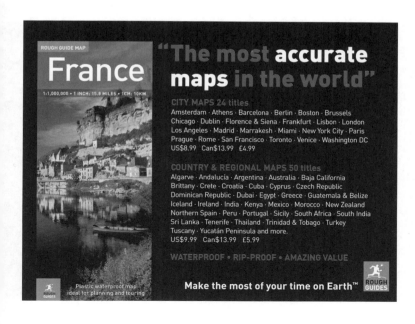

Map symbols

maps are listed in the full index using coloured text

---	Chapter division boundary	⬩	Point of interest
	Motorway	ⓘ	Information office
	Major road	⊠	Post office
	Minor road	🅿	Parking
	Pedestrianized road	◉	Accommodation
....	Tunnel	⚘	Garden
	Railway	⊙	Statue/memorial
- - - - -	Footpath	✡	Synagogue
	Waterway		Church
— —	Ferry route		Building
⊠	Gate		Market
)(	Bridge	◯	Stadium
	Boat		Cemetery
✈	Airport		Park/National park
Ⓜ	Metro station		Beach

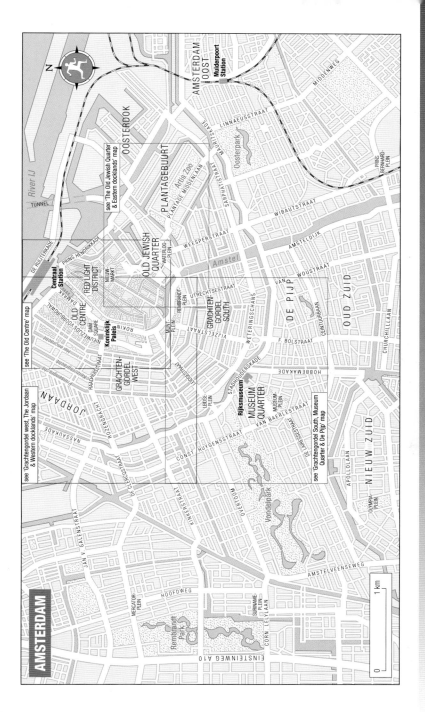

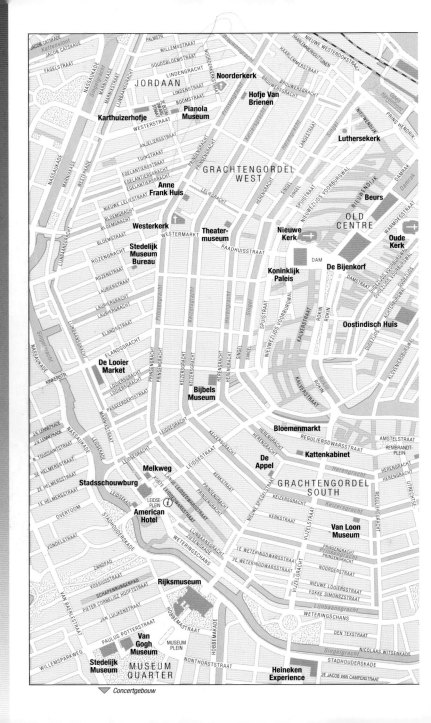

JORDAAN

Noorderkerk

Hofje Van Brienen

Pianola Museum

Karthuizerhofje

Luthersekerk

GRACHTENGORDEL WEST

Beurs

Anne Frank Huis

OLD CENTRE

Westerkerk

Theater-museum

Nieuwe Kerk

Oude Kerk

Stedelijk Museum Bureau

De Bijenkorf

Koninklijk Paleis

DAM

Oostindisch Huis

De Looier Market

Bijbels Museum

Bloemenmarkt

Kattenkabinet

De Appel

Melkweg

GRACHTENGORDEL SOUTH

Stadsschouwburg

American Hotel

Van Loon Museum

Rijksmuseum

Van Gogh Museum

Stedelijk Museum

MUSEUM QUARTER

Heineken Experience

Concertgebouw

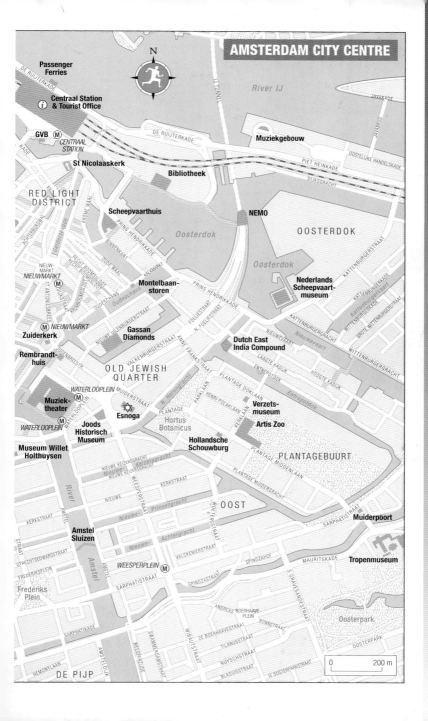

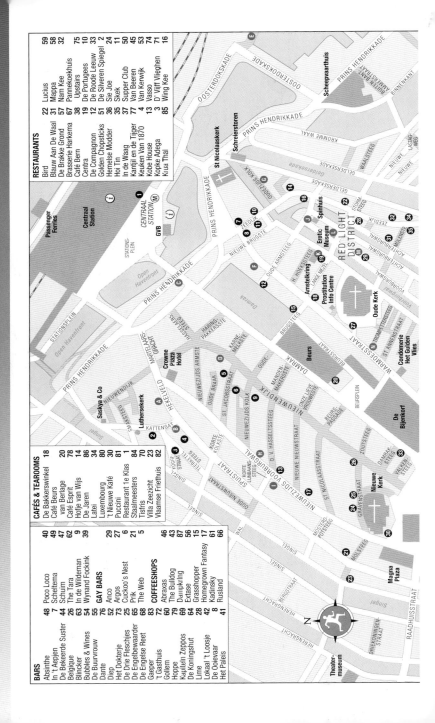

BARS

Absinthe	48
In 't Aepjen	7
De Bekeerde Suster	44
Belgique	26
Blincker	63
Bubbles & Wines	54
De Buurvrouw	55
Dante	76
Diep	52
Het Dokterje	73
De Drie Fleschjes	27
De Engelbewaarder	25
De Engelse Reet	65
Gaeper	68
't Gasthuis	83
Gollem	60
Hoppe	79
Kapitein Zeppos	69
De Koningshut	64
Lime	28
Lokaal 't Loosje	42
De Ooievaar	8
Het Paleis	41
Poco Loco	40
Scheltema	49
Schuim	47
The Tara	62
In de Wildeman	9
Wynand Fockink	39

GAY BARS

Anco	29
Argos	27
Cuckoo's Nest	6
Prik	21
The Web	5

COFFEESHOPS

Abraxas	46
The Bulldog	43
Dampkring	87
Extase	56
Grasshopper	15
Homegrown Fantasy	17
Kadinsky	61
Rusland	66

CAFÉS & TEAROOMS

De Bakkerswinkel	18
Café Beurs	20
van Bertage	78
Café Esprit	14
Hofje van Wijs	86
De Jaren	34
Latei	80
Luxembourg	30
't Nieuwe Kafé	1
Puccini	81
Restaurant 1e Klas	84
Staalmeesters	70
Tisfris	23
Villa Zeezicht	82
Vlaamse Friethuis	

RESTAURANTS

Bird	22	Lucius	59
Blauw Aan De Waal	31	Mappa	58
De Brakke Grond	57	Nam Kee	32
Brasserie Harkema	67	Pannekoekhuis	75
Café Bern	38	Upstairs	10
Centra	19	De Portugees	33
De Compagnon	12	De Roode Leeuw	2
Golden Chopsticks	51	De Silveren Spiegel	24
Hemelse Modder	36	Sie Joe	11
Hoi Tin	35	Skek	50
In de Waag	37	Supper Club	45
Kantjil en de Tijger	77	Van Beeren	53
Keuken Van 1870	4	Van Kerwijk	74
Kobe House	13	Vasso	71
Kopke Adega	3	D' Vijff Vlieghen	16
Kua Thai	85	Wing Kee	

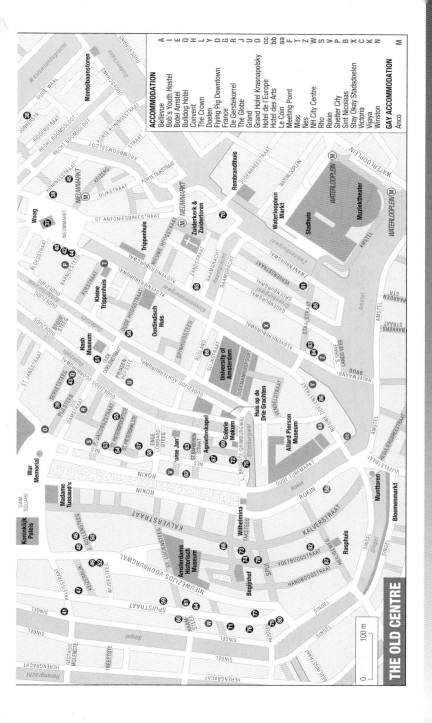

THE OLD CENTRE

0   100 m

ACCOMMODATION

Bellevue	A
Bob's Youth Hostel	I
Botel Amstel	E
Bulldog Hotel	Q
Convent	H
The Crown	L
Doelen	Y
Flying Pig Downtown	D
France	G
De Gerstekorrel	R
The Globe	J
Grand	U
Grand Hotel Krasnapolsky	O
Hotel de l'Europe	cc
Hotel des Arts	bb
Le Coin	aa
Meeting Point	F
Misc	T
Nes	Z
NH City Centre	W
Rho	S
Rokin	V
Shelter City	P
Sint Nicolaas	B
Stay Okay Stadsdoelen	X
Victoria	C
Vijaya	K
Winston	N

GAY ACCOMMODATION

Anco	M

Koninklijk Paleis

Madame Tussaud's

War Memorial

Waag

Montelbaanstoren

Trippenhuis

Kleine Trippenhuis

Oostindisch Huis

Hash Museum

Zuiderkerk & Zuidertoren

Rembrandthuis

Waterlooplein Markt

Stadhuis

Muziektheater

University of Amsterdam

Huis op de Drie Grachten

Allard Pierson Museum

Galerie Mokum

't one Jan'

Agnietenkapel

Amsterdams Historisch Museum

Begijnhof

Wilhelmina

Rasphuis

Munttoren

Bloemenmarkt

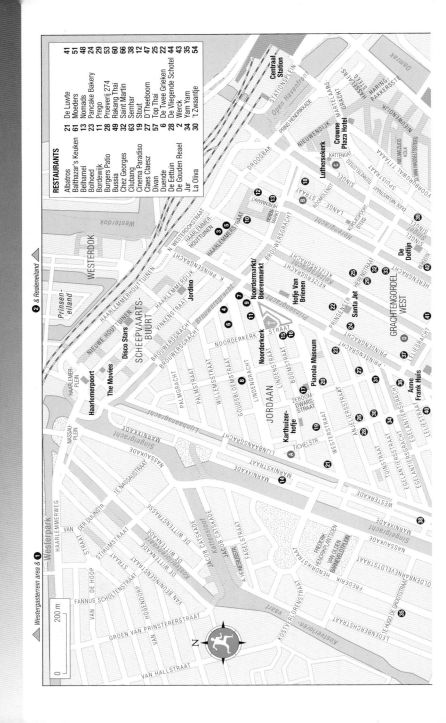

RESTAURANTS			
Albatros	21	De Luwte	41
Balthazar's Keuken	61	Moeders	51
Belhamel	13	Nomads	48
Bolhoed	23	Pancake Bakery	24
Bordewijk	11	Prego	29
Burgers Patio	28	Proeverij 274	53
Bussia	49	Rakang Thai	60
Chez Georges	32	Saint Martin	66
Cilubang	63	Semhar	38
Cinema Paradiso	19	Stout	12
Claes Claesz	27	D'Theeboom	47
Divan	57	Top Thai	25
Duende	6	De Twee Grieken	22
De Eettuin	28	De Vliegende Schotel	44
De Gouden Reael	2	Werck	43
Jur	34	Yam Yam	35
La Oliva	30	't Zwaantje	54

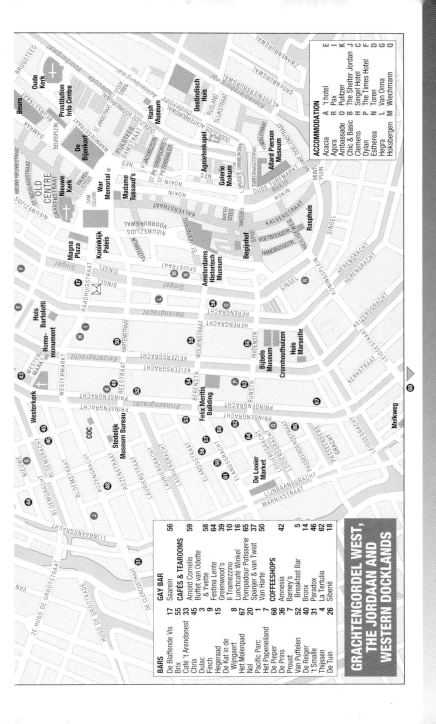

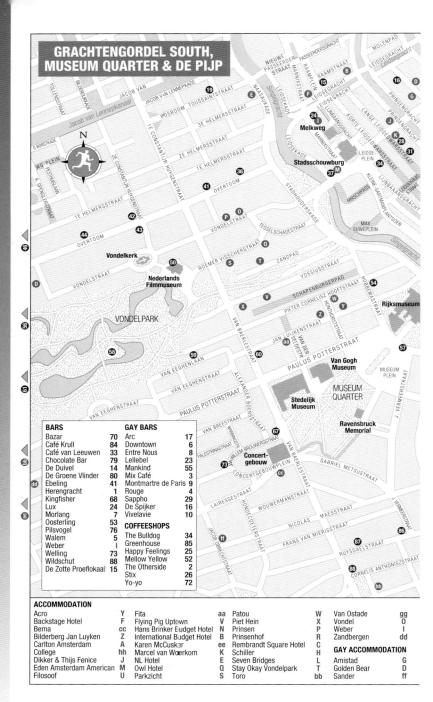

GRACHTENGORDEL SOUTH, MUSEUM QUARTER & DE PIJP

N

Jacob van Lennepkanaal

Melkweg

Stadsschouwburg

Vondelkerk

Nederlands Filmmuseum

VONDELPARK

Rijksmuseum

Van Gogh Museum

MUSEUM PLEIN

Stedelijk Museum

MUSEUM QUARTER

Ravensbruck Memorial

Concert-gebouw

BARS		GAY BARS	
Bazar	70	Arc	17
Café Krull	84	Downtown	6
Café van Leeuwen	33	Entre Nous	8
Chocolate Bar	79	Lellebel	23
De Duivel	14	Mankind	55
De Groene Vlinder	80	Mix Café	3
Ebeling	41	Montmartre de Paris	9
Herengracht	1	Rouge	4
Kingfisher	68	Sappho	29
Lux	24	De Spijker	16
Morlang	7	Vivelavie	10
Oosterling	53		
Pilsvogel	76	**COFFEESHOPS**	
Walem	5	The Bulldog	34
Weber	I	Greenhouse	85
Welling	73	Happy Feelings	25
Wildschut	88	Mellow Yellow	52
De Zotte Proeflokaal	15	The Otherside	2
		Stix	26
		Yo-yo	72

ACCOMMODATION

Acro		Fita	Y	Patou	aa	Van Ostade	gg
Backstage Hotel	F	Flying Pig Uptown		Piet Hein	V	Vondel	O
Bema	cc	Hans Brinker Budget Hotel	N	Prinsen		Weber	I
Bilderberg Jan Luyken	Z	International Budget Hotel	B	Prinsenhof	R	Zandbergen	dd
Carlton Amsterdam	A	Karen McCuskar	ee	Rembrandt Square Hotel	C		
College	hh	Marcel van Woerkom	K	Schiller	H	**GAY ACCOMMODATION**	
Dikker & Thijs Fenice	J	NL Hotel	E	Seven Bridges	L	Amistad	G
Eden Amsterdam American	M	Owl Hotel	Q	Stay Okay Vondelpark	T	Golden Bear	D
Filosoof	U	Parkzicht	S	Toro	bb	Sander	ff

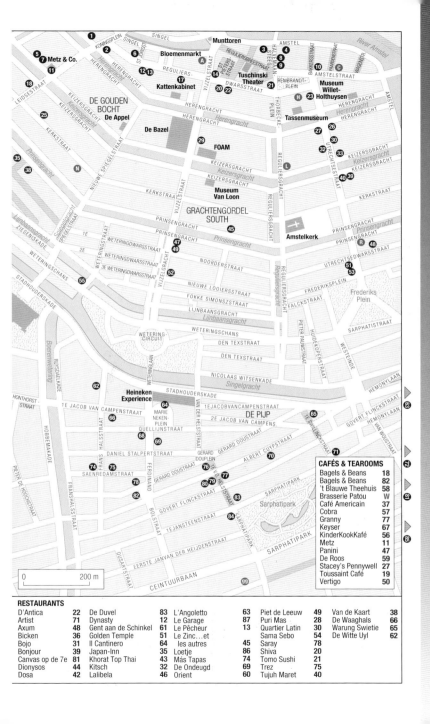

CAFÉS & TEAROOMS

Bagels & Beans	18
Bagels & Beans	82
't Blauwe Theehuis	58
Brasserie Patou	W
Café Americain	37
Cobra	57
Granny	77
Keyser	67
KinderKookKafé	56
Metz	11
Panini	47
De Roos	59
Stacey's Pennywell	27
Toussaint Café	19
Vertigo	50

RESTAURANTS

D'Antica	22	De Duvel	83	L'Angoletto	63	Piet de Leeuw	49	Van de Kaart	38
Artist	71	Dynasty	12	Le Garage	87	Puri Mas	28	De Waaghals	66
Axum	48	Gent aan de Schinkel	61	Le Pêcheur	13	Quartier Latin	30	Warung Swietie	65
Bicken	36	Golden Temple	51	Le Zinc…et	64	Sama Sebo	54	De Witte Uyl	62
Bojo	31	Il Cantinero		les autres		Saray	78		
Bonjour	39	Japan-Inn	35	Loetje	45	Shiva	20		
Canvas op de 7e	81	Khorat Top Thai	43	Más Tapas	86	Tomo Sushi	21		
Dionysos	44	Kitsch	32	De Ondeugd	74	Trez	75		
Dosa	42	Lalibela	46	Orient	69	Tujuh Maret	40		

0   200 m

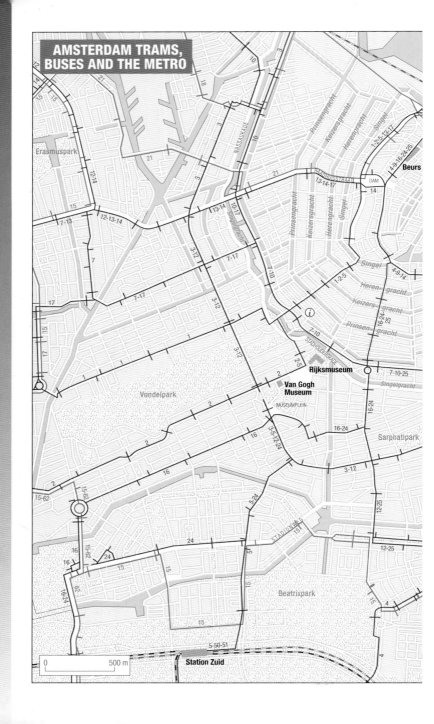

AMSTERDAM TRAMS, BUSES AND THE METRO

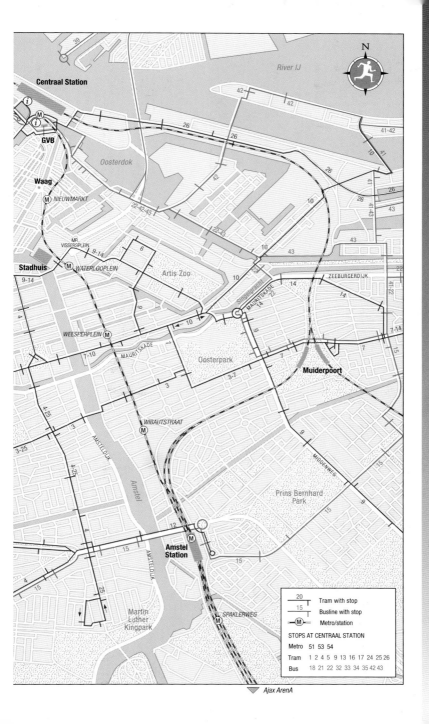

THE OLD JEWISH QUARTER & EASTERN DOCKLANDS

N

0 — 200 m

see 'Zeeburg' map ▲ Ⓐ, ❶, ❷ & ❸

▲ De Gooyer Windmill

▲ ⓭, ⓮ & Ⓑ

Waag

Montelbaanstoren

Nederlands Scheepvaartmuseum

Museum Werf 't Kromhout

Gassan Diamonds

OLD JEWISH QUARTER

Zuiderkerk

Pintohuis

Rembrandthuis

Mozes en Aaron Kerk

Dokwerker

Esnoga

TunFun

Joods Historisch Museum

Waterlooplein Markt

Stopera

Stadhuis

Muziek-theater

Waterlooplein

Jewish Memorial

Museum Willet-Holthuysen

Hermitage Amsterdam

No 58

River Amstel

Dutch East India Compound

Artis Zoo

PLANTAGEBUURT

Verzetsmuseum

Hollandsche Schouwburg

Auschwitz Monument

Wertheim-park

Hortus Botanicus

Oosterdok

OOST

⬤ D & E

⬤ ⑰